Humanism and the Urban World

Humanism and the Urban World

LEON BATTISTA ALBERTI
AND THE RENAISSANCE CITY

Caspar Pearson

THE PENNSYLVANIA STATE UNIVERSITY PRESS
UNIVERSITY PARK, PENNSYLVANIA

Frontispiece: Benozzo Gozzoli, *Saint Augustine Leaves for Milan,* fifteenth century. Sant'Agostino, San Gimignano, Italy. Photo: Scala/Art Resource, New York.

Library of Congress Cataloging-in-Publication Data

Pearson, Caspar, 1974-
    Humanism and the urban world : Leon Battista
    Alberti and the Renaissance city/Caspar Pearson.
       p. cm.
Includes bibliographical references and index.
Summary: "Explores Italian Renaissance writer and
architect Leon Battista Alberti's complex and sometimes
ambivalent attitudes toward the concept of the city, and
relates them to his broader intellectual positions"—
Provided by publisher.
ISBN 978-0-271-04855-0 (cloth: alk. paper)
  1. Alberti, Leon Battista, 1404–1472—Criticism and
    interpretation.
  2. Alberti, Leon Battista, 1404–1472--Philosophy.
  3. Alberti, Leon Battista, 1404–1472. De re aedificatoria.
  4. Cities and towns.
  I. Title.
  II. Title: Leon Battista Alberti and the Renaissance city.

NA1123.A5P43 2011
720.92—dc22
2011003075

The Pennsylvania State University Press is a member of
the Association of American University Presses.

It is the policy of The Pennsylvania State University
Press to use acid-free paper. Publications on uncoated
stock satisfy the minimum requirements of American
National Standard for Information Sciences—
Permanence of Paper for Printed Library Material,
ANSI Z39.48–1992.

This book is printed on Natures Natural, which contains
50% post-consumer waste.

Contents

Acknowledgments

Many people have assisted with the production of this book. Jules Lubbock first suggested that I study Alberti, and he remained an excellent and supportive advisor thereafter. Thomas Puttfarken and David Hemsoll both read my earliest work and offered constructive suggestions. Jo Wallace Hadrill helped me a great deal with my Latin, and Paul Gwynne critiqued some of my ideas. My colleagues in the Department of Art History and Theory at The University of Essex have given me useful advice and assistance. Professor Peter Vergo has been a supportive head of department, granting me the time to bring the manuscript to completion. A Leverhulme Trust Study Abroad Studentship allowed me to spend time in Rome; although the grant was for a different project, I continued to work on Alberti while there. I would like to thank the staff of the British School at Rome, particularly the librarians, then director Andrew Wallace Hadrill, and Assistant Director Susan Russell. I also thank the staffs of the library of the American Academy in Rome, the Warburg Institute Library, the British Library, and the University of Essex Library. Eleanor Goodman was supportive of this project from the start, while Julie Schoelles has been a wonderful and meticulous editor. All errors and oversights are entirely my own.

INTRODUCTION

"Everyone relies on the city," wrote Leon Battista Alberti, "and all the public services that it contains."[1] This statement, delivered in such a matter-of-fact manner, indicates the exceptional importance of cities in the society in which Alberti lived. His world was an urban one. He was born in Genoa, knew Venice as a child, was educated in Padua and Bologna, and subsequently lived and worked in Rome, Florence, Mantua, Rimini, and Ferrara. Fifteenth-century Italy, divided into a patchwork of city-states, boasted what was arguably the most developed urban society in Europe at the time. Moreover, Italy offered a wide variety of urban experiences, with cities of radically different sizes, architectural styles, and climates, located in areas with highly diverse geographical and environmental features.

Alberti would have known merchant cities such as Florence, courtly ones like Urbino, maritime ones such as Naples and Venice, and, of course, Rome itself, the *urbs*, city of the church, with the international crowd of clerics, administrators, and diplomats that it attracted. Furthermore, power within the city-states was exercised in a variety of ways. Dukedoms, nominal republics, and marches rubbed shoulders with kingdoms and straightforward tyrannies. The everyday world of Alberti and his contemporaries was thus deeply engaged with the problems of cities and the peculiarities of urban life: defensive walls, water provision, sewage, drainage, public health, order, policing and crime, thoroughfares, streets and services, relations between neighbors, the search for privacy, and the beauty and impressiveness of buildings. It was a world permeated by government, administration, and law, a place where notaries prospered.[2] It was also a world in which the practicalities of power, the figure of the leader, and competing forms of governance were keenly felt issues and where political strategies were often implemented with remarkable ruthlessness.[3]

In the elite humanist circles in which Alberti moved, a renewed interest in the ancient past had led to a reexamination, and often exaltation, of the urban society of antiquity. Ancient texts described a sophisticated urban milieu, while across Italy the ruins of Roman civilization bore enigmatic witness to the great cities of the past and suggested standards for future attainment. It was against this background that Alberti, a humanist scholar and practicing architect, wrote his treatise on architecture, *De re aedificatoria*. The treatise cannot be dated with precision, and it may be that Alberti continued to work on it until he died. That at least a portion of it was completed and made known to Pope Nicholas V before his death in 1455 seems certain. *De re* was the first architectural treatise to be written since ancient times—since, that is, the treatise of the Augustan architect Vitruvius. Yet Alberti's text is much more than an elaboration or commentary on Vitruvius's treatise. Rather, a combination of extraordinary learning, practical experience, and theoretical rigor results in a strikingly rich and original work that Alberti's contemporaries regarded as an outstanding achievement of Latin prose.

The Treatise

Alberti's treatise is, of course, very much concerned with the city. That is not to say that Alberti offers a specific model and tells the reader how it must be constructed in every detail. He describes no fantasy city, such as the Sforzinda that was later imagined by the Florentine architect Filarete, and none of the ten books of his architectural treatise is devoted to the city as an entity in its own right. Rather, Alberti produced a text that aims to systematically embrace the art of building in its totality.[4]

Basing his divisions on the Vitruvian triad, Alberti devoted the first half of his treatise to what Vitruvius called *firmitas* (stability) and *utilitas* (usefulness). Thus, he discusses *lineamenta* (lines and angles, although this is hardly an adequate translation) in Book I, materials in Book II, and construction in Book III. Books IV and V focus on building types, discussing public works and the works of individuals, respectively. The greater part of the treatise's second half concerns the final element in the Vitruvian triad: *venustas*, or, in Alberti's terms, *pulchritudo* (beauty) and *ornamentum* (ornament). Book VI deals with ornament in a general sense, Book VII with ornament to sacred buildings, Book VIII with ornament to public secular buildings, and Book IX with ornament to private buildings. Finally, Book X is taken up with building restoration, prevention of damage, and a lengthy section on water.

It is only in the course of this discussion that the city is considered, as and when it impinges on Alberti's argument. When Alberti does speak of the city, he does not, as it were, always speak of the same one, for the many urban situations that he discusses do not belong to a single "ideal" city that he advocates. Rather, each is bound up with the phase of the argument at which it appears. Indeed, were he writing about a single ideal city, Alberti's proposals would sometimes appear contradictory. He discusses tyrannies, kingdoms, and republics, cities where the people are separated by class and those where they are mixed together. Sometimes he outlines urban situations inspired directly by the contemporary situation of late medieval Italy, while at other times he seems to be speaking of a far-distant city of antiquity, replete with showgrounds, theaters, and temples to different gods. Yet to acknowledge the open nature of Alberti's discourse, and the absence of specific models within it, is not to say that his text is neutral regarding the city or that it does not manifest areas of preference. His work is full of judgments, sometimes apparent and at other times less so.

Certainly, scholars have long felt the urge to attribute a city to Alberti and have discussed his urban thought in some detail. Inflected by traditional views of Alberti and the Renaissance, Alberti's city has largely been considered a republican one. Alberti has occasionally emerged as an enthusiast of the city who envisaged an egalitarian community founded, in both its social and aesthetic aspects, on the idea of harmony—that concept so frequently held as a keystone of Renaissance thought and art. Thus, Eugenio Garin, the scholar who would later effect a startling transformation in Alberti studies, wrote that "Alberti contemplates an earthly city that is as harmonious as one of his palaces, where nature bends herself to the intentions of art just as would the obedient *pietra serena* of the Florentine hills."[5] Some authors have emphasized the social inclusiveness of Alberti's vision and the citizen-based principles on which it is founded.[6] Moreover, there has been a tendency to stress the rational nature of his thought and to contrast this with the "higgledy-piggledy" character of medieval urbanism.[7] He appears as the instigator of a *conscious* planning that addresses questions of ethics and human interaction, as well as rational ordering and aesthetics. As one scholar puts it, "In *De re aedificatoria* the city is the place in which individual citizens pursue virtuous activities; more than that, for the first time the city is considered to be a collection of buildings and of open spaces consciously designed and related to one another, a collection that allows the citizens to bring order to their society through their participation in its affairs."[8]

Alberti thus appears to be a visionary in two ways: first, in his rational approach to urban planning, which considers not only buildings but also their relationships to one another and to spaces (that is to say, the city as a whole, which is more than just the sum of its parts), and second, in his progressive political and social vision, which, founded on the principle of citizen participation, relates built form to social institutions and ethical positions. This image of Alberti contains much truth and has largely prevailed, although there have been dissenting voices. But it is true to say that the widespread revisionism to which Alberti has been subjected has until recently been less evident in the field of architectural and urban history than elsewhere. Moreover, interpretations of Alberti's city have often been closely related to dominant narratives of the Renaissance, and particularly of Renaissance Florence, as well as to Alberti's own historical reputation.

Alberti in Historiography

Alberti's reputation has a long pedigree both at home and abroad. For instance, a copy of his architectural treatise had reached England by 1487, only a year after its publication in Florence, transported by then bishop of Durham and protonotary apostolic John Shirwood.[9] In 1726, the treatise, which had already appeared in French and Spanish, reached a wider English public with the publication by James (Giacomo) Leoni of an English translation.[10] Thus, when William Roscoe wrote in his 1796 *Life of Lorenzo de' Medici* that Alberti warranted "particular notice as one of the earliest scholars that appeared in the revival of letters," he was speaking of someone who was already well known, at least in architectural circles.[11] Roscoe went on to list some of Alberti's achievements, commenting particularly on his versatility as an author, but concluded that his real contribution was to be found in his writings on architecture. "His principal merit is certainly to be sought for in his useful discoveries and his perceptive writings," Roscoe argued, "[for] he was the first author who attempted practical treatises on the arts of design, all of which, but more particularly his treatise on architecture, are allowed to exhibit a profound knowledge of his subject." This achievement, Roscoe predicted, "will long continue to do honor to his memory."[12]

In this last particular at least, Roscoe was correct, for Alberti's reputation was to increase dramatically in the following two centuries. His enhanced standing can be connected to a burgeoning interest in the culture of fifteenth-century Italy. More specifically, it closely parallels the rise of an idea about history that was only really developed in the nineteenth century but has become a cornerstone of Western historical thought— the Renaissance. In his *Die Kultur der Renaissance in Italien*, published in 1860, Burckhardt famously singled out Alberti as a man who perfectly exemplified the qualities of his age. With his assertion that "men can do all things if they will," Alberti seemed to sum up the development of the individual, which Burckhardt considered such a crucial aspect of the Renaissance.[13] His greatness had not been the result of birth or privileged status but had been attained, Burckhardt maintained, through his own talents. Indeed, Alberti, like that other great man of the Renaissance Leonardo da Vinci, was an illegitimate child who had been forced to make his own way in the world against the odds. He had excelled in all manner of activities, physical and intellectual, and his many writings, particularly the treatise on architecture, stood as a testament to his abilities. Burckhardt famously dubbed Alberti *uomo universale*.

This label determined a line of scholarship that has persisted for more than a century. In her 1863 novel *Romola*, George Eliot described Alberti as a "robust, universal mind, at once practical and theoretic, artist, man of science, inventor, poet"; a succession of authors followed suit.[14] Joan Gadol's 1969 monograph, written over a century after the publication of Burckhardt's work, was unambiguously titled *Leon Battista Alberti: Universal Man of the Early Renaissance* and began by characterizing Alberti as "a representative of that Renaissance type which Burckhardt calls the 'universal man.'"[15] The most recent biography of Alberti, Grafton's *Leon Battista Alberti: Master Builder of the Italian Renaissance*, translates to *Leon Battista Alberti: Un genio universale* in Italian.[16]

One can see why the idea has had such an extraordinary life span. Put simply, it's true. The range of Alberti's activities can hardly fail to astonish anyone who contemplates them. The breadth of his interests and expertise extends well beyond that of a typical humanist scholar of the period. Moreover, while Alberti himself may be the ultimate source of Burckhardt's account, it is clear that some of Alberti's contemporaries were also struck by his versatility. His friend Lapo da Castiglionchio the Younger wrote, "I so praise his genius that I would compare no one with him. I wonder at his genius to such an extent that it seems to bespeak I know not what for the future. For his genius is of this sort: to whichever area of study he puts his mind, he easily and quickly excels the others."[17] It is thus interesting that, despite this focus on his universality, important aspects of Alberti's work were largely ignored for a long time. Perhaps, when contemplating Alberti, we can become too dazzled by the fact of his universality—and by a certain conception of his life that has been present in historiography—to really examine the specifics of his work. Because Alberti's biography is well known and has been amply set out elsewhere,[18] I shall rehearse its details only briefly.

Alberti's Life

Battista Alberti was born in Genoa in 1404 into a great exiled Florentine house. The Alberti had been dominant players in the Florentine political scene of the fourteenth century and had extensive commercial interests across Europe and in the Levant. Their business survived their exile, and Battista's father, Lorenzo, was a very wealthy man.[19] His mother was a Genoese widow, probably of noble birth, whom his father never married. When Battista was two years old, Lorenzo took him and his brother Carlo (also illegitimate) away from Genoa to avoid an outbreak of plague. The same outbreak claimed the boys' mother.

As a "natural son," Battista was at the top of the hierarchy of illegitimate children. Although his father did not take the step of legitimizing his sons, as he could have done, they were nonetheless fully integrated into family life.[20] Battista was educated by the famous humanist teacher Gasparino Barzizza at Padua. There followed a degree in law at Bologna, although this was interrupted by the death of Battista's father. His uncle, who had been left to provide the boys' inheritance, died soon afterward, and there began a prolonged period of difficult relations with some of the other Alberti who were reluctant or unable to pay the boys their due. An anonymous vita—now recognized as Battista's autobiography—tells us that the strain led to physical and mental breakdown. The author ascribes this to his own zealous overwork and to the poverty and poor treatment that he endured at the hands of his relatives:

> His limbs were weak and thin, the strength of his body was exhausted, his vitality and endurance were almost gone, and finally he was stricken with a terrible affliction. As he was reading, the keenness of his eyesight suddenly failed, and he was overcome with dizziness and pain while a roaring and loud ringing filled his ears. The doctors decided that these things were the result of exhaustion; they warned him again and again not to continue in his laborious studies. He did not obey them, but again consumed himself for love of learning, and as he began to do more work than his constitution could stand, fell into an illness worthy of memory. For at this time he could not recall the names of the most familiar things, as if these would be of no further use to him, but he retained a miraculously firm grasp of anything he saw. On the physicians' orders, then, he did give up his legal studies, which had so greatly taxed his memory, just as they were about to bear fruit. Since, however, he could not live without intellectual occupation, he turned to physics and mathematics; these he was sure he could cultivate freely, for he could see that they exercised intelligence rather than memory.[21]

Battista Alberti did recover and shortly thereafter embarked on a career at the papal curia in Rome, in the service of various cardinals and in the college of abbreviators. He took minor orders and was possibly ordained a priest. At any rate, he was awarded benefices that ultimately ensured his financial independence. However, the rift with certain members of the Alberti family—above all the two cousins charged with the payment of his inheritance, Benedetto di Bernardo and Antonio di Ricciardo—worsened. It is a theme to which Alberti alludes time and again throughout his writings with marked bitterness.

For most of his adult life, Alberti was based in Rome, although he made extended stays at Florence following the lifting of the ban on some of the Alberti in 1428, and at many of the courts of central and northern Italy, where he claimed some of the most celebrated, and some of the most autocratic, rulers of the day as patrons. Alberti distinguished himself early on as a brilliant Latinist. Indeed, like Michelangelo, he began his career with a fake, his comic play *Philodoxus*, which he wrote under the name of Lepidus and successfully passed off as a Roman original. But Alberti was also an early champion of the vernacular. Indeed, he not only wrote a number of his most important works in Tuscan but also composed the first grammar of that language; organized a prominent Tuscan poetry competition, the Certame Coronario; and was the first, along with his friend Leonardo Dati, to compose a Tuscan poem in hexameters. In doing so, he entered into a polemical debate with many of the most prominent scholars of his day and pitted himself against the orthodox view, which did not regard the vernacular as capable of producing great literature.

Alberti's writings covered an astonishing breadth of subject. Early Latin works include the *Philodoxus* as well as *De commodis litterarum atque incommodis*, a treatise on the troubles facing young scholars. He composed four major moral dialogues in the vernacular: the *Theogenius*, *Della famiglia* (De familia), *Profugiorum ab aerumna libri*, and *De iciarchia*. The *Della famiglia* (On the family) must be judged one of the greatest works of the age, confronting many of the most pressing issues of the day while utilizing the dialogue form to preserve their complexity and avoid simplistic resolutions.

Throughout the 1430s and 1440s, Alberti penned his *Intercenales*, or *Dinner Pieces*,[22] a collection of Latin fables and short stories that often reveal an extraordinary creative energy and an acute, darkly ironic sense of humor. Much the same can be said of his comic "novel" *Momus*. Then there are the treatises on painting, sculpture, and architecture, each one the first of its kind to be written since antiquity and each profoundly original. In addition, Alberti was a poet, wrote short treatises on horses and on law, and completed an important work on cryptography. He seems also to have been the first, in his *Apologi centum*, to have revived the Aesopian fable.[23]

As we have seen, Alberti was a mathematician, having taken up the subject while recovering from the breakdown suffered in his youth.[24] His *Ludi rerum mathematicarum* demonstrates his proficiency, while those parts that deal with coordinate mapping, when taken together with his *Descriptio urbis romae*, make Alberti the ancestor of modern surveying techniques. A contemporary source refers to him as the equal, in both mathematics and astronomy, of the great astronomer Paolo Toscanelli.[25] Moreover, Alberti was an enthusiast of practical knowledge and a technologist. He tells us in his autobiography that he never ceased looking at things for himself, visiting craftsmen and inquiring of their craft. He employed Genoese divers in an attempt (in good measure successful) to raise a sunken Roman barge from the bed of Lake Nemi. Toward the end of his life, we find him filled with enthusiasm for the "German inventor who recently, by means of moveable type characters, made it possible to reproduce more than 200 volumes from one original text in 100 days with the help of no more than three workmen."[26] Perhaps most famously, Alberti became, in his maturity, an architect, designing some of the canonical works of the fifteenth century and helping to establish the *all'antica* style in Italy.[27]

This brief and selective overview of Alberti's activity gives some indication of his impressive range. In this sense, it is hardly surprising that the idea of his universality has long followed hard at his heels. Yet, insofar as it has become formulaic, the term sometimes seems to obscure the specifics of Alberti's thought rather than to illuminate them. Alberti was, for a long time, bound to a Burckhardtian, "heroic" idea of the Renaissance, which he was traditionally seen to personify. For it was Burckhardt, elaborating on Michelet's sketch, who bequeathed the lasting characterization of the Renaissance as a progressive era exemplified by great men.[28] In doing so, of course, he was reviving a narrative structure that was popular during the Renaissance itself and had its origins in classical civilization. As Anthony Grafton has pointed out, Burckhardt's account of Alberti was fundamentally based on the latter's autobiography, in which Alberti had in turn sought to cast himself in the mold of the great man of ancient times.[29] The heroic concept of the great man subsequently became central to most accounts of the Renaissance. Even Engels, who was hardly an exponent of the importance of individuals in the historical process, wrote enthusiastically of the Renaissance as a period of universal "giants," exemplified by Leonardo.[30]

A heroic image of Alberti could be employed to a number of ends. In Girolamo Mancini's major monograph of 1882, for example, Alberti became a symbol of the Risorgimento. Mancini explained in the preface that he considered it a citizenly duty to restore Alberti, who had been such a great benefactor to the *patria*, to the fame that he deserved. For not only was Alberti an important figure in the emergence of the Italian vernacular and a man gripped with the spirit of Italian renewal, but his own life and treatment by posterity seemed to parallel Italian history. After all, it was not long after Alberti's death that there began "the fatal period of servitude to foreigners." Alberti was forgotten. "He had taught the way in which men, families, and nations become preeminent, prosper, and resist calamities," Mancini observed. "They did not listen and the descendants paid by measure of tears and blood for the faults of the ancestors."[31] Alberti's works and reputation, we are told, dwindled into obscurity and were revived only when Italy herself began her revival toward the end of the eighteenth century. Mancini closed the book, just as he began it, with a patriotic, autobiographical note: "In the first flush of youth I set out to find information about him [Alberti], and fancying to tell his life story I girded myself up to put the much-desired project into action. Then, for a long time, I was prevented from realizing my youthful design by family affairs, private matters, and the patria, the rebuilding of which required the work of all its sons and which was served by me on town and provincial councils, in Parliament, and with arms in the volunteers' corps."[32]

The years spent in the archives researching Alberti's life, it is implied, were part of an act of patriotic duty similar to those listed above. Mancini's archival work was of no little consequence. A brilliant and thorough scholar, he unearthed documents and works by Alberti that formed the basis on which modern studies were founded. His overall view of Alberti was also influential for the literature that followed. Alberti was later singled out again as one of the great figures in Italian culture when his *Momus* was republished with an Italian translation by a fascist press.[33]

Alberti, the Renaissance, and Architectural History

Alberti was thus connected at an early stage to a rather heroic conception of the Renaissance, portrayed as one of the first to throw off the shackles of the Middle Ages and usher in modernity. Subsequent developments in Renaissance historiography sometimes served to reinforce this idea. Perhaps the most dramatic of these was the postwar view of the Renaissance pioneered by Hans Baron, which emphasized the importance of "civic humanism" as exemplified by the writings of Leonardo Bruni. This idea of the Renaissance was broadly positive and sometimes teleological, as can be seen from Baron's *The Crisis of the Early Italian Renaissance*, written in the direct aftermath of the Second World War and published in 1955. Writing in the tradition of Sismondi, Baron argued that Florence's lone defense of her republic against the Milanese tyranny of Giangaleazzo Visconti from 1400 to 1402 was a crucial moment in the formation of the

Renaissance and, by implication, in the history of the world. With the rest of Italy under the Milanese yoke, the Florentines developed a political culture and discourse based on the liberty they so treasured, which went on to form the basis of modern political thought. Baron's language is emotive. He describes the Florentines' "heroic defiance" of the "triumph of tyranny" as the "Athens on the Arno" stood "alone to confront one of those challenges of history in which a nation, facing eclipse or regeneration, has to prove its worth in a fight for survival."[34] Baron is quite explicit about the influence of the recent war on his writings, saying,

> One cannot trace the history of this explosive stage in the genesis of the states-system of the Renaissance without being struck by its resemblance to events in modern history when unifying conquest loomed over Europe. In a like fashion, Napoleon and Hitler, poised on the coast of the English channel and made confident by their victories over every relevant power but one, waited for the propitious time for their final leap. . . . This is the only perspective from which one can adequately reconstruct the crisis of the summer of 1402 and grasp its material and psychological significance for the political history of the Renaissance, and in particular for the growth of the Florentine civic spirit.[35]

Baron, moreover, spells out the process of historical evolution, linking the Italian city-states to those of ancient Greece and arguing that they reflected the modern system of nations in embryo. "The issue," he writes, "was an alternative between two diametrically opposed ways into the future. One possible outcome would be a system of equal states including princedoms and republics—an equilibrium of forces making Renaissance Italy in some respects akin to the Greek pattern of independent city-states and, in other respects, a miniature prototype of the modern western family of nations."[36]

Alberti was not a major figure in Baron's scheme, since his writings did not much resemble those of Salutati, Bruni, and the rest. Indeed, in a perceptive essay, Baron explored the extent to which Alberti's thought diverged from that of his "civic humanist" predecessors.[37] Nonetheless, Alberti was sometimes called a civic humanist by scholars who did not give much consideration to his political thought. More generally, this postwar version of the Renaissance sustained the idea of the period as a leap toward modernity, in which the narrow constraints of the Middle Ages were left behind. The Renaissance, Baron appears to suggest, was nothing less than the ancestor of Western democracy. Such a framework did not provide much impetus to reassess Alberti's thought, since it continued the tradition of a positive, progressive Renaissance, the movement to which Alberti had become inextricably bound.

The greater part of Alberti scholarship for a long while adhered to the figure cut by Burckhardt. Many of the dominant narratives of Renaissance scholarship and sometimes, by extension, of Alberti himself, were markedly teleological. Their final destinations may have diverged (modern unified Italy for Mancini; the twentieth-century Western democracy for Baron), but they shared the view of the Renaissance as essentially forward looking and progressive. Time and again, the Renaissance has been characterized as one of the great periods of history and specifically linked with both classical civilization and the Enlightenment. Voltaire, for example, ranked the age of the Medici—along with those of Pericles, Augustus, and Louis XIV—as one of the great peaks of history. Walter Pater, who strongly emphasized the link between the Renaissance and the classical period, also connected it to the Enlightenment, pointedly including an essay on Winkelmann in his famous volume *Renaissance*.[38] More recently, the historian George Holmes titled his excellent 1969 study on Florentine fifteenth-century humanism *The Florentine Enlightenment*. He went further still, calling his first chapter "The Humanist Avant-Garde" and thereby implicitly connecting the Renaissance not only with the Enlightenment but also with the cultural developments of the late nineteenth and early twentieth centuries—the birth of modernism itself.[39]

This idea of the great periods of history provides a clue in understanding the enduring image of Alberti. For it was, above all, in the sphere of cultural history that periods were generally judged to have been exceptional or not. The very idea of the Renaissance, in its modern sense, grew out of the fledgling discourse of the history of art and architecture, rather than history proper. Alberti, as an architect, architectural and artistic theorist, and urbanist, accordingly occupied a place of great importance. Indeed, it can hardly be missed that those periods of history typically identified as "great" in these narratives—ancient Greece and Rome, the Italian Renaissance, and the Enlightenment—coincide more or less exactly with key phases in the development of "classical" architecture. As the author of *De re aedificatoria*, Alberti thus provides a crucial historical link, connecting the culture of his own period, through Vitruvius and the architectural principles of the ancient builders, to that of the ancient world, and bequeathing this legacy to the academicians, treatise writers, and architects of the Enlightenment.

Urbanism

These great historical periods, it should be stressed, typically have been seen as pinnacles not only in the history of architecture but also in the history of the city. Civilization, not unreasonably, has been viewed as an outgrowth of the *civitas* and, by extension, the *urbs*. Thus, in the introduction to the 1952 text *Golden Ages of the Great Cities*, Sir Ernest Barker writes,

> The purpose of this book . . . has been to assemble (as it were on a necklace or in a coronet) a collection of historical essays on the dozen or so most famous cities of Europe, as they were at the time of their highest civilization and the peak of their cultural influence. There is a reason, and a cogent reason for this concentration on the city. Etymology is sufficient to teach us that the city (*civitas*) is the nursing mother of civilization. The Greek city-state, or *Polis*, was the original fountain of the notion of a free political society composed of equal citizens living together in fraternity under a system of ordered justice. The city-state, or *civitas*, of Rome was the source of our notions of civilization, or "civility" (or in other words the way of life which belongs to cities); and another Latin word for city—the word *urbs*—has produced the tradition of "urbanity," that is to say of grace and good manners in social intercourse. A book on the golden cities of Europe, as they stood at their prime, is accordingly also a book on the sources and springs of European civilization.[40]

Of course, Renaissance Florence is represented in the subsequent pages in an essay by Harold Acton, along with the other cities that one might expect to see. Acton argues that during the fifteenth century, "Florence was the centre of human culture, second only to Athens in its influence on European civilization."[41] Again, the overall conception of the work, written during the cold war, is teleological. The final city discussed is New York, the modern city par excellence, which was in the process of cementing its takeover from Paris as the cultural center of the Western world.[42] New York, center of culture and beacon of liberty, stands as the inheritor of a long civic and cultural tradition that begins in democratic Athens and travels by way of republican Florence.[43] That such narratives still have life is amply demonstrated by recent events. It is surely no accident that the British government's Urban Task Force, chaired by the high-profile architect Lord Rogers of Riverside, titled its 1999 report *Towards an Urban Renaissance*. Aside from the reference to Le Corbusier's *Vers une architecture*, the title employs the word "renaissance" both to signal the rebirth of the city and to associate it with what is seen as a great period in urban history. This message is spelled out in the first paragraph of the report's opening chapter: "From Hellenic Athens and classical Rome, to renaissance Florence and Georgian London, history is rich with examples of towns and cities which embodied the best of urban tradition. These were the places which stimulated new ideas and transacted knowledge. They inspired generations in terms of their design, their economic strength and their cultural diversity. They live on as a reminder of the vital links which can be forged between city and citizen."[44] Here again is the familiar narrative employed by historians and art historians since the eighteenth century, aimed directly at influencing urban planning in Britain at the start of the twenty-first century. The great eras of history are also seen as the great eras of the city, just as they were for Voltaire, Burckhardt, and Engels, to name but a few. Even Ruskin would have recognized the story, although he would have interpreted it differently.[45]

Florence

The historical reputation of Renaissance Florence is of particular importance here because of its effect on ideas about Alberti as an urbanist. The Renaissance has been thought of as a pinnacle of urban history in two specific ways: first, it witnessed the flourishing of the actual city, generally exemplified by Florence, and second, it witnessed the creation of a body of theoretical writing about the city, as exemplified by *De re aedificatoria*. It is perhaps not surprising then that the boundaries have on occasion become blurred and that Alberti, the son of a prominent Florentine family and a eulogist of Florentine art and architecture, has sometimes been seen as advocating a city organized along Florentine lines. Westfall, for example, strongly implies that Florence and its civic-humanist political philosophy were at the base of Alberti's speculations:

> The architectural treatise contains an extremely advanced consciousness of activity as a positive virtue, and it is permeated with the belief that civic activity which involves all citizens in the actions of the city brings order to the city. Alberti acquired this belief in Florence. The individual, the city, and virtue were among the main issues under discussion among the humanists in Florence when he arrived for his first extended residence in his *patria* in 1434. During the two decades that followed he argued that the individual must actively use his talents and that the city should be his arena.[46]

There is double cause to be cautious here, for not only is the idea of Alberti as a "civic humanist" highly questionable, but the image of Renaissance Florence is also far from contentious.[47] Historians of Florentine art and architecture have, perhaps understandably, tended to idealize their accounts of the city, connecting its cultural flourish to the "republican" constitution—sometimes in a rather nonspecific way.[48] The effect of such ideas on perceptions of Alberti might be seen in Samuel Y. Edgerton's important 1976 study *The Renaissance Rediscovery of Linear Perspective*, in which Renaissance Florence is discussed under the heading "Alberti's Florence." Edgerton does not examine Alberti's urban theory here, but he does draw a direct link between Florence and Alberti's character and ideas. "The miracle of Renaissance art and thought," he writes, "including the advent of linear perspective, owed in large measure to the unique institution of the Italian city-state, with its republican form of government. The relatively small size of these Italian states itself encouraged individuality by making possible frequent and easy communication between the lowliest citizens and the top-level governmental administrators, for new ideas to find reception and reward, and for unorthodox opinion to enjoy tolerance. Indeed, the city-state fostered a general feeling that any citizen could make his fame and fortune through the exercise of pure intelligence."[49]

The claim that the formulation of the rules of linear perspective owed in large measure to the republican form of government in Florence, though not absurd, is nonetheless rather startling. One wonders how it could then be possible that so much high-quality mathematical and artistic theory emerged from, for instance, ducal Urbino. Such accounts of Florence must be considered rather partial. As many historians have pointed out, one could equally construct an image of Florence as a city with quite staggering disparities of wealth, where the poor were harshly treated and where few, in reality, enjoyed political rights.[50] Nor was life guaranteed to be pleasurable for the rich, for whom factional struggles could be devastating. The image of Florence as a society offering a kind of equality of opportunity, where anyone could make their fame and fortune on the basis of sharp wits and enthusiasm, would seem, at the very least, to be overstating the case. The purpose of this book is not to rehash debates about the historiography of Renaissance Florence, nor to brand the city, in a simplistic manner, as having been essentially "nice" or "nasty." We should be aware, however, of the effects that idealizing scholarship can and have had on our image of Alberti as a Florentine and as an urbanist.

This is not to deny that Florence made a strong impression on Alberti. The exile of his family came to an end in 1428, and he became acquainted with his patria soon afterward. The famous preface to the Tuscan version of his treatise on painting, *De pictura*, amply testifies to the enthusiasm that the city inspired in him. He addressed the work to Brunelleschi, who had succeeded in constructing the vast dome of Florence Cathedral without recourse to wooden centering—a previously unheard-of feat of engineering. "I used both to marvel," Alberti writes, "and to regret that so many excellent and divine arts and sciences, which we know from their works and from historical accounts were possessed in great abundance by the talented men of antiquity, have now disappeared and are almost entirely lost. . . . Consequently I believed what I heard many say that Nature, mistress of all things, had grown old and weary, and was no longer producing intellects any more than giants on a vast and wonderful scale such as she did in what one might call her youthful and more glorious days." Alberti's introduction to Florence, however, caused a change of heart:

> But after I came back here to this most beautiful of cities from the long exile in which we Albertis have grown old, I recognized in many, but above all in you, Filippo, and in our great friend the sculptor Donatello and in the others, Nencio, Luca and Masaccio, a genius for every laudable enterprise in no way inferior to any of the ancients who gained fame in these arts. I then realized that the ability to achieve the highest distinction in any meritorious activity lies in our own industry and diligence no less than in the favours of Nature and

of the times. I admit that for the ancients, who had many precedents to learn from and to imitate, it was less difficult to master those noble arts which for us today prove arduous; but it follows that our fame should be all the greater if without preceptors and without any model to imitate we discover arts and sciences hitherto unheard of and unseen. What man, however hard of heart or jealous, would not praise Filippo the architect when he sees here such an enormous construction towering above the skies, vast enough to cover the entire Tuscan population with its shadow, and done without the aid of beams or elaborate wooden supports? Surely a feat of engineering, if I am not mistaken, that people did not believe possible these days and was probably equally unknown and unimaginable among the ancients.[51]

The youthful Alberti was clearly impressed by the city and enthused by the architectural and artistic accomplishments of his Florentine compatriots, going so far as to argue that they had surpassed even the ancients.[52] Such enthusiasm must surely bear on Alberti's urban thought, but we should not consider this preface the last word on his position regarding Florence. It must be remembered that it is a dedicatory piece of writing and is naturally laudatory in tone. One must balance Alberti's enthusiasm with his remark later in life that he never managed to feel truly at home in his patria. "I am like a foreigner there," Battista says in the *De iciarchia*. "I went there too rarely, and lived there too little."[53] Florence was undoubtedly of great importance in shaping Alberti's urban thought, but that does not mean that we should understand his attitude toward it as one of straightforward approval.[54] Much less should Florence be considered the model for an ideal city that Alberti advocates in *De re aedificatoria*.

Recent Scholarship

It is no exaggeration to say that Alberti studies have undergone a revolution in the last forty years. Led by Eugenio Garin's pioneering article of 1972, many scholars have radically reassessed Alberti's reputation and position. Having discovered some previously unknown *Intercenales* (the short "dinner pieces" written by Alberti throughout the 1430s and 1440s), Garin began to see Alberti as a "disquieting, unforeseeable, and bizarre writer," constantly engaging in "games of wild fantasy and stylistic affectations."[55] Rather than the positive, civic-minded individual he had sometimes been made to appear, Alberti stood out for his pessimism and sense of existential crisis. The effects of Garin's intervention may hardly be overstated; one distinguished scholar has recently described Garin's writings on Alberti as constituting the most important judgments on Alberti since those of Cristoforo Landino in the fifteenth century.[56] Unsurprisingly, many scholars followed Garin's lead, and a vigorous revisionist current developed in Alberti scholarship.[57]

Alongside this reassessment, and to a large extent stimulated by it, there has been an ever greater focus on particular aspects of Alberti's oeuvre. Light has been shed on many hitherto dark corners, and some of the texts that were traditionally considered less important have received more attention. There is now a journal titled *Albertiana*, the Fondazione Centro Studi Leon Battista Alberti has been established in Mantua, and Alberti's writings continue to appear in new editions and translations. Indeed, since the centenary celebrations of 2004, the field of Alberti studies has rather exploded and a series of major conferences and exhibitions has stimulated an exponential rise in new publications.

It might seem surprising that any one figure could sustain the kind of attention that Alberti has received in recent years. That it has been possible in Alberti's case is testament to one thing above all: the stunning richness of his writings. Alberti, it must be emphasized from the beginning, was a writer of extraordinary brilliance and originality.[58] We should not mistake him for an architect and theorist of the arts who also produced some minor literary works. Nor should we characterize him as a kind of humanist hack, adept at stringing together commonplaces and churning out derivative treatises. On the contrary, Alberti ought to be recognized as a major figure in the literary history of Italy and Europe—a highly original Latin stylist who also developed a fundamentally new kind of vernacular literature.[59] Alberti's writings turn an acute and sophisticated eye on man and the world, regarding them in all of their moral and intellectual complexity.

One can readily see why increased attention has been paid to Alberti's literary output in recent decades. Apart from the rediscovery of a number of the *Intercenales*, a growing interest in literary irony and ambiguity from the mid-twentieth century provided fertile ground for a new appreciation of Alberti's works. Moreover, some of the most prominent features of his writings cohere closely with those things that have been of greatest interest to postmodernist critics—for example, his intertextuality and his persistent authorial self-reflection. Much insight has been gained from the approach, pioneered by Roberto Cardini, that conceives of Alberti's writings as a form of literary mosaic that may be dismantled by a patient scholar. Such an approach, which strongly foregrounds intertextuality, appears to be sanctioned by Alberti himself in a passage of the *Profugiorum ab aerumna* in which a character uses a mosaic floor as a simile for literary composition.[60]

It is quite understandable that the reassessment of Alberti's writing has taken place largely, although by no means exclusively, in Italian. While Alberti's literary contribution was for a long time rather ignored, this was perhaps less the case in Italy than elsewhere. Certainly, Anglophone scholarship—with some important exceptions—tended for a long time to regard him as, above all, an architect and theorist of the arts, relegating his literary works to an inferior position. Italian, quite naturally, remains the language of Alberti scholarship today, and the majority of newly published material has appeared in that language.

The renewed attention paid to Alberti has resulted in some important reassessments of his relationships with a number of cities. Among the great many contributions, we might single out Luca Boschetto's *Leon Battista Alberti e Firenze*, the first major study of Alberti's interactions with Florence. Stefano Borsi has produced a series of publications that deal with Alberti's relationship with Rome and Naples; these works are of crucial importance and demonstrate astonishing scholarly erudition. Borsi's writings fizz with new ideas, arguments, and speculations of many different kinds. Christine Smith and Joseph F. O'Connor's recent examination of Rome under Nicholas V is likewise a monumental achievement of scholarship that must be considered indispensible, while many publications by Alberto Cassani have cast new light on Alberti's approach to architecture.

Momus

One of the most important results of the reassessment of Alberti has been a new focus on his comic "novel" *Momus*. Having remained in relative obscurity for centuries, the *Momus* is now hailed as a unique and brilliant masterpiece, one of Alberti's most significant achievements. It has appeared in new editions and recently in English translation for the first time ever. Satirical in intention, *Momus* undoubtedly takes aim at the papacy and the curia. Scholars have successively rolled back the presumed date of its composition so that it is now no longer seen to target only Eugenius IV but perhaps even the entire papacy of Nicholas V as well. It is likely that Alberti's work on *Momus* overlapped to some degree with his work on *De re aedificatoria*.

Momus is the story of a minor deity, the god of harsh and biting criticism. Although lowly in status, Alberti tells us, Momus is a thoroughly unique individual entirely unlike any other god or man. He is not simply a contrarian but despises gods and men in equal measure. Alberti relates an intricate narrative in which Momus, having offended the gods and challenged the position of Jupiter, is awarded the same punishment suffered by Prometheus. Desperate to avoid this, Momus takes flight and falls through a hole in the heavens. He finds himself in Etruria, where he must live as an exile among men and where he instantly invents new ways to pursue his vendetta against the gods. He becomes first a poet who tells only of the immoral ways of the gods, and then a philosopher in the cynic mode, arguing that gods do not exist, or none such as would pay the slightest heed to human beings. In a short period of time, Momus succeeds in reducing a formerly pious people to a nation of atheists.

The gods ultimately decide that it would be less risky to bring Momus back to heaven than to allow him to continue his activities on earth, and thus he is restored to his old dignity. However, he is not the same individual as he was before. Having learned from men the arts of simulation and dissimulation, Momus prospers as a courtier and is able to convince Jupiter, in revenge for his ill treatment at the hands of men, that the world should be destroyed and replaced with a new and superior version. Momus's strategy eventually comes unstuck as he allows his mask to slip. This time he does not escape the wrath of the gods and ends up castrated and chained to a rock in the ocean with only his head above the surface of the water.

Momus is animated by a pervasive satirical energy that is directed at all and sundry: gods, mortals, philosophers, and particularly, in the form of Jupiter, the figure of the ruler. There is a clear debt to Lucian, and Alberti explains early on that he wrote in a consciously ironic style. The reader should both laugh and learn; although his manner may be comic, Alberti says that he will address subjects of the utmost seriousness. Given the playful nature of the text, it is not surprising that the interpretation of *Momus* should have proved difficult. We are continually left uncertain as to where the author's irony begins and ends. *Momus* reveals an intense interest in the notion of dissimulation, the adoption of masks, cunning speech, and the issue of appearances that are at variance with reality. It appears to be marked by emotional ferment and contradictory sentiments of bitterness, mockery, self-doubt, and exultation. The text feels distinctly subversive, even if we might sometimes struggle to identify exactly what is at stake. It also feels, just as Alberti says of Momus himself, as though it is rather different from any other work of the period. It has been suggested that Alberti proposes here a radically new form of humorism.

In a pioneering essay, Manfredo Tafuri suggested that *Momus* is a crucial text for understanding Alberti as a theorist of architecture. Indeed, he asserted that *Momus* stands in a dialogue with *De re aedificatoria* and that each work must be read with an eye to its counterpart. Arguing from this premise, Tafuri succeeded in turning received wisdom on its head: Alberti was not the architectural brain behind Nicholas V's *renovatio* of Rome but was instead a dissident figure, one who was highly skeptical of the pope's architectural schemes. Tafuri observed that a close reading of *Momus* and *De re* together remained to be undertaken but would likely be highly remunerative. Many steps have since been taken toward this end, and Tafuri's view has largely prevailed. The current study makes frequent reference to *Momus*. More broadly, the principle that Alberti's architectural theory and his literary output are strongly interrelated shall be observed here. Alberti's architectural thought has sometimes been treated as though it may be entirely separable from his more literary work. However, an attentive reading of the texts does not support such a view.[61]

That is not to say that there are not methodological advantages to be had by concentrating on individual works. Françoise Choay's structuralist reading of *De re* considers the treatise apart from Alberti's other works, as a fundamentally distinct order of writing, and constitutes one of the major recent contributions to our understanding of Alberti as an urbanist. Choay argues that Alberti does not offer an ideal city in *De re* but rather is concerned with generative rules for the entire built domain. An ideal city may well exist, she argues, in the *Theogenius* or the *Della famiglia*, but not in *De re*. Such has more or less become the orthodoxy regarding Alberti and the city, and many scholars have since dismissed the term "ideal city" altogether, arguing that it is inapplicable not only to Alberti but to the fifteenth century in general.[62]

It is certainly true that Alberti does not propose an ideal city in *De re*, nor does he do so in any of his other works. The issue of the city for Alberti, one senses, was too complex for such reductive treatment. Moreover, he was not interested in unobtainable ideals but in what might truly be achieved. Alberti was born in exile, and we might speculate that for exiles the city became a "question" in a way that it was not for ordinary citizens. Excluded from their patria, exiles were forced to turn a more objective eye on the other cities of the peninsula—to compare one city to the next, consider the advantages and disadvantages of each, and ask what really constitutes a functioning and attractive urban environment. Precisely this point is raised in the *Della famiglia* when the young humanist Lionardo asks the elderly Giannozzo how he would choose a city in which to live in a foreign land. "How would you be able to tell whether the city is suitable in every respect?" Lionardo inquires. "Would it not be difficult to recognize, not to speak of finding it?"[63]

Giannozzo replies with a lengthy discourse in which he enumerates those features that one should search for in the good city. It should have a healthy environment, not be too exposed to enemy attack, be sited in fertile land without the need to import necessities, and be free from disease, easy to withdraw from in emergencies, and populated with honest and wealthy citizens. Most of all, it should be justly administered, something that in itself will protect from "enemy attack, adversity, or the wrath of God."[64] This prompts Lionardo to ask, "Where is one ever to find a city with so many marvelous qualities? Unless you think Venice is less lacking in these virtues than any other city, for I know you enjoy living there. As for me, I certainly think such a city would be difficult to find." "Nevertheless," maintains Giannozzo, "I should look for it, for I should not want to be sorry later because of my negligence. I should settle in the city where the best and the largest number of the things I mentioned are to be found."[65] This type of pragmatic formulation is typical of Alberti's thinking.

It should be no surprise, then, that he does not offer us an ideal city. Alberti does, however, offer a range of proposals and considers a number of different urban situations, some of which cohere well with one another. His speculations regarding the city have a remarkable richness, the same richness that pervades a great deal of his thought. Indeed, Alberti's general reluctance to reduce the tensions inherent in intellectual positions and his tendencies to highlight ambivalence and to explore oppositions are some of the things that make him an important and compelling thinker.

Any student of Alberti must confront difficult problems of interpretation. Time and again, scholars have commented that Alberti often appears to face in two directions at the same time. On the one hand, there is the Alberti who repeatedly states that man is born to be of use to his fellow man, a staunch defender of the active life with supreme confidence in reason and the value of the liberal arts. There is Alberti the builder, literally remaking the city according to humanistic principles. However, these facets of Alberti's character are balanced by others: Alberti the disillusioned skeptic, the bitter and wounded exile and orphan, the man who despairs of human nature and detects *vanitas* in man's supposedly great undertakings. These binary opposites can feel unsatisfactory, and many scholars have, from time to time, spoken of the need to restore Alberti to a unified whole. Yet it is hard to read Alberti's works without the impression that he is indeed, in many ways, a divided thinker. The reader must also keep in mind that Alberti's works are many and various, comprising a number of different orders of writing and produced for different purposes. Many Albertian works touch on common themes, but they cannot be read as though they might constitute a single text.

Like all humanist writers, Alberti makes frequent allusion to antique literature. He was fond of the maxim he derived from Terence *nihil dictum quin prius dictum* (nothing is said which has not been said before), and a considerable portion of his writings is made up of material that could be described as commonplace. This complicates matters for the reader, who is sometimes left wondering whether Alberti is speaking his mind or merely going through the motions, saying the kind of things that "everyone" said. There is a temptation to dismiss much of Alberti's discourse (for example, when he writes about town versus country) as being *merely* the reiteration of commonplaces. Where topoi are employed, it has sometimes been suggested, we will learn more about Alberti's attitudes toward writing than his attitudes toward the subject being discussed. Yet this approach does a kind of violence to Alberti's creations. While his works do indeed contain material that has been taken from ancient and other sources, they must also be considered as wholes—texts that are animated by their own particular driving force. In reality, all language, as Alberti is fond of reminding us, has a history. All language is made up of things that have been uttered before, and all utterances have the potential to drag their histories along behind them. Alberti must be read with an eye to his own arguments and to the consistency of his positions.

DESTRUCTION

I will . . . go forward with my history, and speak of small and great cities alike.
For many states that were once great have now become small: and those that were
great in my time were small formerly.
—Herodotus, *Histories* 1.5

Disasters, Natural and Man-Made

It is a commonplace of historical writing that cities, and the civilizations
they support, will be subject to periods of rise and fall. Long before the
formulation of the laws of thermodynamics, human intuition suspected
that anything that is composed of parts must eventually break up, and
cities are perhaps the most complicated assemblages that mankind has
created. Throughout history, cities constantly appear to pass in and out
of being—expanding, contracting, undergoing destruction and reconstruction. Each city holds within itself not only the possibility (some might say
inevitability) of its final destruction but also that of its total transformation,
of upheaval and reinvention. The inhabitants of fifteenth-century Italy,
living on a peninsula that was dominated by city-states of various sizes, can
hardly have been immune to such feelings.

The cities of medieval and Renaissance Italy were ephemeral entities, simultaneously fragile and resilient, and subject to continual change,

terrible catastrophe, incredible resurgence, and rapid reversals of fortune. As Lauro Martines has written, "Cities and the problems of cities have haunted the European imagination since the twelfth century. Already then cities routed imperial armies in northern Italy and were in turn reconquered or razed to the ground, only to spring forth again a few years later— larger, more combative, and more populous. Urban vitality seemed at times a function of temporary defeat: strike down a city and you were sure to call forth—at all events in Italy—a still more formidable enemy."[1] In a region where individual city-states waged frequent and often indecisive wars against one another, foreign armies regularly fought sustained campaigns, and the pope tussled for power with the emperor, most city-states could expect to experience the threat of imminent destruction at some point. Indeed, many underwent conquest by an enemy and would themselves, in turn, subject some lesser city; as Martines points out, defeat and resurgence were almost given features of urban life.

Of course, soldiers did not constitute the only threat to the city-states. Accidental and natural disasters were frequent and often devastating. Fire, whether started purposefully or not, posed a serious risk to all cities. Villani tells us that in 1304 an outbreak of fire resulting from factional violence destroyed more than 1,700 buildings in Florence. The fire raged through the center of the city, where all of the most important things were, and those buildings that were not burned were looted.[2] In 1333, Florence was hit by a devastating flood that destroyed many of the bridges over the Arno and wreaked havoc on the city.[3] Furthermore, many parts of Italy were troubled by earthquakes. In 1349, with Italy still reeling from the plague, a terrible earthquake visited destruction on the cities of Perugia, Orvieto, Spoleto, L'Aquila, and Borgo San Seplocro, among others. In Rome, it brought down the campanile of San Paolo Fuori le Mura and parts of the Torre del Conte and Torre delle Milizie.[4] During Alberti's own lifetime, earthquakes continued to shake the peninsula with regularity.[5]

Natural disasters in the country could lead to shortages of food and illness in the cities. Sometimes it might have seemed as though disaster followed upon disaster, with storms, flooding, famine, and pestilence appearing in rapid succession. The year 1456, during which Alberti may still have been completing his treatise, stands as an example. In April, a fierce hailstorm, centered on Terra di Lavoro, damaged all manner of vegetation in the kingdom of Naples, especially the wheat and barley. In the country around Ferrara, the crop was destroyed by flooding. In the summer, a hurricane devastated the Florentine countryside, uprooting trees, destroying buildings, and claiming more than twenty lives. Autumn saw the grape harvest in the kingdom of Naples ruined on account of excessive moisture. Newly sown seeds, meanwhile, were wiped out by heavy rains. At Florence, the Arno burst its banks and flooded the city. During the night between December 4 and 5, the kingdom of Naples was rocked by an immensely powerful earthquake. The next month, Terra di Bari suffered a snowstorm of unprecedented ferocity, which killed livestock and destroyed the olive harvest. Famine followed throughout the greater part of the peninsula, with plague close behind.[6]

It is difficult, if not for the most part impossible, to measure the effects of these events on the mentalities of individuals in the late Middle Ages. However, it seems fair to speculate that they were often powerful. While from a historical perspective we might marvel at the cities' resilience and powers of renewal, those who lived through sackings and conquests must have been deeply affected by the violence they witnessed. Moreover, each time an army approached the city walls, from the point of view of the citizens, it would surely have threatened permanent, as much as temporary, destruction. Similarly, natural disasters, even when relatively small and localized, could be profoundly affecting. As Jussi Hanska has observed, "Such local natural disasters occurred, and indeed still do occur, fairly often. There was not a generation that did not experience some kind of natural disaster. Most likely such disasters did happen not only once, but several times. The frequency and potential loss of lives caused by even small-scale disasters hence had a long-term effect on the mentality and activities of the people."[7]

Ruins and the Fragmented Past

Beyond the natural and man-made disasters that could be witnessed firsthand, Italy furnished ample evidence of those that had occurred in the past. Alberti himself occupied a city of ruins. As a resident of Rome, he would have been reminded on a daily basis of the potential for even the greatest of civilizations to meet with disaster. Large areas of the city, although within the third-century Aurelian walls, lay abandoned and had given way to farmland. The shells of great buildings were sometimes inaccessible on account of the impassable undergrowth around them. To the horror of Alberti and some of his humanist contemporaries, the despoliation of ruins continued apace. Some great structures were so entirely buried and ruined that almost nothing of their original appearance survived.[8] Moreover, it was not only the physical fabric of the city that had undergone destruction but also the body of knowledge that related to it. The topography of ancient Rome could only be recovered in a fragmentary manner and with great effort. To this end, Poggio sought out inscriptions and Biondo combed ancient texts; Alberti must also have been considered an expert, since he acted as a guide to the ruins during a diplomatic visit by the Florentines Lorenzo de' Medici, Donato Acciauoli, and Bernardo Rucellai in 1471.[9]

In the preface to the *Della famiglia*, Alberti lamented the collapse of the Roman world, recounting how "barbarian nations" and "remote subjected peoples" had become "daring enough to force their way onto your most sacred soil and burn the nest and the very seat of that ancient empire of empires."[10] The lament was part of a call for renewal, and Alberti reflects a typical aspect of Italian humanism in questioning the meaning of the destruction of Roman civilization for his own society. Ruins raised questions not only about the past but also about the present: Could the greatness of ancient civilizations ever be achieved again? Was the culture of antiquity irrecoverably lost, or did it in some way persist in contemporary society? Must all civilizations come to ruin? Manuel Chrysoloras, in his seminal ekphrasis comparing the old and the new Romes, provides a good example of the way in which the past was brought to bear by some humanists on the present. Comparing the ruined to the preserved, Chrysoloras attempted to reimagine the glories of ancient Rome and to emphasize the continuities with his own day. Simultaneously, however, he exposed the yawning gulf that separated his own time from antiquity and revealed quite how much had been lost.

Ruins could also invite speculation about the future, leading one to ponder the ultimate fate of one's own surroundings and to imagine the buildings and cities of the present reduced to ruin in years to come.[11] The Florentine chancellor Coluccio Salutati did just this in a famous passage from his *De seculo et religione*:

> Let us climb the hill dedicated to the holy blood of the Blessed Miniato on the left bank of the Arno, or the two-peaked mountain of ancient Fiesole, or any of the surrounding ridges from which every

cranny of our city of Florence can be fully seen. Let us climb up, pray, and look down on the city walls jutting upward to the heavens, on the splendid towers, on the vast churches, and the splendid palaces. It is difficult to believe these could have been completed even at public expense, let alone built out of private men's wealth, as is the case. But then let us bring our eyes or minds back to each individual structure, and consider what deterioration each one of them has sustained. The Palazzo del Popolo has been admired by all and is, it must be admitted, a superb work; yet through its own weight it is collapsing on itself and is falling apart with gaping cracks both within and without. It already seems to be foretelling its own eventual, gradual ruin. Our Cathedral, a wonderful work with which—if it were ever completed—one would believe no building made by human beings could be compared, was undertaken with great expense and exertion and has now been taken as far as the fourth storey, which the fine campanile reaches too. Nothing could be decorated with marble more beautifully, nothing could be painted or designed more attractively. But the Cathedral has developed a fissure and seems about to end in a state of hideous ruin: soon it will be in need of restoring quite as much as completing.[12]

Salutati imagines an aerial view of his city from San Miniato or Fiesole, rather as Poggio, when opening his *De varietate fortunae*, and Alberti, when undertaking his coordinate mapping, were later to peer at Rome from the Capitoline. By removing himself from the city, Salutati is able to transform it from the setting of his daily activity, the stage of his own intentionality, into an object of reflection. Even as he marvels at the wonders of building that have been performed in Florence, he is struck by the awareness that each of these must end in ruin. More than a simple *vanitas* motif, the passage seems to acknowledge the inherent fragility of the city as a project.

Alberti, Nature, and the Origins of Architecture

Against this background, it is perhaps not surprising that Alberti emerges from his architectural treatise as an author much preoccupied by the potential destruction of buildings and cities.[13] In the last book of *De re aedificatoria*, he considers how both man and nature might pose a risk to the built environment in a passage that expresses many of the sentiments that are to be found throughout the treatise:

> I think that those [problems with buildings] which result from some outside influence are almost too numerous and varied to list. The saying "Time conquers all things" refers to some of them; the batteries of old age are dangerous and very powerful; the body has no defense against the laws of Nature and must succumb to old age; some think even heavens mortal, because they are a body. We feel the sun burn or the shadows freeze; we feel the power of ice and wind. The working of this engine can crack and crumble even the hardest flint; vast storms will tear away and thrust out huge rocks from the highest cliff, so that they will crash down along with much of the mountain. Then there is damage caused by man. God help me, I sometimes cannot stomach it when I see with what negligence, or to put it more crudely, by what avarice they allow the ruin of things that because of their great nobility the barbarians, the raging enemy have spared; or those which all-conquering, all-ruining time might easily have allowed to stand forever. Then there are frequent accidents by fire, lightning, earthquakes, battering of waves and floods, and so many irregular, improbable, and incredible things that the prodigious force of Nature can produce, which will mar and upset even the most carefully conceived plan of an architect.[14]

Here, as elsewhere, Alberti's preoccupation with destruction is bound up with his concept of nature—of both the human and more general kind. Indeed, the idea of nature is at the very heart of Alberti's speculations and strongly inflects his conception of the development of architecture. In considering his approach to the issues of destruction and permanence, it might thus be useful to examine Alberti's account of the very origins of architecture and to consider how this relates to his ideas about nature.

At several places in his treatise, Alberti is keen to stress that architecture arose from fundamentally pragmatic concerns. In the prologue to the work, he observes, "Some have said that it was fire and water which were initially responsible for bringing men together into communities, but we, considering how useful, even indispensable, a roof and walls are for men, are convinced that it was they that drew and kept men together."[15] For Alberti, the need for shelter provided the original impulse to form communities and construct buildings, an opinion that he elaborates elsewhere in his treatise. Early in the first book, he returns to the theme during his discussion of lineamenta. He surmises that, having found a place to rest in a location that was safe from danger, primitive people took possession of the site and divided it into spaces according to function. They then "began to consider how to build a roof, as a shelter from the sun and the rain. For this purpose they built walls on which a roof could be laid—for they realized that in this way they would be the better protected from icy storms and frosty winds." No matter who oversaw this process, and however ornate and diverse buildings may have become, Alberti insists, "I believe that such were the original occasion and the original ordinance of building." Moreover, he adds that "no one will question our account of their [buildings'] origins."[16] Similarly, he starts the fourth book, on public works, by discussing the origins of architecture, speculating that "if our surmise is correct, man first made himself a shelter to protect himself and his own from the assault of the weather. Men's appetite then grew beyond what was essential for their well-being, to include all that would contribute to their unbridled demand for every comfort."[17]

In offering this explanation of the origins of architecture and communities, Alberti explicitly contradicts the account given by Vitruvius. The Roman architect had begun the second book of his *De architectura* by explaining how human beings, who previously were "born like animals in forests and caves and woods, and passed their life feeding on food of the fields,"[18] had been brought into communities by the discovery of fire. After this initial breakthrough, Vitruvius argued, the development of human society was swift:

> They added fuel, and thus keeping it [the fire] up, they brought others; and pointing it out by signs, they showed what advantages they had from it. In this concourse of mankind, when sounds were variously uttered by the breath, by daily custom they fixed words as they had chanced to come. Then, indicating things more frequently and by habit, they came by chance to speak according to the event, and so they generated conversation with one another. Therefore, because of the discovery of fire, there arose at the beginning concourse among men, deliberation, and a life in common. Many came together into one place, having from nature this boon beyond other animals: that

they should walk, not with the head down, but upright, and should look upon the magnificence of the world and of the stars. They also easily handled with their hands and fingers whatever they wished. Hence after thus meeting together, they began, some to make shelters of leaves, some to dig caves under the hills, some to make of mud and wattles places for shelter, imitating the nests of swallows and their methods of building.[19]

Thus, as human beings converged in order to enjoy the advantages offered by the fire, proximity caused them to develop language. The results were dramatic: concourse, deliberation, and a life in common. Sociability led to politics; after politics came building.

Alberti's readiness to contradict Vitruvius has often been commented on. However, it is worth considering what caused him to depart from his predecessor's opinion on this occasion. Vitruvius's account, although starting from the pragmatic premise of the importance of fire, is essentially an idealistic one with deliberation and social concourse at its heart. Politics, one might infer, was for Vitruvius prior to architecture; it was deliberation that created the necessary conditions for the invention of useful disciplines. Alberti, on the contrary, mentions none of these things. Neither deliberation nor concourse, nor even language, is posited as being prior to architecture or necessary for its development. Rather, Alberti characterizes architecture as having developed from an essential condition of man's being in the world: his confrontation with the forces of nature. While Alberti's thinking about nature is far too complex to be summarized briefly, we might for now simply note that in *De re aedificatoria*, nature often appears as a destructive force that threatens the projects of human beings.

Of course, the notion of nature as containing elements that might appear harsh and oppositional to men and their creations is a topos that relates to a strain of Stoic thought. It might also, however, be connected to some of the great Christian thinkers who taught that man's relationship with nature had undergone a fundamental change as a result of the Fall. It had sometimes been argued that following the expulsion from Paradise, man entered into a new order of nature—one that was at best indifferent and at worst actively hostile. Some thinkers went so far as to suggest that the whole of nature had fallen along with man. Alberti never repeats these views. Indeed, the extent to which he was prepared to reason outside of traditional theological frameworks is striking, and theological arguments are rarely discussed directly in his writings. Nonetheless, he does approach the subject of the Fall in an oblique manner in his comic masterpiece, *Momus*.

A large portion of the fourth book of *Momus* is given over to the adventures of Charon, ferryman to the underworld, and Gelastus, the shade of a dead philosopher. Through scheming and dissimulation, Momus has succeeded in persuading Jupiter that the world is fundamentally corrupt and should be destroyed in order to make way for an improved version. To prepare the ground, Heat, Hunger, Fever, and the like start to wipe out humanity with all manner of afflictions, resulting in an unusually large number of shades requiring Charon's services. Learning from the shades that the destruction of the world is imminent, Charon desires to see this great creation of the gods while there is still time. However, he is unwilling to attempt such a hazardous journey alone and finds that not a single shade will agree to guide him. Finally, his gaze falls on Gelastus, the worthy and dogged philosopher who was so committed to the ideal of poverty while alive that he turned up at the Acheron without even the money to pay Charon for the crossing. Charon had enforced the rules and left Gelastus waiting miserably on the bank. Now the ferryman offers Gelastus a deal: he will transport him across the river if the philosopher will first agree to accompany him on his journey to the world. Gelastus has little choice but to accept.

Charon and Gelastus make a peculiar and cantankerous couple as they journey through the world, and much of their time is spent bickering. Charon is particularly incensed by Gelastus's elaborate philosophical demonstrations, maintaining that for all of his learning, Gelastus is incapable of seeing the simple truths that are before his eyes. A good example of how Charon is able to cut the ground from under Gelastus's feet occurs as Charon berates the philosopher for the complexity of his arguments. Not only is Gelastus's speech circuitous in nature, but he has failed, Charon asserts, as a guide; they have gone in a circle and are now back in the underworld. This is a mistake on Charon's part. What he takes for the groans of the dead are in fact the trumpets sounding the watch at a nearby city. And what he believes to be the shade of a king whom he once ferried across the Acheron is nothing but an ordinary wolf—an animal, Gelastus points out, that may be harmful to humans and is not the least bit similar to mankind. However, if Charon is mistaken, Gelastus is more so; while Charon's error relates to phenomena, Gelastus's error regards the essence of things. For Charon understands that wolves and men can indeed be one and the same. This prompts him to tell Gelastus a story of his own:

> "Oh, what a fine philosopher, who understands the ways of the stars but not those of men! Learn from the ferryman Charon to know thyself. I will tell you what I remember hearing, not from a philosopher— for all your reasoning revolves only around subtleties and verbal quibbles—but from a certain painter. By himself this man saw more while looking at lines [*lineamenta*] than all you philosophers do when you're measuring and investigating the heavens. Pay attention: you'll hear something that is very rare indeed.
>
> "This painter used to say that the artificer of a great work had been selecting and purifying the material from which he was to create man. Some said the material was clay mixed with honey, others said warm wax. Whatever it was, people said that he should mold two bronze seals upon man, one on the chest, face, and the other parts seen from the front, and a second one on the back of the head, the back, the buttocks and the parts seen from behind."[20]

The creator made many different kinds of humans and then turned "the defective ones and those marked by flaws" into women. This he did "by taking a little bit from the one and adding it to the other." Using different molds, he made all sorts of other living creatures. However, when his work was finished and he saw that some humans were not pleased with the shape he had given them, he declared that they could take the forms of any other creatures they liked:[21]

> "He pointed out his house, conspicuous on a nearby mountain, and encouraged them to climb the steep and straight road that led to it. He said that they would enjoy there an abundance of good things, but he warned them repeatedly not to go there by any other road. This particular road might seem steep at first, but gradually it would become more level.
>
> "Having said this, he went away. The homunculi began to climb, but immediately some, in their folly, preferred to look like cattle, asses and quadrupeds. Others, led astray by misguided desires, went on detours through the little hamlets they passed. There, in steep and echoing valleys, impeded by thorns and brambles, faced by

impassable places, they turned themselves into assorted monsters, and when they returned to the main road, their friends rejected them because of their ugliness. Consequently, realizing that they were all made from the same clay, they put on masks fashioned to look like other people's faces. This artificial method of looking like human beings became so commonly employed that you could scarcely distinguish the fake faces from the real ones, unless you happened to look closely at the eye holes of the masks that covered them. Only then would observers encounter the varied faces of the monsters. These masks, called 'fictions,' lasted until they reached the waters of the River Acheron and no further, for when they entered the river they were dissolved in its steaming vapor. So nobody reached the other bank unless he was naked and stripped of his mask." Then Gelastus said, "Charon, are you making this up as a game, or are you telling the truth?" "No," said Charon. "In fact, I plaited this rope from the beards and eyebrows of the masks, and I caulked my boat using their clay." [22]

The story is markedly strange and sinister. On the one hand, it relates to a tradition of moral writing in which people face difficult but worthwhile ascents. [23] On the other, it constitutes a highly original variation on the theme of the Fall of Man. [24] The creator offers human beings every opportunity to live a blessed and good life, but many choose not to do so. Some, spurred by foolishness, renounce their humanity and opt instead to live as animals. Others, subject to uncontrollable desires, stray from the right path until they find their progress impeded. There, isolated in the midst of a hostile nature, they transform themselves into monsters. Thus, we learn that many men are not really men at all, but monsters wearing elaborate masks. By use of these masks, they may succeed in passing as human beings right up to the moment of death—but not beyond, for in death everyone will be revealed for what he truly is. Gelastus is clearly taken aback by Charon's story, and we readily understand his hesitant and surprised response. Charon's reply offers him little comfort, and there is a particular force to the mocking tone in which some humans are reduced to the base physicality of hair and clay.

It cannot, of course, be permissible to select a short extract from Alberti's entire oeuvre and argue that it represents views underpinning his architectural treatise. Nonetheless, it must be acknowledged that this passage outlines positions that Alberti took in his works time and again. Charon raises the possibility that much—but not all—of mankind may have strayed from the order of nature, abandoning truth and living a life of fiction.[25] The behavior of mankind and the projects that it pursues, including even the philosopher's quest for knowledge, might thus be aberrations rather than a part of the natural order of things. Of course, one might argue that *Momus* is primarily a comic work and we are by no means dealing with Alberti's real views. It is notable, however, that it is often when speaking of the bizarre, fantastical, dreamlike, and absurd that Alberti appears to really address the fundamental questions of man's existence and the true nature of the world; this is the case not only in *Momus* but also in several of the *Intercenales*. Pithy, cynical, and devoid of all fiction, Charon presents his story to Gelastus as the profound and undressed truth about man.

Augustine, the Fall, and the Origins of the City

Of all the projects of mankind, the city is surely among the most characteristic. It was precisely for this reason that Saint Augustine, in his *De civitate Dei*, had viewed the cities of the world with such suspicion. Indeed, Augustine also considered the origins of cities and gave a far less optimistic account than that of Vitruvius. The first city, he asserts, was founded by a criminal and a sinner: "It is written that Cain founded a city, whereas Abel, a pilgrim, did not found one."[26] Cain, the son of Adam, was of course the first murderer in human history, a fratricide who killed his brother Abel. The city thus arose in the wake of two terrible events: the Fall and the first murder. As Augustine's modern translator R. W. Dyson succinctly points out, "It is clearly Augustine's view that, had the Fall not occurred, the state, and the various devices of coercion, punishment and oppression which we associate with the state, would not have come into existence. They would not have come into existence simply because there would have been no need for them. Man is naturally sociable . . . but he is not naturally political."[27] For Augustine, the city is in one sense a good thing, something that is necessary if fallen man is to cooperate and work toward the common good. On the other hand, since it *is* the thing of fallen man, the city, as the locus of politics, was inherently flawed from the start. It arose from the fracturing of man's most natural social institution: the family. As such, the earthly city has no future to speak of, being nothing to do with God; its destruction is inevitable.

It should be remembered that Augustine was writing in the wake of, and in response to, the sack of Rome of 410. Rebutting the notion that Christianity brought about the city's downfall, he argued that Rome's impiety was to blame for the disaster that Alaric and the Visigoths had inflicted on it. Needless to say, it was not lost on Augustine that Rome's origins also lay in fratricidal strife:

> The first founder of the earthly city, then, was a fratricide; for, overcome by envy, he slew his brother, who was a citizen of the Eternal City. . . . It is not to be wondered at, then, that, long afterwards, at the foundation of that city which was to be the capital of the earthly city of which we are speaking, and which was to rule over so many nations, this first example . . . of crime was mirrored by a kind of image of itself. For there also, as one of the Roman poets says in telling of the crime, "The first walls were wet with a brother's blood." For this is how Rome was founded, when, as the history of Rome attests, Remus was slain by his brother Romulus.
>
> . . . Thus, the strife that arose between Remus and Romulus showed the extent to which the earthly city is divided against itself; whereas that which arose between Cain and Abel demonstrated the hostility between the two cities themselves, the City of God and the city of men.[28]

Of course, Augustine's *civitas* is not exactly the city as we think of it. It is a community and, in the case of the eternal city, a congregation of God, the faithful, the saints, and the angels. Nonetheless, the city (*urbs*) is surely the most characteristic expression of the earthly city. Pitted against the heavenly city and chronically divided even against itself, who would marvel that the earthly city should undergo destruction?

Such views perhaps help account for the difference between Alberti's and Vitruvius's accounts of the origins of architecture and communities. Alberti inhabited an intellectual world that was heavily inflected by Christian thought and the teachings of the church fathers. While he may not express much in the way of conventional religious sentiment, he often seems to share Augustine's pessimism regarding mankind and to view the world as being essentially fallen. Indeed, we might draw a tentative link between Alberti's tale of the masked monsters and Augustine's writings. In the *De civitate Dei*, Augustine tackles the subject of the metamorphoses that were so beloved of ancient writers of myths and fables. He considers Varro's claim that the Arcadians were able to transform themselves into wolves by swimming across a particular pool of water and relates that he has heard of inns where the landladies have the ability to turn unsuspecting persons into beasts of burden. The latter transformations are achieved by disguising potions in pieces of cheese. The landladies then use the beasts that they have conjured to perform such tasks as need doing before transforming them back into humans.

Following this, Augustine turns his attention to Homer's account of Circe's treatment of the companions of Odysseus and the events narrated in Apuleus's *Golden Ass*. Much of this kind of thing may be dismissed as poetic fiction, he argues, and some of it may be the work of demons. At this point, Augustine feels that he must clarify that he is not ascribing to demons the power to effect real transformations. Indeed, demons have no independent powers and cannot do anything at all unless permitted by God. Since God is omnipotent, he could of course effect transformations of these kinds, and since his motives often remain impenetrable to us, it may be that he has reason to do so. Even so, if God should allow demons to appear to effect transformations, it will only be the appearances that are altered, since demons "do not, of course, create real natures. If they do indeed accomplish anything of the kind which we are here considering, it is only in respect of their appearance that they transform beings created by the true God, so that they seem to be what they are not. I do not therefore in the least believe that either the body or the soul can be transformed into the members and lineaments [*lineamenta*] of beasts by the art or power of demons."[29]

Noticeably, several of the features of Augustine's passage appear also in Alberti's *Momus*. Men are transformed into wolves and beasts of burden. Most strikingly, Augustine uses the relatively uncommon word *lineamenta*. This term (which Alberti would have known from Cicero and elsewhere) is also used by Charon when describing the object of the painter's contemplation. It was a term of crucial importance for Alberti's artistic theories. After all, Alberti writes in the preface to his architectural treatise that architecture is made up of two parts: *materia* and *lineamenta*. While materia must be fashioned by the craftsman, lineamenta is the realm of the architect proper and is the subject of the first book of the treatise. Alberti may have been attracted to the passage in Augustine precisely because this word appears in it. We might speculate that he takes several elements from Augustine and uses them to create his own account of the transformation of human beings. What he produces is something entirely new, yet still pervaded by the sense of a fallen world, and a fallen mankind, that is so prominent in Augustine's thought.

Transformations into animals and monsters are also to be found in Alberti's early *Life of Saint Potitus*. Having fled his city (perhaps transported on a cloud), the young martyr-saint Potitus takes refuge in the woods. Here, he is tempted by the devil, who sends him an apparition in the shape of a handsome and authoritative man who extols the virtues of the active life, condemns solitude and poverty, and argues that one must seek fame, glory, and acclaim. Potitus is unmoved by this discourse and realizes that what he sees is not, in reality, a man, but a monster. This monster swells to an enormous size and transforms itself into an ox before it finally disappears. Alberti offers considerable commentary on this episode, explaining that such an apparition, which comes and goes without a trace and leaves nothing good in its wake, may be compared to those "goods" that we acquire from fortune. The ox specifically relates to riches, status, and the acclaim of the plebes. Indeed, Alberti wonders, "what greater monster is there than a man who is lost and corrupted? Certainly none."[30] All other monsters, he argues, are produced by nature, but corrupted man is something altogether different—wicked, cruel, libidinous, jealous, and avaricious. Who would think that a monster like this could be nature's work?[31]

The *Life of Saint Potitus* was to be the first in a series of lives of early Christian martyrs that Alberti was commissioned to write by Cardinal Biagio Molin at some point between 1432 and 1434; however, it was the only life of the series that Alberti completed. It is striking that, while there is much in it that is conventional, Alberti's own intellectual and ethical preoccupations are brought to the fore more than one might expect. As Anthony Grafton has argued, some episodes narrated by Alberti "expressed his personal views so strongly that they challenged the validity of his hagiographical enterprise as a whole."[32] The *Life of Saint Potitus* contains sharp criticism of the contemporary clergy as well as the idle quality of monastic life—the latter put into the mouth of the emperor Antoninus. Indeed, the most wicked characters are not straw men but instead have recourse to some plausible arguments that are elsewhere presented seriously by Alberti. Wise characters in Alberti's dialogues often assert that man is born to be of use to his fellow man. Here, the same argument is made by the devil. This creates in the work a tension between ideas that is characteristic of Alberti's thought. The values of activity, contemplation, fame, and glory all hang in the balance. Potitus prefers a solitary life in the woods, surrounded by wild beasts, to a life in the city, surrounded by men. Nevertheless, he ultimately rejects solitude in order to return to the city and carry out important deeds. Alberti revisits this theme on several occasions, but it cannot be said that his thinking is always firmly resolved in the direction of the city. The pull of solitude remains strong and Potitus's preference for wild animals over humans surfaces more than once.

Alberti on Destruction and Stability

Throughout *De re aedificatoria*, Alberti maintains a marked preoccupation with the potential destruction of the architect's works.[33] It is not hard to see why. Vitruvius had named *firmitas* as one of the three main concerns of the architect, and indeed any architect must ensure that his buildings will stand up, even when the weather gets rough. In Italy, this occurs rather frequently, and today storms, floods, landslides, inundations of snow and ice, earthquakes, volcanic eruptions, and other similar phenomena feature on television news with a certain regularity. Stability must surely be the very first concern of the architect, since every other consideration will be of little consequence if the building cannot stand. Yet Alberti's language often seems to betray a deeper concern. Throughout the architectural treatise, the reader has the sense that the architect operates in a universe pregnant with destructive forces, ones that are especially and singularly bent on the ruin of mankind's creations. Numerous passages illustrate the zeal with which Alberti describes such phenomena. For example, in the first book, he warns against building in a valley between two hills in the following terms:

> It will inevitably suffer the ruinous torrents of rain and swirling floods; by absorbing too much damp, it will always rot; and it will constantly exhale earthy mists so damaging to man's health. In such a place no man could retain any strength, as the spirit wilts, nor any body show stamina, as its joints are weakened; mold will grow on books; tools will rust away, and everything in the stores will decay from excess

of moisture, until it is all ruined. Furthermore, should the sun break through, reflected rays would cause the heat to grow more intense, but if kept out, the shade will make the air coarse and stagnant. What is more, should the wind penetrate as far as that, it would only rage with more violence and fury by being forced through fixed channels, but should it not reach there, the air would become as thick as mud. It would not be unfair then to consider such a valley as a puddle or a stagnant pool of air.[34]

Alberti is probably right. One cannot, however, help but be struck by the image of a malevolent dampness that moves through the house, inevitably destroying everything in its path—rotting the books, rusting the metal, rendering the inhabitants weak in body and in spirit. As if the damp were not bad enough, other forces will conspire in the building's downfall, ensuring that it either bakes in reflected sunshine or enjoys air as thick as mud.

Of course, some sites are preferable to others, but Alberti is scrupulous in pointing out the potential perils of each one. Alberti had many sources from which to draw this material, including Vitruvius, Galen, Hippocrates, Pliny the Elder, and the Roman agricultural treatise writers. Equally, however, Alberti includes many of his own observations. His remarks about the frequency of earthquakes on the island of Procida, where, according to "an ancient poetic legend . . . whenever the giant Typhon . . . turns in his grave, the whole island shakes from its very foundations," derive from Strabo and Servius Honoratus. "The poets," Alberti tells us, "have sung about this because of the violence of the earthquakes and eruptions that plagued that place, and that forced the Eretrians and the Chalcidians, who had once settled there, to flee; similarly other colonists, sent there some time later by Hieron of Syracuse to found a city, also fled through the continual fear of danger and disaster."[35] On the other hand, "we ourselves have seen that stretch of Italy, along the whole range of the Hernician mountains, from Algidus near Rome as far as Capua, repeatedly shaken and all but destroyed by earthquakes."[36] Firsthand observation is similarly brought to bear in the eighth book, where Alberti notes that the hill on which the city of Perugia sits is constantly undermined by a stream, leading to landslides: "This has been responsible for much of the city slipping and falling into ruin."[37]

Apart from ordinary natural forces, some locales may simply be inherently malign. Alberti cites what he calls Plato's assertion that some places "would occasionally be ruled by some divine power or demonic government, which might be either favorably or ill disposed toward the inhabitants."[38] In such places, men may easily lose their minds or kill themselves. Other environments might give rise to health problems and perversions. Alberti claims that he has seen towns where every woman who gives birth finds that "she has become the mother of both man and monster."[39] Sensibly, he advises that one should examine the people and animals of a region, as well as the buildings, in order to form an opinion of the area. If the neighboring buildings are "rough and rotting, it is a sign of some adverse outside influence."[40] The comment echoes that of Giannozzo, the elderly patriarch of the *Della famiglia*, who says that he would choose a city to live in by observing the health of the inhabitants and whether there were many robust old men.[41]

Regardless of location, however, all buildings must undergo trials. Chief among these is time; referring to Theodoric's mausoleum at Ravenna, Alberti notes that even buildings that were constructed well away from slopes have been "buried by the sheer force of time."[42] It is notable that he often speaks of the confrontation between construction and nature in terms that are evocative of battle. Wind and water may "threaten and assault" a building (*immineat atque impetat*) and cause it injury (*iniuria*).[43] Roofs are the weapons with which buildings defend themselves against the harmful onslaught of the weather (*arma nimirum aedificiorum tecta sunt contra tempestatum iniurias atque impetum*).[44] Building stone should be thoroughly tested in preparation for its eternal battle (*certamen*) with the elements.[45] In Book III, Alberti returns to roofs, judging that the "most ancient function of the whole building was to provide a shelter from the burning sun and the storms raging down from heaven," and that roofs are at the forefront of this endeavor. "Nor do I imagine," he writes, "that this would be easy, faced as it is with the unremitting barrage not only of rain but also of ice and heat, and, most harmful of all, wind. Could anyone possibly hold out against enemies so relentless and so fierce for any great length of time?" (Quis tam assiduous tanque acerrimos hostes tollerare uspiam diutius possit?)[46]

Sometimes it is as though natural forces are not merely aspects of the weather but genuinely malevolent forces bent on destroying the works of man. When handing out sound and practical advice about allowing rain to run clear off a roof, for example, Alberti observes that "rain is always prepared to wreak mischief, and never fails to exploit even the least opening to do some harm: by its subtlety it infiltrates, by softening it corrupts, and by its persistence it undermines the whole strength of the building, until it eventually brings ruin and destruction on the entire work."[47] Again, Alberti is correct, but again, his language is striking. The rain here appears as an enemy, a purposive agent that aims at destruction.[48]

Despite this, it would be wrong to conclude that Alberti generally conceives of nature as a malign force that conspires to do harm to mankind. On the contrary, the fault should more properly be seen as originating with man. It is mankind that, in its opposition to nature, courts disaster for itself and for its works:

First, nothing should be attempted that lies beyond human capacity, nor anything undertaken that might immediately come into conflict with Nature. For so great is Nature's strength that, although on occasion some huge obstacle may obstruct her, or some barrier divert her, she will always overcome and destroy any opposition or impediment; and any stubbornness, as it were, displayed against her, will eventually be overthrown and destroyed by her continual and persistent onslaught.

How many examples are there to be seen or read about of the failure of mankind's work to survive, simply because it has come into conflict with Nature?

Who would not mock someone who intends to ride over the sea on a bridge of ships, and despise him not so much for his arrogance as for his folly? The port of Claudius, below Ostia, or that of Hadrian, near Terracina, are works that might otherwise have been expected to last forever; yet now we see them in ruins, their mouths long since choked with sand, their harbors silted up, while the sea with its incessant wrestling continues its onslaught and daily increases its advantage.

And what would happen, do you imagine, to any attempt to hold back and restrain the force of cascading water, or the weight of tumbling boulders? We ought to be careful, then, to avoid any undertaking that is not in complete accordance with the laws of Nature.[49]

The discourse here is clearly that of *vanitas*. Any attempt to oppose nature must have its roots in arrogance and will inevitably be punished; natural forces will always prevail through sheer persistence. For this reason, Alberti repeatedly recommends caution and reflection before any building project is commenced. Approached in the proper way, building may be one of the noblest activities that man can undertake. Approached wrongly, it may be among the greatest of follies—proof of how far man has strayed from the order of nature.

One senses here the influence of the long-standing Christian tradition of the condemnation of ostentatious building projects. One cannot help but be reminded of the biblical story of the Tower of Babel, in which the arrogance and folly of man also inspired the destruction of a great architectural work. God introduced different languages into the world to stop the people from cooperating and trying to match their power to his own.[50] The role played by God in the Babel story seems to be assumed, in Alberti's writings, by nature. Indeed, Alberti visits the venerable topos of *Natura sive Deus* (Nature or God) at several points in his works.[51] After his fall from the heavens, Momus systematically sets about the destruction of mankind's pious faith in the gods, first as a poet who sings only of the gods' foolishness and immorality and then as a philosopher who claims that the gods are either indifferent to the plight of humans or do not exist at all:

> He said that the gods were not to be found, especially gods who took any interest in human affairs. Or maybe, in the end, there was only one deity common to all living things, Nature, whose calling and labor it was not only to govern mankind but also flocks, birds, fish and similar creatures. . . . Whatever Nature fashioned had a proper and pre-ordained function, whether men thought this good or bad, and they could do nothing on their own behalf if Nature was unwilling and opposed them. Many things were believed to be bad which were not bad. Human life was a sport of Nature.[52]

This argument gives rise to a furious debate on the nature of the gods. Momus is roundly attacked by the philosophers but refuses to budge: "He [Momus], stubborn in the midst of all the controversy that had arisen, clung the more doggedly to his own opinion, denying the gods' existence, and finally claiming that men were deceived when they believed there were tutelary gods in addition to Nature, just because they saw orbits altering their motion in the sky. Nature freely and spontaneously carried out her customary, inborn offices with regard to the human race, but she did not need our services at all, and could not be moved by our prayers."[53] At the very least, Momus is engaging in sophistry here. As a god himself, he can be in no doubt regarding the gods' existence. However, there are some genuine similarities between the views of Momus and those of Alberti in *De re aedificatoria*. Moreover, while Momus knows that the gods are real, he is also aware that they care little for the fate of men and that, to all intents and purposes, human beings are indeed at the mercy of nature. Indeed, looked at more closely, the position that Alberti flirts with might not seem so close to the Stoics' *Natura sive Deus* as to Spinoza's *Deus seu Natura*.[54] In a different and more positive context, Lionardo Alberti refers, in the *Della famiglia*, to "natura, cioè Iddio" (nature, that is to say God).[55]

War, Defense, and Destruction by Human Agency

If Alberti was preoccupied by the damage that might be inflicted on buildings and cities by nature, he was especially aware of that which might be perpetrated by humanity. Alberti, who often appears convinced that men tend toward violence and destruction, outlines his position succinctly in the fourth book of *De re aedificatoria* during a discussion of walls:

> For our part, when we think of the power that the walls offer for the safety and freedom of citizens against better-placed and more numerous enemies, we will side neither with those who want their city to be defencelessly naked nor with those who put all their hopes in the structure of the walls. With Plato I say that it is of the nature of a city to expect that at some point in its history it should be threatened with conquest, since it is impossible, either in public or in private life, to curb that desire for possession and that ambition which are due to Nature or to human habits, within any reasonable limits: it has been the single most important reason for all armed aggression.[56]

It is ambition and the desire for possession that spur men on to violence.[57] Again, this refers to a condition of humanity that Christian thought had traditionally connected to the Fall, for the church fathers had taught that before the Fall all gods were held in common. Private property and the avarice that it inspired were thus essentially unnatural. The passage is remarkable for its deeply pessimistic view of the urban situation, with Alberti claiming that every city must inevitably be threatened with conquest at some point in its history. The observation echoes that of Adovardo Alberti in the *Della famiglia*, who complains that history is nothing more than a catalogue of "slaughters and the ruin of cities."[58] Alberti seems to conceive of cities as starting out on the defensive and remaining so forever more, and it comes as no surprise that he lavishes considerable attention on matters relating to defense. When constructing a city, he asks, "who would deny the need to add guard upon guard and defense upon defense?"[59]

Alberti's interest in defense is all the less surprising when one considers the traditions within which he was writing. His most important predecessor, Vitruvius, was a military architect and engineer who stated straightforwardly in his treatise that "the assignment of public buildings is threefold: one, to defense; the second, to religion; the third, to convenience."[60] Vitruvius gave considerable attention to the issue of how best to build walls so as to resist enemy attack and ended his treatise with seven consecutive chapters on such things as catapults, ballistae, siege engines, and defensive stratagems. In Alberti's own day, fortification was not considered to be separate from the rest of the visual arts. Throughout the late Middle Ages and Renaissance, some of the foremost artists and architects of Italy were involved in the construction of fortifications and sometimes even weapons of assault.[61] Defense was very much the proper concern of both the architect and the artist, and Alberti's contemporaries would have shown no surprise at its inclusion in his treatise; indeed, they would most likely have been more astonished had it been omitted. Moreover, there is nothing especially new or modern in Alberti's ideas. Guns were starting to play a role in modern warfare, but Alberti, who was ever interested in new technologies, appears to have taken little account of the special requirements of gunpowder fortification or the possibility of using guns to attack the enemy. Rather, as John Hale says, "he is entirely concerned with defensive strength. . . . He is primarily interested in fortifications as giving protection to a city, and, within the city, to the prince: they are necessary to preserve the urban scene, the physical environment of civic life which fascinates him, and he was not moved to rethink them in a way which would take serious account of the new weapon."[62] It is for this reason that Alberti's treatment of defense is so fascinating—because it is so purely defensive.[63] That is to say, it is not a discussion of military matters in general, nor is it the work of a military expert displaying his knowledge of the most up-to-date methods. Rather, it is born out of anxiety about the possible, or perhaps even *probable*, destruction of the city and is thus aimed at one end: the preservation of the city from attack.

Alberti brings defensive concerns to bear on many aspects of the city, including its location. In this regard, the merits of deserts are extolled, and he notes that "according to Pliny, the only reason why Italy had been invaded by so many foreign armies was the popularity of her wines and figs."[64] Nonetheless, a remote location and the ability to sustain itself will not be sufficient to preserve a city or region from attack, as demonstrated by the example of Egypt.[65] The shape of the city will be determined by defensive needs (as, indeed, the shape of cities often was), with some forms giving greater assistance to the enemy than others. The size may also have defensive implications, as some consider a compact city to be safer. Alberti reminds us that many Italian cities were founded on the sites of *castra*, noting that "a camp is like a city in embryo; and you will find that many a city has been founded on sites chosen by experienced generals for camps."[66] Alberti is, of course, right about the military origins of many cities throughout the Roman Empire, and the analogy between camp and city remains at the forefront of his thinking. Defensive justifications sometimes appear to be paramount in his approach to the city and often take precedence over convenience or beauty. Even when laying out streets, large and winding streets are preferable, in part because "if the enemy gains access [to the town], he will risk injury, his front and flank being exposed as much as his back."[67]

It is striking how, throughout the treatise, Alberti refers to "the enemy" as though it were a constant and essential feature of urban life; he takes it for granted that any city will have enemies who will always be looking for ways to capture, enter, and destroy it. Smaller, "private" streets, he advises, should mostly be built in perfectly straight lines, close to the edges of the houses. We might expect such a prescription from an advocate of order and a "Renaissance man" such as Alberti. Yet he observes with seeming approval that "the ancients preferred to give some of their roads within the city awkward exits, and others blind alleys, so that any aggressor or criminal who entered would either hesitate, being in two minds and unsure of himself, or, summoning up the courage to continue, would soon find himself in danger."[68] Here, then, is a direct example of defensive concerns taking priority over those of order when the plan of a city is being designed. Similarly, smaller streets should connect the larger ones, "not so much to provide a public thoroughfare as to give access to the interlying houses, which will be of benefit both to the houses, by increasing the amount of light they receive, and also to the town, by impeding any hostile element seeking to escape."[69] A large, wide street should run from the harbor through the center of the city, connecting to several neighborhoods, not for the easy movement of goods but because with such a road "a counterattack may be launched from all sides against any intruding enemy fleet."[70] Even the large public squares that seem so much a part of the modern, rationally planned, aesthetically conscious city have a defensive purpose. Among other things, they can be utilized, as they often were in practice, as "places to stockpile timber, grain, and other such commodities, essential for sustaining a siege."[71]

The City in History

Alberti's anxiety about the destruction of cities must have appeared fully justified in light of the histories with which he was familiar. Indeed, if there is one constant regarding the city throughout history, it is surely destruction. As a classical scholar, Alberti would have been all too aware of the number of great cities that had been brought to ruin. Troy had utterly disappeared, Syracuse and Carthage had been famously crushed, and Rome had fallen into chronic decay after the repeated invasion of barbarian armies. Ancient historians, such as Herodotus, detailed the destruction of many cities and regions, while other writers, such as Seneca and even Ovid, often described a turbulent, violent, and destructive world. Meanwhile, biblical history was hardly more comforting, especially as told in the Old Testament. The destructions of Sodom, Gomorrah, and the Tower of Babel (not to mention almost the entire world during the flood) are among the major events in Genesis, used to illustrate moral lessons and, above all, the ultimate power of God. We learn of the destruction of successive cities under Joshua and his successors, as the Israelites inhabit the land of Canaan and battle with their enemies. The besieging and ruination of cities is often discussed in graphic and alarming terms. In Deuteronomy, rules are even laid down as to how the destruction should occur. Some cities are to be partially destroyed and all the males within them killed, but the cities in the lands that God has given to the Israelites as an inheritance are to receive still harsher treatment: "Thou shalt save alive nothing that breatheth: But thou shalt utterly destroy them."[72]

Such passages serve to reinforce the view that war is an essential feature of urban life—that destruction is simply a fact of cities and of man.

With some notable exceptions (such as Ruth and the Song of Songs), destruction, and particularly the destruction of cities, forms one of the major themes throughout the remainder of the Old Testament.[73] From the end of Kings, the narrative is dominated by the destruction of Jerusalem, and destruction is prophesied and described with particular intensity throughout the Psalms, Proverbs, Isaiah, Jeremiah, and Lamentations, rising to a fever pitch in Ezekiel. Indeed, while the Bible contains within it the notion of the holy city, there often seems to be tension surrounding the nature and validity of urban life, a feeling that the city was the work of man and thus inherently flawed and necessarily ephemeral. Even from the earliest times, God had, apart from destroying some cities through his own agency, sanctioned their complete destruction by man, and at times the death of every single thing that lived within them.

Fortuna

Alberti's most profound meditation on the issue of destruction is found in the vernacular *Theogenius*. In *De re aedificatoria*, he specifically refers readers who wish to pursue the issue of destruction further to this dialogue. The *Theogenius* is devoted to a discussion of *fortuna* and *e' casi avversi* (ill luck) and whether and how they might be resisted. As such, much of the treatise is taken up with a consideration of destruction resulting from natural disasters and the violence of man, both of which are characterized as manifestations of fortuna. "It is a constituted law of fortuna to pervert every day new things," says Teogenio in the second book, before enumerating a great list of natural disasters.[74] Many regions and "most noble cities" (*città nobilissime*) have been swallowed up by the sea or collapsed into abysses, while earthquakes have wrought terrible destruction across Europe and Asia.[75] "In the times of Tiberius," Alberti relates, "they say that in one night twelve most great and famous cities in Asia were ruined, and in the times of Nero more noble cities were ruined there: Apamea, Laodicea, Hierapolis, and Colossae. And Tacitus writes that in these times there was in Campania such a violent storm that by the fury of the winds the towns, trees, and every plant in the whole province found themselves uprooted and transported far away."[76]

"We ought not therefore to marvel," concludes Teogenio, "little mortal men and above all the other animals most infirm, whenever some disaster befalls us, when we see entire lands and provinces subjected to total extermination and ruin."[77] Nature, in fact, seeks to kill us at every opportunity and has placed "venom and death" in even the tiniest creatures.[78] Insects and small animals have laid waste to entire regions:

> Justinius and Paulus Orosius the historians write that the people called Obderites, and those named Avienates, fled and abandoned their country, chased by a multitude of mice and little frogs. And M. Varro writes that there was a land in Spain laid waste by rabbits, and in Thessalia another city was similarly ruined by moles. And Pliny recounts how great an infestatious enemy are crickets to the Cyrenaic population. And so you will find in the histories that terrible calamities often befell mortals at the hands of such paltry animals. Neither will you find any animal so hated by all the others as man.[79]

As if these disasters were not bad enough, one must also take into account those that have been caused by man:

> The most brutal man finds that he is lethal to other men and to himself. And you will find that more men have perished at the hands of other men than by all the other disasters that have befallen them. Caesar Augustus gloried that in his battles, without the slaughter of civilians, he had killed men numbering one hundred and ninety-two thousand. Paulus Orosius the historian recounted in part the miseries suffered by mortals just in his own times, and although he was a very concise and succinct writer, yet his books grew into most ample volumes, since he found the people and citizens to have suffered misery worthy of record.[80]

The issue of fortuna lies at the very heart of almost everything that Alberti ever wrote. While many writers addressed the topic of fortuna and the possibility of resisting it, the theme is given a particular force by Alberti, one that was undoubtedly inspired by his own life experience. Although such an explanation may appear simplistic, it should be emphasized that Alberti repeatedly links his own experiences to his moral views. This is perhaps most evident in the *Intercenales*, where he appears as both the writer Lepidus and the dogged scholar Philoponius.[81] These characters take the lead roles in the first two *Intercenales*, with Philoponius, in

"The Orphan," sounding an especially bitter note: "They say that fortune is always hostile to just men, and such was clearly the case with Philoponius. Orphaned as a boy when his father died, Philoponius was exiled from his homeland, deprived of his entire patrimony by his nearest relatives, and even excluded and cast out of the closeness and company of his own family, so that he was forced to beg abjectly from strangers."[82] This lament is clearly autobiographical and reflects Alberti's feelings about his own situation. He had been born in exile, had been removed from the great city of Florence, and was a bastard child. His father had died, and other relatives had withheld much of his inheritance. As we have seen, he claims in the *Vita* that the strain ruined his studies and led to a kind of mental breakdown. So cruel were his relatives, he alleges, that they had even attempted to murder him, and Mancini was able to find a document that he felt might lend this story some support.[83]

Exile and family strife weigh heavily on Alberti's writings. He conceives of a world pervaded by a ferocious fortuna, a force that is capable of undoing all things and bringing any man's life to ruin in an instant. Once again, it is through the medium of the fantastical and the bizarre that Alberti most directly approaches the theme; in his intercenale "Fate and Fortune," a philosopher recounts a dream in which he peers from the top of a mountain into the swirling river of life, populated by divine sparks that are destined to become human souls. The philosopher speaks with some of these sparks, who appear to him as shades. They explain the strategies that are employed by different types of character to make their way through the river of life, revealing that some who hold floats and appear to be doing well are in fact in the greatest danger, while others, who rely on their own reason and prudence, or cooperate and are able to moderate their own desires, or cultivate the liberal arts, fare better. On awaking from his dream, the philosopher summarizes what he has learned: "If I interpret it correctly, I learned that fate is merely the passage of things in human life, which is carried along by its own sequence and descent. I observed that fortune is kinder to those who fall into the river where there chance to be whole planks or a boat. By contrast, I found that fortune is harsh to those of us who have plunged into the river at a time when we must continually overcome the waves by swimming. But we shall not be unaware that prudence and diligence are of great value in human affairs."[84]

The notion of life as a dangerous torrent, which one must handle as best one can, would seem to typify Alberti's view of the world. Life itself appears here in the guise of the harsh forces of nature that bear so heavily on the activity of the architect in *De re aedificatoria*. Fate, which moves along its own course in a thoroughly indifferent manner, is not unlike some of the descriptions of nature given by Momus in his apparently disingenuous polemic against the gods. Fortune, on the other hand, deals differently with each individual, being kinder to those who are lucky enough to find themselves in reasonable circumstances and harsher on those who do not. Nonetheless, this description of man in the world is far from being thoroughly pessimistic. Through cooperation and control of his ambition, man may lessen his hardships and be in a better position to overcome each looming crisis. Moreover, those who invented the liberal arts appear as gods, flitting over the river with winged sandals; they are venerated "because they first fashioned as a great aid to swimmers the planks which you see in the river, inscribing on the various planks the names of the liberal arts."[85]

Below the inventors of the liberal arts, another category of beings is worthy of special praise. They too are lifted high, although their sandals are not as perfect as those of the inventors and they are not entirely raised out of the water. Their special merit lies in having "enlarged the planks by adding fragments to them, and they delight in gathering planks from beneath the rocks and from the furthest bank, in fashioning new planks of similar shape and purpose, and in offering all their works to those who swim."[86] This is surely the category in which Alberti would have placed himself. In the *Profugiorum ab aerumna*, Alberti famously had Niccola di Veri de' Medici describe literary endeavor as a kind of mosaic in which the author located fragments of ancient wisdom and sought to combine them into a new work.[87] Meanwhile, in the intercenale "Rings," Philoponius describes how he had tried to win the favor of Minerva "by drawing select pebbles from the sacred fount, by cleaning and polishing them, and by consecrating them on the altar to adorn the candelabra of Posterity."[88]

In each case, contemporary scholars have little hope of matching the great inventors of the liberal arts, but they are able to make modest contributions of recovered fragments. Sometimes, in "Fate and Fortune," they might even offer new planks altogether. As Alberti emphasizes throughout his writings, the means by which man may elevate himself, to some degree, above the torrents of fate and fortune are the cultivation of *dottrina* and the acquisition of *virtù*. The prizes at stake are *fama* and *gloria*. Of all the contributions that Alberti offered to his fellow swimmers in the river of life, he must have considered his architectural treatise to be among the foremost. Like the very planks themselves, *De re aedificatoria* serves as an aid to edification with the aim of resisting the ruinous forces of the world. Seen in this light, the art of building, far from being a mundane activity, reaches to the very heart of the human condition.

Building

It is ultimately this tension between a seemingly invincible fortuna and a potentially transcendent virtù that drives much of Alberti's thinking. He does not offer trite solutions, and his thought mostly inhabits a liminal space, oscillating between confidence in man's potential on the one hand and a profound and fundamental pessimism toward man and his dealings with the world on the other.[89] In regard to buildings and cities, this pessimism emerges in Alberti's preoccupation with the potential ruin of the built environment. The odds are stacked against the works of man. Such are the variety, strength, and persistence of the forces ranged against them that their destruction is almost inevitable. And yet it must be noted that Alberti's concerns about destruction do not cause him to advocate a Petrarchian withdrawal from the city, even where he comes closest in the *Theogenius*. Much of *De re aedificatoria* concerns the city and assumes an urban setting. Alberti must have been largely convinced of the feasibility of the city, as he certainly was with regard to architecture in general. His enormous and often explicitly stated enthusiasm for architecture, and his intense engagement with his subject, is palpable throughout his treatise. Alberti's concerns about destruction did not dissuade him from his belief in the worthwhile nature of building as an activity; indeed, he repeatedly emphasized its exceptional value and excellence. Neither was he dissuaded from designing and building the works for which he is famous. Rather, he insists in *De re* on prudence. Both patron and architect should think long and hard before executing any plan, delaying construction for as long as possible, repeatedly examining models, and listening attentively to the criticisms and suggestions of others. Such are the number of potential problems and the obstacles to be overcome that it would be better not to build at all than to build something of which one could not be entirely confident in every detail. Such a view, of course, accurately reflects the complexity of construction.

Building, for Alberti, might exemplify man's folly and misunderstanding of his relationship with nature, but it might also exemplify his virtù. In this context, it is worth considering the opening passages of Alberti's vernacular dialogue *Profugiorum ab aerumna*. The participants are Alberti himself (although he remains silent) and two of his Florentine contemporaries, Agnolo Pandolfini and Nicola di Vieri de' Medici. The dialogue opens in the Duomo of Florence, with Agnolo praising the cathedral architecture in the following terms:

> And certainly this temple has in itself grace and majesty; and, as I have often thought, I delight to see joined together here a charming slenderness with a robust and full solidity so that, on the one hand, each of its parts seems designed for pleasure, while on the other, one understands that it has all been built for perpetuity. I would add that here is the constant home of temperateness, as of springtime: outside, wind, ice and frost; here inside one is protected from the wind, here mild air and quiet. Outside, the heat of summer and autumn; inside, coolness. And if, as they say, delight is felt when our senses perceive what, and how much, they require by nature, who could hesitate to call this temple the nest of delights?[90]

Contrary to Salutati's employment of the cathedral as an example of inevitable ruin, Alberti here uses it to illustrate that, approached in the proper manner, buildings may achieve a kind of permanence that is at odds with the general nature of things. Moreover, the building has not only been constructed with perpetuity in mind but has succeeded in creating an environment that is akin to the gentler and more benevolent aspects of nature. Indeed, while poorly considered building projects may stand as prime examples of the folly of "fallen" man, it is as though well-considered ones may actually recuperate a kind of prefallen nature.

Alberti's faith in the potential of building is nonetheless beset by a level of anxiety and doubt. One might, as we shall see in subsequent chapters, say the same of his attitude toward his scholarly activity. As Rinaldo Rinaldi has observed with real insight, behind the much-celebrated Albertian literary "mosaic," there is a continual sense of a suspected *vanitas vanitatum*— a question regarding the ultimate purpose of such an accumulation of knowledge, which hints at a profound and radical skepticism.[91] Moreover, "the tiles of the mosaic, Alberti's sources, end up seeming like the relics of an apocalyptic destruction of knowledge, brought about by time and the foolishness of humans."[92] The same forces that threaten the works of the architect, in other words, have also succeeded in devastating knowledge itself, to the degree that every act of recuperation serves ultimately to reinforce the fundamental unrecuperability of what once existed. Once again, time and human nature conspire to color both the world and man's activities within it with a tragic hue.

Human Nature

At the root of Alberti's ambivalent feelings about cities and other projects of mankind lies a highly pessimistic view of human nature. Alberto Cassani has argued that Alberti's concept of fortuna in the *Theogenius* differs from that of his medieval predecessors in the crucial respect that it is, in large measure, the divided and troublesome nature of man himself that causes him to be subject to the vicissitudes of fortune. This position is spelled out in the Intercenale "Defunctus," where, following his death, Neophronus looks back on his life and comments: "I see that everything which men think permanent, or believe committed to eternity, perishes abruptly, passes away suddenly, and is destroyed in an instant. Human affairs are not opposed by fate and fortune. Rather, human beings are the greatest bane of the human race."[93] Certainly, Alberti comments harshly on human nature in a number of his works, including the *Momus*. After Hercules succeeds in entering heaven, Momus is overjoyed at the thought that all men will seek to emulate him and, because of their nature, will descend into enormous conflict: "What disasters, what sackings of cities, what slaughter of nations do I foresee!"[94] He is glad to stay in exile on the earth among the mortals, enjoying the prospect of seeing "the ocean full of their corpses, their provinces soaked with blood, the stars besmirched with the smoke of their burning cities!"[95] Back in heaven, Mercury recounts how once humans started to make votive offerings, they asked for all sorts of terrible things, including the slaughter and death of their closest family members: "What could be more despicable? They even dared pray for the ruin and destruction of whole cities and provinces."[96] As we saw earlier, Alberti suggests that underneath their masks some human beings might actually be wolves or monsters. Of course, Varro, and subsequently Augustine, was not the only writer who narrated men's transformations into wolves.

This is also the punishment that Jupiter metes out to Lycaon in the very first metamorphosis narrated by Ovid. Lycaon is given this form as a result of his violence, brutality, and impiety:

> His clothes changed to coarse hair, his arms to legs—
> He was a wolf, yet kept some human trace,
> The same grey hair, the same fierce face, the same
> Wild eyes, the same image of savagery.[97]

Various features of this first part of the *Metamorphoses* find echoes in Alberti's tale of the masked monsters and in *Momus* as a whole: the story of a creation, the idea of man as a creature molded from earth, and a Jupiter who seeks to destroy humankind.

Common to these metamorphic narratives is a blurring of the boundaries between men and wolves. Such elision may be found elsewhere in Alberti's writings. In his intercenale "The Wolf," the wolf appears in its traditional role as a savage and merciless predator who wishes to attack a foal. After the wolf is defeated by its would-be prey and finally killed by a shepherd, Alberti tells us that "by this example, I wish it to be understood that among mankind one finds many who, quite similar to wolves, never cease to plague peaceful and quiet citizens with injury and abuse."[98] In the *Theogenius*, Alberti deploys, in the vernacular, Plautus's dictum *lupus est homo homini*—man is a wolf to man.[99] In these passages, we see his more pessimistic face regarding humanity.

Alberti's tale of the masked monsters touches on some of his most acute anxieties about mankind. Many of the themes that animate *Momus* resonate in his other works. Written around the same time as *De re aedificatoria*, *Momus* is pervaded by the notion of destruction, as Jupiter, to whom humans look for care and protection, is intent on destroying his creation and only desists because he has no idea how to construct something better in its place.[100] It is a preoccupation that both texts share and to which many of the arguments in *De re* must be seen as complicated responses.

THE DIVIDED CITY

In the first chapters of Book V of *De re aedificatoria*, Alberti engages most thoroughly with the city as a concept in its own right. However, the discussion is not framed as an examination of the city per se, nor as a comparison between different kinds of cities, although that is in effect what it becomes. Rather, in full accordance with the structural logic of the treatise, Alberti begins Book V, titled "On the Works of Individuals," by discussing "what is necessary or desirable in the case of individuals." Working from the premise that different people require different kinds of buildings, "let us begin," he says, "with the more exalted." These are the people "entrusted with supreme power and judgment," the rulers, who may be divided into two kinds: those who rule alone and those who rule as part of a group. "The one who alone rules over the others," Alberti says, "is he who should have the greatest honor. Let us therefore consider what is appropriate in his particular case." (Dignissimum nimirum oportet esse hunc, qui caeteris praesit solus; quae igitur istius unius gratias fiant, consideremus.)[1]

The precise meaning of this sentence is not immediately clear. Whether Alberti is proposing that the lone ruler is the kind of ruler who is the most worthy of honor, in and of himself—in other words, the best kind—or whether he is simply saying that lone rulers will, by their nature, require the most honors, including the most dignified architectural treatment, is not apparent. The distinction is a fine one but, as we shall see, important. In cities where power is concentrated in the hands of just one person, Alberti asserts, this individual may be of two kinds, either one who "governs reverently and piously over willing subjects, motivated, that is, less by his own gain than by the safety and comfort of his citizens," or one "who would wish to control the political situation so that he could remain in power even against the will of his subjects." The latter is a tyrant, and, Alberti stresses, "each building and even the city itself should differ when under the rule of those called tyrants, as opposed to others who take up their command and care for it like a magisterial office conferred on them by their fellows." As a legitimate ruler, a king will have no fear of his subjects, whereas the tyrant's "own people may be just as hostile as outsiders." Thus, where Alberti concentrated previously on fending off the threat of destruction from nature or a foreign army, when discussing the tyrant's city, he must consider how it may best be fortified "against one's fellow citizens."[2]

The Tyrant's City

Alberti proceeds to outline exactly how the cities of the tyrant and the legitimate ruler diverge.[3] At the outset, the tyrant appears in a negative light as one who seeks power only for himself and is indifferent to the sufferings of his people, while the king rules purely in their interests, as though his power were that of a magisterial office. The subject was a live one at the time that Alberti was writing, but his remarks must be viewed in the context of a long-standing political discourse in which tyranny is condemned and other forms of government, usually monarchy, are approved.[4] This discourse, as Hans Baron has shown, had been reinvigorated and adapted in the circle of the Florentine chancellor Coluccio Salutati (1331–1406) at the beginning of the fifteenth century. An ideological defense of "liberty," as opposed to tyranny, formed an important element of Florentine propaganda during the war with Milan and continued to be developed by humanist chancellors, in particular Leonardo Bruni.[5] Alberti was connected to this circle, and we might expect his text to reflect elements of Bruni's thinking and to proceed with a full-scale denunciation of tyranny.[6] However, as the passage unfurls, the clear conceptual difference between the two rulers is not maintained linguistically or attitudinally.

Throughout most of his description of the tyrant's city, Alberti refers to the authority figure not as a tyrant but as a *princeps*. Yet, toward the end, he seems to return to his original definitions, remarking, "Such are the differences between the town of a tyrant and that of a king."[7] In the second chapter, Alberti employs the term *princeps* throughout. Moreover, he does not condemn the tyrant and his city to the degree that we might expect; his tone even verges on enthusiasm, creating a considerable level of ambiguity.[8] The tyrant, Alberti argues, needs to have the city set out in such a way that he can exercise total control over the people and guard against rebellion, for, given the likely hostility of his own people, "he must therefore fortify his own city against foreigner and fellow citizen alike." Furthermore, "the layout of the fortifications must allow him to receive outside reinforcements, even some of his own men against their fellow citizens."[9]

Noting that the most effective way to protect against rebellion is to divide the city, Alberti proposes that this may best be achieved by the construction of a wall that forms an inner circle within the preexisting city walls: "This wall, I believe, should not run diametrically across the city but should form a kind of circle within a circle. For the wealthy citizens are happier in more spacious surroundings [*laxioribus spaciis*] and would readily accept being excluded by an inner wall, and would not unwillingly leave the stalls and town-center workshops to the food sellers; and that rabble, as Terence's Gnatho calls them, of poulterers, butchers, cooks, and so on, will be less of a risk and less of a nuisance if they do not mix with the important citizens."[10] We are thus presented with the vision of a city forcefully divided along class lines by the very physical means of a wall. The rich would happily desert the city center for the more spacious and salubrious setting of the outer circle, while the center itself would be given over to the "rabble" of the poor. It is an extreme picture of the city, abhorrent to the modern reader and on which Alberti's own position is unclear.[11]

The Theory of the Tyrant

As stated earlier, Alberti swiftly dispenses with his initial tone of condemnation when writing of the tyrant; as the passage progresses, the distinction between the tyrant and the legitimate ruler becomes compromised. This is perhaps unsurprising, for the instability of the distinction is a notable characteristic of the Renaissance literature on the subject. This can be seen particularly in Coluccio Salutati's treatise *De tyranno*, one of the most important texts on tyranny at that time.[12] At the outset, Salutati vigorously condemns tyranny, as one might expect. He defines the tyrant as "either one who usurps a government, having no legal title for his rule, or one who governs *superbe* or rules unjustly or does not observe law or equity; just as, on the other hand, he is a lawful prince upon whom the right to govern is conferred, who administers justice and maintains the laws."[13] His tone, especially when speaking of the lawful prince, is similar to that later adopted by Alberti. On the issue of whether tyrannicide can ever be justified, Salutati notes with approval a number of precedents, including situations in which people were killed merely on the suspicion that they *intended* to become tyrants. He argues, "Anyone who sets up a tyranny may be lawfully resisted, not merely by a party of the people, but by an individual, and . . . such a monster may be put down by force, even to the point of murder."[14]

But Salutati's tone soon begins to change. Having significantly modified the standard defense of tyrannicide, making it more restrictive, he somewhat surprisingly proceeds with a defense of Caesar, who, his modern translator remarks, was certainly a tyrant "according to all [of Salutati's] definitions. . . . His title was defective, his power had been gained by violence and could be maintained only in the same way."[15] Yet the defense of Caesar takes up a very large portion of the treatise and is followed by sections that argue in considerable depth that the murder of Caesar was not justified and that "Dante was right in placing Brutus and Cassius in the lowest Hell as traitors of the deepest dye."[16] What had thus started out as a treatise attacking tyranny moves closer to a defense of a "benevolent despotism,"[17] revealing something of the same ambivalence found in Alberti's text.

Salutati's treatise thus hints at the coexistence of two contradictory strains of thought lying at the heart of the discourse on rulers and tyrants: on the one hand, civic, mercantile view, and on the other, a yearning for authority and a suspicion that only government by a single individual could deliver strength and unity.[18] Perhaps more interesting still, Salutati's initial etymological examination of the word "tyrant" reveals an ambiguity in the very origins of the concept. He states,

> The word "tyrant" is of Greek origin and has the same meaning among both the Greeks and ourselves, in ancient times and now.

> For the word "tyros" is the same as "brave." Now, from the beginning
> . . . every community was governed by kings, and these, as Justinus
> says, were raised to power, not through any arts of popularity, but by
> the well considered judgment of good citizens. Their special func-
> tion was to defend the frontiers of the realm, to rule justly and to
> settle quarrels . . . and since these duties required bravery of mind
> and body, the most ancient Greeks and primitive Italians called their
> kings "tyrants."[19]

It was only after evil increased in the world, Salutati says, that the word "tyrant" was confined to the ruler who abused his powers. This assertion that kings and tyrants were originally one and the same, and that the word "tyrant" simply means "brave," does much to blur the distinction between them. While Salutati does not consciously intend to do so, it is surely implied on some level that the two concepts are not wholly separable—that kings may in fact be tyrannical, and tyrants, to some degree, kingly. The text thus betrays an attraction to the figure of the tyrant, existing uneasily alongside repulsion. Indeed, one might argue that the degree of attention devoted to this figure in the Renaissance is telling, not just of a fear but also of a fascination. Consequently, we should not necessarily assume Alberti's condemnation of the tyrant's city, nor wholly reject his apparent enthusiasm.

Building the Wall

Alberti begins his section on the tyrant's city by referring to some historical precedents. He comments that "Euripides thought the common people to be a powerful adversary in themselves, but totally invincible when they combine deceit and guile."[20] The masses possess enormous strength, which would be irresistible if combined with intelligence. The cunning ruler must thus be able to manipulate things so as to contain this great threat, and this is where the idea of division is advanced. "Carrae in Egypt," Alberti observes, "was a city so heavily populated that when fewer than a thousand people died on a single day, it was considered healthy and thriving; prudently their princes had so divided it up with water conduits that it appeared not as one but as several small towns joined together."[21] Alberti is quite clear as to the reasons for this action. "Their motive, I believe, was not so much to distribute the advantages of the Nile more widely as to reduce the fear of any large-scale popular uprising, and to ensure that any such disturbance might be easily quelled; just as a colossus, if divided into two or more sections, is easier to manage and transport."²² He then cites another example of the effectiveness of division, this time involving the entire country of Egypt: "It was the practice of the Romans never to send a senator to Egypt as proconsul, but to delegate the individual regions to men of equestrian rank. The reason for this, according to Arrian, was to remove the risk of revolution under a single ruler. They also observed that no city was ever free of civil discord when divided naturally either by a river or by being sited on several hills, or if it was partly on hills and partly on a plain."²³

Thus, Alberti suggests that the city be divided by a wall into concentric circles, as the best way of maintaining control. Yet it is important to stress the extremely authoritarian nature of Alberti's proposal, for it is not simply based on the principle of division alone. That is to say, the partition of the city is not, by itself, sufficient. Separation must be actively enforced:

This internal wall should be planned so as to touch every district of the town. As in all other city walls, so especially in this case, the construction must be robust and bold in all its details, and so high as to dominate the roofs of any private houses. It is best to fortify it with battlements and turrets on both sides, and even perhaps a moat, so as to protect the guards stationed along it from either direction. The tops of the towers ought not to be open to the inside, but completely walled, and no more exposed to those on the inside than to the approaching enemy, especially where they overlook a road or the high roof of a temple. I would prefer there to be no route up into the towers except through the walls, and no access from the castle to the walls except where the prince [*princeps*] allows it. No arches, no towers should stand along the roads through the town. There must be no projecting balconies, from which missiles could be thrown at soldiers as they patrol the neighborhood. In short, the whole town should be planned to give the one with supreme power sole possession of all the highest structures, and to make it impossible for anyone to restrict the movement of his men and prevent them from patrolling the town.²⁴

The wall serves not merely to divide the people but also to allow the movement of the tyrant's (or the prince's) troops as they hold the city by force. Hence, it should be fortified and equipped for battle with the citizens, just as the external wall should be fortified to repel an invading army. From the towers and battlements of the dividing wall, the tyrant's troops will be protected from the people and will have the advantages of surveillance, domination of the private houses, and command of the roads and the high roofs of temples. The wall thus stands as the manifest symbol of the power of the ruler, as well as the crystallized representation of the class conflict that underlies the city.

The interpretation of these passages is of considerable importance. It cannot be said that Alberti advocates either a divided city or a tyrannical government as his preferred urban model. Rather, his approach is entirely consistent with his methodology, as he discusses the buildings that will be necessary for the highest citizens, the rulers, whom he divides into those who rule alone and those who rule in groups, further dividing those who rule alone into legitimate rulers and tyrants. Alberti does distinguish the city of the tyrant from that of the king, and he goes on to describe the buildings that are fitting for the republic. As Charles Burroughs has argued, "The concentric city . . . should be regarded not as an ideal city and still less as a feasible project, but as the diagrammatic demonstration of a stage in an argument, to which other considerations and aspects of reality are for the moment not pertinent."[25]

Equally, it cannot be said that Alberti straightforwardly and unambiguously condemns the tyrant and his city, a thing he could easily have done. Indeed, we may wonder, if the tyrant is to be considered an appalling figure, why does Alberti describe his city at all? Why, after some cursory remarks about the harsh nature of tyranny, does Alberti then explain in some detail how one might best be set up and preserved? It is perhaps the introduction of the word *princeps* that most serves to muddy the waters. This was an ambiguous term and had been so even in ancient times. Augustus had adopted the title to persuade the populace of the nonmilitary and benevolent nature of his rule. It preserves a certain vagueness, suggesting simply "principal citizen," "top person," or "chief" rather than indicating a specific position or definite powers. In Alberti's day, it would have had the added nuance of the vernacular *principe*. Of course, some of those called *principe* were to all intents and purposes tyrants, yet the term nonetheless suggested legitimacy.

One is struck by the largely nonjudgmental tone of Alberti's discussion. He recognized that the architect can be of great use to the ruling power, whatever the nature of that power might be. His position is redolent of the modern, technocratic discourse of realpolitik and contrasts strongly with much medieval thinking. As Jonathan White has put it, "Alberti tends no longer moralistically to distinguish *bonum et malum* in the manner of his medieval predecessors Dante and Lorenzetti [in his frescoes of good and bad government], but to theorize 'beyond good and evil' in a pre-Machiavellian, not to say pre-Nietzschean, manner."[26] Rulers of city-states may well have been the chief audience for Alberti's treatise. After all, architects were few and far between, and many of them would have been unable to read Latin.[27] Alberti himself was of course employed, at various times, by Sigismondo Malatesta and Leonello and Meliaduse d'Este, all of whom could arguably be called tyrants. Moreover, contemporary rulers eagerly consumed Alberti's architectural treatise. Lorenzo de' Medici demanded that each chapter be delivered directly to him at Careggi, straight from the printing press and still unbound. When Borso d'Este asked to borrow his manuscript copy, Lorenzo agreed on the condition that it be returned swiftly "because he is very fond of it and reads it often."[28]

Finally, it should be noted that the tyrant's city is one of the most clear and striking images of a city that Alberti produces in the architectural treatise, and one with which he seems particularly to engage. This may simply be because such a city, with its concentric circles, is especially clear in its form and memorable due to its tyrannical nature. Whatever the reason, its portrayal does chime with the politically conservative impulses that are often found in Alberti's writings, where he repeatedly articulates his mistrust of the lower orders.

Class Relations

Alberti's idea of a divided city certainly suggests that he was pessimistic about class relations, and especially about the threat of the "rabble" who would be confined within the inner circle. Mistrust of the poor and of the "crowd" were widely expressed sentiments in this period, while disdain for the irrationality of the plebes is a commonplace of much of the Latin literature that Alberti would have known. In the *Theogenius*, the wise Genipatro asserts that "according to Plato, Axiochus says that the plebes are nothing other than inconstant, infirm, unstable, fickle, simple, frivolous, bestial, slothful, guiding themselves only with errors, always hostile to reason, and full of every corrupt judgment."[29] In Alberti's *Della famiglia*, meanwhile, it is said that the moon governs the behavior of the plebes, along with that of women.[30] A fear of the poor is clearly articulated toward the end of the third book of *Della famiglia* in an exchange between Giannozzo and Adovardo Alberti concerning the subject of friendship:

GIANNOZZO: Personally, what can I say about friendship? Perhaps I could say that the rich find more friends than they want.

ADOVARDO: Nevertheless, I see the rich are envied by others, and it is said the poor are enemies of the wealthy. Perhaps there is some truth in the saying. Would you like to hear the reason?

GIANNOZZO: Yes, go on.

ADOVARDO: Because every poor man tries to become rich.

GIANNOZZO: True.

ADOVARDO: And no poor man can become rich without the corresponding diminution of another's wealth, unless he can grow riches from the soil.[31]

Adovardo here expounds a theory of class relations in which the rich and the poor must necessarily be antagonists, and his argument suggests a proto-Physiocratic view in which wealth in the money economy exists in finite quantity. New wealth cannot be created unless it is grown from the soil; otherwise, the enrichment of the poor must necessarily entail the impoverishment of the rich.[32] Furthermore, Adovardo notes gloomily that "the poor are almost infinite in number" and far more numerous than the rich. "Everyone tries to get more property, each in his own way, through deceit, fraud, and theft no less than through industry," Adovardo explains. He then poses the question "If wealth is besieged by so many pilferers, can it get you friends or enemies?"[33] It is notable that in Alberti's divided city wealth really is besieged; a fortified wall prevents the poor from attacking the rich.

Florence and Rome

Beyond the literary tradition, Alberti's views may have been inspired by the actual conditions of quattrocento cities. Robust commercial economies were magnets for immigrants, and there is ample evidence of anxiety regarding the *gente nuova* in many Italian cities.[34] In Florence, large numbers of laborers came from the surrounding *contado* and even from as far away as Germany to work in the wool and cloth industries, from which the city derived much of its wealth. As a result, there existed a sizeable population of semiskilled and unskilled workers that was liable to create high levels of unemployment and unrest. Worker-based revolts were not common but did occur, the most famous being the revolt of the Ciompi in 1378.[35] Just seven years earlier, a lack of food and the high price of grain had caused wool carders to lead a revolt at Siena.[36] In towns across Italy throughout this period, there was evidence of unrest caused above all by shortages of food and the imposition of charges and taxes by local authorities. Moreover, while workers' organizations, in the rare cases that they arose, were quickly stamped out, a form of radicalism did exist in religious movements such as the Franciscan Spirituals and Fraticelli. Particularly active in Florence, they emphasized the spiritual value of poverty and persisted in asserting that Christ and the apostles had owned no property, even after a papal bull of 1323 branded the teaching heretical.[37]

If conditions in Florence could generate anxiety about class relations and civic disorder, Rome, where Alberti lived much of his adult life, was far worse. Rome was not a commercial city like Florence; much of its economic activity was agricultural, with the *bovattieri* forming the leading guild in the city.[38] Nevertheless, the population of Rome was volatile and often hostile toward the papacy, and power was both exercised and possessed far more precariously than it was in Florence, Milan, Venice, or Naples. Alberti arrived in Rome during the unhappy papacy of Eugenius IV, which saw the storming of the Campidoglio, the proclamation of a republic, and the pope's flight and protracted refuge in Florence. Eugenius left the city in a galley, disguised as a Benedictine monk. Recognized at the last moment, he was forced to cower ignominiously under a shield to avoid the shower of stones that rained down on him as he set sail for Ostia. In the pope's absence, his palaces were looted.[39] Looting was also common during papal interregna, while newly crowned popes often faced volatile crowds along the route of the *possesso*.

Much of the serious violence that occurred in Rome had its origins with the nobility, whose fractious ways have been well documented by historians. Nevertheless, the actions of the common people—themselves a turbulent and dangerous group—might be the most visible expressions of aristocratic maneuvering. A diplomatic dispatch written by Bartolomeo Bonatto, a representative of the marquis of Mantua during the pontificate of Pius II, gives a taste of the level of Roman hostility toward the papal court, as Bonatto explains that he was forced to pay a higher than anticipated rent so that he could live "close to the courtiers, since otherwise I would have to go outside of the area to which they have retreated in order to be safer."[40] This image of a city with sharp divisions between safe and unsafe areas is supported by another diplomatic document dating from the same period. Commenting on the revolt of Tiburzio, the Milanese representative explains that the rebels could not be pursued since they were holed up "in the heart of the city," in the Pantheon, and to send soldiers after them would be "to lead these people [the soldiers] to the slaughter."[41]

Poulterers, Butchers, and Cooks

When identifying the types of people that one might expect to pose a risk and cause a nuisance, Alberti referred to the speech of a character in Terence's play *Eunuchus* (*The Eunuch*). These words must have been well known in humanist circles, primarily because Cicero had cited them in the *De officiis*. There, the Roman orator used them to identify trades that are connected to sensual pleasures and ought, therefore, to be held in contempt:

> Least respectable of all are those trades which cater to sensual pleasures:
> Fishmongers, butchers, cooks, and poulterers, and fishermen,
> As Terence says. Add to these, if you please, the perfumers, dancers, and the whole *ludus talarius*.[42]

Alberti's contemporary, Matteo Palmieri, paraphrases Cicero's words fairly closely in his vernacular *Vita civile*, asserting that "among the trades are [to be considered] dishonest those which harm and are useless to the morals of men and which service unnecessary pleasure, such as taverns, cooks, sellers of cosmetics, schools of dance or other lascivious things, and any game of dice."[43]

Another contemporary, Lapo da Castiglionchio the Younger, who knew Alberti and was his colleague at the curia, wrote disapprovingly in his dialogue *De curiae commodis* of the great number of "cooks, sausage makers [or poulterers], and gourmet food makers" present at the papal court.[44] Alberti, in other words, was employing a commonplace, albeit not one of the most common. Nevertheless, his words were certainly apt and entirely fitting to his purpose. Some of the professions that he mentions were indeed associated with disorder of one kind or another, and it is worth considering them in some depth.

Food Vendors

Starting with the butchers, it is notable that in Florence these tradesmen were traditionally regarded as fractious, violent, reluctant to abide by regulations, and quick to partake in uprisings.[45] The commune preferred not to antagonize them.[46] Although master butchers were guildsmen and sometimes very wealthy, they were also, of course, recognized as individuals who regularly handled animal products and raw meat. In addition to the butchers, Alberti mentions petty confectioners; they, too, seem to have been regarded as problematic in some Italian cities. In Florence, a fourteenth-century statute forbade sellers of bread, wine, meat, cooked fish, or any other comestible from going within two hundred *brachia* of the palace of the captain and podestà.[47] Presumably, such persons were believed to degrade public space through their very presence and perhaps to constitute a security risk.[48] Itinerant traders could, by their nature, be difficult to identify and to subject fully to communal controls. No doubt one of the major sources of contraband goods in most cities, such individuals would often have been associated with criminality and disorder.[49]

It was not only itinerant food vendors, however, who aroused suspicion. Alberti also mentions markets, which were indeed notoriously chaotic places that attracted people of every stripe, including criminals and ne'er-do-wells.[50] Apart from their stalls, where a good deal of selling, and sometimes presumably swindling, took place, markets often played host to taverns. These were locales of both drinking and gambling, and it is no surprise that Palmieri adds them to Cicero's list of trades "that cater to sensual pleasures" (*quae ministrae sunt voluptatum*). Objections to taverns may well have had a political dimension. As Samuel Kline Cohn has argued, taverns provided opportunities for the poor to congregate and "forge their own plebeian culture."[51] Indeed, tavern keepers appear second in number only to wool workers on late trecento lists of people condemned as Ciompi or revolutionaries in Florence.[52] However, the main objection to taverns was moral, as is borne out by the legislation that restricted them. It was not merely that drinking and gambling often led to arguments and fights. Taverns encouraged drunkenness and gluttony, and it was commonly held that where these sins appeared, sexual license was rarely far behind.

This connection among food vendors, gluttony, and sexual depravity is of vital importance in understanding Alberti's description of the tyrant's city. Gluttony signaled uncontrolled desire and abandonment to pleasure. That such abandonment could, and often did, lead to sodomy and pederasty was a common opinion among the preachers of popular sermons, the authors of humanist treatises, and the drafters of civic legislation. Thus, Lapo da Castiglionchio the Younger, who characterizes gluttony as among the worst vices to be found at the papal curia, explains that those who take excessive delight in food and drink "zealously seek out beautiful servant boys to serve the meals, as well as catamites and men whose hair is done a little too finely. They want them to be clothed in splendid finery, smooth and, especially, beardless, in which requirement they follow, I believe, the authority of Alexander of Macedon."[53] Referring to a maxim that was well known among the humanists, Lapo observes that fine food "stirs up most desires for [other] pleasures and especially those of Venus, which cool down when the [gustatory] pleasure has suffered, just as Terence says, without Ceres and Liber."[54]

More prosaically, Florentine legislation of the fourteenth century explains that it is necessary to restrict the activities of taverns because they are places in which "many boys are led into error; they become accustomed to it and convert in their behavior to vices and to foul and protracted sins, which are abominable before God and before men."[55] The countermeasures include the forbidding of foods "pertaining to gluttony or levity" (*pertinentia ad gulositatem sive ghioctorniam*) and a range of fines for tavern keepers who entertain thieves, rascals, prostitutes, and outlaws.[56] The harshest penalty is reserved for those who allow sodomy to take place on their premises; they are to be burned.

Taverns were, of course, natural targets for moralists and popular preachers. The late trecento moralist Paolo da Certaldo characterizes taverns as being at the opposite end of the scale from churches in a moral consideration of buildings.[57] This opinion is also found in the sermons of Fra Bernardino of Siena, who pursues the analogy much further by showing how each element of the church finds its antithesis in one of the constituent elements of the tavern environment.[58] Bernardino expresses a fear that is widely articulated in the literature of the period—that the corrupting power of taverns may threaten the social order. While it is to be desired that no one should frequent taverns, the young especially must be dissuaded, and the highborn young above all.[59] This category was particularly at risk, having both the means to facilitate a gluttonous lifestyle and by far the most to lose from one. By frequenting taverns, the young rich would mix with their social inferiors in an unseemly manner, become corrupted, squander patrimonies, and disgrace families. To clarify, it was not only those who did not practice sufficient restraint in eating who were labeled gluttons; gluttony also concerned the eating of foods that were overly refined and delicate or that were judged unbefitting to the social status of the diner. Sumptuary law existed to some extent to prevent the lowly from eating above their station. More important, however, it sought to limit the extravagance of the highborn, and of highborn youth in particular.

Alberti addresses the issue of gluttony in the *Della famiglia*, the *Cena familiaris*, and the *De iciarchia*, a dialogue in which he makes himself the main speaker. Dispensing advice to the assembled youth of the Alberti family, he warns of the destructive potential of excessive eating and drinking. What results is an acerbic sketch of a gluttonous lifestyle and the moral descent that inevitably results from it. Notably, Alberti is not concerned with the lower orders but with the higher—youths who are often spoiled and easily led into bad ways. Such gluttons swiftly fall prey to a kind of moral degradation that brings disgrace upon themselves and their families, since, as Lionardo comments in the *Della famiglia*, "those whose sons are wicked and lost in iniquity shall not avoid blame or escape shame for negligence."[60] Beyond this, young, inebriated gluttons may pose a real danger to the public. Prone to drunken disputes, they are consumed by envy if they see others succeed, and "they are maddened if they cannot get their own way; they become predators, deprecators, conmen, traitors, and make themselves prey to every kind of corruption."[61] Their lifestyles lead directly to many of the worst vices, including "theft, sacrilege, [and] robbery. They become pimps, poisoners, and lead people, by fraudulence and betrayal, to lose their belongings, their honor, their life, and to sell their integrity and the integrity of their family."[62]

Cooks

Against this background, it is not difficult to understand the contempt for cooks that appears in some of the literature of the period. Like poulterers and butchers, cooks spent their days up to their elbows in raw ingredients and animal products.[63] Lapo makes much of the fact that cooks in curial circles in Rome tended to be foreigners—mostly northern Europeans (that is to say barbarians)—and describes them as "men covered with grease and grime in the middle of the kitchen, embroiled in the smoke and stench."[64] Cooks and tavern keepers must often have been closely associated, and the trecento Florentine legislation that severely restricts the operations of taverns is addressed to both of them: "tavern keeper or cook or anyone known by any other name."[65] Just as taverns were sometimes characterized as anti-churches, it is readily apparent that cooks could be conceived of as anti-priests, men who transformed substances for pleasure rather than for piety. It was this pleasure that the cook aimed to inspire that was the problem. He produced "gluttonous things" (*res gulosas*) and things "pertinent to gluttony and levity" (*pertinentia ad gulositatem sive ghioctorniam*)[66]—things that, in Palmieri's terms, provide "unnecessary enjoyment" (*non necessario dilecto*).[67]

This notion of cooks as being among the lowliest of servants, and of cookery as a morally suspect practice, certainly predates both medieval tradition and Cicero.[68] Plato condemned cookery for being concerned only with pleasure and for having been founded on opinion rather than knowledge. In the *Gorgias*, the philosopher argues that cooks are not guided by coherent, rational principles but simply proceed according to trial and error, aiming to give pleasure to a particular individual at a particular time. Since cooks are unable to offer a coherent account of any principles on which their practice is based, Plato asserts, cookery cannot be a *technē* and belongs rather to the realm of "flattery." Moreover, since cookery is not a *technē* and has no foundation in knowledge, it can have no relationship to the good, the ultimate object of all knowledge. Cookery, therefore, can neither aim for the good nor be guided by it: "I call this flattery, and I say that such a thing is shameful . . . because it guesses at what's pleasant with no consideration for what's best. And I say that it isn't a craft, but a knack, because it has no account of the nature of whatever thing it applies by which it applies them, so that it's unable to state the cause of each thing. And I refuse to call anything that lacks such an account a craft."[69]

Thus, when Alberti speculated about building a wall to enclose the market stalls, workshops, and food sellers, and to confine Terence's rabble of poulterers, butchers, and cooks, his words were well chosen. The issue was not simply that such people represented the lower orders' propensity and willingness for revolt (although they were certainly perceived that way) but that they embodied the urban world's potential to corrupt. The unregulated mixture of substances and persons, pleasure seeking and abandonment to vice, and the dereliction of duty, reason, and the good— such were the things that these tradesmen might be expected to inspire. These ideas must underpin Alberti's advice that they be isolated, a suggestion echoed in the *De iciarchia*. Speaking of corrupted, drunken, and gluttonous youths, Alberti remarks, "Disgrace of the city, they deserve to be taken off to some deserted island so that such a great pest will not corrupt the rest."[70]

The Flight from Trade

Of course, Alberti's views are informed not simply by the idea that the "important citizens" (*cives primarii*) want to live a life untroubled by poulterers. He conjectures that they would also be happier in more spacious surroundings, delivering this opinion as though it is mere common sense and requires no justification. Yet in many places across Italy, a family's presence in the very center of the city was an indicator of its elevated status.[71] Rather than building their homes on spacious peripheries, families vied for coveted plots of land that were close to the symbolically important political and religious centers. Alberti's statement seems to point to his own lack of enthusiasm for much of what urban life entailed; he appears to take for granted that anyone who could get out would do so.

As we have seen, what they would have primarily been fleeing from was trade and commerce—two of the foremost things that we think of as particularly characterizing urban life. It is notable that Alberti gives little attention to commerce or industry in his otherwise wide-ranging treatise. By contrast, he devotes a good deal of attention to agriculture and the arrangement of the farm. Now, the latter was a well-ploughed literary furrow, a topos of outstanding pedigree, while the activities of the wool shop, to understate matters, was not. Nevertheless, one might still expect commerce to feature more prominently in Alberti's text, considering the technical nature of the treatise and the importance of trade in many of the cities with which Alberti was familiar. It is not as though Alberti was a remote intellectual who knew nothing of trade. On the contrary, he came from a large and significant merchant family with international business interests that had earned them a fortune.[72] Commerce is, in fact, discussed more frequently in the *Della famiglia*, where Alberti's dialogical approach makes for a characteristically complex treatment: sometimes commerce is acknowledged as a necessary means of generating income, occasionally it is lauded, and frequently it is denounced. It is worth considering this in more detail.

Merchants and Scholars

The issue of profit making is first raised by Adovardo Alberti when considering how a father must choose a trade for his son. In Florence, he explains, the republican system of government prevents any citizen from acquiring outstanding glory as a military leader, since he might then pose a threat to the republic itself. Regarding the other trades, Adovardo continues,

> Nor does our city place much value on men of letters. In fact, it is intent on profit and wealth. Whether this is due to the country or our ancestors' nature and customs, it seems that everyone grows up to seek profits, every conversation seems to be about money, every thought is turned to gain, and every skill is employed in gathering wealth. . . . Just as Plato, that prince of philosophers, writes that all the customs of the Spartans are impregnated with their desire to conquer, so could I say that in our city the heavens produce keen minds ready to discern profit. The place and custom spur them, not to seek glory above all, but to acquire and save worldly goods and to desire riches.[73]

This comparison between scholarship and profit making informs many of Alberti's discussions of commerce. As one might expect, he routinely accords scholarship a higher value, and there is a certain bitterness in the manner in which he rebukes the Tuscans for their obsession with wealth and their disdain for letters. Later on in the dialogue, Lionardo returns to the subject of amassing profit, having established that it is necessary for the survival and happiness of the family:

> Well then, let us begin to acquire wealth. Perhaps this is a suitable time for this sort of discussion, for the darkness of night approaches. To those of noble and liberal spirit, no occupations seem less brilliant than those whose purpose is to make money. If you think a moment and try to remember which are the occupations for making money, you will see that they consist of buying and selling, lending and collecting. I believe that these occupations whose purpose is gain may seem vile and worthless to you [Battista] for you are of noble and lofty spirit. In fact, selling is a mercenary trade; you serve the buyer's needs, pay yourself for your work, and make a profit by charging others more than you yourself have paid. . . . Lending would be a laudable generosity if you did not seek interest, but then it would not be a profitable business. Some say that these occupations, which we shall call pecuniary, always entail dishonesty and numerous lies and often entail dishonest agreements and fraudulent contracts. They say, therefore, that those of liberal spirit must completely avoid them as dishonest and mercenary.[74]

Once again, moneymaking is characterized in decidedly negative terms as something that will appear "vile and worthless" to the scholarly Battista. This is not the end of the story, however, since Lionardo in fact contends that "those who judge all pecuniary occupations in this manner are wrong."[75] If conducted with honesty, business will be a dignified activity. Moreover, money is necessary not only for the family but also for the city, which must be able to call on wealthy citizens in time of need.[76] There follows a lengthy and clearly sincere defense of moneymaking, though Lionardo still contends that "acquiring wealth is not a glorious enterprise to be likened to the most noble professions." He goes on to say, "We must not, however, scorn a man who is not naturally endowed for noble deeds [*quelle molto magnifiche essercitazioni*] if he turns to these other occupations in which he knows he is not inept and which, everyone admits, are of great use to the family and to the state."[77] However acceptable moneymaking may be, and however useful, it is still ranked beneath "nobler" occupations such as scholarship.

The Family Business

For Alberti, the issue of commerce was, of course, inextricably bound up with that of family. The Alberti had been great merchants, and it is no surprise that Lionardo uses his own ancestors' deeds as examples of honest and worthy business dealings. One senses that there was an instinct within Alberti, as a scholar, to denigrate commerce, but that this conflicted with an equally strong desire to honor his family. To dismiss commerce would be to dismiss his own father and his most revered ancestors. The issue is complicated by Alberti's relationship with the two cousins who had deprived him of his patrimony and, as he was later to allege, sought his assassination.[78] These same men would shortly lead the family business into disaster, and it may be that Alberti was already critical of their stewardship.[79] That his grievance against them was not far from his mind is confirmed when Lionardo, in the course of his discussion of professions, notes that literary studies are subject to the assaults of fortune, commenting, "Your father dies; or there are envious, harsh, inhuman relatives; or you may fall into poverty or misfortune."[80]

The desire to assert the superiority of letters may well have been Alberti's reaction to some of his family members making the opposite contention, perhaps especially the two cousins in question. After all, in the intercenale "The Orphan," Philoponius's "impious" and "unjust" kinsmen "foolishly asserted that anyone merited disdain who wished his literary achievements to win him more esteem than wealthy men possessed."[81] To this degree, it is possible that the emphasis on the excellence of the Alberti of former times, and above all their *onestà*, was intended to draw an unflattering comparison with some (but by no means all) of the Alberti of the present day.[82] As so often is the case in Alberti's writings, one is struck by the ambivalent nature of his thought. Where the family is concerned, love, pride, rejection, and fury seem to be subject to an uneasy commingling.

The praise of the Alberti ancestors' commercial dealings makes great play not only of their moral virtues but also of the scale of their enterprise. Lionardo notes that they were "known as very great merchants [*grandissimi mercatanti*] within the borders of Italy and beyond, in Spain, in the West, in Syria, in Greece, and in all ports."[83] The point is an important one, for the difference between petty tradesmen and grand *mercatores* was enormous. Apart from being keenly felt in practice, this distinction enjoyed a sound theoretical pedigree since it was expounded by Cicero in the *De officiis*.[84]

Those who "buy things up by wholesale of the merchants, to retail them out again little by little," Cicero opines, are to be considered mean and no better than ordinary people, "for what they gain is but a very poor business, unless they are guilty of abominable lying, than which there is nothing in the world more scandalous." On the other hand, "as for merchandise, it is sordid and mean, when the trade that is driven is little and inconsiderable; but when it takes in a great quantity of business, and, bringing home goods from every country, sells them out again without lying or deceiving, we can hardly say but that it is creditable enough."[85]

These words form part of the same passage in which Cicero quotes Terence's line about poulterers, butchers, and cooks—the very line that Alberti used when describing the tyrant's city. Commerce on a small scale cannot enjoy prestige since it will only be profitable if it is conducted dishonestly. When it is conducted on a grand scale, by contrast, dishonesty is not essential to profit making. Hence the importance of the size of the Alberti business: size went hand in hand with magnificence but was also a necessary condition for the *onestà* of the Alberti ancestors.

Florence and the Market

Alberti's feelings about commerce may also have been colored by his birth in exile. The emphasis on the Florentines' dedication to profit above all else might reflect Alberti's sense that his family had been driven out by ruthless and greedy merchants who, unlike the Alberti, were not reluctant to place profit before honor. We ought to recall Alberti's remark in the fourth book of *De re aedificatoria* that "with Plato I say that it is of the nature of a city to expect that at some point in its history it should be threatened with conquest, since it is impossible, either in public or in private life, to curb that desire for possession and that ambition which are due to Nature or to human habits, within any reasonable limits: it has been the single most important reason for all armed aggression."[86]

The amassing of profit must be seen as part of the fundamental human impulse for possession—a desire so deeply ingrained in humanity that it cannot be controlled. It would hardly be surprising if Alberti, like Dante, another great Florentine exile before him, viewed the Florentine enthusiasm for profit as an inevitable cause of faction and strife. It is worth remembering that in the tyrant's city, those in the outer circle left the center to the "confectioners" around the forum. Alberti uses Terence's unusual *cuppedinarius* for food sellers but, perhaps making a joke on *cupidus* and *denarius*, renders it *cupidenarius*—someone who longs for money.[87] His divided city might then hold out the prospect of a flight not merely from the marketplace, in the sense of the piazza or forum, but from the market in general—from the destructive exchange of goods and currency.

There is perhaps one final reason why Alberti may have felt an antipathy toward trade: the profits it brings are ephemeral. Like other writers, he often displays a preoccupation with the disappearance of families who had once enjoyed enormous wealth. In the prologue to *De re*, when commending buildings as enduring monuments to their patrons, he asks, "How many respected families both in our own city and in others throughout the world would have totally disappeared . . . had not their family hearth harbored them, welcoming them, as it were, into the very bosom of their ancestors?"[88] Large mercantile economies, then as now, were susceptible to rapid reversals of fortune and spectacular collapse. The risks of long-distance international trade were substantial. Political events could result in the seizure of the overseas merchant's property, and sometimes his person too. Land routes were subject to bandits and sea routes to pirates (hence the Italians' early development of systems of insurance). Moreover, the international merchant operated in a Europe that was still largely feudal and did not always obey the rules of commerce. Kings, dukes, and other nobles could default on debts, leaving the merchant with little or no redress.[89] Florence witnessed some major banking collapses during the fourteenth century, triggered by the English king Edward III's defaulting on loans, and Lionardo specifically refers to the families involved in the *Della famiglia*:

> It seems that in our city no great fortune but our own has ever been preserved long enough to be passed on to one's grandchildren. In just a few days fortunes have gone up in smoke, as people say, and of some of them nothing is left but poverty, misery and infamy. I do not wish to give numerous examples or discuss the reasons or misfortunes which have caused the great wealth of many of our citizens to be dissipated. . . . The Cerchi, Peruzzi, Scali, Spini, Ricci and many other families of our city were at one time powerful and immensely rich. Today, they are still noble and honorable but have suddenly fallen upon evil days, and fortune has reduced some of them to dire straits.[90]

The market, then, might serve only to reinforce the ephemeral nature of the city, to place it in the hands of *fortuna* and to increase the risk of its destruction, the very thing that so troubled Alberti.

At Home with the King and the Tyrant

A close examination of the description of the tyrant's city and its context certainly reveals a richness of meaning, but it does not allow us to pin down Alberti's own position or "view" with certainty. It has sometimes been suggested that the passages concerning the divided city express an aristocratic strain in Alberti's thought, and perhaps the ambivalence that I have identified regarding commerce could be used to back up such an assertion.[91] In truth, however, there is little meaning in branding Alberti aristocratic. The nobles of large Italian cities did not congregate in a single noble "quarter" or abandon the city centers. If one were to attempt to formulate what an "aristocratic" city of the period would have looked like, it would not be the city described by Alberti. Nonetheless, it is worth thinking briefly about what kind of city Alberti's scheme *might* have resembled and to what extent it relates to actual built form. In order to do this, we should consider some of the other features of the city where government is in the hands of a single person.

The actual dwelling place of the ruler is yet another area in which Alberti asserts that the tyrant and the king may be distinguished from each other:

> A royal palace should be sited in the city center, should be of easy access, and should be gracefully decorated, elegant, and refined, rather than ostentatious. But that of a tyrant, being a fortress [*arx*] rather than a house, should be positioned where it is neither inside nor outside the city [*neque in urbe neque ex urbe*]. Further, whereas a royal dwelling might be sited next to a showground, a temple, or the houses of noblemen, that of a tyrant should be set well back on all sides from any buildings. In either case an appropriate and useful guideline, which will lend the building dignity, will be to construct it in such a way that, if a royal palace, it should not be so large that it is impossible to throw out any troublemaker, or, if a fortress [*arx*], not so constricted that it resembles a prison more than the apartment of a fine prince.[92]

Once again, Alberti argues that architectural design will reflect the fact that the tyrant must fear his own people, while the king need not. The king, as the beating heart of the city, will be located in the very center, while the tyrant must skulk on the peripheries, where he will be "neither inside nor outside the city."

Alberti goes on to discuss the arx in greater detail, observing that it had developed as a retreat in times of adversity and had originally been a sacred place, consecrated to religion: "But then tyrants took over the citadel [arx] and transformed a place of piety and religion into one of cruelty and excess, a sacred haven from adversity into a generator of distress."[93] Nonetheless, Alberti does not decline to discuss how an arx might be built and defended. "The most suitable layout for the citadel," he advises, "is for all sections of town wall to be linked in the form of O, which is either in turn grasped, but not enclosed, by a huge C with bent horns . . . from which several radial walls emanate to the circumference. Thus the citadel, as we have just recommended, is neither inside nor outside the town. But if one wanted to give a concise description, one might not go wrong in describing it as a well-guarded back door to the town. . . . The citadel should be threatening, rugged and rocky, stubborn and invincible."[94]

The arx is the place of last redoubt, though not so much for the people of the city as for the ruler. It embodies one of the most important things that the architect may offer to anyone who governs a city: personal security. Indeed, in these passages, Alberti appears to describe how one might largely dispense with people—often characterized as unreliable and irrational—and rely instead on architectural structures for one's safety. As he observes, "A compact citadel is safer than a large one. The former can be entrusted to a few, the latter requires a large garrison; and as a character of Euripides' said, 'never has there been a crowd without some mischievous element'—so here it is safer to put your trust in a few than to risk the perfidy of many."[95] Alberti goes on to explain how one could create an arx that, while defensible by just a few men, would be almost impossible for an enemy to capture. Even so, "since in human life no chance may be left without provision, let there be some secret entrance into the center of the citadel, known only to you, through which entry may be forced with armed men, should you ever be shut out. To this end, it might be worth having a concealed section of wall, laid in clay instead of lime."[96] Strikingly, Alberti addresses the reader directly at several points in this passage. Speaking as though to the ruler of a city-state, he describes how one might build a lifeline in a world in which no one can be fully trusted. The arx is a necessary refuge for the ruler and must, as such, be impenetrable. On the other hand, it is possible that the arx could fall into the hands of others. In this case, it is vital that the ruler—"you"—is able to enter it with ease. And this, too, can be accomplished by the architect.

Of course, it is the tyrant who has the greatest need of the arx—greatest, but not exclusive. Alberti understands that other, more legitimate rulers may also require a stronghold and implicitly acknowledges that different forms of power will often have recourse to the same means. As we have seen, the tyrant's arx should not be so restricted that it looks more like a prison than a fortress, and a royal palace should not be so open that it cannot be secured. However, Alberti goes much further in blurring the distinction between the two rulers when he remarks that "since it is expected of a royal household that it should differ from a fortress in almost every respect, and certainly in the most important ones, the palace must be linked to a fortress, so that in emergencies a king will not be without a fortress, nor a tyrant without a palace for his entertainment."[97] Behind their magnificence, kings will have to deal with the cut and thrust of exercising and maintaining power; in front of their realpolitik, tyrants will need to erect a façade of magnificence and legitimacy. The real differences between these rulers would appear to consist of accidents as much as essence.

Rome Under Nicholas V

An excellent example of precisely the kind of arrangement described by Alberti can be found in Castiglione del Lago. Here, a predominantly sixteenth-century palace faces onto the town, while linking to a large fortress behind that also connects to the city's walls. However, one of the places that most obviously comes to mind in connection with the tyrant's city is Rome. First, as we have seen, Rome really *was* a divided city in which the papal administration could not always command the center. The notion of two separate and often strongly opposed groupings within the city was firmly established there. As we have seen, Alberti stresses that the tyrant must reside neither in nor outside of the city, and this, of course, was more or less the case with the Vatican. Rome enjoyed an idiosyncratic topography that was harder to comprehend than that of many other cities. Its historical development had left its most important centers—the Lateran, the Vatican, and the Campidoglio—on the peripheries.[98] The Vatican was particularly remote since it was divided from the greater part of the city by the Tiber, had no connecting road to Trastevere, and was reached from the opposing bank by a single bridge.

During precisely the same period in which Alberti was writing his treatise, the Vatican was given new prominence as a papal residence by Pope Nicholas V, very much with security in mind. Nicholas undertook a vast program of urban renewal in Rome, spurred by his decision to hold a jubilee in 1450. His schemes entailed the rebuilding of a number of churches—including large-scale modifications to St. Peter's—as well as the transformation of the Vatican into a fitting papal residence. Indeed, the Nicholan *renovatio* was particularly concerned with the fortification of the Borgo. The Vatican received new walls and was to be linked more closely to the Castel Sant'Angelo. This building itself underwent some considerable renovation, with the addition of four towers, the raising of the height of the central tower, and the addition of a bronze and wooden statue of the Archangel Michael.[99] The walls of the Leonine City and the Borgo were reinforced and made to connect with those of the Vatican, thus creating a genuine fortified citadel replete with its own castle.[100] This last building enjoyed particular attention, since, as Westfall comments, "nearly a century of Roman history had shown the strategic importance of the Castel Sant'Angelo; each pope entrusted it to his most faithful officer, the cardinals considered it their last redoubt during a papal interregnum, and the people of Rome weighed its possible role in any turmoil they might plan or undertake."[101]

On the far bank of the Tiber, then, Nicholas sought to shore up papal authority and security by connecting his palace to a stronghold.[102] He fortified the entire area and, according to the account of his biographer Giannozzo Manetti, had plans to rejuvenate its economic activity. The Borgo under Nicholas might indeed have become "like a small town," a city in embryo, just as Alberti recommends for the arx.[103] Certainly, Nicholas had good reason to be preoccupied with his safety, only narrowly surviving the conspiracy of Stefano Porcari in 1453. Alberti was a keen observer of these events and famously wrote about them in his *De Porcaria coniuratione*. He appears to have rather admired Porcari in some respects, particularly for his unswerving commitment to gaining "liberty" for his city. Nonetheless, he was in no doubt as to what a successful conspiracy would have meant: "The final step would be looting and slaughter all over the city. Porcari had decreed that the whole papal crowd should be exterminated. He said he wished to act so that within the city walls, there would be no more need to fear the chief—his teeth would truly have been drawn."[104]

Alberti's attitude in this instance is not easy to construe. We might speculate that he was sympathetic to Porcari's critique of the papacy and thirst for liberty but that he disapproved of Porcari's methods of obtaining it and his desire for innovation. In any case, Alberti shows himself to be all too aware of the difficulties of the popes, commenting, "I understand that some can conclude that everything is now out of hand. I remember the time of Eugene. I have heard about the troubles of Boniface and have read of the difficulties of many popes. . . . From another angle, I find the pope's majesty obviously solid. . . . Hence I am not much afraid of external aggression. I also think the plague of internal evils will die down. My understanding of the matter, however, and my conclusions, are far from settled."[105]

"Majesty" (*maestas*) was key to the pope's ability to govern the city.[106] As we have seen, Alberti was attentive to this idea in *De re aedificatoria* and fully understood that architectural treatment was capable of both conferring and reducing it. He suggests that the ruler should not appear fearful of his own citizens, arguing that in constructing the arx "it is necessary to cater to both defense and attack, yet in such a way as to make it appear that your sole concern is for the former."[107] Fortresses and citadels must indeed have been commonly presented in such a manner, but no one was fooled as to their real purpose. As Nicolai Rubinstein has written, "Ever since the early years of the signorial regime, the building of fortresses was considered to be characteristic of its tyrannical nature; indeed, it was the most visible manifestation of the power of a tyrant who, as Savonarola put it much later, 'per forza sopra tutti vuole regnare [desires to rule over everyone by force].'"[108] As recounted by Manetti, Nicholas was quite clear in his deathbed speech that he had built fortifications "against external enemies and against those at home who desire revolution, daily conspiring to lay waste and arising to do great damage to ecclesiastical governance."[109] Alberti perhaps had this in mind when he commented in *De Porcaria* that "people say that it becomes the chief's duty to guard his threatened life, yet also that it offends his majesty to have to take such precautions."[110]

Alberti, Nicholas V, and the Renovation of Rome

The issue of Alberti's relationship with Nicholas V has been the subject of intense scrutiny in recent scholarship and has undergone radical revision.

The view of Alberti as the architectural brain behind Nicholas's *renovatio* of Rome was first set out by Georg Dehio in 1880 and remained current for a century. However, in 1984, Manfredo Tafuri was able to turn this argument on its head.[111] He contends that Alberti, rather than standing at the heart of Nicholas's projects, was a marginalized figure, ill at ease with the pope's grandiose schemes and excluded from his council. Tafuri maintains that when read together, *De re* and *Momus* offer a sharp critique of Nicholas's building schemes. Other scholars have since elaborated on Tafuri's sketch, and it now seems beyond question that Nicholas and his *renovatio* are the central target of Alberti's satire in *Momus*.[112] As has been demonstrated in a thoroughly convincing manner, *Momus* takes particular aim at Nicholas's building projects. In the text, Jupiter wishes to destroy the world without the least idea of how to construct a better one to replace it; this must surely be seen as a comment on Nicholas's program of urban renewal. Juno, subject to an *aedificandi libido* (lust for building), uses the gold from the votive offerings of human beings to construct a triumphal arch, which collapses almost immediately.[113] This may be connected to the collapse of the great tower that Nicholas built at the Vatican and perhaps also to the caving in of the vault of the church of San Teodoro.[114] Further examples abound.[115]

In *Momus*, Jupiter is unable to distinguish good counsel from bad, and both he and Juno are quick to listen to incompetent "experts" and advisors. Some scholars have seen in this an attack on Giannozzo Manetti, the humanist scholar who was close to Nicholas and eulogized him in a posthumous account of his life. Manetti adopts some of Alberti's architectural vocabulary when describing Nicholas's building schemes, and this has sometimes been taken as evidence that Alberti was the architect responsible for them. However, recent scholars have argued that Manetti sometimes uses Alberti's language precisely in order to defend Nicholas against Alberti's direct criticisms. In this view, Alberti is seen as initially having had high hopes for the Nicholine pontificate and as having been involved in the *renovatio* at an early stage.[116] Alberti would then have become disaffected upon realizing the direction of the pope's politics and perhaps upon seeing his own advice ignored (a hypothesis for which there is strong evidence in *Momus*). It has even been suggested that Alberti was displaced, in his position as architectural advisor, by Manetti, a man whom Alberti considered to be entirely lacking in competence in the field of architecture.[117]

This type of account locks Alberti and Manetti into a polemical battle regarding the nature of Nicholas's pontificate and his program of urban renewal. Sections of *De re* would form part of this polemic, while other key components were Alberti's *De Porcaria coniuratione*, Manetti's biography of Nicholas, and *Momus*. It has been speculated that the latter two works were composed more or less simultaneously, or that *Momus* was written in direct response to Manetti's defense of Nicholas.[118] At issue was not only Nicholas's building program but also the nature of his rule, for Alberti's satire in *Momus* does not stop at characterizing Jupiter's building projects as wrongheaded and unsound. Rather, these are the manifestations of a tyrannical ruler. Nicholas, it has been argued, developed a new conception of the papacy that was fundamentally authoritarian. Not only did he gather ecclesiastical power to himself in an unprecedented manner, but he also sought to dominate the city of Rome to a degree that many found unacceptable. Trampling on the fundamental liberties of the Romans, Nicholas allegedly sought to turn them from citizens into subjects (a major complaint of Porcari to which Alberti seems to be sympathetic). The pope's policies were underpinned by apocalyptic themes, which, some scholars have argued, also play a central role in *Momus*, where Alberti subjects them to savage irony.[119]

Christine Smith and Joseph F. O'Connor have recently argued with great force and erudition for Alberti's opposition to Nicholas's policies. They assert that "Alberti does not just point out Nicholas's foibles and those of the Roman curia, as has been said. Instead, *Momus* confronts a new vision of the papacy developed in an abundant apologetic literature under Nicholas V, including Manetti's biography of the pope. Alberti pushes the imagery and claims of this literature to their illogical conclusions. By proclaiming the triumph of folly he hopes to ward it off."[120] Chief among the absurdities that Alberti identified in the Nicholan conception of the papacy was the pope's apparent desire to assume the place of God, which Alberti subjects to satire in *Momus*. He appears to present Nicholas's building schemes as vainglorious, rash, and overbearing—accusations that Manetti is keen to counter. Smith and O'Connor have demonstrated that Manetti relied on the Aristotelian virtue of magnanimity, as interpreted by Thomas Aquinas, in order to defend his patron.[121] From this perspective, Nicholas did not build for his own glory but rather for that of the church, and his magnanimity was manifested as magnificence in his architectural schemes. It was imperative that he should construct large and expensive buildings, for only these unusual sights would be able to arouse the wonder of those who saw them and thus draw them to the faith. Nicholas's own defense of his building schemes, as reported in his testament, appears to be rather more frank. The pope was concerned above all with the shoring up of ecclesiastical authority by means of fortification and the construction of buildings of overwhelming size. Smith and O'Connor have brilliantly demonstrated that there existed in the Middle Ages a complicated relationship between magnificence and authority, in which large buildings and fortifications were often recognized as effective means of overwhelming or intimidating a population and thereby asserting control. "Manetti," they argue, "defends Nicholas against the charge of tyranny by casting the building projects as proof of magnificence. But the sophisticated reader who knew historiography and the incipient political theory developed from Aristotle's works would have understood that magnificence could be a euphemism for manipulation. Alberti was such a reader."[122]

In light of these arguments, it is not difficult to believe that Alberti was taking aim at Nicholas's fortifications when he wrote of the tyrant's city in *De re*, as Charles Burroughs has suggested.[123] Furthermore, as Stefano Borsi has shown, Alberti foregrounds the conflict between the papal crowd and the citizens of Rome in *De Porcaria*. Indeed, Alberti demonstrates a marked sympathy with Porcari's view that under Nicholas it was impossible to live as a citizen and that the Romans were marginalized in favor of foreigners. One may hardly say then that Alberti argues in favor of tyranny in *De re*. Quite to the contrary, when taken together with *De Porcaria* and *Momus*, the passages on the tyrant's city appear to form an energetic condemnation of tyrannical government, specifically that of Nicholas.

However, these passages also serve as an examination of how architecture might both embody and express power and how urban topography might bear on political stability. As we have seen, Alberti claims that no city will be free of discord if it is divided by a river or if it stands on a plain but includes areas of different heights. As Borsi observes, Alberti here draws a universal principle from what appears to be a concrete feature of both Florence and Rome. Alberti lived in Rome in the parish of Santi Celso e Giuliano, in the area of Banchi, just across the river from the Castel Sant'Angelo and the Borgo. Thus, Borsi argues, he would have been in the perfect position to observe how important it was to dominate the Ponte Sant'Angelo. Indeed, Alberti lived where the city of the Romans met the city of the clerics. From his vantage point, he would have been able to see the fortifications rising emblematically around the Leonine City on the other side of the bank, "and the author of *De re* knew very well what significance was attached to initiatives of that sort."[124] Alberti's preoccupations with the instability of the two cities with which he was particularly familiar—Florence and Rome—are thus at the center of his speculations regarding the divided city. It is no coincidence that an Intercenale that considers both is titled "Discord." While it seems that Alberti was strongly opposed to many aspects of Nicholas's pontificate, this relationship was undoubtedly a complex and multidirectional one. His consideration of the tyrant should perhaps be perceived as an intellectual meditation on a problem—viewed in all its complexity—that was stimulated by events in the city in which he lived.[125]

THE LIMITS OF POWER

In the previous chapter, we saw Alberti consider stern architectural intervention in the city, physically preventing the populace from rising up against its masters. This discussion may be connected to a critique of the policies of Nicholas V in Rome. Yet there is also a modern and calculated aspect to Alberti's discussion, something approaching a science of power, insofar as it ostensibly claims a kind of dispassionate objectivity. Burroughs is right when he asserts that the divided city is not in fact an ideal city or a feasible project. As has been said, Alberti does not at any stage describe one single ideal city, and many of his proposals would be contradictory.[1] Nevertheless, the divided city does represent a kind of ideal political situation or system. It may not be a feasible or a desirable project, but it illustrates an ideal set of power relations and stands as an example of the capacity of architecture to enforce a political order.

Eugenio Garin has made some useful remarks concerning Alberti in this context.[2] Commenting on the divided city, he observes that,

> in point of fact, [Alberti] makes a distinction between the new principalities and kingdoms and the free republics. The new principalities must seek refuge in the mountains and defend themselves with fear and suspicion, while the free populations may inhabit the comfortable cities in the plain. But apart from this, Alberti's town is built

to stress class differences, and to accommodate a precise political structure within its walls and buildings. Thus the architect becomes the regulator and coordinator of all the town's activities according to a free restatement of the Aristotelian concept. Alberti presents architecture as the art of arts, the queen and the sum of all others. Town planning is not just connected with politics, it is part and parcel of political activity, almost its highest expression.[3]

Garin goes on to quote Alberti's famous definition of the architect, given in the prologue to *De re aedificatoria*: "Him I consider the architect, who by sure and wonderful reason and method, knows both how to devise through his own mind and energy, and to realize by construction, whatever can be most beautifully fitted out for the noble needs of man, by the movement of weights and the joining and massing of bodies. To do this he must have an understanding and knowledge of all the highest and most noble disciplines."[4]

Alberti thus describes the architect as a man who requires extensive knowledge of all sorts of matters, although he later restricts this considerably.[5] As Garin says, throughout the treatise, Alberti stresses the all-encompassing nature of architecture, its ability to regulate and to transform almost every facet of life. Indeed, one cannot help but be struck by the extent of the architect's terrain in *De re*, as evidenced by the sheer number of matters that are discussed. We should remember that Alberti's was the first treatise on architecture since ancient times. In this sense, he is trying to recover an order of knowledge from a multitude of fragments—literally the fragments of buildings and texts. Yet the treatise does not feel like a mere exercise in recovery but rather like the creation of something autonomous and self-sufficient, something that is new. Alberti, one senses, is offering an entire plank to the swimmers in the river of life, and it promises to be the most important of all.

Alberti was clearly aware that the order of knowledge in which he dealt could constitute a kind of power and that those who exercised power would find it of interest.[6] Throughout the *Momus*, the architect is counterposed to the philosopher as a figure who likewise has a claim to profound knowledge, not just about building but also about the running and governing of things.[7] As Anthony Grafton has effectively demonstrated, Alberti had to be ever mindful of his career, and his treatise must, in part, be seen as a demonstration of the feats that architects could perform for the rulers of cities. To that extent, it is like a long and elaborate equivalent of the famous letter that Leonardo da Vinci sent to Ludovico Sforza, detailing the wonders he could perform in peace and at war. Beyond the construction of walls and fortresses, however, what could Alberti offer to the ruler?

One answer might be "clarity." Alberti's treatise holds out the prospect of a city that could be known better than those that actually existed. A good portion of Alberti's intellectual activities was connected to the placing, mapping, fixing, and measuring of things, making things visible, quantifiable, and graspable according to a consistent and rational system. Alberti was the first to formulate the rules of mathematical perspective in writing, a system that allows space to be accurately represented and objects to be positioned in the "correct" relation to one another.[8] He suggested that painters might employ a squared veil in order to rationalize spatial relationships. Alberti also authored the *Descriptio urbis romae*, a description of the topography of Rome thought to have been completed by 1444, which represents the first accurate records of the coordinates of the city's major monuments, walls, and river. This mapping was achieved by the use of an instrument that Alberti developed especially for the purpose. The *Descriptio* does not rely on perspective but presents an alternative method of systematizing spatial relations, not as they appear from a realistic point of view but as they "actually are." A method of coordinate mapping is outlined in the treatise on mathematical games, in the *Descriptio* Alberti explains how to use the coordinates to create an image on paper.[9]

Thus, to some degree, the divided city must be viewed as another spatial system, effecting the placing and fixing of the various elements of a city: *cives primarii*, *turba*, and *princeps*. This strict arrangement would make clear the position and proportions of these groups as well as their relationships to one another. In this sense, Alberti is outlining a system of power that relies on spatial knowledge and gains control over the elements of the city by separating them and making them visible.

House and City

According to Alberti, "The city is like some large house, and the house is in turn like some small city." To this extent, he thinks of the spaces of the city just as the spaces of grand houses were often thought of, in reality and in literature. Alberti was fond of this maxim and, observing that a house is really a city in miniature, he advises that "with the construction of a house, therefore, almost everything relevant to the establishment of a city must be taken into account: it should be extremely healthy, it should offer every facility and every convenience to contribute to a peaceful, tranquil, and refined life."[10] Earlier in the treatise, Alberti suggests that the rooms of a house might be considered as miniature buildings.[11] The royal household should have a complex arrangement resulting in different categories of people more or less sticking to their prescribed areas:

> There are clearly two types of dining room, one for free men and one for slaves; then there are bedrooms for married women, young girls, and guests, almost all being single rooms. . . .
>
> [The dining rooms, storerooms, and so on] should be kept separate, lest excessive contact between guests and attendants detract from the dignity, comfort, and pleasure of the former or increase the insolence of the latter. . . .
>
> In a royal household the quarters of the wife, the husband, and the servants should be kept quite distinct, and each should contain its own services and whatever might contribute to its grandeur, to prevent the number of servants in any one quarter from causing confusion. . . . Each should therefore be allocated its own zone and *area*, and accommodated within its own pavilion, with its own separate roof. Yet they should be linked by a covered walkway, so that when teams of domestic servants are rushing to perform some task, they appear not as if summoned from some neighboring house, but as though stationed there at the ready. The prattling and noisy hordes of children and housemaids should be kept well away from the men, as should the servants with their uncleanliness.[12]

Although speaking of a royal household, Alberti is clear that private houses should strive to imitate this model. Indeed, he returns to this theme once more when prescribing the arrangement of a country house, considering in some detail the setting out of all the rooms, including the areas for women; the husband's and the wife's chambers, with the former leading to the study and the latter to the wardrobe; the grandmother's room; rooms for boys, girls, and nurses; guest rooms; and rooms for young men and sons of sixteen or seventeen years of age. Alberti's precepts are meant to apply, so far as is possible, to humbler citizens as much as to the rich.[13] Unsurprisingly, both the house and the city use the division and arrangement of space to impose a moral order. Each aims to produce a particular way of life, social and familial hierarchy (manifested in the house in the arrangement of the quarters allocated to various ranks of servants as well as to the family members), and efficiency in day-to-day activity.

A prime concern in the arrangement of space is sexuality. Alberti makes clear that the disposition of rooms in his country house aims in part to keep young women from mingling too much with men and that this will be achieved by surveillance, with the ways to all parts of the house leading from a central area. Similarly, he would have the monastery set out in such a way as to preserve chastity, again relying primarily on surveillance to accomplish this. Here, "measures should be taken not just to dissuade the occupants from violating their chastity, but (more importantly) to make it impossible. For this reason all entrances must be barred, to prevent them from being entered, and those which are open must be watched, so that no one can loiter there without arousing suspicion."[14] Even contact between husband and wife, whether in the home of patrician or prince, would be regulated by and expressed in architecture, according to Alberti's proposals, since "the apartments of his wife should be kept entirely separate from those of the prince, except for the most private rooms and the chamber containing the marriage bed, which should be common to both."[15] Later he asserts that "the husband and wife must have separate bedrooms, not only to ensure that the husband be not disturbed by his wife, when she is about to give birth or is ill, but also to allow them, even in summer, an uninterrupted night's sleep, whenever they wish. Each room should have its own door, and in addition a common side door, to enable them to seek each other's company unnoticed."[16]

Hygiene

Speaking of the various texts of the Renaissance that approach the problem of the ideal city, Garin comments that three major priorities can be discerned throughout: "public hygiene, internal security, and defense against external attack." Behind these urban schemes, one can detect "the epidemics every day renewed, the popular disorders, the struggles for supremacy, the sieges, the sacking of towns, famine. It is thus that treatises on urbanism become treatises on politics."[17] It is hardly surprising that hygiene should be a central preoccupation for Alberti and other treatise writers, since the issue quite naturally was, and remains, at the heart of urban living. Inevitably, public hygiene was the subject of a good deal of civic legislation during this period. Controls were essential, for without them life in the cities would have been unbearable.[18] Moreover, such measures were seen as necessary to prevent the spread of plague. While disasters on the scale of 1348 did not occur frequently, recurrent plagues were simply a fact of life in the Italian cities and must have played upon the mind of the entire citizenry. As a child, Alberti had been terrified for his father's safety during an outbreak in Venice.

Throughout the treatise, Alberti is preoccupied with health, the choosing of healthful sites, proximity to waters, animals, vapors, and the quality of air.[19] Similarly, he is concerned with the treatment of sewage and drinking water, as well as communal drainage, all of which have an effect not only on the layout of the house but also on the placement of buildings in relation to one another.[20] None of this is remarkable. Returning once more to Alberti's tyrant's city, we can immediately see that hygiene is a factor here, too, in the eagerness of the *cives primarii* to escape markets, food sellers, poulterers, butchers, and cooks. This passage seems primarily to address security concerns, but it clearly also relates to hygiene. Food trades, particularly those that dealt with animal products, were naturally associated with health risks. Butchers' shops were strictly regulated and often faced restrictions during the warm summer months.[21] Moreover, it was often considered that unhygienic practices could give rise to plague. The closure of butchers' shops was sometimes the first action taken by the authorities at the onset of an epidemic.[22] Some believed that butchers released pestilential vapor into the air that had been trapped in the carcasses of animals.[23] Meanwhile, cooks might also have been associated with dirt and disease in the late medieval period. To take an example from far afield, Chaucer, in the general prologue to *The Canterbury Tales*, describes a cook as beset by a diseased growth, which, though it is difficult to construe the author's apparent irony, seems somehow to be connected to his trade.[24]

Alberti's passage bears a certain resemblance to the formulations of civic ordinances that dealt with the use and disposal of animal products. We might take as an example a bull of Martin V dated 1425, which Alberti, who was both a papal abbreviator and somebody preoccupied by the urban problems of Rome, may well have known. Here, it is stated that the office of master of the streets (*magistri stratarum*) must be revived, in large part because of the harmful effects of certain trades on the city: "And (as indeed we gather) some of the citizens, residents and inhabitants of the city [Rome] and the above mentioned district, namely food vendors, fishmongers, cobblers, tanners, and various artisans, inhabiting places and also workshops in the city and exercising their crafts there, do not fear to throw into and conceal in the streets, roads, ways, and public and private places meat, intestines, heads, feet, bones, blood, not to say rotting skins, meat and fish, and other fetid and rotting things of this kind."[25] Such legislation was more typical than remarkable. Already in 1288, a Bolognese statute reveals many of the same preoccupations, ordering that "no one throw or cause to be thrown into the piazza of the commune of Bologna or in the crossroads at the Porta Ravennate, any stinking or dead animals or rotting fish or shellfish or any filthy or stinking thing or foodscraps, sweepings, dung or prison filth. Item, that no butcher, or anyone else, is to slaughter . . . any animal within four houses of the piazza, nor to pour onto it the blood or intestines of any animal. . . . And whoever contravenes any of the above . . . is to be fined 40s for each occasion."[26]

More generally, there was a widespread belief in the Renaissance and the Middle Ages that the poor and members of marginalized groups were both the cause and the carriers of plague.[27] Alberti's citing of the food trades in a passage ostensibly concerned with controlling the security threat of the "rabble" suggests a connection in his mind between civil disorder and disease, and, conversely, between public hygiene and the disciplined society.[28] The preoccupation with contagion that exists throughout the treatise might be seen as concerning contagions of two different kinds: the spreading of disease and the disorderly and uncontrolled mixing of persons.[29]

Alberti clearly understood that people who live in unsanitary conditions pose a health risk to others. He notes early on in the treatise, "The Genoese colony of Pera, on the Black Sea, is always prone to disease, because slaves are daily brought there sick of soul and neglected of body, wasting away from idleness and filth." In the same passage, he observes that some places "are so unprotected that when strangers arrive from some foreign land, they often bring with them plague and misfortune; and this may be caused not only by arms and violence, or the work of some barbarian or savage hand: friendship and hospitality may also prove harmful."[30] The unregulated mixing of persons may thus have serious health implications, and such concerns surely bear on those parts of the treatise in which Alberti considers various forms of segregation. He rarely cites medical or sanitary issues in this regard, but his observation about the Egyptian city of Carrae, where he judges that the numerous channels that seemed to bring the benefits of clean water to the populace were probably more valued for their function in separating the people, demonstrates that he was well aware of the fluidity of the distinctions among public health, public order, and division of the city in urban planning.

In the seventh book, Alberti diverges somewhat from the ostensibly neutral tone of his treatise when he recommends the zoning of cities. Foreigners, he contends, may corrupt the state, and they should not be permitted to mix freely with citizens, on the grounds of order and security. "Personally," he says, "I prefer the Carthaginian system: while they were not unreceptive to foreigners, they would not allow them the same privileges as their own citizens; they permitted them access to certain roads leading to the forum, but denied them any view of the more private parts of the city, such as the dockyards and so on."[31] Zoning, however, should not be restricted to foreigners:

> Mindful of this precedent, we should divide the city into zones, so that not only are foreigners segregated into some place suitable for them and not inconvenient for the citizens, but the citizens themselves are also separated into zones suitable and convenient, according to the occupation and rank of each one.
>
> The charm of a city will be very much enhanced if the various workshops are allocated distinct and well-chosen zones. The silversmiths, painters, and jewelers should be on the forum, then next to them, spice shops, clothes shops, and, in short, all those that might be thought more respectable. Anything foul or offensive (especially the stinking tanners) should be kept well away in the outskirts to the north, as the wind rarely blows from that direction, and when it does, it gusts so strongly as to clear smells away, rather than carry them along.[32]

The Republic

Alberti is no longer discussing the city of the tyrant here, as is evident from his placing of the more respectable things in the center and the fouler ones on the peripheries. Indeed, the tyrant's city takes up only a small part of the treatise, and Alberti also considers the republic. As has already been noted, he is hardly an "advocate" of tyranny, or even monarchy, as a preferable mode of government. Moreover, strongly republican sentiments do appear in his works, including *De re aedificatoria*. In Book IV of the treatise, Alberti makes a number of proposals about how the state should be governed; these are remarkable in that they somewhat deviate from his previously neutral tone and sound, broadly, republican:

> There is no respect in which man differs more from man, than that which differentiates him so markedly from the beasts: his power of reason and his knowledge of the noble arts, and also, if you wish, his prosperity and good fortune. Few mortals stand out and excel in all these gifts at once. Herein lies our first distinction: a few individuals stand out from the entire community, some of whom are renowned for their wisdom, good counsel, and ingenuity, others well known for their skill and practical experience, and others famous for their wealth and prosperity. Who would deny them the most important roles within the state? And so to these men of outstanding ability and great insight should be entrusted the care of government. They should administer divine matters according to the principles of religion, set up laws to regulate justice and equity, show us the way to a good and blessed life, and keep watch to protect and eventually increase the authority and dignity of their fellow citizens. When they have been worn out, as may happen, by the years, and are inclined more to a life of contemplation than one of action, they might agree upon a suitable, useful, and necessary policy, and then should entrust its execution to those of practical experience who are free to put it into effect, so that they in turn can bring benefit to their country. Meanwhile, the latter, having undertaken their task, should dutifully carry it out with dexterity and diligence at home, and with application and patience abroad: they should give judgment, lead armies, exercise their own strength and diligence, and husband those of their men. Finally, they will acknowledge that were the means to carry out their functions not available, their efforts would be frustrated, and the next in line are therefore those who, either by working the land or by trading, supply those means. All other citizens should, within reason, owe allegiance to and respect the wishes of the ruling group.[33]

Alberti seems to offer an opinion here, not as to how things might be done but as to how things *should* be done, advocating rule according to ability. There are, of course, echoes of Roman republicanism in this view; it also sounds rather like a Florentine recipe for government. It is those men who are particularly wise and ingenious, or skillful and experienced, or wealthy and prosperous who should have care of the state. In contrast to the tyrant, the rulers whom Alberti describes here are to administer the *res publica* for the benefit of their fellow citizens, dispensing justice and ensuring equity. When they reach old age, they will require rest and retire from the active life of affairs, settling into contemplation. They will entrust their duties to the following generation, again basing their choice on ability. Those who create wealth and produce food are the next in importance, as without them, the plans of the rulers would come to nothing. Finally, it is the duty of all other citizens to show allegiance to the ruling group.

While Alberti is far from offering a comprehensive theory of government, there is genuine republican sentiment in this passage—republicanism of a markedly conservative stripe. After all, the claim that government should be in the hands of those who are the most able, who will by and large coincide with the wealthiest, is hardly radical. In a sense, Alberti is saying little more than that the ruling group should be the ones to rule, and provides an ideological justification for their position. As Alberti observes, "There is no respect in which man differs more from man, than that which differentiates him so markedly from the beasts: his power of reason and his knowledge of the noble arts, and also, if you wish, his prosperity and good fortune." To propose that rulers should be those most gifted with prosperity and good fortune, who are also likely to have been well schooled in the noble arts and may thus appear to have advanced powers of reason, is simply to assert that the upper classes—or *cives primarii*—should govern the state. After all, whoever rules is really, by definition, he who is most blessed with good fortune, and ruling groups across Italy would no doubt have believed that Alberti's description applied exactly to them. Meanwhile, the duty of the great mass of people is to remain loyal to the ruling group, rather than to hold them to account. This is not to discount the republican quality of Alberti's thought here, especially where he goes on to talk about citizens "presiding over domestic councils." Certainly, his discussion of government is far from anything found in Filarete. But there is little doubt that government is to remain in the hands of only a few. Having set out the divisions between men, Alberti proceeds to discuss "what is appropriate for the people as a whole, what for the rather few important citizens [*paucioribus primaries civibus*], and what for the many less important ones."[34]

Nonetheless, there is, in this conservatism, a kind of radicalism. Michel Paoli has noted in the passage from *De re* an affinity with the political views espoused by Alberti in his late dialogue *De iciarchia*.[35] Here, Alberti is at pains to distinguish between those few who have knowledge and the many who do not. The latter are volatile and subject to unreason, and it is thus natural that they should be ruled by the former (just as in the *Profugiorum ab aerumna* it is argued that reason should rule the passions in the well-balanced soul). This results in a natural hierarchy in which the wisest and richest citizens govern the republic in the common interest. Furthermore, it is the duty of these citizens to ensure the longevity of the natural order by resisting innovation and by educating the youth so that they will respect tradition and acquire the competence to govern in their turn.[36] As Paoli demonstrates, Alberti elaborates on these themes in a number of the *Intercenales*.[37]

As has been noted by many scholars, the *De iciarchia* is marked by strongly anti-Medicean sentiments. Alberti's position regarding the Medici seems to be a complex one that changed throughout his life.[38] However, he implies throughout the *De iciarchia* that Medici rule has disrupted the natural order in the republic, excluding traditional members of the oligarchy from real participation in government. In this, there is a kind of parallel with Alberti's objections to the regime of Nicholas V; people are effectively denied the right of citizenship, and ancient liberties are dispensed with.[39] This opposition to Medici dominance might be seen as motivating many of the antipolitical positions that Alberti takes in his moral dialogues, including the *Theogenius* and *Profugiorum*.[40] There, he asserts that involvement in a corrupt government implicates the participant in immoral actions. Moreover, such regimes will only accommodate those who readily assent to the will of the dominant faction or family. It is for this reason that Agnolo Pandolfini, in the *Profugiorum*, refuses to go to the government palace to give advice to the Signoria.[41]

Alberti thus argues for greater inclusiveness in the governing of the republic. It should be emphasized that he does not advocate widening the social makeup of the ruling group but rather favors the readmission of those families who had been excluded by the Medici.[42] As we have seen, Alberti was distrustful of the lower classes and often condemned their desire for change in the social order. He saw their thirst for innovation (or *novitas*) as being among the greatest threats to any state. Here again, Alberti's political and architectural thought appears to constitute two sides of a single coin. New building that has not been well planned, and may therefore fail to reach completion, is condemned. Also denounced is the thoughtless destruction of preexisting structures, the ineptitude of modern architects (in both *Momus* and *De re*), the mania for piling up stones, and the desire to build oversized or excessively ostentatious buildings. Similarly, new modes of government, innovations in the laws, departure from the practices of one's forefathers, personal ostentation, and the desire to elevate oneself above others are all characterized as evils to be avoided. In this sense, the Medici were guilty of innovation, suppressing time-honored practices in order to put themselves above others. Nicholas V likewise attempted to bring about a new conception of the papacy and to remake the city of Rome—projects that Alberti appears to characterize in *Momus* as absurd and inevitably doomed to failure. Notably, given the closeness of Alberti's views in the passage from *De re* to those in the *De iciarchia*, we might say that he harks back to the government of Florence before the era of Medici dominance—that is, back to the fourteenth century and to the golden age of his family.

The Institutions of the Republic

In the fifth book of *De re*, where the issue of government is addressed directly, Alberti speaks of the republic in earnest. As we have seen, he divides states into those ruled by one man alone and those by several, and having discussed the cities of the tyrant and the king, "it now remains," he says, "for us to deal with what is needed when control is not in the hands of one individual, but of several at the same time. Here government is either entrusted collectively to the magistrates or distributed among them. The republic consists of the sacred (involving divine worship, over which the clergy preside) and the temporal (involving the well-being of society, over which the senator and the judge preside at home, and the generals and admirals abroad). Each of the above should have two separate types of abode, one for official business, the other a place to retreat with his household."[43]

The buildings that Alberti goes on to describe certainly conjure up the idea of a free state. For instance, he speaks of the *palestra* as a place where philosophical conversation might take place. Moreover, he advises, "Should you wish to establish public auditoria and schools, places for the wise and learned to meet, position them where they are equally accessible to all."[44] He describes the senate, in which "every measure must be taken to ensure that a group of citizens may be pleasantly received, decently treated while present, and conveniently dismissed" (although it must also be fortified), and mentions the chamber of justice.[45] There follows a lengthy section on military camps, in which Alberti speaks in condemnatory tones about tyranny: "As for stationary camps set up specifically to sustain a siege, their requirements will be very similar to those mentioned for the citadel of a tyrant, which is an object of constant hatred for the citizens; indeed, there can be no form of siege harder to bear, than to keep a citadel under constant watch, and to await continually the opportunity to release all the pent-up hate by its destruction."[46] Thereafter, he proceeds to talk about the magistrates, who include "the quaestor, collector of taxes and public revenues, and so on. These will require the following: a granary, a treasury, an arsenal, an emporium, dockyard and stables. On this topic there is seemingly little to be said, but what there is, is important. The granary, treasury and arsenal must of course be located in the center, in the most crowded part of the city, where they will be better protected and more accessible."[47] This statement makes it abundantly clear that Alberti is no longer speaking of the divided city of the tyrant. After all, as Luigi del Fante has commented, placing the arsenal, treasury, and granary in the central circle of that city would furnish the "rabble" with all of the means for a revolution.[48]

The City in Books VII and VIII

When Alberti speaks of the city in Book VII, which concerns the ornament of sacred buildings, he is clearly not thinking of the tyrant's city. Rather, his words evoke the image of a pleasant city, given over not only to utility but also to beauty and recreation. In fact, he implies that if the city were pleasant enough, it may render means of compulsion unnecessary. Citing an ancient example of wealthy people being forced to move to a newly founded city, he observes that "any neighbor, or even foreigner, would do this of his own free will, if he knew there was somewhere that he could lead a healthy and happy life, among honest citizens of good character."[49] Alberti appears to have such a city in mind throughout Book VII and into Book VIII, which deals with ornament to public, secular buildings. Here, he describes a sequence of important buildings in a section that has sometimes been interpreted as an imagined journey through a kind of ideal city.[50] And indeed, he does speak in terms of journeying. Just as if approaching an ancient Roman city, Alberti begins Book VIII with a consideration of sepulchers and watchtowers. He then says that "next we must enter the city" (*sequitur ut intra urbem ingrediamur*), as though he were leading us through the gate.[51]

Alberti first directs his attention to roads and bridges. Plato's preference for spaces at crossings where nurses could meet with their children is noted. Moreover, "the presence of an elegant portico, under which the elders may [stroll] or sit, take a nap or negotiate business, will be an undoubted ornament to both crossroad and forum."[52] The nurses, Alberti conjectures, will be more diligent in their duties because they are exposed to the public gaze, while the presence of elders will deter the young from bad behavior. Next, he moves to the forum, insisting that the currency market should be the most splendid.[53] There follow triumphal arches, show grounds (divided into theaters, circuses, and amphitheaters), and parades in which youths and elders might exercise, with sitting rooms "where distinguished citizens and philosophers might debate noble topics."[54] Then come the portico for litigation, the comitium, the curia, the library, and baths.

This does provide a picture of a city. It is hardly a complete city, being concerned only with nonreligious buildings (sacred buildings are considered in Book VII), and still less an ideal city. The interpretation of Book VIII as presenting a humanist city in which the library is central and wisdom prevails, would seem to capture one aspect of Alberti's thought here. Arguably, however, he is more concerned with the logic of his treatise, describing in turn the chief public secular buildings and discussing their ornament, just as he says he will.[55]

Nonetheless, there is a marked optimism in Alberti's approach to the city in Book VIII. He seems here to be convinced of the civilizing effects of the *civitas* in a way that he is not elsewhere. He evidently enjoys the idea of the elders resting and transacting business at crossroad porticoes. The notion that their presence will moderate the behavior of the youth clearly demonstrates a belief that concourse of people in the city, and *public places* in which the citizens may mix, can have a restraining, humanizing effect. He says as much when discussing show grounds. These had been strongly condemned by a number of writers, including, at some length, Saint Augustine, and Alberti clearly felt obliged to acknowledge this. However, he gives these opinions remarkably short shrift and notes instead that "Moses is praised for being the first to gather his entire nation into a single temple on feast days, and for bringing them together at set times to celebrate the harvest. His motive, I might suggest, was but the desire to cultivate the minds of the citizens through concourse and communion, and to make them more receptive to the benefits of friendship. Thus to my mind our ancestors established show buildings within their cities as much for functional reasons as for any festivity or pleasure."[56] Again, here is the idea that the city can civilize and that concourse can make people better citizens. In the same spirit, the parades and "sitting rooms" Alberti envisages allow for the elders and wise men to congregate and exchange ideas, and for the young to play and take exercise. Thus, when Alberti talks about the city in general, as he does in these books, it is much more like the republican city than any other.

Cities Ancient and Modern

It is notable that the city Alberti describes in Books VII and VIII is an antique one.[57] There is something of a far-off quality to it, as Alberti enumerates the building types he knew of through classical literature and the ruins of ancient Rome. He acknowledges this himself when he laments that the theaters, circuses, and amphitheaters he describes in such detail are no longer built in the society in which he lives. On the one hand, Alberti must be seen as arguing for a renewal (as he does specifically in the case of show grounds here, and regarding Italy as a whole in the preface to the *Della famiglia*). On the other, this far-off ancient city provides him with a free argumentative space in which his misgivings about society and human nature may be put aside. It thus allows him to pursue the particular phase of his argument, here concerned with ornament.

The tyrant's city appears in Book V, where Alberti is considering not ornament but utility, that is, building types and function. Social considerations necessarily impinge on this discussion, and his tone is far more pessimistic. The tyrant's city is not a far-off vision, but arises very much out of the concrete conditions of late medieval Italy. Although Alberti is generally repelled by it, he also seems to find some aspects of it attractive. This attitude relates to his pessimism regarding society and his consciousness of the instability of Florence and Rome.[58] When Alberti considers flight from the city center, he characterizes it as something that anyone who could would happily do. Indeed, even when Alberti sounds more optimistic and when he speaks of the republic, the attraction of class segregation and abandonment of the city still persists. In fact, in his discussion of the republic, he turns first to the dwellings of the rulers, writing,

> The family home should correspond to the character on whom he has modeled his life, whether king, tyrant or private citizen. There are certain buildings most suitable to this class of person. Virgil puts it brilliantly: "The house of father Anchises lay withdrawn, screened by trees." He understood that leading citizens would best have houses well away from the common crowd and working masses, for their own sake and for their families'. One reason for this was the delight and charm of living among open spaces, gardens, and country pleasures; in addition, it would prevent the lusty youth of a family so varied and large, of whom hardly any would live on his own, from being spoilt by the meat and drink of other men's tables, or from giving husbands cause for complaint; what is more, it will protect patrons from being unduly disturbed by the persistent flattery of well-wishers. I have noticed that the wisest princes have withdrawn not only beyond the range of the crowd but outside the city altogether, to avoid being continually plagued by common people with little motive behind their visits. And what is the use of all their wealth, if they are unable to take occasional time off to relax and laze?[59]

Even in the discussion of the republic, the common people appear irritating and infestatious, and the city is a place where the young will be corrupted. Alberti's remark about young men giving husbands cause for complaint touches again on the notion that cities provide for a dangerously unregulated mixing of persons. Withdrawal from the city to a place where one may relax and occasionally laze is a thoroughly good thing. In fact, in Book VII, where Alberti speaks of a pleasant city divided into different districts, segregation is not far from his mind. For it is here that he turns to consider the control of foreigners (discussed earlier) and the zoning of the citizens themselves: "Some might prefer the residential quarters of the high born to be quite free of any contamination from the common people. Others would have every district in the city so well equipped that each would contain all its essential requirements; thus it would be quite acceptable to have common retailers and other shops mixed in with the houses of the most important citizens. So much for this subject. Clearly utility demands one thing, and dignity another."[60] This statement appears even-handed, yet Alberti's neutrality is to be doubted. Having the poor around, it suggests, offends the dignity of the rich; it is only for the sake of utility that one might consider it.

The Failure of Politics

Much can be said about Alberti's politics, but in the end we struggle to pin him down. This should perhaps not surprise us, since unidirectional interpretations of Alberti's thought rarely fare well. Moreover, in *De re aedificatoria*, Alberti is ostensibly concerned with the provision of buildings for whichever institutions exist, rather than speculating about which institutions *should* exist. Although he does take positions, they are often implied and dissimulated. As has often been observed, his thought does not appear to be that of a "civic humanist." More fundamentally, however, Alberti appears to have been profoundly skeptical of the feasibility of politics. In this regard, it is illuminating to consider that *Momus* seems to have been intended as a political treatise. There are obvious reasons for which Alberti might have wanted to dissimulate in his satire of a pope; nonetheless, *Momus* is more than just a satire on Nicholas V. This extraordinary work, so multiform, ironic, and difficult to decipher, suggests that Alberti found it difficult to approach the charged arena of politics directly. This compares strikingly with his forthright treatment of the family. In *Momus*, Alberti's cynicism and disenchantment sometimes even verge on a kind of violence.

It is in this work that Alberti's celebrated sketch of the vagabond appears. Momus entertains the gods with stories of his exile on earth and claims that of all the ways of life he sampled, he preferred that of the vagabond to all others. What follows is a kind of Lucianesque paradoxical encomium of the *erro*. Although these pages are sometimes dismissed as having no significance beyond that of a mere ironic joke, Michel considered them to be the most brilliant that Alberti ever wrote.[61] The passage may have been largely influenced by Lucian's *Parasite*, where, in a typical humorous inversion, it is argued that it is better to be a sponger than a wealthy man. However, Alberti's vagabond is quite different from the urbane parasite presented by Lucian and offers a somewhat more sinister and subversive portrait. For Alberti, the vagabond's destitution implies a kind of power; regular people are strangely reluctant to bandy words with this figure, whose total rejection of ordinary aspirations implies a sharp critique of the urban lifestyle.

The vagabond is presented as the person who is ultimately best placed to enjoy urban space: "The theatres belong to vagabonds, the porticoes to vagabonds—in fact every public space belongs to vagabonds! Others wouldn't dare sit in the forum and bicker with a slightly raised voice. Afraid of the raised eyebrows of their elders, others don't dare do anything lawless or immoral in public, they'll do nothing of their own free will and choice. While you, vagabond, will lie lounging around the forum, shouting freely, doing whatever takes your fancy."[62] Alberti, it might be remembered, recommends in De re that spaces should be created for the gathering of elders, whose presence would restrict the exuberance of youth. Here, by contrast, he extols the freedom of one who has escaped such constraints and distinguished himself from the rest, who do "nothing of their own free will and choice." Commenting on this passage, Anthony Grafton has argued that "Alberti, in short, conjures up the sturdy beggar as a specter at Alberti's own feast—the ghost whose obtrusive presence disrupts the calm order of his ideal city, whose body interferes with the clean lines of the stone platforms on which his temples stand, and whose voice breaks the public quiet. It is hard to see this comment as directed more against Nicholas [V] than against the ideal urban order evoked in On the Art of Building."[63]

One might go further. As we have seen, the urban order implies a political one, and Alberti's ghost disturbs this feast as well. Indeed, the vagabond illustrates the limitations of political strategies and controlling mechanisms. The powers that be, even at their most authoritarian, struggle to maintain a grip on him. As Momus says, "When a bad prince reigns, others will escape and wander in exile; you [vagabond] will frequent the tyrant's citadel."[64] The vagabond has no class allegiance and should not be considered part of the vulgus. Indeed, he despises all equally, regardless of social status: "Only in the discipline (as I may call it) and art of beggary did I not encounter anything which displeased me in the least. You see naked beggars lying down in the open air and on the hard earth: you scorn them; you despise them with the mob; you are revolted. But watch out that the beggars don't scorn and despise both you and the mob!"[65]

Of course, Alberti's vagabond is not a real beggar sprawled in a late medieval Italian piazza. He is a figure from classical literature, as *all'antica* as the *opus reticulatum* patterning on the Palazzo Rucellai, and he relates to a particular strain of cynic thought. In creating this character, Alberti deploys a literary topos to a far greater extent than he engages with the realities of urban poverty. The vagabond is comic and also described as meriting contempt. And yet he is effective in casting doubt on precisely the kind of urbanistic strategies that Alberti considers in *De re*. Moreover, a close reading of the passage on the tyrant's city reveals an unexpected but instructive kinship with the sketch of the vagabond, since both have their origins in the parasite topos.

When identifying the poulterers, butchers, and cooks that the important citizens would desire to escape from, Alberti refers to Terence's description of the rabble in the play *Eunuchus*. This particular passage, as we saw earlier, had been incorporated by Cicero into the *De officiis*. It seems likely that fifteenth-century writers such as Lapo da Castiglionchio the Younger and Matteo Palmieri referred to this source, since their own treatment of the subject is very close to that of Cicero. Alberti, on the other hand, clearly had not only the *De officiis* but also the *Eunuchus* in mind when he wrote *De re*. He is the only author to name Gnatho, the character in the play who speaks of the rabble. Gnatho is a parasite, a formerly wealthy man fallen on hard times, and in the passage quoted by Alberti, he is extolling the virtues of the parasitic life. Indeed, he explains that he wants for nothing since he had patronized the food traders to such a great degree while he was wealthy that they now provide him with everything he needs. He contrasts his condition with that of another formerly wealthy man, who unlike himself has fallen into a miserable state, and he describes how, as they approached the market together, all of the traders rushed out to greet him: "Our conversation lasted till we came to the market. Up run all the tradesmen delighted to meet me, fishmongers, butchers, pastrycooks, sausagemakers [or poulterers], spratsellers . . ."[66]

The similarities to Alberti's language confirm his reliance on Terence's text. He also speaks of the *macellum* and includes, in a slightly modified form, Terence's word for a food trader, *cuppedenarius*. Alberti was thus fully aware of the context of Gnatho's words. Some of Gnatho's discourse is similar in content to that which Lucian was later to give to the parasite Simon, who seems to have inspired Alberti in the creation of his vagabond. For example, Gnatho offers to teach his companion how to become a successful parasite, hoping that just as philosophers have disciples who are called after them, "so hangers-on may be called Gnathonists" (*ut parasiti ita ut Gnathonici vocentur*).[67] This type of joke, in which the parasitic life is considered an "art" or "discipline" that can be taught, is the kind of thing of which Lucian was also fond, and it is likewise present in Alberti's treatment of the *erro*.

It is interesting that in Alberti's discussion of the tyrant's city, when he seems to engage closely with the realities of late medieval political life, the antique figure of the parasite should make an appearance. Indeed, it is also intriguing that Gnatho should be present in the midst of this image of extreme authority. For Gnatho is a mobile character, one who, as it were, looks both ways. Neither slave nor patrician, he is of less determinate class, someone who "gets away" with things. Gnatho is much cleverer than the wealthy man to whom he is attached, and he comes off well at the end of the play. He is the kind of indeterminate and guileful character whom authority struggles to maintain a grasp on—something he shares with the vagabond. At the very moment that Alberti depicts an urban and political order in which the will of the ruler is utterly dominant, Gnatho's intrusion casts doubt on the feasibility of any such thing.

Alberti was a political thinker of great importance, and his works touch on themes that were amplified in the following century by writers such as Machiavelli and Erasmus.[68] Despite this, he does not offer the reader a well-developed theory of government. This should not surprise us, since his thinking seems to include a profound skepticism regarding politics. This skepticism does not merely concern specific political systems but brings into question the nature of politics itself. It is, however, far from total. Alberti clearly sees the merits of various systems of governance and is prepared to pursue them, intellectually, to quite a considerable extent. Ultimately, however, he seems unwilling or unable to fully reconcile his thoughts on the subject, and this attitude toward politics, to some extent, necessarily becomes an attitude toward the city.

4

BEYOND THE CITY

Alberti, in a number of works, characterizes the country and the city as
binary opposites. Not only is each the antithesis of the other, but one is
often judged to be superior—namely, the country. It is a fact that has every
appearance of being thoroughly banal. Such sentiments were already common currency in antique literature. The opposition between town and
country, urban and rural, is a literary trope, a familiar topos, among the most
common of commonplaces. As such, it is connected more to literature than
to the realities of rural life or to town-country relations; when it is deployed
by a humanist, one is likely to find out more about writing than farming.
By the fifteenth century, the topos was already sufficiently well worn to
become a target for satire.[1]

It would not be unreasonable to conclude that when Alberti writes in
this vein, there is not much to be learned either from or about him. His
"preference" for the country is exactly what one would expect. It is a literary exercise, an imitation of the antique for its own sake, quite transparent
to anyone who knows their genres. Such passages of writing cannot be
treated as documents that contain reliable information about what went
on in the country or about Alberti's "real" attitude toward it. Alberti, it is
sometimes argued, was simply saying the kind of thing that "everyone"
said, and to attach any real significance to it would be naïve.

This view involves an oversimplification. Alberti's imitation of the
antique is not in dispute, nor is his propensity for polished allusion and

literary play. His discussion of town-country relations *is* self-conscious and formulaic, just as we might expect. But this does not tell us everything there is to know about it or even very much. It should hardly require stating, but something's being a topos does not render it devoid of meaning. The literary waters in which Alberti swam were thick with commonplaces; it is their adoption and use that should interest us. Of course, many commonplaces become such because they express sentiments that are fundamental to a culture's thinking, ideas that maintain their currency across time. Alberti was part of a literary culture that sought to create a modern form of writing that was, ironically, based on the antique. We should hardly be surprised that he and his contemporaries adopted not just antique words but entire blocks of language, thoughts, and arguments. The recognition that Alberti himself characterized his work as the assemblage of fragments has formed the basis of an entire, and very fruitful, scholarly approach to his writings.

There is a temptation to view Alberti as if the identification of his sources is the proper end of reading his work, either an end in itself or perhaps an activity that is sufficient to reveal the "meaning." As we have seen in previous chapters, there is certainly much to be gained from such identification. Yet ultimately, the text is not reducible to the sum of its sources. It constitutes a different entity—one that is animated by a logic of its own. As Rinaldo Rinaldi has put it, in the act of identifying sources, scholars risk arriving at the same outcome as Democritus does in the third book of *Momus*. Here, the philosopher "dissects and identifies the parts of an animal, without, however, succeeding in finding the brain."[2] Alberti's writing must be read, above all, with a view to its overall coherence and that, while we must pay attention to topoi, we cannot simply dismiss large sections of his work as mere literary play. After all, all language is made up of other language, and this need not overly alarm us.

Closely related to these considerations is the issue of the degree to which Alberti's statements correspond with an actual state of affairs. Is his account of the country somehow diminished if it is not entirely true or accurate? Does it become correspondingly less meaningful or less interesting? Certainly, any attempt to use Alberti's writings to gain an accurate sociohistorical picture of central Italian rural life in the fifteenth century would not fare well. But this is not the object of this chapter or indeed this book. Rather, we are concerned here with Alberti's thought, specifically his urban thought. Ultimately, it is the way in which the country is used to reflect on the city that is of prime interest. The extent to which Alberti's writings relate to actual contemporary practice is highly significant, but it is not a criterion by which passages of writing are to be judged relevant or redundant.

The Country

The country was important to the class of high-ranking Florentine families to which the Alberti belonged. Such families typically held extensive country possessions, sometimes of a fairly diverse nature. The chief purpose of country estates was not to provide a place for reflection but to produce goods and money. Farm produce could feed and sometimes clothe the family. It could also be sold at a profit, while lands, mills, country inns, village shops, and so forth could be rented out. Beyond this, possessions in the country provided security. Most obviously, they allowed for the diversification of investments. In addition, they offered refuge during times of plague or upheavals in the cities. However, they seem also to have been viewed as vital elements in the preservation of family status and identity. In her groundbreaking study of Florentine villa culture in the fifteenth century, Amanda Lillie, focusing on the Strozzi clan, has demonstrated how the various branches of the family almost never sold their *casa da signore*, or main country residence. Indeed, there appears to have been a general reluctance to sell any family lands, all of which, but most especially the *casa da signore*, must have been viewed as integral to family identity.[3]

A number of key points arising from Lillie's careful archival analysis deserve to be stated clearly. First, the most important estates owned by high-ranking Florentine families tended to be ancestral seats. Second, involvement in both urban and rural life was typical of such families in the fourteenth and fifteenth centuries. Third, the fifteenth century did not, at least as regards the Strozzi, witness a turning away from urban life and a return to the land. As Lillie puts it, "It could be further argued that there was no need to return to the land because they had never (at least not since the thirteenth century) left it."[4] Typical of most Strozzi in this period were diverse systems of property management, ambitions to own both town and country property, and a willingness to let out their town houses during times of financial hardship. This indicates a mixed economic and domestic life that included urban and rural elements alike. It seems legitimate to assume that much the same would have been true for other Florentine families of equivalent age and status.

Despite Alberti's fame as an urbanist, perhaps the first modern urbanist, a real eulogy of the city never appears in his works. Moreover, Alberti devotes very little of his architectural treatise to commercial or industrial buildings, which are characteristic of the city. He does not describe any kind of factory or industrial machinery and only briefly mentions the shop.[5] By contrast, the country does receive a eulogy, and the farm warrants extensive discussion. While Alberti never wrote a treatise dedicated to the city, he did write one concerning the farm, albeit a brief and stylistically uncharacteristic work. The *Villa* is a short, didactic treatise on farming that may have been penned in the late 1430s and draws inspiration from Hesiod's *Works and Days*.[6] Alberti uses the word *villa*, here and elsewhere, to denote a farm or farm estate, and the emphasis is placed firmly on the idea of productivity. Indeed, the treatise opens with the admonition "Buy your villa to feed the family, not to give pleasure to others."[7]

This work stands as a good example of how literary imitation and sincere engagement with his own society need not be mutually exclusive in Alberti's writings. The treatise imitates antique sources yet also clearly articulates a view regarding country property that was widely held at the time. Indeed, Alberti specifically states that the country house itself is of relatively little importance; it is the land that matters.[8]

Buying and Selling

Alberti's ambivalence regarding urban commerce seems to underpin much of the argumentation he deploys regarding the country. It is precisely from a critique of the market that Giannozzo Alberti sets out his argument in favor of country living in the third book of *Della famiglia*. This book is on household economy, and Alberti says in the preface that he took Xenophon's *Oeconomicus* as his model.[9] The bulk of the dialogue takes place between the old patriarch Giannozzo and the young humanist Lionardo, each of whom presents very different views about the relationship between the individual and society. Giannozzo is a particularly complex character, and, as we shall see, the way in which he is interpreted, and his place in the dialogue appraised, has a crucial bearing on how we assess Alberti's view of the country. His is the voice of the quintessential thrifty Florentine patriarch, and in the third book of *Della famiglia*, he instructs the younger Alberti on the art of managing the family and household.

In the course of the discussion, Lionardo asks Giannozzo how he would feed the family and whether he would buy food and other essentials from the market from day to day. Giannozzo replies in the negative:

GIANNOZZO: Certainly not, for it would not be good management to buy them. Do you think that one who sells something sells what he could keep longer? Do you think he gets rid of the best or the worst?

LIONARDO: The worst; whatever he does not think he can keep well. But at times one sells good and useful things for need of money.

GIANNOZZO: I admit it; but if he is wise, he will sell the worst first. And if he sells the best, will he not try to sell it for more than it cost him? Will he not try with all his shrewdness to make it seem better than it is?

LIONARDO: Often.[10]

Giannozzo says that he would prefer instead to "have in my house whatever can be kept without danger and without great effort" and to sell any surplus or anything that could not be kept. Lionardo asks how such a thing is to be achieved, and Giannozzo replies, "I shall tell you. I should try to own property which could provide my household with grain, wine, firewood, yarn, and similar things at a lower cost than I should have to pay if I bought them at the market. I should also have flocks, pigeons, and chickens raised on it; even fish."[11]

It is at once apparent that Giannozzo's real complaint is against the "commodity" in the Marxian sense—an item alienated from producer, seller, and consumer alike. Goods bought at the market are likely to be of inferior quality, he argues, for otherwise they would not be sold. There is no guarantee that the food on sale has been grown with any interest or care, but rather it is more likely that the producer had only profit in mind; in either case, its origins are obscure. Even if the produce is of high quality, its price will increase merely on account of its being for sale, and the vendor will try to market it as better than it is. Thus, Giannozzo asks Lionardo, "Well then, do you not see? When one buys, he pays more and risks getting something which has been adulterated, will not keep, and is not very good. Am I right? And even if there were no other reasons, it would still be better for me to have everything I need on my own property rather than look for it elsewhere, for having tried these things over the years I should then know how they are and in what season they are good."[12] In contrast to the commodity, the things that an individual produces himself, with which he has direct concern and over which he exercises care, are likely to be good. The commodity is here explicitly presented as a thing of the city and contrasted with the country life. For despite Giannozzo's impeccable bourgeois credentials, his wealth, and his extensive experience in business matters, he is clearly advocating a form of self-sufficiency.

This characterization of the city as the place of commodities is an accurate one, especially in regard to those cities that were centers of international trade. All manner of goods passed through them. In Florence, not only luxuries but sometimes even essential foodstuffs had to be imported from overseas, since the *contado* could not always support the urban population.[13] The Renaissance has been described as both the birth of the commodity, by Marx, and the birth of the individual, by Burckhardt. As Margreta de Grazia has pointed out, "There is one thing . . . which Burckhardt's subject and Marx's object have in common: each excludes the other. Burckhardt's individuated subject is cut off from objects; Marx's commodified object is cut off from subjects."[14] Giannozzo's words seem to express an awareness of, and a genuine disquiet about, a separation of this kind.

We may note that toward the beginning of the dialogue, Alberti's dying father, Lorenzo, says that he is not excessively troubled by the thought of death but that "it grieves me to leave the sweetness of life, the pleasure of your company and of talking to you and my friends, the pleasure of seeing my possessions. I should not want to be deprived of these before my time."[15] For Lorenzo, his possessions still appear to be very much a part of who he is, a piece of his identity of which death will rob him. In another sense, the Alberti had been robbed of a great deal of their possessions as a result of their exile, a fact that is much lamented throughout the *Della famiglia*. Notably, it is not so much the loss of wealth or the possessions themselves that seems to grieve the family but rather the loss of a corresponding identity that these possessions conferred, and the resulting feeling of rootlessness.

The country offers an alternative to this kind of uneasy separation. Those who live in close connection to the land are not rootless and self-contained consumers. They are intimately involved with the production of the goods they use and can invest their care in them. When Lionardo asks how Giannozzo could achieve his self-sufficient farm—given that if one were to rent the lands, the proprietor would reclaim them when they became profitable, and managers would need to be found and paid—Giannozzo responds, "For this very reason as well as many others, I should buy the land with my money, so that it would belong to me, to my children, and to my grandchildren. In this way I could have it fertilized and cultivated with greater love so that at the proper time my heirs might enjoy the fruit of the plants and labors I had put into it."[16]

The personal nature of the bond with the land is thus emphasized. Whereas rented property would remain separate and ephemeral—a commodity to be used, abandoned, and exchanged according to its profitability and the condition of the market—land that is owned becomes, in a sense, a part of the owner and his family. It is this relationship of care, of personal interest across generations, that helps ensure the goodness of the produce. It is also this relationship that confers status and identity on the family members themselves, anchoring them to a place and lending them security against the vicissitudes of fortune.[17] This connection among places, things, and identity, as well as the grief caused by the loss of these possessions as a result of exile, seems to be alluded to directly in the exchange that follows. Lionardo wonders where a property that could furnish a whole range of produce might be found (displaying considerable agricultural knowledge in the process). "To get good wine," he comments, "you need sunny slopes; to get good wheat, you need an open plain with soft, loose earth; good firewood grows in rough, mountainous terrain; meadowlands should be soft and moist. How, then, would you find a place which combined so many diverse characteristics? Tell me, Giannozzo, do you think one can find many places suitable for vineyards, grain, woods, and grazing? And if you found them, do you think you could get them at any but a high price?"[18]

Giannozzo agrees that such a thing would be difficult but insists that it is not impossible. "Unfortunately," he concedes, "you are right. And yet I remember that in Florence there were many landowners, including some members of our own family like *messer* Benedetto, *messer* Niccolaio, *messer* Cipriano, *messer* Antonio, and others, who had lands where you could not wish for anything better. They were situated in fertile country with pure air, rare fogs, no strong winds, good water, everything pure, healthy, and lovely to behold."[19] This memory, however, soon becomes a lament: "But let us not talk of these possessions which seem more like manors or castles than farms. Let us not think at the present moment of the magnificence of the Alberti family. Let us forget those proud and ornate structures which today are in the hands of new masters. Many who see them as they pass by sigh and wish they could find there once again the ancient courtesy and welcome for which we Albertis were known."[20] Giannozzo thus introduces a great rural past for the Alberti. In their heyday, the family had enjoyed magnificent country possessions, and they had been anchored by their land, with which they were closely identified.

Land and Money

Alberti returns to these themes later in the work, when Giannozzo is drawn into a debate with Adovardo about whether wealth is better possessed as land or money. Adovardo advances a strongly capitalist defense of the money economy, using arguments similar to those that Poggio Bracciolini put into the mouth of Antonio Loschi in his *De avaritia*.[21] Adovardo contends, for instance, that "everything has its roots in money or is nourished by it. No one can doubt that money sustains all occupations." Indeed, "if money, then, takes care of all these needs [the needs of the family] why should we bother to manage anything else but our money?"[22] He finishes by reminding Giannozzo that money has served the Alberti well in exile. For while their property had to be abandoned to strangers, they were able to take their money with them, and those who were possessed of money fared far better in exile than those who were not. This reminds us that the Alberti exile is at the very heart of the discourse about property and identity. The production of Alberti's well-crafted prose is driven by a question of the utmost seriousness: How does a family survive a disaster?

In replying to Adovardo, Giannozzo reiterates many of the views we have already encountered earlier in the book. First, he argues, a level of self-sufficiency is not only convenient but provides one with a pleasure that money simply cannot buy: "I will insist that if I had money I should still lack many things which I could not buy promptly when needed with due regard to quality and low price. Even if they should cost little, I should still like the pleasant task of managing my properties myself and harvesting what I need rather than to have to look after my money continuously, struggling to find various things from day to day and spending more for them than if I had stored them in my house."[23]

Once again, Giannozzo invokes a more fulfilling relationship to objects, which may be gained through rural self-sufficiency. He goes on to attack the money economy of the city as being tricky and changeable, touching on one of the major themes of Alberti's writings—the ephemerality of the city (and, indeed, of all human projects) and the likelihood of its destruction. Only in the country, he seems to argue, can stability, permanence, and security ever be found. He asks Adovardo,

> If in present conditions you find that you have lost less money than property, do you therefore think that money can be preserved more easily than property in ordinary times? Do you think a fortune in ready cash is more stable than one in lands? Do you think income from money is more useful than the income you derive from farmlands? Is there anything easier to lose, more difficult to save, more dangerous to handle, more bothersome to get back, and which vanishes, disappears, goes up in smoke more easily? Is there anything else more susceptible of the above difficulties than money?[24]

Money fortunes, just like the cities in which they are made, can be destroyed overnight. Indeed, Giannozzo categorically states that "nothing is less stable or less enduring than money." He continues,

> It is incredibly difficult to save money. It is a task filled with suspicion, danger, and misfortune more than any other. Nor is it possible to keep money locked up in any way. If you keep it under lock and key in secret, it will be of no use to you or to your family. . . . I could go on telling you of the dangers which threaten money; thieving hands, bad faith, bad advice, adverse fortune, and numberless other things of this nature can swallow any sum in one gulp, consume all of it so that you will not even see its remains or ashes.[25]

Possession of land, he argues, is far more secure and enduring, for the land itself cannot be destroyed and will remain your possession, even if it falls into the hands of others:

> You must consider, Adovardo, that neither theft, nor rapine, nor fires, nor sword, nor the perfidy of mortals, nor—what else dare I say?— thunder, nor lightning, nor God's wrath can deprive you of your lands.

If this year they were struck by hail, or if the seed was destroyed by too much rain, frost, wind, heat, or drought, you will have better luck next year; if not you yourself, then your children and grandchildren. How many orphans, how many citizens have found lands more useful than money! There are endless examples of this. And how many bankrupts, pirates, and thieves have filled their gorge with Alberti money! They have amassed great, unbelievable sums and wealth through our losses. If only that money had been spent in buying pastures, woods, or even lands on the slopes of mountains, for then at least they would still be called ours, and we could still hope to get them back if times change.[26]

This emphasis on the indestructibility of land is particularly significant in light of the anxiety concerning the destruction of the city that is present in Alberti's work. It seems that whereas he believes that the city—any city—will almost certainly face destruction, the land, which is the essential component of the country, simply *cannot* be destroyed. Any misfortune that befalls the land is temporary, and even if the owner gains no pleasure or profit from it throughout his own life, it can be passed on to future generations who may have better fortune.[27] Giannozzo says that had the money taken from the Alberti in their exile been invested in land, these possessions "would still be called ours." That is to say, they would still, in a sense, be owned by the Alberti and would continue to confer status and identity upon them, a grounding in the world, which had been so painfully removed by their exile.

The Self

A key inference from Giannozzo's position seems to be that only the country creates proper conditions for the full realization of what we might today call "selfhood." The self of the city is a circumscribed one, isolated and remote, who is likely to have an unsatisfactory relationship with the objects that he uses and possesses. He must buy the things he needs and, as such, does not invest the same kind of care in them. As a result, these objects are inferior, less useful, and less pleasurable to him than they might otherwise be. The isolated self, it is implied, is not authentic or fulfilled. For it is precisely this "care" that binds man to the world, grounding him in places and objects.[28]

The self-sufficient farmer (whether real or imaginary) will be more complete and fulfilled, someone who is connected to the food he eats, the produce he grows, the equipment he uses, and the land he farms in a genuine and authentic manner. The country is thus portrayed as the place in which selfhood can be achieved—the place where one can be oneself.[29] The second major theme is that of security and durability, which again impinges on the notion of "selfhood." For not only is the country indestructible and resistant to change, but it can support an enduring dynastic identity that lasts beyond one's own lifetime—hence the repeated reference to the benefit of land to one's children, grandchildren, and beyond. And since the land cannot easily be mutilated or destroyed, such an identity will have an enduring foundation.

Many of these themes, or versions of them, are present in the antique sources from which Alberti gained much of his agricultural knowledge. Cato, Varro, Columella, and Pliny the Elder, among others, all assert the supremacy of agriculture over trade and commerce, as well as its priority in human history.[30] Indeed, Cato begins his agricultural treatise by observing that "it is true that to obtain money by trade is sometimes more profitable, were it not so hazardous. . . . The trader I consider to be an energetic man, and one bent on making money; but as I said above, it is a dangerous career and one subject to disaster. On the other hand, it is from the farming class that the bravest men and the sturdiest soldiers come, their calling is most highly respected, their livelihood is most assured."[31] A similar sentiment is found in Hesiod's *Works and Days*, where, commending the agricultural life, the poet comments,

> Less worry comes from having wealth at home;
> Business abroad is always insecure.[32]

Both Lionardo and Giannozzo agree on this point during their discussion of the country. Lionardo at no point attempts to counter Giannozzo's eulogy to rural life, but joins in enthusiastically. Comparing agriculture to commerce, he asserts,

> Is there a man who would not get pleasure from the villa? The villa gives much honest, safe profit. It is a known fact that other occupations expose you to a thousand dangers, trouble you with worries, and cause many losses and regrets. If you buy merchandise, you must

exercise great care: when you have it shipped, you are beset by fears; while you keep it in stock, you incur danger; when you are selling it, you are filled with anxiety. If you sell it on credit, you are troubled with suspicion and encounter difficulties when you try to collect; if you barter, you may be tricked. The same is true for all other transactions, which only cause you endless worry and anxiety.[33]

He then embarks on his own eulogy of the country life, which is worth quoting at length:

> Only the villa is grateful, generous, safe, and true above everything else. If you cultivate it with love and care, it will never seem to it that it has repaid you sufficiently, and it adds reward upon reward. In the spring the villa gives you infinite pleasures: plants, flowers, perfumes, and songs. It strives to make you happy, it smiles at you and promises a great harvest, fills you with hopes and pleasures. How generous you will find it in the summer! It offers you different fruits at different times; it never leaves your house without its bounty. Then comes the autumn. Now the villa gladly rewards your labors and care with marvelous gifts and profits, and with what love it repays you a dozenfold [he lists the autumn produce]. . . . Not even in winter does the villa cease being generous. . . . It will offer hares, wild goats, and deer for you to hunt, overcoming the cold and force of winter in the pleasures of the chase. I shall not speak of the chickens, the lambs, the cheese, and other delicacies which the villa raises up for you and conserves throughout the year. The villa gives you everything you need at home; it does not let you be seized by melancholy, but gives you pleasure and profit. And if the villa requires any of your labor, it does not in so doing wish you to be sad, troubled, or worried, nor does it fatigue and torment you like other occupations. The villa likes your work and exercise to be full of pleasure, something that is most useful—no less for your health than for the cultivation of the land.[34]

As well as echoing passages from Xenophon and Cicero, these words are reminiscent of Hesiod's and Virgil's depictions of the farmer as the happy beneficiary of the generosity of the land.[35]

Giannozzo commends Lionardo for his words, asking, "What else can one say, Lionardo? You could never adequately express how good the villa

is for the health, useful for living, and convenient for the family."[36] Unlike
Lionardo, however, he pursues another favorite theme of the ancient poets
and agricultural writers: the contrasting wickedness and unpleasantness
of the city. On the farm, he says, one need not "fear the deceitfulness of
debtors or administrators. Nothing is done in secret, everything is open
and visible to all. You cannot be tricked and do not have to use the services
of lawyers or witnesses. You do not have to bring suit in court or do other
similar bitter or worrisome things which cause you so much anguish if you
wish to prevail that most times it would be better to lose."[37]

The country is here portrayed as simple and honest. This image is
directly opposed to the immorality and complexity of the city—an environment full of trickery and deceit, ruthless competition and animosity. If
one is to survive, he must engage in thoroughly unpleasant activities, such
as litigation, which will cause him just as great displeasure as would the
result of not having undertaken the action. This use of legal proceedings
as an example of the city's unpleasantness is consistent with the healthy
medieval tradition of disdain for lawyers. It is also interesting when one
bears in mind the author's legal training as well as the role that lawyers
must have played in the loss of his inheritance. It seems that Alberti perhaps wished to contrast the man-made law of the city—often imperfect
and unjust, used to mediate bitter enmities and control hostility—with the
natural law of the country, which consists of simple justice, doing good,
being moderate, and following nature and the rhythms of the seasons.[38]
Again, this would seem to echo Virgil's words:

> The fruit his boughs, the crops his fields, produce
> Willingly of their own accord, he gathers;
> But iron laws on tablets, the frantic Forum
> And public archives, these he has never seen.[39]

Giannozzo follows his attack on the city and its legal wrangles by saying,
"Add to this the fact that you could go to your villa and live there in peace,
maintaining your family and taking care of your own affairs. On holidays
you could sit in the shade and talk pleasantly of the ox, the wool, the vineyards, or the sowing, without hearing gossip, complaints, or other cursed
things which plague those who dwell in cities, where you are continuously
beset by suspicion, fear, slander, injustice, quarrelling, and other things

too ugly and horrible to mention or remember."[40] The simplicity of the country and the lack of hostility involved in agriculture are reflected in the language of that place. Country discourse is presented as direct and practical, whereas in the city, the discourse is that of gossip, slander, and quarrelling—modes of speech that partake of immorality, pride, and vanity. It is striking how Giannozzo describes this urban discourse as a kind of onslaught, a terrible deluge of unpleasant noises that continually rains down on the individual.[41] This imagery is reminiscent of Alberti's fears concerning the destruction of the city in *De re aedificatoria*, particularly his descriptions of natural forces bombarding buildings. However, in this case, it is the individual who is bombarded rather than the city.

The same sentiments feature throughout Alberti's writings. In his early *De commodis litterarum atque incommodis*, probably penned in 1428, he similarly describes how the scholar must struggle to survive within the ocean of malicious and insincere discourse that fills the city:

> If we judged correctly what is the expertise of highly educated men, perhaps flattery, sarcasm, and unscrupulous cunning would not outweigh the knowledge possessed by men of modesty and candor. Yet, at present the crowd is more pleased with malice than with righteousness, with deception, frivolity, and insolence than with humane and modest conduct, and it is the crowd without whose approval the man of learning can never escape poverty. The crowd, unable itself to beat the cunning bent on conquest and pillage with which their masters enter into lawsuits, when they see schemer colliding with schemer, glorify the one who wins by more successful scheming. Thus, if an unscrupulous learned legalist takes up an unjust case, they will call him a great master, the best of men, and a great friend. They have come to think deception a virtue, they admire the art of creating a mask and a false image as a remarkable mobilization of knowledge, and they believe that malice and wickedness and deliberate misinformation are derived from recondite knowledge.[42]

The masses "never waver in their hatred of sincerity," while wealth and respect come only "to the one who practices deceit."[43] Meanwhile, knowledge of good, pure, and useful things "is despised and rejected in an ignorant and ugly way by the people of the city."[44] It seems that Florence (which Alberti may have visited by this time) is the city that he has in mind, for he writes that

> it seems to be the nature of men in cities to be big talkers and nasty gossips, but they are most brazen and evil-minded in our Tuscan towns. There they mock everyone, defer to no one, speak wildly, and behave with insolence. I think I should actually give some credit for this to our people and to Tuscany. In the Tuscan cities, because of their ancient liberty, it is permitted to say and do things which, to those raised under tyrants, would seem carelessly spoken or intemperately done. It is the glory of liberty, and its consequence, that, as long as you obey the laws, you can choose your own pleasures and your own course.[45]

This passage appears to be ironic, implying that the freedom granted by republican rule is above all the freedom to behave badly and indulge in slander. The notion that the city is home to trickery and false words, exemplified by litigation, is also present in the *Theogenius, Profugiorum, Momus, Della famiglia,* and other texts. As we have seen, man's slide into insincerity and dissimulation is characterized in *Momus* as the result of an originary decision to stray from the God-given order of nature.

If, in the city, one is tormented by the continual noise, the posturing, and the argument, and enveloped by the "ugly and horrible" discourse, country folk are free of this deluge. Giannozzo says, "You can talk with pleasure about anything while all others listen to you willingly and with enjoyment. Everyone has some useful things to say about agriculture. If you should make a mistake in planting or sowing, everyone would be willing to teach and correct you. Tending the fields does not give rise to envy, hatred, or ill-will."[46] Essentially, everyone in the country would be keen to help you and to share their knowledge. You need not disguise your mistakes, for others will eagerly correct you without trying to take advantage. They will wish you success and not be resentful of your achievements, whereas in the city it appears that any activity will make you enemies, and any success will breed envy. Lionardo, who is young, humanist, and progressive, does not oppose Giannozzo but rather continues to praise the country, although he refrains from attacking the city: "At the villa, moreover, you enjoy beautiful days in the open air under a clear sky. You enjoy delightful views of tree-covered hills, green valleys with clear springs and streams, water running, bubbling, disappearing among the green tufts of grass."[47]

It is noticeable that Lionardo's enthusiasm for the country consists mainly in the praise of nature and the productivity of the land. Giannozzo's enthusiasm, on the other hand, is of an altogether more profound nature, going beyond these inanimate things and encompassing also what he characterizes as the different kinds of speech and actions that are associated with each environment. Giannozzo describes the country as "a real paradise, by God!" and seems to perceive much of its excellence as deriving from its dissimilarity to the city: "Even better, at the villa you can avoid the noise of the city, the tumults in the public square, the struggles in the Government Palace. At the villa you can hide from the crimes and wickedness of the many evil men who, in the city, are always before your eyes, fill your ears continuously with gossip, and go through the streets shrieking and bellowing like maddened, horrible beasts. How wonderful it is to be at the villa! No happiness can equal it!"[48]

Politics

This mention of upheavals in the piazza and the government palazzo brings us once again to the theme of politics. Like many ancient writers on farming, Giannozzo characterizes politics as one of the key evils of the city. There is no sense here of the piazza and the palazzo as places where great deeds are performed, where the assembled people carry out their civic functions and duties; rather, the political center of the city is a stage for ruthless competition and perpetual strife. Ironically, the man who lives surrounded by animals in the country will be more fulfilled and more completely human, whereas in the city, political activity, surrounded by people, causes humans to become like animals, "shrieking and bellowing like maddened, horrible beasts." Giannozzo thus seems to express the deep skepticism regarding politics—the sense that it is something unnatural—that lies behind much of Alberti's thinking. Alberti also returns here to a theme that he had explored in one of his earliest works, the *Life of Saint Potitus*, as he relates how the young martyr-saint withdrew to a wood and judged it better to live among ferocious, wild beasts than among the "cruel, impious, and monstrous men, of which almost every city is full."[49]

The view of the city as the place of politics, and thus a corrupted place, is forcefully spelled out in an earlier passage in the *Della famiglia*. When Lionardo asks Giannozzo whether he considers it an honor to hold a government office, he replies, "Not at all, my dear Lionardo, not at all, my dear children. It seems to me that nothing is less worthy of being considered an honor than taking part in the government."[50] We know that Giannozzo speaks from experience, because he explains upon entering the dialogue that he was at the government palace at dawn that very day in order to speak up for a friend of his.[51] Nonetheless, the life of the statesman is to be avoided:

> It is a bothersome life, filled with suspicion, labor, and servitude. What difference do you see between those who work for the state and servants? They must scheme, beg this person, bow to another, strive against a third, and quarrel with a fourth. Their life is filled with endless suspicion, envy, enmity, insincere friendships, and abundant promises and offers. Everything is nothing but lies and vanity. The more you are in need, the less likely you are to find one who will keep his word or promise. Thus all your efforts and hopes will suddenly come to naught, bringing you grief, harm, and ruin.[52]

Nothing, Giannozzo says, can be gained from office. "Of what use is it to you," he asks, "except in that it gives you the chance to plunder and be overbearing with a certain amount of impunity?"[53] An endless stream of people will come before you with various demands, aggravating and possibly corrupting you: "You will be surrounded by quarrelsome, miserly, and unjust men who will fill your ears with suspicions, your soul with cupidity, and your mind with fear and unrest."[54] Your own affairs will be neglected, while your office will not allow you to complete your public duties as well as you would like. You will be at the center of many conflicting opinions, and whichever you choose, the result will be unhappy. Giannozzo explains, "Everyone believes . . . his opinion [is] better than that of others. Whether you follow the mistaken opinion of the majority or the arrogant opinion of the few, you will cover yourself with infamy. If you strive to please one, you will displease a hundred more. Oh, it is a fury not known, a wretchedness not avoided, an evil not hated by everyone as much as it deserves."[55]

Damning as these indictments may be, there is nothing especially shocking about them; rather, they rehearse somewhat standard criticisms of political activity and corruption. The tone does, however, intensify as Giannozzo warms to his theme:

> O madmen, O vain, proud tyrants, you excuse your own vice by saying that you cannot suffer others less rich, but perhaps of more ancient lineage, to be your equals, as justice requires. You cannot live without oppressing lesser citizens and thus you desire power. And what do you do, O fools, to acquire power? You are mad, for you expose yourselves to every danger and risk death. You are beasts, for you deem it an honor to be surrounded by evil men. . . . You deem it an honor to be numbered among plunderers. You deem it an honor to associate with, and support, men who are servants but whose wishes you yourselves must satisfy. What bestiality! You are men worthy of hatred if you take pleasure in the perversity and sorrow which go together with public office and administration.[56]

These are strong words. The vocative seems out of key with the urbane quality of much of the rest of the dialogue. Giannozzo appears to describe political ambition as a kind of mania—a disease even—that causes a person to abandon reason and do all manner of foolish and risky things. Cities, it seems, are to be associated not merely with plague but also with mental illness. The country might thus be a place to which one flees from both the plague and diseases of the mind.[57] In the *Vita*, Alberti draws a parallel between envy—which he often associates with political activity and urban life in general—and disease, observing of himself that "he described envy as a sort of invisible disease, the most insidious of plagues, for it enters by the ears, by the eyes, by the nose, by the bones, by the very fingernails into the soul, to burn there with invisible flames, and even some who think themselves untouched may be wasting away."[58]

Returning to Giannozzo's attack on politics, however, the most striking passage is the one that directly follows those quoted above:

> Unless cruel and bestial by nature, what joy can one feel when he must continually listen to the complaints, laments, and sobs of orphans, widows, and unfortunate wretches? What pleasure can one feel when all day long he must welcome hordes of coarse men, swindlers, spies, slanderers, thieves, and scandalmongers, but must guard himself against them at the same time? What peace can one

have who every night must twist men's arms and limbs [*le braccia e le membra*], hear pain-racked voices cry out for mercy, and yet must persist in horrible cruelties and must be the butcher and the mangler of human limbs [*membra*]? How abominable it is just to think of it.[59]

This passage is disturbing on account of the strong evocation of the very physical realities of torture: twisting, mangling, and butchering. Undoubtedly, these words express a genuine and deeply felt horror, which is manifested not least in the emphasis on human limbs. The repetition of the word "limbs" (*membra*) in a single sentence suggests a particular force.[60] Stylistically uncharacteristic, this sentence stands out in the text, and the repetition perhaps indicates the extent to which this fear and disgust was personal to the author and not merely another position in an argument. Notably, in the *Life of Saint Potitus*, the cruel and wicked emperor—who extols the active political life—orders that the saint be mutilated limb by limb (*membratim*).[61] It is vital that we remember that torture and violence, both public and secret, were a continual presence in the urban life of the Renaissance.[62] Torture was a real threat, something that could happen to a person suddenly and easily. A key part of Giannozzo's dislike of the city would seem, then, to derive from a sense of fear and ongoing violence that is too awful to articulate fully.

Transparency

This points to a further negative aspect of the city. Although torture could be a public spectacle, the type referred to by Giannozzo, which is described as taking place at night under the watch of politicians, has a marked ring of secrecy. Cities might appear to be places of clandestine activities, veils, and uncertainties. They are, after all, constructed from walls, buildings, and doors—things that serve to obstruct and control vision. We should remember, by contrast, Giannozzo's assertion that in the country "nothing is done in secret, everything is open and visible to all."[63] Alberti, as we have seen, was interested in vision and the means by which entities might be made known visually. The urge to make the city visible—a legible and graspable entity—sometimes manifests itself in *De re aedificatoria*, particularly where he considers various forms of zoning. Such ideas might betray an impulse to do away with the illegibility and obstructed visibility, the maze of walls and streets that may hide dangerous and horrific things.[64] The country is the opposite of the city in this respect. It is the place not of walls but of open spaces. Visibility is unimpaired; one can see across the fields and far into the distance. If the terrain is open, any person approaching can be spotted long before he arrives.

When speaking about the country, the characters in the *Della famiglia* use a profusion of words connected to clarity and purity. Two passages already quoted stand as good examples. Giannozzo describes the old Alberti possessions as "situated in fertile country with pure air [*aere cristallina*], rare fogs [*rarissime nebbie*], no strong winds [*non cattivi venti*], good water [*buone acque*], everything healthy and pure [*sano e puro*], and lovely to behold."[65] Later, Lionardo declares that "at the villa . . . you enjoy beautiful days in the open air under a clear sky [*quelli giorni aerosi e puri, aperti e lietissimi*]. You enjoy delightful views of tree-covered hills, green valleys with clear springs and streams [*quelli fonti e rivoli chiari*], water running, bubbling, disappearing among the green tufts of grass."[66]

Air quality was, of course, a priority for Alberti in his architectural treatise. In the *Della famiglia*, there once again seems to be an analogy between health and morality. In the country, both air and water are pure and transparent; in this sense, they are analogous to the pure and transparent nature of country life, where everything is open. While the city is a place of illusions, the country is the home of clarity. Giannozzo talks of the city, and particularly political activity within it, as being full of false promises and false friendships, of honors that seem great and yet are worthless, of temptations that cause a loss of all sense and perspective. In the city, amid the disorienting and overpowering noise and the thick air that obscures vision, nothing is as it seems. In the country, by contrast, everything is as it seems; the simple rhythms of agricultural life and the seasons are free from falsehood.

City Versus Country

As Giannozzo's praise of the country gives way to an assault on the city, Lionardo stops joining in and asks him, "Are you saying it is better to live in the country than in the city?" Giannozzo affirms, "Personally, my children, yes I do praise country living for those who wish to live with less vice, melancholy, and expense, and enjoy better health and greater happiness."[67]

Yet, when asked whether he would recommend raising children in the country, he says no; the world is full of bad people, and urban living is the best way to learn the ways of the wicked. One must observe such people, for "one who does not know the sound of the bagpipe cannot very well judge whether or not the instrument is good."[68] This assertion finally draws some protest from Lionardo, who counters,

> In the city, Giannozzo, the young also learn to become civilized. They learn honorable professions, observe things which make them scorn vice, and see more closely the beauty of honor, the delights of fame, and the divineness of glory. They also learn how sweet it is to be praised and respected, and have the reputation of a virtuous man. The young are awakened by these excellent things, are moved and encouraged to seek virtue, and gladly undertake arduous tasks worthy of immortal glory. Perhaps these excellent things are not to be found at the villa amongst trees and clods of earth.[69]

The defense of the city as the center of social and civic values is exactly what we might expect from the humanistic Lionardo. The country may offer peace, but the city offers honor, fame, and glory, ranked by the humanists—not least Alberti—among the highest prizes attainable by man. Giannozzo does not dismiss Lionardo's argument out of hand, but he is clearly unconvinced. "Even so, my dear Lionardo," he says, "I am not sure whether it is better to raise children in the country or in the city. Let it be as you say, let each place have its own usefulness. Let the cities create their great dreams: high office, power, and renown; and let the villa have tranquility, peace of mind, freedom, and health."[70] Outwardly, these words have the appearance of a compromise. However, Giannozzo has already condemned high office and power at some length, and he finishes this part of the discussion by remarking, "Personally, if I had a farm like the one I have described, I should spend a good part of the year there and manage to have the pleasure of feeding my family well and abundantly."[71]

Interestingly, this is the only opposition that Lionardo mounts to Giannozzo's praise of the country. Both characters are in almost complete agreement about the benefits of rural life; their opinions diverge rather around the nature and value of the city. The true counterargument to Giannozzo's position is voiced not during the discussion of the country but in the earlier debate on politics and participation in government. Following Giannozzo's passionate outburst, Lionardo engages in a lengthy defense of political activity and civic values. It is true, he says, that some people become involved in politics simply to gain immoderate power over others, and they are to be condemned. Also frowned upon are those "who have been brought up in [our] country's ancient tradition of freedom . . . filled with bitter hatred against all tyrants," but who are "not content with the liberty enjoyed by all, [and] would want more freedom and license."[72] Yet these are not the only people to enter politics; some desire only peace and the praise of their fellow citizens. Indeed, Lionardo implies, political participation is a duty of the good man, for "neither can republics endure if all good citizens are satisfied only with the tranquility of their own private life. Wise men say that good citizens must attend to affairs of state and bear the burden of public office, without heading idle gossip."[73] They must do this not only for the benefit and safety of their fellow citizens but also to prevent the republic from falling into the hands of the wicked.

Lionardo sums up his argument by saying,

> So, you see, Giannozzo, your commendable ideal of a secluded, honest life cannot be followed by those who thirst for glory, although it may be noble and excellent in itself. Fame crowns those who attend to public affairs, not those who enjoy the leisure of private life. Glory is to be gained in the forum, for only in the people's midst is praise nourished by the voice and judgment of honorable men. Fame avoids solitude and private places and presides over the people assembled in parliament. It is there that it gives luster and glory to the names of those who, rising above ignorance and vice through long study and strenuous efforts, break through the darkness and cause people to acclaim them.[74]

When the Alberti are allowed back in Florence, they will be ready to take part in government. Giannozzo again sounds a conciliatory note, expressing his hope that the young Alberti will do just this, and win glory in the process. Immediately, however, he adds a markedly anti–"civic humanist" qualification: "Nevertheless, I remind you that you must never neglect your private affairs for those of the republic."[75]

Speaking for Alberti

Whichever character can most readily be identified as Alberti's mouth-piece obviously has a crucial bearing on how we assess the author's attitude toward both the town and the country. Some have chosen to see Lionardo as expressing Alberti's real views, in line with a conception of Alberti as a progressive, civic-minded humanist. Guarino, for example, argues that Lionardo "obviously becomes Alberti's spokesman in this discussion," and says of Giannozzo's condemnation of politics that this "obviously does not reflect Alberti's civic humanism. It expresses the disillusionment of a man who feels he has been unjustly persecuted. Lionardo will oppose these views."[76] Yet this is an oversimplification of Alberti's work. As many commentators have pointed out, Alberti used the dialogue to present opposing points of view without explicitly endorsing either.[77] Indeed, one of the most fascinating aspects of the *Della famiglia* is the extent to which the text takes a dialogical form, presenting a number of conflicting arguments without any final resolution.

What then of Giannozzo, the advocate of country living? How does Alberti treat this character? Giannozzo seems to a large extent to be an accurate portrait of the Florentine patrician and his preoccupation with management. On the other hand, he sometimes appears comical. His claim that "it is a corrupt inclination of young men to prefer pleasure to work and the company of spendthrift youngsters to that of thrifty, old managers" is one example.[78] On another occasion, we find Lionardo laughing rather mysteriously in response to Giannozzo:

LIONARDO: Very well. What do you think is most important as far as health is concerned?

GIANNOZZO: The air, which you must use as you find it, whether you like it or not.

LIONARDO: And then?

GIANNOZZO: Other things necessary to sustain life, like food. Among these you must number good wine. My dear Lionardo, you laugh.

LIONARDO: And you would settle in a place having all these things?[79]

Lionardo appears to be amused by Giannozzo's concern for wine but pulls himself together and goes on with the conversation, ignoring Giannozzo's remark about his laughter. It is hard to say with any certainty, but it does appear that from time to time Lionardo finds Giannozzo humorous.

Nonetheless, Alberti clearly held Giannozzo in very high regard, for he strongly praises him in the opening pages of the *Profugiorum*. Niccola tells Agnolo Pandolfini that both he and Battista consider only two men to be ornaments to the *patria*, fathers of the senate, and true moderators of the republic: Pandolfini himself and Giannozzo Alberti, whose qualities, Niccola says, are expressed in the third book of *Della famiglia*. These two men are elder statesmen of unrivaled authority and integrity.[80] Yet there is also a tragic side to Giannozzo. The grief and loss that he feels as a result of his exile are palpable throughout the dialogue and sometimes lead to disenchantment, particularly where politics and the city are concerned.

Giannozzo's bitterness stems from a weary acquaintance with what are characterized as the annoyances of urban, "civilized" life. He has a sense of having been wronged, and this animates his suspicion of high ideals such as glory, as well as his desire for a kind of simplicity. For like the pastoral, so the form of the georgic, on which Giannozzo bases his praise of the country, contains an implicit criticism of "civilized," complex wisdom and discourse, matching it against a purer wisdom of simple things and practical living.[81] It is no coincidence that Giannozzo is not a man of letters, and this fact is repeatedly stressed throughout the work.[82] Giannozzo frequently refers to the other characters as "you men of letters" and exchanges some rather sharp words on the subject with Adovardo. During the discussion of the relative merits of money and land, Giannozzo tells him, "I am right to think you men of letters are too contentious. There is nothing so certain, so plain, so clear that you cannot make it doubtful, uncertain, and difficult with your subtleties. But now, whether you wish to argue with me as you are pleased to argue among yourselves or whether you really want to know my opinion on this subject, I must answer you, more to make you happy, Adovardo, than to defend any opinion."[83] Adovardo protests his innocence. He adds that "personally, I should not want to give up the study of letters which delights me," and claims to be unable to counter Giannozzo's arguments.[84] Nonetheless, he continues to do so, and Giannozzo observes, "I am glad to see you pretend to give way only to fortify your position with wiles rather than strength." Yet Giannozzo agrees to continue his argument, saying, "I do not fear your snares, although perhaps I should."[85]

Certainly, the assembled company thinks of Giannozzo as someone unacquainted with letters, and it does not necessarily expect eloquence or wisdom from him, for Lionardo asks Adovardo, "Why do you keep staring, Adovardo, as if you were amazed at Giannozzo's words? If you had heard his previous arguments, you would admit that his statements are like divine oracles."[86] Adovardo, meanwhile, seems reluctant to give way in this debate about educated as opposed to practical wisdom and indulges in exactly the kind of underhanded argument of which Giannozzo accuses him. Lionardo asks him directly, "Do you think, Adovardo, that it would be a mistake to accept Giannozzo's opinion regarding good management?" Adovardo assures him, "On the contrary, it would be a mistake not to accept Giannozzo's judgment as true." Yet he adds with sophistic dexterity, "However, Lionardo, at times it seems to me that it is not wrong to have doubts regarding certain things, even though they may be true."[87]

The Escape from Rhetoric

Giannozzo, as a practical, unlettered enthusiast of the country, provides an interesting critique of learned, humanist discourse. Again, it is tempting to say that Alberti, a man of letters par excellence, should be identified with the other characters. Yet Giannozzo is treated sympathetically in relation to this point, whereas Adovardo is guilty of all the accusations leveled at him. In fact, we should not be surprised that Alberti's cynical and ironic outlook should lend him some sympathy with a critique of his own practice.[88] The *Della famiglia* displays throughout a fascination with discourse, with the tensions and animosities between different positions, and with the possibility that dialogue provides for dialogical readings and ambivalent outcomes. Battista himself, when asked by Lionardo what he and his brother are thinking about, responds, "I was thinking how varied and unpredictable a discussion is."[89]

In reply, Lionardo acknowledges that eloquent speech is a complicated thing that does not necessarily have simplicity and sincerity as its only aim. This tells us two important things. First, we should not rely on the characters' pronouncements in the *Della famiglia* as clear statements of anyone's point of view, least of all Alberti's. Second, Alberti may indeed have felt that there was something insincere about "civilized" modes of speech and humanist rhetoric, just as Giannozzo asserts, and that the distinction between the pure discourse of the country and the wily and illusory discourse of the city, which Giannozzo alludes to, was a real one. Of course,

Giannozzo's persistent assertion that his own speech is straightforward and not rhetorical is itself a rhetorical position—although it is more properly Alberti rather than Giannozzo who is taking it.

Scholarly language becomes the object of criticism in the *De commodis*, where it sometimes appears dry and unnatural. It is in the *Momus*, however, that the discourse of scholars is subjected to mockery. Momus himself makes fun of the philosophers during his exile on earth, and a number of philosophers are satirized in various ways.[90] Intriguingly, however, the speech and wisdom of Gelastus, who at some level stands for Alberti himself, are also regularly belittled by a skeptical Charon as he trudges through the world carrying his boat on his back.[91] For example, when Charon is feeling particularly exasperated by Gelastus's philosophizing, he asks him how exactly philosophers are thought to be wise. "Surely you're not asking in what our wisdom consists?" Gelastus responds. "In fact, we know everything: the causes and movement of the stars, rain and lightning; we know about the earth, heaven and the sea. We are the inventors of the finest arts; our counsels are like legislation, prescribing that which conduces to piety, to a just mean in life and to goodwill among men."[92]

Charon appears interested. Is it, he asks, a principle of philosophy that man should work for the benefit of his fellow man, helping and supporting him wherever possible (something that Alberti himself asserts)? Gelastus enthusiastically agrees. And is it then a duty to alleviate the troubles of those you live with, helping them and lightening their cares? Again, Gelastus, happy to see that Charon at last understands the philosopher's art, strongly agrees. Charon answers, "Well, if this is your duty and principle, help me carry this heavy boat!"[93]

The Spider

There is no reason to disassociate Alberti with Giannozzo's position. If anything, it is stated rather more forcefully than the counterarguments. If, however, Giannozzo is on one level a wronged and tragic figure, who rails against the wickedness and evil of the city, he also perhaps has a dark side. He may well abhor the deceitful and sinister carryings on of the urban environment, but this is not to say that he does not contribute to them. Throughout the dialogue, he is portrayed as cunning and even ruthless, ever mindful of thrift and ever pessimistic, secretive, suspicious of his fellow citizens, and committed to pursuing selfishly his own interests and those of his family.[94] Moreover, in detailing how the family is to be managed, he appears to be manipulative and controlling, ensuring that he knows of everything that occurs and directing events according to his own choosing. In a key passage, Giannozzo uses a simile to describe his position as head of the family. He says to Lionardo,

> Well then, you men of letters, when you talk of the prudence neces-sary in life you give the example of the ants and you say that from them we must learn how to provide today for tomorrow's needs. When you establish a monarchy, you follow the example of the bees. You say they obey only one and strive for the common weal. . . . Allow me, then, to follow your commendable and noble custom. Allow me to use some similitudes of my own, not so appropriate as yours, but not altogether incongruous, and I shall be able to explain more clearly and almost paint before your eyes those qualities I think necessary to the head of the family.
>
> You have seen how the spider [*ragno*] arranges the threads of his web in rays, so that each one of them, no matter how long, finds its beginning, its root, its point of origin in the center, where that most industrious animal [*industrissimo animale*] dwells. Once it has spun its web, it dwells there alert and diligent, so that if any of the threads, no matter how minute or distant, is touched, it feels it immediately, rushes there, and takes care of everything. This is what the head of a family should do. Let him study his affairs and arrange them so that they all depend on him, originate with him, and find support in the safest places. Then let him stay there in the center, vigilant and ready to hear and see everything, and if something should require his attention, let him take care of it immediately.[95]

This seems to present a menacing portrait of a controlling and sinister patriarch, yet it is worth considering the history of the topos that is being used. The example of ants as creatures that show foresight in planning for the future is widely found in ancient sources. Similarly, bees were given a great deal of positive attention by ancient writers—Virgil's fourth *Georgic* is entirely devoted to them—who routinely saw them as examples of natural monarchies led by a single king (as it was not discovered that the chief bee was a queen until the seventeenth century).[96] The spider, however, is more problematic. Spiders have today often taken on negative associations, and for modern people, being described as spider-like may be viewed as a bad thing. Yet we should not be too hasty in applying this interpretation, for in the ancient sources with which Alberti was familiar, spiders are generally seen in a positive light.[97]

Pliny the Elder praises bees, ants, and spiders along the same lines as Giannozzo. All three species are industrious and intelligent, although bees, which "have been created for the sake of man," are held in the highest esteem of all.[98] Nonetheless, the spider "deserves even exceptional admiration." Pliny goes on to praise the great skill with which the spider constructs its web and the success with which it "conceals the snares that lurk in its chequered net."[99] Although it is described as a hunter, this appears to have heroic rather than negative connotations, as the author details how spiders hunt small frogs and lizards,[100] "giving a show worthy of the amphitheatre when it comes off." Just like Giannozzo's spider, this animal "watchfully and alertly" waits for its prey and runs to it, and "when the web is torn it at once restores it to a finished condition by patching it."[101]

This kind of praise occurs frequently in classical literature, leading Ian C. Beavis to comment that "although some spiders were somewhat unpopular [in the ancient world] for making the interior of houses untidy with their webs, the attitude toward spiders in antiquity (except, of course, for the venomous *phalangia*) was generally a favorable one. They were noted for their industry and hard work, as displayed in their weaving, and were regarded as comparable in this respect with bees and ants." Beavis adds that "it is interesting that amid all this eulogistic material there is no hint of spiders being considered as unattractive in appearance or in habits."[102] On top of this, we may note that the texts written around Alberti's time in which bees and spiders play a significant role consider spiders in a positive light. For instance, in Luigi Guicciardini's *Dialogue of Bees and Spiders* (c. 1529) spiders receive quite exceptional praise on account of their intelligence. In Edmund Spenser's *Fairie Queene* (1590), both bees and spiders stand for different kinds of artistic creation, with the poet seen as spinning his tales in the same artful manner as the spider spins its web.[103]

However, this does not amount to conclusive evidence that Alberti meant the image of the spider to be a purely positive one. As Beavis notes, there was one kind of spider that was looked upon with fear and hostility: the venomous *phalangia*. The distinction between harmless and poisonous spiders was clear in classical literature, for they were often denoted by different words.[104] However, in Italian, there is no word for *phalangia*; instead, *ragno* denotes both kinds of spiders. A key source for Alberti may have been Aristotle, whose remarks Alberti's in some ways resemble, and who discusses both varieties of spiders. Authors often refer to the bee, spider, and ant together, as does Aristotle in his *History of Animals*. He says that these three are "among the most industrious," adding that the spider is especially "ingenious" and noting the monarchical form of bee society, as well as the ants' propensity to store for the future.[105] Interestingly, however, Alberti's description does not so much resemble Aristotle's account of ordinary spiders as it does his account of the *phalangia*. Aristotle writes,

> There is a . . . third kind of these [*phalangia*], the most skilful and smoothest. It weaves by first stretching thread to the extremities in every direction, then it lays down the radii from the middle (it takes the middle with fair accuracy) and on these lays down the woof, so to speak, and then weaves them together. Now the bed and storage of prey she arranges elsewhere but she does her hunting at the centre where she keeps watch. Then when something has fallen in and the centre has been moved, first she binds it round and enwraps it with webs until she has made it helpless, then she lifts it up and carries it away, and if she happens to be hungry she sucks out its juice (for that is what she gains from it), but otherwise she sets out on the hunt again, after first mending the broken part. And if anything has fallen in meanwhile, she first goes to the centre, and from there goes back to what has fallen in, just as from the beginning.[106]

Like Giannozzo's spider, this creature arranges the web so that everything emanates from the center and has its origin there; the spider always retains its central position, rushes to whatever falls into its net, and deals with it instantly, while diligently maintaining the fabric of the web. It also feasts, in a rather horrific way, on the juice of its victims.

It does not seem overly fanciful to propose that both kinds of spider bear on Alberti's description of the *paterfamilias*. Again, he overtly follows Aristotle in ranking the bee, spider, and ant together in excellence and industriousness; yet what he describes sounds not only like the benign spider but also like the venomous one.[107] Alberti had in fact described the spider in sinister tones in his *Musca*, a short, Lucian-inspired, comic praise of the fly. Here, he relates how the noble and joyous fly is cruelly destroyed by the cunning and solitary spider. Spurred on by its thirst for knowledge, the fly goes to inspect the spider's web and "falls into the trap of the cunning spider, skilled in all the martial arts, [and] is crushed in an unjust contest. . . . The spider uses long Sabine lances, and is more learned in throwing its nooses than Alanus, who seized Triad, king of Armenia in the fray of battle; remaining hidden, it does not, however, dare to go forth from its fort into the duel it has prepared, before it sees the enemy folded in its web and utterly stifled."[108] Alberti goes on to describe how the "monster" dispatches the fly and any of its family who come to save it with "great cruelty," and how, although the fly may sing in the web, it is unable to move the heart of the wicked spider. Here, then, the spider is certainly menacing and cruel. Furthermore, in the same text, Alberti argues that bees have been overrated by the poets and that ants are responsible for the destruction of cities. It must be remembered, however, that Alberti begins the *Musca* with the claim that he is imitating Lucian, and he finishes with a comic coda: "Scripsimus hec ridendo et vos ridete." (We wrote this laughing—now you laugh too!)[109]

The image of Giannozzo's spider takes on further significance when we recall Alberti's assertion that a city is really a large house and a house a small city. If we are to see the head of the household as menacing, controlling, manipulative, and secretive, then he surely becomes analogous to the sinister figure of the tyrant.[110] Salutati, in fact, had at some length drawn parallels between the despotic ruler and the head of the household, arguing of the despot's rule that "its ultimate purpose is similar to that of the house-father."[111] The association of the head of the household and the tyrant, in which both are characterized as figures of central authority who rule in a despotic fashion according to their own will, was thus an established one. We have seen that the tyrant had a particular relationship to architecture, how he could arrange the city in such a way as to dominate it completely, and how readily he could adapt architectural knowledge to the exercise of power and control. It is notable that just as the tyrant dominates his city and the patriarch his house, so the spider dominates his web; all are architectural constructions. Indeed, two texts that Alberti's description of the spider resembles—those of Pliny the Elder and Aristotle—both make reference to the architectural nature of the spider's activities.

In fact, all of the animals of which Giannozzo speaks, along with the swallow (also used by Vitruvius as an example of a natural builder),[112] had long been associated with construction. As Martin Kemp has observed,

"The three particular animals (swallow, bee, and spider) . . . had been busily active throughout classical Antiquity and the Middle Ages, building their nests, cells and webs at the behest of the many philosophers who had been concerned with the vexed problem of animal intelligence."[113] Spiders, however, are associated not just with construction and weaving but sometimes with geometry as well, and with architecture in a more "intelligent" sense.

Pliny devotes much attention to the building activities of bees, but these are discussed in terms of construction rather than architecture. On the topic of the spider's web, by contrast, he enthuses, "With what architectural skill is the vaulting of the actual cave designed!" (Specus ipse qua concamaratur architectura!)[114] Aristotle talks of how the spider "lays down the radii from the middle (it takes the middle with fair accuracy)," and his modern translator explains that "here is employed the word for making a logical postulate, or an approximation in drawing a geometrical figure."[115] This idea is repeated by Aelian, some of whose words again sound rather similar to those of Giannozzo:

> It seems after all that Spiders are not only dexterous weavers after the manner of Athena the Worker and goddess of the Loom, but that they are by nature clever at geometry. Thus, they keep to the center and fix with the utmost precision the circle with its boundary based upon it, and have no need of Euclid, for they sit at the very middle and lie in wait for their prey. And they are, as you might say, most excellent weavers and adept at repairing their web. And any thread that you may chance to break of their skilled and delicate workmanship they repair and render sound and whole again.[116]

The spider, with its architectural and geometrical sense, seems to prefigure not only the tyrant but also the architect, or perhaps the tyrant who employs architecture to his particular ends. It relates to the architect in his capacity as arch-manipulator, as overseer and regulator of every aspect of the city and its activities. It is also significant that, just as the tyrant in *De re aedificatoria* would have recourse to all kinds of secret passages and contraptions (listening tubes, sections of wall set in lime, and so on), the head of the family, Alberti says, would require similar devices. He advises,

There should also be a more private side door, for the master of
the house alone, to enable him to let in secret couriers and messengers, and to go out whenever the occasion and circumstances
demand, without the knowledge of his household. To these I have
no objections. I would also recommend the inclusion of secret hiding
places, concealed recesses, and hidden escape routes, known only to
the head of the family, where he might keep his silverware and clothing in difficult times, and even hide himself, should the situation
become so grave.[117]

While such proposals seek to address a key problem of the Renaissance
city—the lack of privacy that resulted from people often living in very
close proximity—as well as Alberti's ever-present security concerns, they
also express a certain point of view about how the individual political male
must act. It is as though the nature of cities is such that one must be devi-
ous in order to survive, for nobody can be trusted, even within one's own
family. Giannozzo is just such a head of the family. The example of the
spider sheds some interesting light on his character, though it does little
to simplify the process of interpretation. It might be argued that he is both
menacing and menaced, both oppressor and oppressed. Giannozzo is himself, to some degree, the type who engages in selfish and manipulative
behavior and the dark dealings of the city. Yet he also wishes to flee to the
country.

Alberti's ambivalent position regarding secrecy in *De re* is of great
importance. In the *De commodis*, he remarks that "there is a special sort of
pleasure in avenging injuries, in plotting and conspiracies, in assaults and
battles that lead to your overcoming enemies by your own powers; still
hostile conspiracies and hatred are extremely painful."[118] Alberti was, of
course, the author of an important work on cryptography, the art of writing
secret texts. Moreover, as we have seen, although he seems to crave plain
and open discourse, his own writing is full of irony, masks, and personae.[119]

Some of Alberti's works are in dialogue form, whether featuring real
characters or imaginary ones; Battista himself occasionally appears as a
character. The *Philodoxus*, Alberti's first work, was originally "published"
under the name of Lepidus as a work of Roman comedy. When Alberti
claimed the piece as his own, the issue of its authorship in some ways grew
more complex. *Philodoxus* begins with a lengthy autobiographical foreword

in which Alberti (or rather the literary character Alberti) tells the familiar tale of his study of law, the hardships that followed his father's death, and the abuse he suffered at the hands of his relatives. He explains how the text came to be published under the name of Lepidus and ends with an evocation to the reader to "defend your friend, Leone Baptista Alberti, of all men the most devoted to scholars; defend me, I say, from the slanders of the envious."[120] There subsequently occurs another foreword, this time by the fictional author Lepidus, who again tells us about himself and the circumstances in which the play was written. Then follows the comedy, a morality play in which the characters perform an allegorical function. Notably, Alberti gave Lepidus a life outside of the play, and as we have seen, he appears as a character in the *Intercenales*. Indeed, Lepidus is the protagonist of the very first of the *Intercenales*, "The Writer," where Alberti uses the character in an unmistakably autobiographical way. Alberti claims in his foreword to the *Philodoxus* that once it became known that he was the author, many who had praised the play when they believed it to be the work of Lepidus disdained to do so any longer. The implication is that Alberti's act of masking was necessary to prove his talent in the face of hostility and that by doing this he revealed the prejudice of his critics; when he unmasked himself, he unmasked them also.

In the *Vita*, Alberti reveals himself to be preoccupied with controlling the way he was perceived by others. Of course, the *Vita* itself is part of this preoccupation. Autobiography was unusual at this time and is more extraordinary in Alberti's case since he was only around thirty-four years old when he wrote it. Once again, he takes on a persona, this time an anonymous one, and can write about himself almost as a character. The attempt to control his own image must be judged a brilliant success. Burckhardt, who suspected that Alberti might be the author, made this the foundation of his account of him, the influence of which has already been demonstrated. Alberti writes of himself,

> He was always examining his own conduct, checking it again and again to make sure there was nothing there to make anyone even suspect any ill of him, and he used to say that slanderers inject the worst of evils into human life. . . . Therefore he wanted everything in his life, every gesture and every word, to be, as well as to seem to be, the expression of one who merits the good will of good men, and he would say that, as in everything, so especially in these three things

one should take the utmost care, adding art to art to make the result seem free of artifice—how one walks in the street, how one rides, and how one speaks; in these things one should make every effort to be intensely pleasing to all.[121]

Alberti thus presents himself as one who put great effort into appearing effortless, who was intensely conscious of his own speech and even of the way he walked. It is interesting that Alberti should have written these things down, given that his appearance of effortless grace would only be effective so long as people genuinely believed it to be effortless. Yet Alberti clearly took great pride in this act of artfully presenting an appearance. It was not, it seems, enough to do it successfully; he wanted people to *know* that he was doing it—to recognize what we might call his *sprezzatura*. This must be recognized as a further example of Alberti's self-fashioning, for attention to one's gait and other forms of public deportment had been an important issue in ancient Greece and was a preoccupation of the Roman orators.[122]

Alberti obviously saw rigid self-control and the ability to disguise his feelings as being among his most important attributes. "He himself was by nature quite irascible and had a quick temper," Alberti writes, "but he deliberately repressed his rising indignation immediately."[123] Another one of Alberti's characters who learned to do this was Momus. As the god of biting criticism, Momus could not restrain himself from giving vent to his feelings and expressing his true self. His own exile was caused by the goddess Deceit, and it was on the earth that he learned to show a different face to the world. "The fellow who wants to master the arts of trickery and deceit and cunning treachery really needs to spend some time with men!" he reflects. "But if there's one agreeable thing I've learnt from bitter exile it's this: I've come out of the experience a clever and careful skin-changer and dodger; I've become an expert at simulation and dissimulation."[124] Recalled once more to heaven to sit among the gods, Momus reasons with himself that he must adopt a novel strategy and mask himself behind a new persona: "What will that mask be, Momus? I must show myself to be a friendly fellow, of course, easygoing and affable. I must learn how to be useful to everyone, how to humor people indulgently, receive them with good cheer, entertain them graciously, and send them away happy. Can you do something so completely against your own nature, Momus? Yes, I can, as long as I want to."[125] From this point on, Momus will present a mask to the world that will hide his true feelings, though in himself he will remain unchanged:

> What next? Shall I then forget my deep-rooted and almost congenital habit of doing harm? No; but I will control it silently, and I shall preserve my old zeal against my enemies, using, however, another way, a new method for entrapping and hurting them. I have come to the conclusion that men who have to live and do business among the multitude must never in their heart of hearts blot out the memory of an injury they have sustained, but they must never make public their anger at this offence. Instead, they must be time-servers, practicing simulation and dissimulation.[126]

Like these men of affairs, Momus will remain vigilant, gathering information on each person and making sure that he knows the dealings and weaknesses of each one. "By the same token," Momus reasons, "such men must themselves always hide their own enthusiasms and desires by adroit techniques of pretense. Watchful, skilful, armed and ready, they should wait for an opportunity to avenge themselves and not miss it when it presents itself. They should be forever mindful of their own interests. . . . They will account everyone's words as equally untrustworthy. They will trust no one, but they will pretend to trust everyone. They should fear no man, but should train themselves to applaud and flatter everyone while in their presence."[127]

This portrait of the man of affairs is somewhat reminiscent of Giannozzo's arachnid patriarch—who lies still in his web, making sure that everything is known to him so that he may choose the right time for decisive action— and of the tyrant in his fortress, surrounded by listening devices and secret getaways. It is also, simultaneously, evocative of the men of political action whom Giannozzo so despises:

> In short, it will be advantageous above all to call this one thing to mind over and over again: hide all your plans carefully and well, covering them with signs of trustworthiness and innocence. I shall carry this off brilliantly once I get used to molding and shaping my words, expressions, and my whole appearance so that I seem identical to those who are deemed good and meek, even though I am completely different from them. Oh, what an excellent thing it is to know

how to cover and cloak one's true feelings with a painted façade of artificiality and studied pretence![128]

One cannot help but be struck by the similarities with another of Alberti's characters: the Battista of the *Vita*. He, too, learned to control the face that he presented to the world, but clearly never forgot the offenses he received; the attack by his relatives is alluded to throughout his writings. He was irascible by nature but learned to control his anger, just as Momus, when provoked by the goddess of wisdom, "although he took bitter offence at this, had decided to simulate and dissimulate in every situation, and so he dispatched Minerva with gentle speech and mild words."[129] Of course, Momus is an antihero in a comedy that specifically claims to be ironic, and it would be wrong simply to read him as a figure for Alberti himself. Yet he seems to embody the side of Alberti that scorns society, the city, the leaders of men, and even men themselves. Despite his simulations, Momus is one of the few characters in the comedy who can be judged authentic. His behavior is terrible and lacking in all morality, yet it is often he who sees the truth of the world.[130] His bitter and scornful words reveal gods and mortals as they really are. Men are venal, selfish, violent, and aggressive, or else, like some philosophers, pompous, grandiose, and full of empty words. The gods are lazy, stupid, and greedy, ever competing for their ruler's favor. Jupiter's arrogance and vanity prevent him from ruling properly, and he strives not to be good, just, and wise, but merely to seem so.

However, it is Momus's authenticity that leads to his downfall, for ultimately he is unable to maintain his strategy of simulating and dissimulating. Frustrated with the foolish ways of the gods, he cannot help but speak out against them. The moment that he shows his authentic self, in a world where all admire false images, he is doomed. Alberti seems to consider that falsehood and deception are necessary parts of living among others, and one must assume masks and personae in order to survive. Yet the country offers the vision of escape to an environment of clarity and truth where the masks can be cast aside, where words and feelings genuinely coincide. It is ironic that Alberti should feel this urge to escape from masks and symbols, for he is the author of an early autobiography, a person who wrote under pseudonyms, turned himself into a literary character,[131] adopted the symbol of the winged eye, and named himself Leone. Alberti, we might judge, was the most symbolic of all. Yet we should also recall that unlike either Jupiter or Momus, the Buttosta of the *Vita* strove not only to "seem" but also to "be."

Truth and Fiction in the Country

Giannozzo's account of country life is not entirely fanciful, to the extent that his preoccupations coincide to a considerable degree with those of contemporary landowners of his class. Indeed, his very interest in the country and his assumption that the ownership and management of land forms part of the concerns of the family are typical rather than unusual. He desires that country property should be, above all, productive. He emphasizes the contribution that crops and other products can make to household economy. Land is presented as a means of diversifying investment and providing financial security. Country estates are seen as an important ingredient in securing familial and dynastic identity.

Layered on top of this, however, is a raft of different concerns that relate to Alberti's own intellectual positions and that are mediated through commonplace literary motifs (although they may also reflect the types of things that people of Alberti's class sometimes said). Here, praise for the country ceases to have the same kind of connection to reality but rather becomes part of a polemic against certain aspects of urban life; politics is perhaps foremost among its targets. Alberti's treatment of the subject also provides a means to consider different forms of discourse and whether urban discourse is somehow insincere, raising interesting questions about humanist rhetoric. As we have seen, this touches on the issue of dissimulation. Moreover, it poses—but does not finally resolve—the question of the value of the humanistic goals of fame and glory and how avidly the individual should seek them.

THE SUBURBS AND OTHER PLACES

As we have seen, in the *Villa*, rural property is viewed exclusively in terms of productivity. In the *Della famiglia*, Giannozzo conceives of the farm in a similar way. However, he also repeatedly talks of the enjoyment and pleasure that he would gain from working the fields and even tells Adovardo that should his farm not be highly profitable, it would still be worth owning for pleasure. The tone is no longer the somber and admonitory one of Hesiod but is rather that of the Roman writers Cato, Varro, and Columella. A statement from one of Varro's characters seems to express Giannozzo's opinion exactly: "The farmer should aim at two goals, profit and pleasure; the object of the first is material return, and of the second enjoyment. The profitable plays a more important role than the pleasurable."[1]

Although Giannozzo is keen on self-sufficiency as an ideal, his perspective very much remains that of the Florentine patrician who owns property in both town and country. He asserts that he would be content to remain largely in the country and that "a farm should be such that a whole family could live on it the entire year without having to add more than a bit of salt."[2] On the other hand, he would prefer to have property close to the city since this would allow him to visit his villa often and to "spend a good part of the year there."[3] Again, his views appear to accurately reflect the real Florentine situation, where lands close to the city were especially prized.

Giannozzo's praise of farming does not, of course, signify that he welcomed backbreaking agricultural work. Landowners of his station entrusted the work of their estates to laborers, most of whom were tenant farmers. The legal agreements made by proprietors and *lavoratori* could vary considerably, as could the personal relationships between the two classes.[4] A characteristic but by no means ubiquitous arrangement was the sharecropping system known as *mezzadria*, in which the tenant divided the produce with the landlord. Such arrangements could necessitate a close degree of contact between proprietor and *lavoratore*, and this would have been central to the rural experience of many farm owners. For all his love of the country, Giannozzo is certainly not idealistic in his view of the peasantry. Rather, he denounces peasants as being incredibly wicked, deceitful, and sly—always asking for something, always bemoaning their poverty, often taking the best part of the produce and leaving the landlord with nothing but expenses.[5]

Here, again, we encounter a view that was probably quite widely held. Pietro de' Crescenzi, for example, expresses similar opinions in his *Trattato della agricoltura*, written at the beginning of the fourteenth century.[6] This state of affairs was underpinned by economic factors. Wealth tended to drain from the country toward the city, leaving the country in a state of what David Herlihy has termed "liquidity crisis."[7] Tenant farmers were indeed compelled to ask their landlords for many things, since they relied on the landlords' capital injections to keep their operations viable. It may also be true that tenants were given to bemoaning their poverty. As Herlihy points out, most *mezzadria* arrangements were initiated by a loan from the landlord, which the tenant sometimes struggled to repay. In such cases, poverty became the tenant's primary defense. Alberti may have shared Giannozzo's opinions regarding rural *lavoratori*. As Luca Boschetto has shown, he was repeatedly involved in legal action against the tenants of his benefice at San Martino a Gangalandi. The vigor with which Alberti, who appears in his writings as one who disdained money, pursued these sometimes indigent peasants is quite startling.[8]

Villas

The vast majority of Florentine villas may have been geared toward production, but some were not. This distinction found expression in Florentine modes of tax assessment, with the *catasto* of 1427 differentiating between those properties that were productive, or that supported a productive family, and those that were surplus.[9] A similar distinction appears in Alberti's architectural treatise, where he observes that "country houses may be divided into those inhabited by gentlemen and those by workers of the land, and further divided into those built mainly as a business and those intended more for pleasure."[10] Alberti speaks of the villa with great enthusiasm in *De re aedificatoria*, since the architect will have a freer hand in the country. In words that are reminiscent of Giannozzo, he asserts that "here everything is more open, whereas the city is restrictive."[11]

As we might expect, the productive villa receives an extensive treatment that goes beyond architecture to also take in farming. Alberti starts with the buildings designated for workers and then moves on to those of overseers and owners. The farm is described in great detail, including where it should be situated, how the farmyard should be set out, what should be grown, what tools will be needed, and how livestock and fish should be treated. Alberti displays considerable agricultural knowledge, much of which he gained from the ancient Latin texts on farming. He then goes on to describe the villa of the wealthy that is purely for pleasure, adding, "Some would maintain that he [the master] should have one villa for summer and another for winter."[12] The setting for such a villa should take greater account of dignity than of the fertility of the soil, he says, and he proceeds to describe a lavish country house that is suitable for entertaining guests on a grand scale:

> It should have easy access from the fields, and a generous reception area for the arrival of guests; it should be in view, and have itself a view of some city, town, stretch of coast, or plain, or it should have within sight the peaks of some notable hills or mountains, delightful gardens, and attractive haunts for fishing and hunting.
>
> . . . There should be a large open area in front of the gates for chariot and horse races, its dimensions greater than the distance a young man could hurl a javelin or fire an arrow. Likewise within the gates there should be no shortage of semiprivate spaces, walkways, promenades, swimming pools, areas both grassed and paved over, porticoes, and semicircular loggias, where old men may meet for discussion in the welcome winter sun, and where on holidays the family might pass the day, and where in summer grateful shade may be found.[13]

Such a house would have many separate apartments for family and guests, men and women, young and old. This conception of the villa is far removed from the ideal of rural self-sufficiency and would seem openly dependent on urban capital for its existence. With its swimming pools and area for chariot races, it appears to be a building of far-off antiquity. The villa is here conceived of in specifically aesthetic terms, as a thing that should be viewed. Moreover, the land is also conceived of aesthetically, now somewhat in the sense of a land*scape*. Mountains, plains, gardens, or stretches of coast here become objects to be looked at and enjoyed. First in the list of things that might constitute desirable views for villas, however, are cities and towns. This in itself is interesting since it points to the extent to which the villa still stands as a kind of refuge from the city. Indeed, some of its power to delight must rest in its ability to transform the city from a place of everyday life into a distant piece of aesthetic scenography, thereby reinforcing the viewer's sense of removal from his or her urban existence.

Refuge and Contemplation

Alberti seems to have been of the opinion that a beautiful landscape could have positive effects on the soul. In the *Vita*, he suggests that viewing such prospects might actually cure disease. The notion of the beneficial effects of withdrawal to the country on the soul is present in much of his discussion about villas. More broadly, it has been suggested that the fifteenth century witnessed a gradual shift in which the villa replaced the monastery as the most important setting for contemplation.[14] Whether one agrees with this or not, the country is certainly connected to the contemplative life in some fifteenth-century literature, including a few of Alberti's treatises. One need only think of the *Theogenius*, where all of the characters who are morally good and spiritually developed are exiles who live outside of the city.

A prime example is Genipatro. Genipatro lives in the woods, somewhat in the manner of Saint Potitus. There, he spends his time studying nature and reading the classics. His hands, Alberti tells us, "were callused through the exercise of cultivating his garden, where every day he gave some hours to his health."[15] Extolling the virtues of solitude, Genipatro rehearses the usual list of flatterers, traitors, and immodest men who infest the city and says that in the woods he is free from such molestation. He voices the commonplace maxim that he is never less alone than when he is by himself, explaining that he will always have the great authors for company. In this way, he is able to attain superior knowledge of both the world and himself. "Should I wish to know the reasons and principles behind the various effects produced by nature," he says, "should I desire a method by which to discern the true from the false, should I search to know myself and together to understand the things produced in life in order to thenceforth recognize and revere the father, the first and greatest master, originator of so many marvels, I am not without the most sacred philosophers. From these I gain satisfaction and feel myself becoming better and more learned every hour."[16] Setting up the same kind of dichotomy that appeals to Giannozzo, he tells the rich and arrogant Tichipedo, "Your greatness and civic pomp, the frequency of many *salutatori*, will never please me more than my quiet solitude."[17]

Alberti clearly feels the enticing pull of the contemplative life in this dialogue, but he cannot be viewed as a thinker who generally favored *otium* and solitude over action and concourse. Indeed, it may be that, like Lorenzo Valla, Alberti would have regardless conceived of contemplation as a form of action. After all, activity is highly valued in many of his works, and his own life involved a greater degree of activity—the raising of sunken Roman barges, the erection of buildings, and so on—than did those of many humanists. Whatever the merits of solitude and a life spent among nature, these things are not, ultimately, "solutions" to the problems of the human condition. Agnolo Pandolfini effectively says so in the *Profugiorum ab aerumna*.

Agnolo's statement is of particular interest because he is a character whom Alberti deliberately associates with Giannozzo, and who was very much connected to the idea of retreat. He was a senior and respected elder statesman, but according to Vespasiano da Bisticci, he had withdrawn from government affairs immediately following the exile of Palla Strozzi. Alberti is keen to emphasize this aspect of Agnolo, having some messengers arrive at the start of the dialogue to request that he go to the government palace to advise the Signoria. Agnolo pointedly refuses, responding that the Signoria will only want him to say that which they want to hear. We know that Agnolo possesses a fine villa, because Niccola di Vieri de' Medici mentions it at one point, observing, "If I were to have a building so well adapted and so magnificent, in a place so agreeable and so salubrious as you, Agnolo, I don't know where I would spend the greater part of my days other than only there."[18] Nonetheless, Agnolo argues that retreat to the land will never provide the best protection against adverse fortune: "They say that one finds no payer more very faithful than the earth. That which you might entrust to her, according to the precept of Hesiod, she pays back not in equal but in greater measure. You will find your industry and vigilance more faithful still, in particular that which you place in honest and worthy things, when the heavens and every fate disposes itself in these matters to satisfy your merits. Never was *virtù* without the prize of praise and favor."[19] The attainment of virtù should remain the foremost goal of the individual.

The Hortus

Given Alberti's often stated preference for moderation in all things, it is not surprising that he should have been attracted to the idea of the *hortus*, a building located between city and country. Even Momus, in the *tabellae* that he presented to Jupiter, recommended that the prince should usually seek out a middle way between opposing positions. The hortus appears to be perfectly suited to a man of Alberti's intellectual makeup. It is discussed in the ninth book of *De re aedificatoria*, where Alberti presents it precisely as a kind of architectural *via di mezzo*:

> There is one type of private building that combines the dignity of a city house with the delight of a villa—a topic passed over in previous books, and saved until now. This is the suburban *hortus*, something that, I feel, must not be overlooked on any account.
>
> . . . There was a saying among the ancients: "Anyone who buys a farm should sell his house in the town." And also, "If your heart is set on city life, you need no country business." By this they meant, perhaps, that a *hortus* was the best solution. The physicians advise us to breathe air as clear and pure as possible; this, I do not deny, may be found in an isolated hilltop villa. On the other hand, urban, civic business requires the head of the family to make frequent visits to the forum, curia, and temples. To do this easily you need a house in town; yet one may be inconvenient for business, the other damages health.[20]
>
> Generals used to shift camp lest the stench prove too offensive. What then would you expect of a city, full of festering piles of filth

which have accumulated over the centuries? This being the case, of all buildings for practical use, I consider the *hortus* to be the foremost and healthiest: it does not detain you from business in the city, nor is it troubled by impurity of air.[21]

The reflections on the city are consistent with those that are either expressed or implied earlier in the treatise. The urban environment is not a healthy one. Indeed, since it is full of festering piles of filth that have accumulated over hundreds of years, it is very much the locus of bad air—precisely the thing that was widely held to cause illness and plague in the fifteenth century. We have previously seen how issues of this kind are bound up with social concerns about the lower orders that lead Alberti to contemplate the separation of classes and a move to the more spacious peripheries of cities. We have also seen how the physical diseases of the city find their correlation in mental diseases, and how the country can help one to avoid both and perhaps even offer a remedy.

Alberti stipulates that the hortus should be equipped with all of the uplifting delight of the villas, which he has described in the fifth book. His evocation of lawns, meadows, groves, and limpid springs is reminiscent of the language used by Giannozzo and Lionardo when describing the country—language that is redolent of clarity, purity, and salubriousness:

It is useful both to have the city close by and to have places to which you withdraw easily and do what you will. [Et urbi sane vicina iuvant facilesque recessus, ubi quae libeant, ex libidine liceant.] A place close to town, with clear roads and pleasant surroundings, will be popular. A building here will be most attractive, if it presents a cheerful over-all appearance to anyone leaving the city, as if to attract and expect visitors. . . . I would make the road leading up to it rise so gently that visitors do not realize how high they have climbed until they have a view over the countryside. Meadows full of flowers, sunny lawns, cool and shady groves, limpid springs, streams, and pools, and whatever else we have described as being essential to a villa—none of these should be missing, for their delight as much as for their utility.[22]

Particularly striking is the notion of the hortus as a place where you may do what you will—a place, in other words, that is free from the restrictions of urban society. It is a place of utility, but also a place of delight.

Suburbia

The hortus is, of course, essentially a suburban building. Alberti does not refer to a *villa suburbana* or use any word that is coextensive with it, but this is clearly what he has in mind. It is a fact that has not gone unnoticed by scholars. The modern historian of the city Lewis Mumford felt that "just as one finds the earliest evidence of the back-to-nature movement in Piero di Cosimo's paintings, so one finds an esthetic and psychological justification of suburban development in Alberti's treatise on building." Here, the notion of a house that is conveniently situated for town and country "sounds the true suburban note." Referring to the passage (quoted above) in which Alberti describes the delights of the landscape around the hortus, Mumford notes, "As for the esthetic attributes of both house and site, Alberti's first perceptions might almost stand as the classic last word."[23] Above all, Alberti's treatment of the hortus tells of "an attempt to achieve liberation from the sometimes dreary conventions and compulsions of an urban society: an effort, given the necessary financial means, to have life on one's own terms, even if it meant having it alone."[24] The suburb, Mumford argues, embodies the modern ideals of personal freedom and liberty— things that may not be readily available in the city.

In this sense, the hortus is able to offer something of the contemplative withdrawal and delight in nature that is so extolled in the *Theogenius*, while maintaining the necessary links with the city. As Genipatro says, "It is for sure the greatest happiness to be able to live without any regard for these fleeting and fragile things of fortune with a spirit free from the many contagions of the body, and away from the uproar and annoyance of the lower classes [*plebe*] in solitude, conversing with nature."[25] More prosaically, and indeed practically, Alberti remarks in *De re aedificatoria* that he would not want the surroundings of his suburban hortus "to be so busy that it is never possible to come to my door without being properly dressed."[26] Here, he indeed appears to express what would later become the very quintessence of the suburban outlook and a certain kind of bourgeois attitude toward space.

Suburbs, of course, did exist in fifteenth-century cities. Leonardo Bruni characterizes them as an essential feature of the cityscape in his *Laudatio Florentiae urbis*: "The villas are more beautiful than the distant panorama, the suburbs more handsome than the villas, and the city itself more beautiful than its suburbs."[27] This hierarchical description, in which each element outshines the previous ones, clearly characterizes the city center as the place of greatest magnificence. A little later, Bruni elaborates this image further:

> The city itself stands in the center [of its territory] like a guardian and lord, while the towns surround Florence on the periphery, each in its own place. A poet might well compare it to the moon surrounded by the stars, and the whole vista is very beautiful to the eyes. Just as on a round buckler, where one ring is laid around the other, the innermost ring loses itself in the central knob that is the middle of the entire buckler. So here we see the regions lying like rings surrounding and enclosing one another. Within them Florence is first, similar to the central knob, the center of the whole orbit. The city itself is ringed by walls and suburbs. Around the suburbs, in turn, lies a ring of country houses, and around them the circle of towns.[28]

It is instantly noticeable that Bruni conceives of the city as a series of concentric rings, just as Alberti was later to do—albeit in a rather different way. Bruni's clear assertion of the primacy of the city, however, contrasts with Alberti's rather more nuanced view. A reader of Alberti's text might come away with the impression that the suburbs are quite the best place to be, away from the noise and filth of the city center. Bruni does not characterize the city in this way at all, and far from dwelling on festering piles of filth, he specifically mentions that Florence is the cleanest of cities.

Fifteenth-century suburban villas still do exist. It has even been conjectured that Alberti had a hand in the design of the Medici villa at Fiesole, which stands today.[29] Of course, quattrocento suburbia was not the same thing as modern suburbia. The most famous of Renaissance suburban villas are those that belonged to the Medici and to Agostino Chigi—magnificent dwellings that have nothing of the bourgeois or petty-bourgeois connotations of twentieth-century suburbia. This last example points to another obvious context for Alberti's speculations. Rome was not like the central knob in the middle of a buckler; its topography was altogether messier. The large *disabitato* of the hills meant that an extensive area of land was given over to cultivation and pasture but remained within the city walls. As a result, the division between town and country was not clear and precise. Just as in Florence—and most cities—many inhabitants of Rome had strong connections to the country. Indeed, it seems that even people of relatively humble station often owned some land that could be cultivated. Twice yearly, generally in late spring and at the time of the vintage, there was a mass exodus from the city as people flooded to their small holdings and country properties. Justice had to be suspended from mid-June until late August for the harvest, and again for the vintage in early autumn.[30] The hortus may have had a particular appeal for the inhabitants of a society that mingled town and country in an imprecise manner.

Neighborhoods and Peripheries

Alberti does not exactly advocate leaving the city center to live in a suburban hortus. Instead, he probably felt that the *cives primariis* should ideally have recourse to several kinds of buildings: a town house, a hortus, and a villa or villas dedicated to pleasure or productivity, possibly in a range of different terrains. Nonetheless, the hortus sounds like a more or less permanent residence, or at least one that could be lived in for substantial periods of time. After all, it is the best solution for one who has business in both town and country. Its proximity to the city means that working life can continue undisturbed. Moreover, it spares one from the serious health risks that must be endured when living in the city.

This notion of the well-off citizens taking up residence outside the city or on its peripheries is interesting in the context of actual fifteenth-century urban topography. In reality, important families in most cities found it vital to maintain their presence in the very heart of the city, close to civic institutions and symbols of power. Patronage networks often militated against social zoning, resulting in neighborhoods that consisted of all social classes and in which myriad familial, business, and other kinds of links connected people of different stations. Neighborhood identity was very strong in many cities and was often inextricably bound to the presence of important families. Thus Benedetto Dei, in his chronicle of the 1470s, is able to conceive of the topography of Florence in terms of its important citizens, describing one street as "leading from Bancho di Casavechia to Bancho Bencivenni."[31] Similarly, a member of the Bonsi family describes his dwelling in a 1427 *catasto* entry as being in the Via della Cuculia, "tra' Serragli."[32]

Neighborhood identity was also strong in Rome, as Alberti knew well. Eugenius IV had failed to curtail the power of the nobility and was forced to agree to a set of city statutes in 1446 that conceded a significant level of autonomy to nobles who controlled neighborhoods in the city. Nicholas V confirmed these statutes as one of his first acts upon becoming pope.[33] The strength of neighborhood identity is reinforced by the fact that interneighborhood fighting could break out in many cities. The attack on Drago Verde in Florence by the militia of Lion d'Oro following the revolt of the Ciompi is just one such example. In fact, neighborhood identity could sometimes override civic identity. The fourteenth-century chronicle of Donato Velluti records that the nobility and guildsmen of the Oltrarno, perceiving themselves to be unfairly taxed and not sufficiently represented, threatened to "cut the bridges and make a city for ourselves."[34] This was not an idle threat, and the Signoria quickly gave in.

The idea of living in a hortus does not contradict that of belonging to a neighborhood. After all, in Florence, each district of the city was associated with its own area of the *contado*, and it seems that property owners gravitated toward lands that were administered by their own urban district. Nonetheless, Alberti gives very little regard to the notion of neighborhood in his writings. In Book VII of *De re aedificatoria*, he discusses the division of the city into twelve zones. However, shortly thereafter, he considers whether the rich and the poor should live in entirely different areas. When Alberti considers the hortus and other ideas about class separation and gravitation to the peripheries, his writing evokes the sense of a desired escape from much of what neighborhoods entail: restriction, proximity to others, lack of privacy, and complex bonds and relationships. The very closeness of neighborhoods is one of the things that necessitates the construction of secret entrances and exits to a palace for its master's use. Outside of the city, as we have seen, Alberti conceives of things as being far more relaxed and open. With their complex networks of loyalties and power relations, neighborhoods might appear messy and impenetrable, entities that could generate discord or violence within the city. A clearer separation of the classes was perhaps more intellectually appealing.

As it happens, there is some evidence that traditional neighborhood structures were beginning to break down in the fifteenth century, at least in Florence. Samuel Cohn has argued that following the defeat of the Ciompi, the dissolution of the typical medieval "*Gemeinschaft* of rich and poor" gave way instead to a new "class geography" as monumental buildings and piazzas opened up in the city center.[35] However, the result was rather the opposite of what Alberti envisaged since, in reality, it was the poor who were pushed to the peripheries. Indeed, the peripheries of many fifteenth-century cities seem to have enjoyed the same prestige as those of modern cities. The hortus, which might stand at some remove from the city walls, is not to be associated with these outlying districts.

Villas and Ideology

The importance of Alberti's writings on villas does not rest on the extent to which they accurately reflect relations between the city and the country in the city-states of fifteenth-century Italy. It is the extent to which they shed light on Alberti's own attitudes—particularly his attitudes toward the urban world—that is of importance here. In literature, the villa is often a point of departure for an argument, and Alberti certainly uses it to polemicize against those aspects of the city that he dislikes. Through discussion of the villa, he is able to negotiate a number of ideas about environment and well-being, the balancing of privacy and convenience, and the extent to which one should engage with the masses. The villa has long stood as a kind of ideal that can be used to throw light on the urban situation—whether or not such light really helps one to see accurately. James Ackerman has gone further, asserting that "the villa is . . . a paradigm not only of architecture but of ideology; it is a myth or fantasy through which over the course of millennia persons whose position of privilege is rooted in urban commerce and industry have been able to expropriate rural land, often requiring, for the realization of the myth, the care of a laboring class or of slaves."[36]

The villa may well entail a kind of fantasy, particularly as it appears in literature. For Alberti, however, it must be acknowledged that this fantasy is particularly strong. Indeed, one could argue that it becomes the basis for an entire ideal regarding domestic architecture. For Alberti urges that a town house, "as far as the limited space and light will allow, . . . should assume all the delight and charm of a villa."[37] Contrary to what has sometimes been claimed, Alberti seems to give the villa priority over the urban town house.[38] This is not to say that Alberti was not an enthusiast of "the more shady, and softer delights of the city," but it does indicate that he tended to favor the pleasures of more open spaces.[39] Furthermore, he is not merely speaking about the habitations of the rich, for the less wealthy may also benefit from a villa:

> For their own buildings, humbler folk should follow the example
> of the rich and emulate their magnificence, as far as their resources
> allow, though this imitation must be dampened, so that financial

considerations are not sacrificed to pleasure. Their villas, then, should provide for the ox and herd almost as much as for the wife. They want a dovecote, fish pond, and so on, not for pleasure so much as for profit. Yet the villa should be pretty enough to ensure that the mother of the family will enjoy living there and will give careful devotion to its domestic upkeep.[40]

The villa is, then, a building type of exceptional importance for Alberti. He appears to view at least some degree of withdrawal from the city as desirable or even necessary. Moreover, there is some suggestion that the city might be improved to the extent that urban living could become somewhat less urban, and rather more like the country.

6

THE BEAUTIFUL CITY

Beauty was a topic of crucial importance to Alberti. Indeed, it was so important that he devoted almost the entire second half of his architectural treatise to the subject (or rather to both beauty and ornament, which he considered to be separate but related entities). Mindful of Vitruvius's stipulation that all buildings should be "built with due reference to durability, convenience and grace" (*firmitas, utilitas,* and *venustas*),[1] Alberti addressed the first two in Books I to V of his treatise. In the first chapter of Book VI, having reiterated his methodology and attacked Vitruvius's confused terminology, he signals that it is time to turn to the third: "Of the three conditions that apply to every form of construction—that what we construct should be appropriate to its use, lasting in structure, and graceful and pleasing in appearance [*ad usum apta, ad perpetuitatem firmissima, ad gratiam et amoenitatem paratissima*]—the first two have been dealt with, and there remains the third, the noblest and most necessary of all [*omnium dignissima et perquam valde necessaria*]."[2]

The claim that graceful and pleasant appearance is "the noblest and most necessary" part of the triad marks a significant departure from Vitruvius, who made no hierarchical distinction among the three elements. Alberti consolidates this position at the start of the following chapter:

> Now graceful and pleasant appearance, so it is thought, derives from
> beauty and ornament alone, since there can be no one, however surly

or slow, rough or boorish, who would not be attracted to what is most beautiful, seek the finest ornament at the expense of all else, be offended by what is unsightly, shun all that is inelegant or shabby, and feel that any shortcomings an object may have in its ornament will detract equally from its grace and from its dignity.

Most noble is beauty, therefore, and it must be sought most eagerly by anyone who does not wish what he owns to seem distasteful.[3]

As Westfall points out, "Alberti accepted all three conditions [of Vitruvius's triad] (although he substituted the term *aptum* for *utilitatis*)," but in the sixth book, "Alberti abandoned Vitruvius' definition of beauty and with it his terminology. He replaced his own meek 'pleasant and delightful to the sight' with the forthright term beauty (and ornament—pulchritudino et ornamentum), and he proceeded with his definitions."[4] Beauty and ornament thus form the subject of Books VI to IX, with the tenth book reserved for building restoration, damage prevention, and a lengthy discussion of water.

The Functions of Beauty

According to Manetti's account of Nicholas V's deathbed speech, the pope defended his building activity by arguing that it served a serious religious purpose. The minds of ordinary people, he argued, are fickle and inconstant. When they hear learned men explain to them the legitimacy of the church's supreme authority, they will be persuaded—but only for a short time. Later, their belief, based on shallow foundations, will begin to fade away. For this reason, the church must have recourse to large and impressive buildings, ones that look eternal, as though they were built by God. Such sights will serve daily to reinforce the faith in the minds of those who see them.[5]

In *De re aedificatoria*, Alberti advances a somewhat similar argument. However, he is not concerned that buildings should be *magni* but rather that they should be beautiful. The difference is crucial. As we have seen, Alberti critiqued Nicholas's architectural schemes partly on the basis that they were overblown and aimed at a kind of coercion. Beautiful buildings operate in a different way. Beauty, Alberti argues, is the quality that is able to endow both secular and religious institutions with authority, as the ancients clearly understood. "What remarkable importance our ancestors, men of great prudence, attached to it [beauty] is shown," he says, "by the care they took that their legal, military, and religious institutions—indeed, the whole commonwealth—should be much embellished; and by their letting it be known that if all these institutions, without which man could scarce exist, were to be stripped of their pomp and finery, their business would appear insipid and shabby."[6]

Alberti, however, sees the power of beauty as extending well beyond the shoring up of institutional authority, and he develops the argument in a new and radical direction:

> In addition, there is one particular quality that may greatly increase the convenience and even the life of a building. Who would not claim to dwell more comfortably between walls that are ornate, rather than neglected? What other human art might sufficiently protect a building to save it from human attack? Beauty may even influence an enemy, by restraining his anger and so preventing the work from being violated. Thus I might be so bold as to state: No other means is as effective in protecting a work from damage and human injury as is dignity and grace of form. All care, all diligence, all financial consideration must be directed to ensuring that what is built is useful, commodious, yes—but also embellished and wholly graceful, so that anyone seeing it would not feel that the expense might have been invested better elsewhere.[7]

Commenting on this passage, Jan Bialostocki has written, "Thus we learn that beauty and dignity are the best weapons against destruction. It is a truly bold view, quite unknown—as far as I know—in theoretical literature before or after Alberti."[8]

Bialostocki's observation is a crucial one, for Alberti is indeed stating that beauty may protect a building—and presumably, by extension, a city—from attack. He does not state this in the manner of a chance observation or characterize protection as a fortunate but supplementary quality of beauty. Rather, he carefully asserts and then reiterates in the clearest manner possible that no other means is as effective in protecting an architectural work from the enemy. Beauty may be employed as a strategy to combat the threat of destruction, which, I have argued, dominates Alberti's urban thought. Given his assertion that "with Plato I say that it is of the nature of a city to expect that at some point in its history it should be threatened with conquest," his ascription to beauty of the power to calm aggressors must be considered highly significant.

Moreover, this notion of beauty as a remedy against aggression is not merely stated once and then forgotten, for Alberti returns to it on two further occasions. In the eighth book, when discussing funerary monuments, he writes, "It is not quite clear whether monuments intended to last for ever should be built of noble or cheap material, because of the danger of theft. But the ornate certainly delights, and, as we have mentioned already, there is no means more effective in protecting an object and preserving it for posterity."[9] In the final book, he again makes reference to works that "because of their great nobility the barbarians, the raging enemy have spared."[10]

Destruction and Experience

Alberti demonstrates a profound belief in the psychological impact of architectural form in these passages. Yet, as Bialostocki notes, his argument raises a number of difficult questions. "It is startling," he observes, "that Alberti expressed such an opinion, he who wrote the *Descriptio Urbis Romae*, who directed the restoration of many early Christian churches in Rome, and was therefore well acquainted with the fate Roman works of art and architecture, although invested with a superior beauty, had to suffer."[11]

Alberti would have seen evidence of the destruction of such works all over Italy. In *De re aedificatoria*, he lists many buildings of the ancients that had been destroyed and laments the poor condition of some that were still standing.[12] Moreover, he must have been only too aware that beautiful buildings, paintings, and sculptures were regularly damaged or destroyed during his own lifetime as cities were laid siege to and sacked.[13] Constantinople fell in 1453, while Alberti was writing his treatise.[14] Presumably, he would have been familiar with accounts of the destruction that followed. Indeed, the same city provides a good example of how the evidence of sacks and similar phenomena might lead one to take the exactly contrary view to Alberti. Commenting on the Venetian-led sack of Constantinople in 1203, the Byzantine chronicler Niketas Choniates had written, "Not a single structure was spared by these barbarians who were borne by the fates and hated the beautiful."[15]

Bialostocki notes that Alberti mourned the destruction of "our temples, our altars, our theatres" at the hands of the barbarian in the preface to the *Della famiglia*. "This proves that his idea about beauty and dignity as weapons against destruction conveys not so much his experience as his hope. How can it," Bialostocki wonders, "be fitted into Alberti's system of thought?"[16] The question is indeed perplexing, but it should be noted that the physical evidence could be interpreted in more than one way. It is true that the ramshackle and depleted city of fifteenth-century Rome bore powerful witness to an immense destruction—that of both the city itself and the broader Roman world. On the other hand, ancient Rome had not been leveled. Some things still stood, much more in Alberti's day than in our own. When Alberti lamented the destruction of temples and theaters in the *Della famiglia*, his familiarity with Latin literature allowed him a good idea of the kind of structures that had been lost. Nevertheless, beyond the rhetorical context of the *Della famiglia*, he might also have been struck by the fact that those buildings that had survived tended to be monumental in nature, including temples, theaters, and amphitheaters. In other words, it was not, for the most part, *insulae* and other lesser buildings that could still be seen in Rome, but rather those structures that had been constructed with an eye to beauty and dignity.[17]

Beauty and Ornament

However Alberti interpreted the evidence, it is clear that we will need to examine his aesthetic theory in some detail if we are to understand his ideas about the power of architectural beauty. The issue of beauty is addressed directly in *De re aedificatoria*, although the passages that do so tend to be brief. Indeed, Alberti seems somewhat ill at ease when examining beauty itself, no doubt because he felt that a visual matter such as beauty could not be adequately grasped through the medium of words. Following the passage in which he describes the power of beauty to resist attack, he proceeds to provide definitions of beauty and ornament, warning from the start that it is not a topic that lends itself easily to discourse:

> We could perhaps understand the precise nature of beauty and orna-
> ment, and the difference between them, more clearly in the mind
> than my words could explain [*fortassis animo apertius intelligemus quam*

verbis explicari a me possit]. For the sake of brevity, however, let us define them as follows: Beauty is that reasoned harmony [*ratione concinnitas*] of all the parts within a body, so that nothing may be added, taken away, or altered, but for the worse. It is a great and holy matter; all our resources of skill and ingenuity will be taxed in achieving it; and rarely is it granted, even to Nature herself, to produce anything that is entirely complete and perfect in every respect.[18]

It emerges from this that beauty derives from the relationship between the parts of a work, and that relationship should constitute a "reasoned harmony," or *ratione concinnitas*. Beauty is thus an inherent property, essential to the work itself. It will be achieved when it is not possible to add or subtract anything except to the detriment of the work. The achievement of beauty is difficult and will require skill and ingenuity, and its attainment is likened to—or rather actually *is*—the attainment of a kind of perfection. Finally, it is something that will be recognized in the mind—perhaps through visual imagining?—far more easily than it may be understood through language. Following this, Alberti turns to ornament and explains how it differs from beauty:

"How rare," remarks a character in Cicero, "is a beautiful youth in Athens!" That connoisseur found their forms wanting because they either had too much or too little of something by which they failed to conform to the laws of beauty. In this case, unless I am mistaken, had ornament been applied by painting and masking anything ugly, or by grooming and polishing the attractive, it would have had the effect of making the displeasing less offensive and the pleasing more delightful. If this is conceded, ornament may be defined as a form of auxiliary light and complement to beauty. From this it follows, I believe, that beauty is some inherent property, to be found suffused all through the body of that which may be called beautiful; whereas ornament, rather than being inherent, has the character of something attached and additional.[19]

The Rules of Architecture

Alberti's words suggest that beauty ranks higher than ornament, which is something that is applied to enhance a work in which the beauty is in some way deficient. However, as Elisabetta Di Stefano has demonstrated, this hierarchy should not be overstated. As an auxiliary light to beauty, ornament may be understood simultaneously as both additional and integral. Thus, it is able to render the pleasing more delightful.[20] In any case, the production of both beauty and ornament will depend on the architect's adopting a consistent set of principles and proceeding according to reason, as Alberti spells out in the remainder of the chapter:

> Anyone who builds so as to be praised for it—as anyone with good sense would—must adhere to a consistent theory; for to follow a consistent theory is the mark of true art. Who would deny that only through art can correct and worthy building be achieved? And after all this particular part concerning beauty and ornament, being the most important of all, must depend on some sure and consistent method and art, which it would be most foolish to ignore. Yet some would disagree who maintain that beauty, and indeed every aspect of building, is judged by relative and variable criteria, and that the forms of buildings should vary according to individual taste and must not be bound by any rules of art. A common fault, this, among the ignorant— to deny the existence of anything they do not understand. I have decided to correct this error; not that I shall attempt (since I would need detailed and extended argument for it) to explain the arts from their origins, by what reasoning they developed, and by what experience they were nourished; let me simply repeat what has been said, that the arts were born of Chance and Observation, fostered by Use and Experiment, and matured by Knowledge and Reason.[21]

Architecture appears here very much as a *technē*, something that depends on a consistent theory and is open to rational interrogation. Beauty and ornament, which Alberti again characterizes as the most important parts of architecture, must rely on some "sure and consistent method and art" (*certa et constans . . . ratio atque ars*). This statement is advanced in opposition to those who claim otherwise and maintain a kind of aesthetic relativism— whoever they may be. Alberti attacks the notion that the criteria by which the beauty or any other aspect of a building may be judged might be relative. He dismisses the idea that architecture should not be bound by rules and that the forms of buildings should be determined merely by individual taste, and he ascribes these opinions to the ignorant and to those who lack understanding. This position is, of course, fundamental to

Alberti's enterprise since, were it not the case, it would hardly be possible to produce an architectural treatise that was anything more than a technical construction manual or a collection of subjective opinions. Indeed, Alberti's words here sound like a response to actual criticisms that he might have encountered when he let it be known that he intended to produce a treatise that would constitute an all-encompassing theory of edification.[22]

Alberti makes bold claims in these passages and consequently raises our expectations. What, we want to know, *are* the rules of beauty? And what are the nonrelative and invariable criteria by which beauty may be judged? Can Alberti really provide a universally applicable formula that will remain true for every case? Can he even furnish a set of rules that, if we follow them precisely, will guarantee that we will produce something beautiful—despite his having told us that beauty may only be achieved with difficulty and is hard to understand through verbal means? There is also a puzzling aspect to the way that he finishes the chapter. Why, when he declares that he will correct the opinions of the ignorant, does he find it necessary to add that he will not provide a history of the arts from their origins, and why does he then devote the next chapter to a discussion of architecture's development from its beginnings in Asia, through its advancement in Greece, to its ultimate maturity in Italy?

The answers to these questions are not straightforward. We might begin by considering Alberti's brief history of architecture. According to Alberti, architecture first flourished in Asia, where wealthy kings demanded lavish buildings to reflect their exalted status. As the Asians' experience in building grew, they were able to compare one building to another and to "discern differences in number, order, arrangement and exterior appearance. . . . In this way they learned to appreciate the graceful and to spurn the ill-considered."[23] The next phase of development occurred under the Greeks, who examined the buildings of the Egyptians and Assyrians and realized that ingenuity and skill drew more praise than did expenditure of wealth. Consequently, they aimed to display the maximum possible ingenuity in the design of their buildings and looked to nature for their inspiration. Again, they carefully compared one building to another, and they "performed all manner of experiment, surveying and retracing the steps of nature."[24] From this process, they derived many important precepts.

Architecture reached its maturity in Italy, where the Italians also looked to nature and based their buildings on animals. In this way, "they found that grace of form could never be separated or divorced from suitability for use"—an early instance of a kind of functionalist aesthetic. As the dominion of Rome grew, building schemes became ever more ambitious, but opulence was tempered by a natural frugality. Alberti explains, "Their concern and enthusiasm for building continued unbroken, until eventually they probed so thoroughly into the art that there was nothing so recondite, concealed, or abstruse as not to have been explored, traced out, or brought to light."[25] They strove to endow every structure they built with beauty, even down to the drains. The Romans were assisted in this not only by the knowledge that they obtained from the Greeks but also by many excellent precepts that were handed down to them by the native Italian Etruscans.

The purpose of this narrative—aside from its patriotic intent—is to show that the principles on which ancient Roman buildings were constructed were derived over many centuries by many thousands of architects. They are the fruits of endless consideration and comparison of different buildings and their components, of a constant striving for ingenuity, of the investigation and imitation of nature, and of empirical experimentation and reasoned criticism. The precepts that guided ancient Roman architects, in other words, were precious and hard-won, the results of centuries of collaborative work—things that no individual could ever hope to deduce from scratch.

In the first chapter of the sixth book, Alberti says that he "grieved that so many works of such brilliant writers had been destroyed by the hostility of time and of man, and that almost the sole survivor from this vast shipwreck is Vitruvius, an author of unquestioned experience, though one whose writings have been so corrupted by time that there are many omissions and many shortcomings."[26] Famously, Alberti goes on to attack Vitruvius's style and his mixture of Greek and Latin terminology, finally concluding that since Vitruvius's treatise is incomprehensible, it can be of no practical use. The precious precepts that guided ancient architects have therefore, in their verbal form, been lost—swept away in the apocalyptic destruction of ancient culture. They are still, however, obtainable from ancient buildings. Indeed, Alberti notes, "examples of ancient temples and theatres have survived that may teach us as much as any professor, but I see—not without sorrow—these very buildings being despoiled more each day. And anyone who happens to build nowadays draws his inspiration from inept modern nonsense rather than proven and much commended methods. Nobody would deny that as a result of all this a whole section of our life and learning could disappear altogether."[27]

This lamentable state of affairs, Alberti tells us, is what caused him to press ahead with his treatise. His own recovery of the principles of ancient architecture was achieved with difficulty and effort, since in the absence of reliable texts he had to derive his knowledge from the analysis of buildings. He carefully examined any ancient building that attracted admiration and "never stopped exploring, considering, and measuring everything, and comparing the information through line drawings [*lineamenta picturae*], until I had grasped and understood fully what each had to contribute in terms of ingenuity or skill."[28] Thus, when Alberti speaks of rules that must be followed, he is mostly referring to the rules that he has derived from Roman buildings—the same rules that the ancients honed throughout the centuries. Alberti ends his brief history of architecture by emphasizing exactly this point. "Through the example of our ancestors . . . and through the advice of experts and constant practice on our part," he asserts, "thorough understanding may be gained on how to construct marvelous buildings, and from that understanding well-proven principles may be deduced; rules that should not be ignored by anyone eager—as we all should be—not to appear inept in what he builds. These we must set down, as was our undertaking, and explain to the best of our ability."[29]

This returns us to our earlier question: Of what kind are the rules that Alberti says we must follow, and are there precise rules for the creation of beauty? Will Alberti furnish us with a precise set of measurements and describe how every single detail must be arranged in, say, the building of a basilica? Or will he provide general principles that are capable of guiding us in any particular instance? The answers to the last two questions are yes and no: "These principles either direct every aspect of beauty and ornament throughout the building or relate individually to its various parts," Alberti writes. "The former are derived from philosophy, and are concerned with establishing the direction and limits to this art; the latter come from the experience of which we spoke, but are honed, so to speak, to the rule of philosophy and plot the course of this art. These latter ones have a more technical character, and I shall deal with them first, saving the former more general rules for an epilogue."[30]

Alberti will, in fact, provide a multitude of rules that concern the individual parts of a building. Columns, for example—the "principal ornament" in the entire *res aedificatoria*—will be the subject of extensive discussion, with precise rules regarding bases, shafts (length, width, entasis, and so forth), and capitals. These rules include specific measurements, mathematical proportions, and geometric forms. The same goes for entablatures and all manner of other architectural features. So important did Alberti consider precision to be in these matters that he twice asks that the copyist use words rather than numerals when describing measurements, so as to avoid any errors. To this degree, Alberti provides rules that we can—and indeed should—follow if we are to create beautiful buildings. On the other hand, there is another type of rule concerning beauty—general rules that, Alberti says, are derived from philosophy. Even if they ultimately guide the precise, technical rules, the general rules are less tangible and altogether harder to define. They do not concern the individual parts but the entire work, including, presumably, the overall arrangement of the parts. Discussion of the general rules is put off until the ninth book.

It has sometimes been remarked on that despite Alberti's ranking of ornament as subsidiary to beauty, it is nevertheless to ornament that the titles of Books VI to IX refer.[31] Perhaps this should not surprise us, since one is on firmer ground providing fixed rules regarding the parts of columns than rules concerning beauty in general. Are we thus to understand Alberti's division of rules into two types as corresponding to the division between beauty and ornament? Do the specific, technical rules that relate to the parts of buildings govern ornament, while the general philosophical rules concern only beauty? Again, the answers seem to be yes and no. By far, the majority of the specific measurements and other details that Alberti provides relate directly to ornament. On the other hand, when he explains how to determine the plan of a building, he clearly approaches the issue of beauty since he is, in fact, defining essential aspects of the building itself.

However, beauty must result from a type of perfection that includes all of the parts—every aspect—of the building. As such, it can ultimately be the result only of rules of the general, philosophical variety. And Alberti has, in fact, already supplied one of these, or at least a criterion by which beauty can be recognized: the work should be such that nothing may be added to or removed from it, except to its detriment. Whether Alberti's maxim is of any practical use in the process of architectural design is thus debatable. Ultimately, it simply begs the question of how we are to recognize what is better and what is worse.[32]

Ornament

As we have seen, Alberti defines ornament as something additional, something that may be used to remedy any defects in the inherent beauty of a building. This being the case, it follows that a good building will likely be restrained in its ornamentation, for if it is well made, its beauty will need little enhancing. Alberti is understandably cautious regarding opulence and lavishness. His own argument demands this of him, as did his cultural and intellectual background. Condemnation of luxury, opulence, and the excessive ostentation of wealth were constants in the writings of ancient moralists and the contemporary sermons of preachers. These sentiments gained legal expression in sumptuary law and popular expression in bonfires of the vanities. The connection between opulence and excess on the one hand, and parsimony and rectitude on the other, was so standard as to hardly require stating.[33] As Alberti observes, "I notice that the most prudent and modest of our ancestors much preferred frugality and parsimony in building as in any other matter, public or private, judging that all extravagance on the part of the citizen ought to be prevented and checked, and that both admonitions and laws were issued to this end with the utmost vigor and persistence."[34]

As we might expect, Alberti pays close attention to issues of decorum and is critical of inappropriate building materials and excessive displays of wealth. Naturally, this relates to a hierarchy of building types—perilous waters that Alberti himself had to navigate in the course of his own career as an architect. Private buildings should not, in general, outshine public ones, nor secular outdo sacred. These were live issues in Italian city-states, especially in Florence with its republican constitution. We might consider Cosimo de' Medici's rejection of Brunelleschi's scheme for the Medici palace, apparently on the basis that it would have aroused envy. Perhaps it was not simply the size of Brunelleschi's project that disturbed. It could also have been that the architect's design diverged very conspicuously from that of other palaces in the city. Perhaps it was articulated by *all'antica*-style orders. Maybe it even incorporated expensive stones or marble. Alberti, of course, did build a palace façade in Florence with pilasters and other *all'antica* features, as well as with elements that referred to Florentine tradition and also to the Palazzo Medici. In the same city, he completed one of the Renaissance's most prominent colored marble facades at Santa Maria Novella.

One gains a sense of the real delicacy of the issue of ornamenting private buildings when Alberti addresses the subject in Book IX:

> Everything is best when it is tempered to its own importance. And if you want my advice, I would rather the private houses of the wealthy were wanting in things that might contribute to their ornament, than have the more modest and thrifty accuse them of luxury in any way. Nevertheless, the need to hand down to posterity a reputation for both wisdom and power is universally accepted (for that reason, as Thucydides said, we build great works, so as to appear great in the eyes of our descendants); equally we decorate our property as much to distinguish family and country as for any personal display (and who would deny this to be the responsibility of a good citizen?).[35]

The serpentine nature of Alberti's discourse here testifies to the sensitivity of the subject. He was not altogether against opulent materials, even in private building, provided that they were used sparingly. Of course, temples could be accorded the greatest license, yet even here Alberti notes that opinions vary. Some advocated making the temple as opulent as it could possibly be. On the other hand,

> Cicero follows Plato's teaching, and holds that citizens should be compelled by law to reject any variety and frivolity in the ornament of their temples, and to value purity above all else. "Let us have," he added, "some dignity for all that."
> I could easily believe that in their choice of color, as in their way of life, purity and simplicity would be most pleasing to the gods above; nor should a temple contain anything to divert the mind away from religious meditation toward sensual attraction and pleasure. Yet, to my mind, with temples as with other public buildings, provided it in no way diminishes their solemnity, it is thoroughly commendable to attempt to execute wall, roof, and flooring skillfully and elegantly, and to make them as durable as possible.[36]

Famously, Alberti proposes the use of darkness and candlelight to create a sense of awe.[37]

The position that Alberti takes most frequently is that ingenuity trumps expenditure and should be the most sought-after quality in architecture.

He clearly favors moderation, with varying degrees of license being considered appropriate to different building types. "If I were to sum up the whole question," he concludes, "I would say that sacred buildings ought to be so designed that nothing further may be added to enhance their majesty or cause greater admiration for their beauty; the private building, on the other hand, must be so treated that it will not seem possible to remove anything, because everything has been put together with great dignity. To the others, that is, the profane public, must be left, I feel, a position midway between these two."[38] This adaptation of Alberti's own maxim does not cohere particularly well with his earlier definition of beauty, but it nonetheless effectively conveys his position.

Ornamenting the City

Alberti's principles regarding ornament seem mostly to have been formulated with buildings in mind. However, he does address the ornamentation of the city as a whole, albeit briefly, at the start of Book VII. At issue is the arrangement of buildings in such a way as to enhance the appearance of both the city and its surrounding region. "Plato," he notes, "preferred the urban center and the surrounding countryside to be divided into twelve districts, each with its own temple or chapel. For our part, we would also include crossroad altars, courts for lesser judgments, garrisons, racecourses and recreation grounds, and other similar facilities, provided sufficient homes flourish in the surrounding countryside to warrant them."[39]

While the site should be taken into account and even an abundance of citizens may act as an ornament, it is ultimately the arrangement of parts that is judged all important. Just as Quintilian recommends for a well-crafted speech, cities should be regulated by *ordo*. "The principal ornament to any city," writes Alberti, "lies in the siting, layout, composition, and arrangement of its roads, squares, and individual works: each must be properly planned and distributed according to use, importance, and convenience. For without order there can be nothing commodious, graceful, or noble."[40]

This leads Alberti into a discussion of zoning, which we have already touched on. In the course of his treatment of public buildings—both sacred and profane—he examines many things that relate to the fundamental structure of the city: walls, watchtowers, gates, roads, bridges, and fora, among others. Sometimes his maxims are of a general nature, such as his recommendation that "apart from being properly paved and thoroughly clean, the roads within a city should be elegantly lined with porticoes of equal lineaments, and houses that are matched by line and level.[41]

At other times, Alberti is far more specific. The contemporary forum, for example, should be a double square, surrounded by a portico with a height of not more than a third, and not less than two-sevenths, of the width of the forum. The height of the base of the portico should be one-fifth of the portico's width, and so on. The best place for an arch will be at the meeting of a royal road (*via regia*) and a forum or square. Alberti describes such arches, along with towers and other structures, in detail.[42] There is much that could be taken from the books on ornament, especially Books VII and VIII, if one were to attempt to build an "Albertian" city. Alberti includes some fairly specific recommendations regarding streets and other urban infrastructure, as well as their design and arrangement. Yet even here, he does not offer an ideal city but rather provides a set of rules and maxims that could, in truth, serve for the building and planning of numerous different cities.

Beauty

So much, as Alberti might have said, for ornament. In the fifth chapter of the ninth book, he finally returns to the subject of beauty, the investigation of which is described as very difficult:

> Now I come to a matter with which we have promised to deal all along: every kind of beauty and ornament consists of it; or, to put it more clearly, it springs from every rule of beauty. This is an extremely difficult inquiry; for whatever that one entity is, which is either extracted or drawn from the number and nature of all the parts, or imparted to each by sure and constant method, or handled in such a manner as to tie and bond several elements into a single bundle or body, according to a true and consistent agreement and sympathy [*recta et stabili cohesione atque consensu*]—and something of this kind is exactly what we seek—then surely that entity must share some part of the force and juice, as it were, of all the elements of which it is composed or blended [*aut coherescat aut immisceatur*]; for otherwise their discord and differences would cause conflict and disunity.[43]

If this is a difficult matter in most fields, Alberti continues, it is especially so in architecture, which is by nature a complex discipline involving the arrangement of a great many parts. He will proceed by examining beauty in nature. "The great experts of antiquity," he observes, "have instructed us that a building is very like an animal, and that Nature must be imitated when we delineate it. Let us investigate, then, why some bodies that Nature produces may be called beautiful, others less beautiful, and even ugly."[44]

Alberti goes on to say that things of entirely different appearance may be deemed equally beautiful, making it obvious that there is no single form of beauty. Nonetheless, beauty is not merely a subjective quality:

> When you make judgments on beauty, you do not follow mere fancy, but the workings of a reasoning faculty that is inborn in the mind. It is clearly so, since no one can look at anything shameful, deformed, or disgusting without immediate displeasure and aversion. What arouses and provokes such a sensation in the mind we shall not inquire in detail, but shall limit our consideration to whatever evidence presents itself that is relevant to our argument. For within the form and figure of a building there resides some natural excellence and perfection that excites the mind and is immediately recognized by it. I myself believe that form, dignity, grace, and other such qualities depend on it, and as soon as anything is removed or altered, these qualities are themselves weakened and perish. Once we are convinced of this, it will not take long to discuss what may be removed, enlarged, or altered, in the form and figure. For every body consists entirely of parts that are fixed and individual; if these are removed, enlarged, reduced, or transferred somewhere inappropriate, the very composition will be spoiled that gives the body its seemly appearance.

Everything that Alberti says here is entirely consistent with the principles outlined in Book VI. He now places particular emphasis on the natural capacity of human beings to recognize and be excited by beauty and excellence and to recoil from the ugly. This is not, Alberti stresses, the result of whimsy, but of a reasoning faculty that he appears to consider universal. From what he has said already, he asserts, it is clear that "the three principal components of the whole theory into which we inquire are number [*numerus*], what we might call outline [*finitio*], and position [*collocatio*]."[45] Beauty, then, is a matter of finding a perfect balance with regard to the number of parts, the defined shape of these parts, and the position in which they are placed. But this is not the whole story. There remains something that arises from the "composition" and "connection" of these three: "a further quality in which beauty shines full face: our term for this is *concinnitas*; which we say is nourished with every grace and splendor. It is the task and aim of *concinnitas* to compose parts that are quite separate from each other by their nature, according to some precise rule, so that they correspond to one another in appearance."[46]

The term *concinnitas* has been the subject of much debate by scholars. Its exact meaning has been disputed, and there seems to be no adequate translation into English or indeed any language; hence it is often left in the original Latin.[47] It is an example of Alberti once again taking a word from rhetoric and applying it to architecture, for Cicero uses it on several occasions to describe a well-composed speech.[48] Robert Tavernor argues that Alberti was combining two terms used by Vitruvius, *symmetria* and *dispositio*, under a single heading. Nonetheless, he warns that *concinnitas* cannot be interpreted as merely equivalent to these and says that this assumption has led some scholars astray.[49] Indeed, Alberti himself may have understood *concinnitas* in a number of senses, for he uses the word throughout his writings, including in vernacular works where it appears in the Italianized form *concinnità*. Often the context is different and the meaning is open to two or more interpretations.[50] In *De re aedificatoria*, however, Alberti clearly invests the term with great significance, for he writes,

> When the mind is reached by way of sight or sound, or any other means, *concinnitas* is instantly recognized. It is our nature to desire the best, and to cling to it with pleasure. Neither in the whole body nor in its parts does *concinnitas* flourish as much as it does in Nature herself; thus I might call it the spouse of the soul and of reason. It has a vast range in which to exercise itself and bloom—it runs through man's entire life and government, it molds the whole of Nature. Everything that Nature produces is regulated by the law of *concinnitas*, and her chief concern is that whatever she produces should be absolutely perfect. Without *concinnitas* this could hardly be achieved, for the critical sympathy of the parts would be lost.[51]

Alberti thus extends the significance of concinnitas well beyond the boundaries of architecture to the entire world. It regulates the perfect harmony between different entities, not just in the physical sense but in all things: "It runs through man's entire life and government." In terms of architecture, then, concinnitas is that perfect harmony among all the parts that derives from nature. Alberti confirms this by stating, "If this is accepted, let us conclude as follows. Beauty is a form of sympathy and consonance of the parts within a body, according to definite number, outline, and position, as dictated by *concinnitas*, the absolute and fundamental rule in nature. This is the main object of the art of building, and the source of her dignity, charm, authority, and worth."[52]

Architecture and Nature

Of particular interest is Alberti's insistence that the rules of architecture are taken from nature. Indeed, concinnitas, which is "the main object of the art of building," is itself "the fundamental rule in Nature." As we have seen, Alberti claims that ancient architects were guided by nature and that the Romans based their buildings on animals.[53] The orders are the product of the study of nature, as is their correct application:

> They realized that numbers were either odd or even; they employed both, but the even in some places, the odd in others. Taking their example from Nature, they never made the bones of the building, meaning the columns, angles, and so on, odd in number—for you will not find a single animal that stands or moves upon an odd number of feet. Conversely, they never made openings even in number; this they evidently learned from Nature: to animals she has given ears, eyes, and nostrils matching on either side, but in the center, single and obvious, she has set the mouth.[54]

For a building to be beautiful, it should therefore imitate nature.[55] Presumably, the same goes for the city as a whole. In many ways, this is not surprising. It coheres well with the praise of the country found in many of Alberti's works and with his descriptions of the delightful surroundings of villas. Indeed, among the pleasures of being at the villa is not only that one is surrounded by nature but also that one may enjoy the aesthetic qualities of a prospect on a distant landscape. In the *Della famiglia*, Alberti's characters speak straightforwardly of "natura, cioè Iddio." Then again, we saw that nature could also be a harsh and oppositional force, especially as it appears in the *Theogenius* and some parts of *De re aedificatoria* and *Momus*. This binary view is, of course, typical of medieval thinking, which tended to differentiate between a *natura naturans* and a *natura naturata*. Clearly, where Alberti characterizes nature as containing the fundamental principles of architectural design, it is nature as a giver of norms that is being evoked. This is nature of the perfect and, so to speak, "unfallen" kind. In any case, as we have seen, man's problems with nature appear to be mostly the fault of man. In Alberti's thinking, nature's perfection remains mostly constant.[56] However, this position is perhaps not fully resolved, and this too is unsurprising since a kind of unresolved dualism is inherent in medieval thought regarding nature, and in a great deal of modern thought as well.

Flowers and Stones

Nature's relationship with architecture is not unproblematic. While these two entities might, in *De re*, exist in harmony, in *Momus* they enter into opposition. The issue finds its clearest expression in two exchanges between Gelastus and Charon during their journey through the world.[57] Charon, who has spent all of his time in the gloom of the underworld, is overwhelmed by the beauty of nature:

> Charon's senses—his sight, hearing and other senses—were unbelievably acute. So when the fragrance of the flowers that filled the meadow reached his nostrils, he felt so much pleasure and wonder in gathering and contemplating those flowers that he could hardly be torn away from them. But Gelastus warned that they had too long a journey ahead of them for Charon to indulge in the childish pleasure of picking flowers. They had far more important things to do, and the mortals had so many flowers that they trod them under foot even when they didn't want to. This was the last thing Charon wanted to hear, but he thought he should obey his guide.
>
> So they forged on. Charon feasted his eyes on the pleasant variety of nature, on the hills, valleys, springs, rivers, lakes and other similar features, and began to ask Gelastus from what source this great abundance of precious things had come into the world.[58]

Gelastus seizes upon the chance to treat Charon to a philosophical demonstration, but it leaves the ferryman utterly cold. What a complicated way, he comments, to explain something so simple. Eventually, they arrive at the city and make their way to the great theater that stands there. As we may remember, Jupiter had decided to destroy the world and replace it with a better version. In preparation for this destruction, all manner of misfortunes had been visited on humanity. The great number of shades who consequently arrived at the Acheron had prompted Charon's visit to the world in the first place. Meanwhile, mankind had reacted to these misfortunes by constructing a huge theater to appease the gods. This was a fantastic work of architecture—vast, richly ornamented in the most elaborate manner, and filled with giant columns of Parian marble and statues of every god:

> When they reached the middle of the theatre, Gelastus said, "So, Charon, what do you think?" Charon answered that the theatre and its decorations were nothing compared with the flowers he'd picked in the meadow. He professed himself amazed at how men placed more value on things that the vilest hands could accomplish, rather than on things that defied understanding. "You spurn flowers," he said; "shall we admire stones? Everything about a flower is beautiful and pleasing [*in flore ad venustatem, ad gratiam omnia conveniunt*]. In these man-made constructions, you won't find anything wondrous apart from the wondrous extravagance of misplaced labor."[59]

Nature, then, exemplified by the flowers of the meadow, is seen as the source of true beauty. Its simplicity contrasts sharply with both the discourse of men and the things that they build. Thus, it is a poor reflection on human beings that they pay no attention to the flowers but are impressed by great buildings. Despite the enormous effort that goes into the construction of such buildings, these structures can in no way match the beauty of nature, as expressed in a single small flower.[60] Indeed, buildings of this kind are really monuments to wasted effort. Notably, while this passage can be understood in a very literal sense, there is surely also an analogy at work between grandiose buildings and the complex arguments constructed by Gelastus.

First and foremost, however, there appears to be a serious condemnation of architecture here. Moreover, it is one that finds a kind of echo in *De re*. In the second chapter of Book VI—the crucial chapter in which Alberti gives his definition of beauty and says that it might protect a building from attack—he also praises flowers. "When we gaze at the wondrous works of the heavenly gods," he argues, "we admire the beauty we see, rather than the utility that we recognize. Need I go further? Nature herself, as is everywhere plain to see, does not desist from basking in a daily orgy of beauty— let the hues of her flowers serve as my example."[61] If this sounds close to *Momus*, so does what follows: "But if this quality is desirable anywhere, surely it cannot be absent from buildings, without offending experienced and inexperienced alike. What would be our reaction to a deformed and ill-considered pile of stones, other than the more to criticize it the greater the expense, and to condemn the wanton greed for piling up stones? To have satisfied necessity is trite and insignificant, to have catered to convenience unrewarding when the inelegance in a work causes offense."[62]

Just as in *Momus*, there is a kind of comparison drawn between flowers and stones. Flowers appear supremely beautiful, while misplaced ideas have caused stones to be piled up wastefully. It is one of the instances in which one senses most clearly a direct form of dialogue between the contemporary *Momus* and *De re*. Indeed, the passage in *De re* helps to illuminate Charon's harsh criticisms. Presumably the real problem with the theater is that it is not good architecture in the Albertian sense. It relies on vastness, opulence, and expense to achieve its impact, perhaps lacking the true beauty of concinnitas.[63] In this sense, it could even be considered a *lapidum strues informi et inconcinna*, an expression of the arrogance and perversity of mortals. Of course, it is not only the mortals who are impressed. The gods are also awed by the theater—but then again, in *Momus* the gods mostly appear stupid, corrupt, venal, and lacking in real understanding.

Charon's cutting remarks thus should not be considered a condemnation of architecture per se, but of bad, vainglorious architecture. Nonetheless, they leave an aftertaste of uncertainty, a lingering doubt as to whether buildings can ever really equal the perfection of nature. Indeed, one might question why building should be undertaken in the first place, since the perfection that it aspires to already exists in nature. In Book IX of *De re*, Alberti explains how the architect must ensure that the most minute elements of a building "are so arranged in their level, alignment, number, shape, and appearance that right matches left, top matches bottom, adjacent matches adjacent, and equal matches equal." Following this maxim, he observes, the ancients sometimes decorated their buildings with identical statues, "so similar to one another that we might claim that here nature herself has been surpassed; since never in her works do we see so much as one nose identical to another."[64] However, even if Alberti is being entirely serious, the case is a marginal one. In the normal run of things, nature will not be surpassed.

Cathedrals and Groves

At this point, we might think back to Agnolo Pandolfini's description of Florence Cathedral. As Christine Smith has pointed out, it is the only praise—in fact, the only architectural criticism—of a modern building that Alberti has left to us. In this passage, too, there is an analogy with nature, as Agnolo observes that "here is the constant home of temperateness, as of springtime: outside, wind, ice and frost; here inside one is protected from the wind, here mild air and quiet. Outside, the heat of summer and autumn; inside coolness."[65] This *nido delle delizie* recreates the qualities of a benevolent, natural *locus amoenus*, a refuge in which there is constant spring. Strikingly, it serves as a protection against another type of nature, now conceived of in its inimical form. The well-considered and beautiful cathedral is, appropriately enough, able to constitute something like a prefallen nature. The balance and moderation of its design produce a temperate environment that contrasts with the extremes of heat and cold outside. Of course, the cathedral must also be a refuge from the surrounding extremes of the city.

Interestingly, while Alberti begins the *Profugiorum* by describing building in natural terms, he opens his earlier dialogue, the *Theogenius*, in the opposite way, discussing nature in terms of architecture. Teogenio says,

> But let us sit, if so it pleases you, here among these myrtles, a place no less delightful than your most vast and sumptuous theaters and temples [*i vostri teatri e templi amplissimi e suntuosissimi*]. Here there are columns fashioned by nature inasmuch as you see most upright trees. Here, from the sun above, we are covered by the most joyous shade of these beeches and firs, and hereabouts, wherever you turn, you see a thousand most perfect colors of various flowers, interwoven among the green, shine forth in the shade and outdo the great luster and brightness of the sky; and from whatever direction the breeze moves toward you, from there you will sense the sweetest odors come to please you. And then the gaiety of these little birds, which you see

in your presence with their most painted and ornate plumes—who would not be delighted by them? How beautiful are these creatures which from time to time come to greet me with new songs praising the heavens! And this neighboring pure and silver spring, witness and judge in part to my own studies, always helps me forward, inasmuch as it winds coaxingly about me; now hiding itself among the foliage of these most fresh and charming little grasses, now with its waves raising itself and sweetly murmuring, beautiful to behold, it bows and greets me again. Now very happy and most calm, it opens itself to me, and suffers that I gaze at and contemplate myself in it. Furthermore, here no jealous person, no bad-mouther, no false deprecator—here, nobody wicked perturb, our peace and quiet. But let us sit down.[66]

The motif of the flowers as expressions of nature's absolute beauty is used again here, but this time, Alberti extends the description to the trees, the birds, the grass, and the stream. Once again, this environment is a refuge, in part from physical forces (it shades from the sun) but mostly from the terrible ways of other men, from envy and bad-mouthing. It is primarily a refuge from the city.

However, this grove is also clearly analogous to a building, with its "columns fashioned by nature" and its natural decoration. Indeed, in the comparison of the grove to "vast and sumptuous theaters and temples," there is an implied contrast between natural beauty and grand architectural schemes, which is close to that articulated by Charon. Presumably, a building such as Florence Cathedral is qualitatively the opposite of the grand theater that Charon so disdains, and stands instead as an example of good architecture—one that embodies the properties of Teogenio's grove. Hence it is able to serve as a refuge, both from harsh natural forces and from the negative aspects of the city. Unlike the theater described in *Momus*, it is a building that remains within natural limits. If the entire city were to be constructed according to these same principles, we might speculate, the urban situation would be very different.

Beauty and Rhetoric

We have already seen how living in the country might benefit the mental health of an individual and how, conversely, living in the city might endanger it. This would seem to be good enough reason to construct the city according to natural principles. However, it does not fully illuminate Alberti's remarks that beauty has the power to save buildings from destruction. Does his claim imply that beauty is able to exert the power of persuasion? If so, should we consider Alberti's concept of beauty to be analogous to rhetoric? Like all humanists, Alberti was highly engaged with the subject of rhetoric. His knowledge of the Latin orators was profound, and in his writings he demonstrated that he was himself an expert practitioner. As Christine Smith has shown, his praise of Florence Cathedral is a rhetorical structure of some sophistication, and Michael Baxandall famously demonstrated the centrality of rhetorical ideas in *De pictura*. The word *concinnitas* itself, as employed by Cicero, is a rhetorical term, as are many of the other terms used by Alberti to develop his aesthetic theories.[67]

Christine Smith has argued that Alberti was inspired by Christian rhetoric, as conceived of by Saint Augustine. This type of eloquence sought to persuade men to forsake vice for virtue by appealing to the emotions. She points to Alberti's description of the temple in *De re aedificatoria* as a building that seeks to move the soul of the one who experiences it, in a manner that is fully consistent with Augustine's principles:

> There is no doubt that a temple that delights the mind wonderfully, captivates it with grace and admiration, will greatly encourage piety. To the ancients a people seemed to be truly pious when the temples of the gods were crowded.
>
> This is why I would wish the temple so beautiful that nothing more decorous could ever be devised; I would deck it out in every part so that anyone who entered it would start with awe for his admiration at all the noble things, and could scarcely restrain himself from exclaiming that what he saw was a place undoubtedly worthy of God.[68]

The profound impact of the properly ornamented and sufficiently beautiful temple on the spectator perhaps sheds light on why Alberti believed that architectural beauty could save a work from attack. A beautiful building would be able to exercise the power of persuasion over an enraged enemy. Its effect might be like the most persuasive eloquence, addressed to the emotions, where it seeks to overwhelm the soul with pleasure and a sense of moral purpose. In that way, a beautiful building could perform a range of didactic functions: instilling piety, recommending virtue over vice, perhaps even calming an aggressor.

It is interesting that one of the very first claims in Augustine's *De civitate Dei* is that even the barbarians were respectful of the holy Christian places and that those who took shelter within them were spared:

> The shrines of the martyrs and the churches of the apostles are our witnesses; for during the sack of the city they sheltered those who fled to them: both their own people and strangers. Thus far the bloodthirsty foe raged, but no farther. There, his savage fury acknowledged its limit, and those of the enemy who were merciful conducted thither those whom they had spared.... Indeed, whenever those savage men, who elsewhere raged in the usual fashion of an enemy, came to the place where what the rules of war would have permitted elsewhere was forbidden, all the ferocity with which they smote was curbed, and their greed for captives subdued.[69]

According to Augustine, such a thing was unknown in any previous war. It is difficult to substantiate the truth of these claims, but the logic would seem to be that the barbarians (who were themselves Christians, albeit Arians) recognized something inherently good in the Christian places. It is as though the spirit of Christianity was a sort of universal language, able to speak to all men across whatever divisions existed between them. In the same way, it would seem that Alberti considered beauty to be a kind of common language, or perhaps something that intervened *prior* to language. And Alberti does, of course, refer to beauty as *hoc divinum*.

Beauty and Music

Clearly, there is an analogy between the well-composed building and the well-composed speech. Alberti's aesthetic theory in *De re aedificatoria* can indeed be related to rhetorical concepts, but not exclusively. There is also a Pythagorean and even a Platonic element in Alberti's ideas, though by no means can he be considered a "Neo-Platonist."[70] It is the Pythagorean to which I would like to turn now.

Alberti names Pythagoras only twice in his treatise, and one of those times is simply to describe one of his students. The second mention of

Pythagoras is more significant. In the course of a discussion of *finitio*, he writes, "For us, the outline is a certain correspondence between the lines that define the dimensions; one dimension being length, another breadth, and the third height. The method of defining the outline is best taken from those objects in which Nature offers herself to our inspection and admiration as we view and examine them. I affirm again with Pythagoras: it is absolutely certain that Nature is wholly consistent. That is how things stand." Alberti then explains how music embodies ideal, harmonic relationships that are also applicable to architecture, asserting that "the very same numbers that cause sounds to have that *concinnitas*, pleasing to the ears, can also fill the eyes and mind with wondrous delight. From musicians therefore who have already examined such numbers thoroughly, or from those objects in which Nature has displayed some evident and noble quality, the whole method of outlining is derived. But I shall dwell on this topic no longer than is relevant to the business of the architect. Let us therefore pass over what relates to the modulations of a single voice or the rules of the tetrachord."[71]

Alberti goes on to describe musical relationships in some detail and says that "architects employ all these numbers in the most convenient manner possible: they use them in pairs, as in laying out a forum, place, or open space, where only two dimensions are considered, width and length; and they use them also in threes, such as in a public sitting room, senate house, hall, and so on, when width relates to length, and they want the height to relate harmoniously to both."[72] Alberti, of course, claims in the *Vita* to be an accomplished musician, and one of the characters in his *Profugiorum* refers to him as such. None of the musical theory to which he refers, however, relates to contemporary practice. It is all derived from ancient sources.

Pythagoras is well known for his belief that music could stir human emotions, and it is said that he demonstrated his theory in practice. He used music to treat physical conditions as well as negative emotions, including grief, anger, pity, envy, fear, depression, torpor, and violence.[73] Different emotions were to be treated with different rhythms and melodies, using above all the correct musical mode. Saint Basil describes how Pythagoras was able to halt a drunken revel simply by commanding the flute player to change to the Doric mode. The company quickly sobered up and skulked home, feeling ashamed.[74] Iamblichus tells a similar story of Pythagoras's ability to calm drunkenness and also details how Empedokles was able to avert a murder by calming passions with music.[75] Similar anecdotes regarding Pythagoras, such as his pacifying an enraged dictator with a song, would have been known to Alberti. We should also note Alberti's recounting of the belief that the bite of the tarantula could be cured by music:

> [The bites] may be treated with a remedy of Theophrastus, who maintained that snakebites could be healed by the sound of the flute. Musicians caress the ears of the afflicted with various forms of harmony, and when they hit the right one, the victim will leap up as though startled, and then, through joy, straining every nerve and muscle, will keep time to the music in whatever manner takes his fancy. Some of the victims will, as you may see, try to dance, others to sing, while others will exert themselves attempting whatever their passion and frenzy dictate, until they are exhausted; they continue to sweat for several days more, and only recover when the madness, which had taken root, has been totally satiated.[76]

This emphasis on musical harmony caressing the ears of the afflicted and calming their madness is reminiscent of the Old Testament story of David, who was able, by playing his lyre, to relieve Saul from the effects of the evil spirit sent by God to torment him. David, of course, became a great builder, constructing the city of Zion on God's orders.

There are further examples of music affecting the passions that may have influenced Alberti, not least the stories of Orpheus and Amphion. Orpheus's adventures were particularly well known, for they occur in both Virgil's *Georgics* and Ovid's *Metamorphoses*. Among the most popular episodes of Orpheus's life were his playing music to the animals and his journey into the underworld to retrieve his wife, Eurydice. Virgil describes his descent thus:

> Even the jaws of Taenarum he braved,
> Those lofty portals of the Underworld,
> And entering the gloomy grove of terror
> Approached the shades and their tremendous king,
> Hard hearts no human prayer can hope to soften.
> His music shook them: drawn from the very depths
> Of Erbus came insubstantial shades,
> The phantoms of the lightless. . . .
>
> .   .   .   .

... More than this,
The very halls of Death and inmost dens
Of Tartarus were awestruck, and the Furies,
Their dark-blue locks entwined with writhing snakes;
Cerberus stood with his three mouths agape,
And the gale that drives Ixion's wheel was stilled.[77]

Orpheus was able to enter into Hades unharmed because of the power of his music. He even overcame the hard-hearted Pluto, who remained untouched by any prayer, and pacified Cerberus himself. Indeed, all horrors of the underworld were temporarily suspended; Ixion's wheel stood still, and for a moment, hell ceased to be hellish.[78]

Orpheus remained a popular character in medieval literature, although he does not appear in Renaissance art as much as one might expect.[79] He was often associated with Amphion, whose myth is less documented in classical sources but was regularly repeated in medieval texts. Amphion was often credited with the invention of music; the best-known story about him related how he had built the walls of Thebes by charming the stones into place with the power of his music. In discussing these two characters, medieval writers often used language that is strikingly similar to Alberti's passage regarding the power of architectural beauty to pacify an enraged enemy. Macrobius, for example, associating the mythical musicians with Pythagorean ideas, says,

Every soul in this world is allured by musical sounds so that not only those who are more refined in their habits, but all the barbarous peoples as well, have adopted songs by which they are inflamed with courage or wooed to pleasure; for the soul carries with it into the body a memory of the music which it knew in the sky [that is, the music of the spheres], and is so captivated by its charm that there is no breast so cruel or savage as not to be gripped by the spell of such an appeal. This, I believe, was the origin of the stories of Orpheus and Amphion, one of whom was said to have enticed the dumb beasts by his song, the other the rocks. They were perchance the first to attract in their song men lacking any refinement and stolid as rocks, and to instill in them a feeling of joy. Thus every disposition of the soul is controlled by a song. For instance, the signal for marching into battle and for leaving off battle is in one case a tune that arouses the martial spirit and in the other one that quiets it.[80]

The idea that music could win over the most cruel and savage people was thus well established. We should at this point recall Alberti's words that "there can be no one, however, surly or slow, rough or boorish, who would not be attracted to what is most beautiful."[81] Other texts reveal still more similarities to Alberti's thinking. Orpheus and Amphion are discussed in the commentary to an anonymous late fourteenth-century French poem (attributed to Evart de Conty) called the *Chess of Love*. The commentary is concerned largely with the theme of the harmony of the cosmos and the human body, and it discusses music at some length. "We should know," the commentator says, "that Orpheus and Amphion were two very wise ancient musicians, not only of harmonic music . . . but also of great discretion, intelligence and the beautiful speech corresponding to these qualities. . . . Because then Orpheus and Amphion by their pleasant music and their melodious eloquence often led the proud, the avaricious, and the madmen who live like animals, hardened in soul and vices and long stubborn in them, back to the path of reason and of good and virtuous life, the ancient poets pretended that mountains and stones followed these musicians."[82]

The emphasis here is not so much on the legends of the musicians charming stones and other inanimate objects, which are dismissed as poetic fictions, but very much on the fact that they won over savage and hostile men, persuading them to forsake vice for virtue. This was done not only by their music but also by their eloquence—a combination of the two arts that we have particularly associated with Alberti's notion of architectural beauty. It is also notable that the commentator speaks of "madmen who live like animals," for Alberti likewise employs this image when attacking the city. In the *Della famiglia*, we should recall, he decries the "wickedness of the many evil men who, in the city, are always before your eyes, fill your ears continuously with gossip, and go through the streets shrieking and bellowing like maddened, horrible beasts."[83] A literary tradition thus existed that ascribed to music the power to calm savage and aggressive persons, and it employed terms very similar to those used by Alberti when discussing architectural beauty. He does not recount the legends of Orpheus and Amphion in his own works, but it is interesting that his friend Cristoforo Landino had him tell their stories as a character in his *Disputationes Camaldulenses*. Outlining the various ways of interpreting texts, "Alberti" says,

> Finally we may interpret something through an allegory: which happens when we do not comprehend merely what the words signify,

but something else hidden under a figure. The poet writes that the stones were so moved by Amphion's lyre that they freely placed themselves in the walls of Thebes when they were being built. In this figure what else do we understand but that by the eloquence of a very wise man the people of Boetia (who up to that point had been as stupid as stones in the face of any reasoning and exceedingly hardened against every humanizing influence) came out of the forests and marshes into the city and afterwards freely submitted themselves to extensive laws for the common good.[84]

It is noteworthy that in a panegyric written by a Hungarian student to his teacher, Guarino of Verona, in 1454, Amphion appears as an example of the power of the arts to refine the semisavage *hominem naturalem* and enable him to become a civilized inhabitant of a town.[85] Horace writes about Orpheus and Amphion in similar terms, stressing how their eloquence and music led to the establishment of laws, towns, and settled life:

> While men still roamed the woods, Orpheus, the holy prophet of the gods, made them shrink from bloodshed and brutal living; hence the fable that he tamed tigers and ravening lions; hence too the fable that Amphion, builder of Thebes's citadel, moved stones by the sound of his lyre, and led them whither he would by his supplicating spell. In days of yore, this was wisdom, to draw a line between public and private rights, between things sacred and things common, to check vagrant union, to give rules for wedded life, to build towns, and grave laws on tables of wood; and so honour and fame fell to bards and their songs, as divine.[86]

Alberti, it seems, believed that architecture could do the same.

Music thus furnished abundant examples of how the arts could strongly affect human behavior. Alberti is hardly the first to suggest that architects might use the same numbers as musicians.[87] However, he does seem to go beyond this, claiming that the same harmonies will produce pleasure in each case—as though musical harmonies could actually be perceived visually.[88] The extent to which he believed in this notion seems to have been borne out by his own architectural practice. In addition to the musical proportions that can be found in his buildings, Alberti actually refers to music in regard to the Tempio Malatestiano. In his famous letter to Matteo de' Pasti, who was charged with executing the work, he warns, "You see from whence the measurements and the proportions of the pilasters are born: that which you change puts into discord all that music."[89]

Of course, this is not to say that the pleasure to be had from visual harmony that derives from the same numbers as musical harmony is the pleasure of recognizing the musical "origin" of the numbers. Being aware that a visual harmony might derive from the same numbers as a musical harmony has nothing to do with its enjoyment. Indeed, knowing that any kind of harmony is derived from numbers is thoroughly irrelevant to the resulting pleasure. It is the harmony itself that causes the pleasure, and one need know nothing about how the architect or musician created it.[90]

Of course, what good music and good architecture share is that both are governed by concinnitas, the "absolute and fundamental rule in nature." In the *Profugiorum*, there are clear analogies among nature, music, architecture, and rhetoric (Agnolo's oratory is praised in the same kind of terms as is Florence Cathedral). Alberti could have found confirmation of the links among these disciplines in the discussion of musical modes in Plato's *Republic*. Is it not true, Socrates asks Glaucon, that if "rhythm and mode must conform to the words and not vice versa, then good rhythm follows fine words and is similar to them, while bad rhythm follows the opposite kind of words, and the same for harmony and disharmony?" Glaucon agrees and further assents to Socrates's proposition that the words, in turn, "conform to the character of the speaker's soul." In this case, Socrates argues, "fine words, harmony, grace and rhythm follow simplicity of character— and I do not mean this in the sense in which we use 'simplicity' as a euphemism for 'simple mindedness'—but I mean the sort of fine and good character that has developed in accordance with an intelligent plan." This principle, moreover, can be applied to other, analogous fields: "Painting is full of these qualities, as are all the crafts similar to it; weaving is full of them, and so are embroidery, architecture and the crafts that produce all the other furnishings. Our bodily nature is full of them, as are the natures of all growing things, for in all of these there is grace and gracelessness. And gracelessness, bad rhythm and disharmony are akin to bad words and bad character, while their opposites are akin to and are imitations of the opposite, a moderate and good character."[91] Here, Plato demonstrates the connection of good speech, music, and many other arts, including architecture, to the good and upright soul. Moreover, he stresses that only good music should be allowed in the republic, for good music (and other arts) has the power to improve men, while bad music will do the opposite.

In the *Vita*, Alberti describes how he himself has been cured of physical illness by music and the sight of beautiful landscapes and flowers. "With a fever upon him," he writes, "and streaming with cold sweat the whole time from the pain in his body, he summoned musicians and struggled for almost two hours to overcome the effects of the wound and the vexation of the pain by singing." Later, he explains that "the sight of blossoms, flowers, or especially pleasing places often restored him from sickness to health."[92] Perhaps, then, concinnitas could be a cure for man's maladies, a redeeming force for a species that had left the order of nature.[93] In that sense, it could provide the foundation for an architecture, and a city, that was yet to come.[94]

Conclusion

At the heart of Alberti's writings, there is, as we have seen, a tension surrounding the issues of fame, glory, fate, *fortuna*, and *virtù*. Equally pressing, if not so explicitly articulated, is the issue of truth and the failure of appearance and reality to fully coincide. It is perhaps for this reason that Alberti sometimes has recourse to bizarre and visionary imagery. One senses a genuine attempt to get under the skin of things. The disturbing tale in which Charon describes a strange version of the Fall of Man is an example of precisely this kind of writing. Here, the attempt to penetrate the surface, to see beyond the skin, is almost literal, as Charon lifts the mask on a good portion of humanity.

Scholars have, in recent years, been preoccupied with the notion of dissimulation in Alberti's writings. Alberti treats the theme recurrently and insistently and, of course, engages in his own *simulatio* and *dissimulatio*. It is impossible not to find Alberti's own face, to some extent, behind many of his characters' masks: Lepidus, Philoponius, Gelastus, Momus, and others. As we have seen, Alberti seems to relish taking on these personae while simultaneously craving a world that is governed by transparency. Simulation and dissimulation appear to be the necessary tools for an inhabitant of human societies—that is to say, of cities. The town versus country commonplace is employed as part of a polemic in this regard, one that reveals both the speech and the actions of men in cities to be altogether too complex to be trustworthy. As Momus discovers, simulation and dissimulation are essential for men of affairs who live among the multitude (*intra multitudinem atque in negotio vivendum sit*). It is the condition of being surrounded by dissimulators that necessitates dissimulation on one's own part.[1]

The reference to men who are *in negotio* is important in this regard, since, as we have seen, business appears to embody many of the most problematic areas of urban life for Alberti. He conceives of the urban market as an inherently untrustworthy place in which people are tricked. More than that, however, it is a place where values begin to float freely, where a person passes his life into the hands of others, relying on objects with which he has no connection and of whose origin he is ignorant. He steps outside of the natural social bond of the family, into the far more contentious one of the city. Alberti's treatment of commerce is nuanced, but it is fair to say that he frequently characterizes it as the antithesis of scholarship. The exceptionally high value placed on scholarship by Alberti, an arch scholar himself, is hardly surprising. Yet he subjects even the discourse of the scholar to robust scrutiny, starting from the *De commodis*. Giannozzo and Adovardo's exchange on the subject remains within the bounds of affability but is nonetheless tense.

Alberti often appears skeptical of the ability of language to resolve the disjuncture between appearance and reality. One sometimes senses that he desires a radical clearing away of misleading appearances, a kind of apocalyptic destruction of falsehood. This occasionally enters into his writings in the form of violent imagery—for instance, Charon caulking his boat with clay from the dissolved masks of deceiving monsters and plaiting ropes from their hair.[2] In the *De iciarchia*, Alberti again resorts to the imagery of the mutilation and destruction of the body when revealing deceiving "monsters," asking, "Who can look upon a slanderous deprecator, a defamer, and not be horrified by his fury? Worst of men! They ought to be pursued by the entire populace, not, I say, with bow and arrows, but with ropes and flaming torches. They should be roasted until their bones are left entirely bare, so that no pretence may yet stay hidden within that monster."[3]

Christine Smith has pointed out that the introduction to every book of *Momus* emphasizes the extent to which the protagonist imperiled the very fabric of the universe.[4] Momus, we are told, "nearly drew men, gods and the whole machinery of the world into utter calamity."[5] Indeed, Alberti promises, "You will see how the salvation of mankind, the majesty of the gods and the government of the world were brought almost to a final crisis."[6] This destructive aspect of Momus—his preternatural ability to hasten the Apocalypse—must surely be connected with his role as truth-teller.[7] Momus's irrepressible habit of blurting out the truth threatens to destabilize an entire order that is predicated on the fact that appearance and reality do not coincide.

Of course, *Momus* is a kind of treatise on politics, and this fact is in itself revealing. The multiform and complex nature of the text, and the difficulties that we encounter in trying to interpret it, point to the charged nature of the issue at hand. The stakes could not be higher. Politics holds out the prospect of the *bene e beato vivere*, of a life in common governed by high principles and guided throughout by *dottrina*. Alberti offers not simply a critique but also a serious engagement. Momus's *tabellae* outline a mode of governing in the interests of the common good. Based on the characteristically Albertian principles of finding a middle way between opposites, they urge Jupiter to strive not only to seem good but to actually be so. Both here and in the *De iciarchia*, as well as elsewhere, Alberti exhibits a certain faith in the potential of politics. However, it must be said that his faith is far from constant or total. Giannozzo's skepticism remains, and insofar as it regards politics, it also regards the city.

All of the preoccupations enumerated above have a bearing on Alberti's thinking about the city. He repeatedly considers the notion of a kind of withdrawal from the urban world, or at least from aspects of it. Villas, rural and suburban, are of course prominent in this discourse. Alberti also expresses interest in the idea of zoning, thereby removing inhabitants of the city from the worst aspects of urban life. In the tyrant's city, this becomes bound up with the image of an extreme political order, the establishment of a kind of total power that is manifested in architectural terms and is indeed sustained by the architect. And yet none of these propositions quite convince. For all the attractions of the villa, the city remains central to life in fifteenth-century Italy. Alberti's commitment to action renders it not only necessary but also desirable. Meanwhile, the slippery figure of the *erro* casts doubt on the ultimate ability of political systems to enforce an order—even systems as draconian as the tyrant's city. For in good times and bad, the vagabond lounges in the piazza and even frequents the tyrant's citadel.

The republic is similarly beset by problems, which Giannozzo seems to view as irresolvable. The question, of course, is whether it is ever possible to eliminate rivalry, enmity, bitterness, and suspicion, and whether men can be convinced to act out of concern for the common good rather than personal interest. These were real problems within Tuscan communes, beautifully illustrated by Lorenzetti in his frescoes of good and bad government. Where the elderly Giannozzo sees factionalism and pain, the young, humanist Lionardo sees an opportunity for the attainment of the highest goods: praise, fame, and glory. Alberti also sought these prizes, but there is some question in his writings as to whether, putting aside all rhetorical positions, they are worth pursuing. After all, the good man is unlikely to get a hearing in the city, or so Alberti often says. Scholars are deprecated in Florence, where only profit is valued. This is not to deny that fame and glory frequently appear as the highest achievements to which man may aspire—apart from the attainment of *virtù*—but the desire for them sometimes appears to be tinged with a sense of *vanitas*.

Alberti's thought was deeply imbued with rhetorical concepts, as demonstrated on many occasions. Yet there is also a side of Alberti that seems antirhetorical, that wants to attack rhetoric, even as he is unable to step outside of it. Perhaps it is unfair to single out rhetoric in this regard; it might be more accurate to say that the problem is language as a whole. Paul-Henri Michel, and more recently Branko Mitrović, has observed insightfully that Alberti often appears to distrust words.[8] He was, of course, one of their most skilled manipulators and as such understood the inherent ambiguity in language—its ability to express more than one thing simultaneously, even things that oppose each other. It is an ability that Alberti himself exploited with dexterity. He sometimes even seems to regard words as possessing a kind of danger. This skepticism toward language is opposed, in *De re aedificatoria*, to an extraordinary faith in numbers, and we might remember that during his breakdown as a youth, Alberti gave up his study of law and pursued the study of mathematics—with seemingly therapeutic consequences.

In this regard, the claims that Alberti makes for the power of beauty take on an enhanced significance. Visual beauty is not dependent on verbal reasoning or persuasion but seems in some fundamental sense to be prior to them. It derives from exactitude, from number and line—things that do not partake of the ambiguity inherent in language. Indeed, it is as though beauty is able to cut through the fog of language and to penetrate, ironically, beyond appearance to the most fundamental kind of reality. Concinnitas appeals to a reasoning faculty within us that allows us to recognize the true, harmonic order of the universe; as Alberti says, it is the fundamental rule of nature.

The idea that buildings, cities, and, by implication, everything that man does should be guided by concinnitas has important implications. Concinnitas runs through man's entire life and government, or at least should do so. Yet, as we have seen, Alberti sees the lives and government of the masses as being fundamentally unsound, guided by foolish desires, arrogance, perversity, and ignorance. The cut and thrust of day-to-day life reveals not so much an all-embracing harmony as a ubiquitous disproportion: immoderate desires, lack of reason, and so forth. There can surely be no greater evidence that much of humanity, in Alberti's view, had stepped outside of the order of nature. For what would a society governed by concinnitas be if not a return to nature, not in the sense of living in the woods but in the sense of embracing the natural harmony that human beings are universally capable of recognizing? The status of the city in relation to nature would itself appear to be a matter for debate. As Alberti says in the *De iciarchia* (in direct contradiction to Aristotle), while the family is a natural social institution, cities "were perhaps constituted by chance, and for no other reason than only to be able to live together with sufficiency and comfort."[9]

We have seen that nature plays an exemplary role in Alberti's aesthetic theory, particularly in the form of flowers. Trite as it may sound, one could perhaps consider the beautiful city, conceived along Albertian lines, as a reconciliation between nature and culture in the purest sense. The works of man would embody the fundamental rule of nature. In a more literal sense, Alberti does appear to want to "naturalize" the city, or at least to bring elements of nature into it. Town houses should approximate villas as far as possible. One might consider a hortus to be a means of living in both city and country simultaneously. Alberti envisages public sitting rooms being available for distinguished citizens and philosophers, "with unrestricted views of the sea, mountains, lakes, or any other pleasant scene."[10] As we have seen, he appears to believe that the sight of both nature itself and architecture that embodies concinnitas can have curative properties for human beings.

The contrast between the verbal and the visual is also found in the story that Charon recounts to Gelastus. Charon is clear that he did not hear his story from a philosopher and that philosophy is nothing but subtleties and verbal quibbling. Rather, he heard it from a painter who "by himself . . . saw more while looking at lines than all you philosophers do when you're measuring and investigating the heavens."[11] The painter's knowledge was gained by looking at lineamenta (*contemplandis lineamentis*), making it far superior to anything that one might hear from a philosopher. Indeed, sight appears to be the crucial faculty for perceiving the nature of man in this story, for it is only by looking closely at the eyeholes of the masks that one might discern the beast beneath. In the *Vita*, Alberti says of himself that "he could also recognize the faults of a man on sight alone."[12] If Charon's statement that painters can discern more in the contemplation of lineamenta than philosophers can in measuring the heavens actually expresses Alberti's own view, then it is a radical statement indeed. If we are to understand it, we must give some consideration to what exactly the painter was contemplating.

Lineamenta are the subject of the first book of *De re* and thus stand, in Alberti's view, at the heart of the entire *res aedificatoria*. There have been several attempts to formulate exactly what Alberti intends by this term. The proposal that lineamenta refer to ground plans, though enticing, cannot ultimately be accepted. After all, Alberti also speaks of the lineamenta of a window frame, and in the *De iciarchia*, he refers to the *lineamenti* of the human body.[13] A compelling account of the matter has recently been provided by Branko Mitrović. In the preface to *De re*, Alberti argues that a building is a kind of body that, like other bodies, consists of lineamenta and matter. Mitrović argues that Alberti is specifically referring to Aristotle's position that material objects consist of form and matter.[14] While materiality is the realm of the artisan, lineamenta are the product of *ingenium*. Hence, Mitrović posits, "Alberti's lineaments, *lineamenta*, are . . . the properties which constitute the architecturally relevant similarity between a building as a material, three-dimensional, spatial object and that same building as conceived in the mind of the architect. They are the content of drawings and models by which the architect's idea is conveyed to builders."[15] An object's lineamenta will be established by "determining the disposition of lines and angles; they are contemplated with human cognitive capacities independently of the matter in which they are instantiated."[16] Ultimately, Mitrović argues that a knowledge of lineamenta constitutes the knowledge of shape, since this is what the lineamenta define. This is the knowledge possessed by the painter, a knowledge that is nonverbal and superior to philosophy.

Although the notion of lineamenta is developed in *De re*, it cannot be seen as exclusive to architecture. As is evident from Charon's story, painters are also well versed in lineamenta. Alberti strives to emphasize the common ground between painters and architects in *De re* and indeed names painting as the only discipline besides mathematics in which he requires the architect to be an expert. In the final chapter of Book VI, Alberti says that "what follows principally concerns the rules of *lineamenta* [*rationes lineamentorum*]; it is of the greatest importance, and may give great delight to painters."[17] In the first chapter of Book VII, he reiterates that his inquiry will be of use to painters and notes a little further on that in making a statue from bronze, gold, and silver, the man who casts it will attend to the respective weights "while the sculptor looks to the lineaments." [18] A knowledge of lineamenta thus appears to be something like a common foundation of the visual arts. [19] In Charon's story, Alberti clearly imbues the visual arts—and specifically the understanding of lineamenta—with an exceptional epistemological value. Those who are skilled in making images and who understand shapes and lines can see beyond the appearance of things to the reality beneath. [20] Implicit in Charon's story, of course, is the age-old analogy between artistic creation and creation by God. As a second type of creator, the artist is able to see into the secrets of the world and humanity and to discern the true nature of things. [21] As seen in *De re*, the architect is also able to use lineamenta to reform human beings and cure them of their violent ways.

The power of beauty appears to be a neat solution to the problems of the city—a necessary redemption, as it were. Yet it is legitimate to question whether it is adequate. Manfredo Tafuri, examining Alberti's notion that beauty might protect a building from an aggressor, comments that "it is impossible not to detect a desperate note in such formulations. The 'weak force' of *concinnitas* is pitted against unconquerable evil." [22] Perhaps this view underestimates Alberti's faith in concinnitas. He does not describe it as a "weak force," but rather as something that impinges on every aspect of mankind's being in the world. And yet one cannot help but share Tafuri's skepticism. However Alberti may have chosen to interpret the physical evidence of Rome or any other city, he must have been aware that experience did not bear out his claims. Given the scale of violence and destruction described in Alberti's writings, and the ubiquity of vice and unreason, beauty does indeed seem like a flimsy defense. Alberti states his claim about the defensive power of beauty on three occasions in the architectural treatise, and he must have believed it to some extent. It is difficult, however, to imagine that he had no doubts. As with the goals of fame and glory, one sometimes senses that beneath Alberti's very real belief in the value of architecture lies a sense of *vanitas*.

Ultimately, Alberti's doubts regarding the city reflect his doubts regarding man. Again, Charon's creation story is illuminating. Commenting on the passage in his *Rinascite e rivoluzioni* of 1975, Eugenio Garin noted pithily, "Nobody has noticed that some decades before Giovanni Pico della Mirandola composed the famous hermetic opening of the oration in praise of man, Alberti had already written the parody." [23] The remark is a perceptive one, for Charon's story does indeed read as a parody. Where Pico describes the great potential of man, Alberti presents us with his immediate failure.

In contrast to Pico's assertion that man may attain divinity, in Alberti's text, man's pretensions dissolve into a mess of hair and clay. Indeed, Charon's disparagement of philosophical wisdom would seem to be part and parcel of this position. The painter perceives more in the study of *lineamenta* than all philosophers do when measuring and investigating the heavens.

Here, Alberti appears to dismiss the wisdom of the philosopher-astronomer who gazes at the heavens. Yet this figure had been, par excellence, the image of the medieval man of wisdom.[24] Moreover, the notion that man's special dignity was signaled by his *rectitudo*, by his standing upright and gazing upon the heavens—the greatest work of the creator—was a commonplace that predated Christianity. It appears in Cicero, and Vitruvius utilizes it in his account of the origins of architecture, ascribing the invention of building in part to the fact that men had "this boon beyond other animals, that they should walk, not with the head down, but upright, and should look upon the magnificence of the world and of the stars."[25] By the first century B.C., this was already a well-worn truism. Alberti employs it himself in the *Della famiglia* and again in the *Profugiorum*, although the context is not straightforward in either case.[26] In the *Momus*, however, he deliberately seeks to undermine it, and in so doing signals an attack on the dignity of man. When challenged by Charon as to what philosophers actually know, Gelastus had specifically claimed that they knew about the stars and the heavens. Charon here dismisses such knowledge as mere pretension. Man enjoys his lofty verbal quibbles about the stars but, as we have seen, tramples over the flowers without a second thought. As the naturalist Stein in Joseph Conrad's *Lord Jim* puts it, "Sometimes it seems to me that man is come where he is not wanted, where there is no place for him; for if not, why does he want all the place? Why should he run about here and there making a great noise about himself, talking about the stars, disturbing the blades of grass?"[27]

Charon likewise characterizes man as a creature whose folly runs from top to bottom and from macrocosm to microcosm. Viewed from a different perspective, one of man's greatest virtues, his investigation of the world, might only be proof of the extent to which he is at odds with nature. As Teogenio says in the *Theogenius*, "The other animals are content with what befits them: only man investigates new things, and, in so doing, corrupts them. . . . What foolishness of mortals that we want to know when, how, for what reason, and to what end every institution and work of God exists. And we want to know what matter, what form, what nature, what force pertains to the sky, the planets, the intelligences; and we want a thousand secrets to be better known to us than to nature."[28] In the *Theogenius*, this denunciation of man's appetite for knowledge becomes a denunciation of his building activity as well, with the extraction of natural resources characterized as a violation of nature.

The true depth of Alberti's skepticism regarding the dignity of man is difficult to judge. Christine Smith has argued that in *Momus*, Alberti is ultimately able to reaffirm man's dignity, and it is true that the work ends with Jupiter's reading of the *tabellae* in which Momus's wisdom is contained. Indeed, one could argue that man's dignity is affirmed in every work that Alberti ever wrote. His late *De iciarchia* endorses positive participation in the republic and the pursuit of fame and glory as the highest of prizes. Alberti's faith in reason and in *virtù* is unwavering, and it informed his life as well as his work. His letter to Matteo de' Pasti in which he dismisses the opinion of a certain Manetto regarding a cupola and states that he would rather place his trust in the architects of the Pantheon—and in reason above all—bears powerful testament to this belief. In all of Alberti's moral dialogues, the seemingly unending problems with which man is faced eventually find solutions of one kind or another. Virtù, above all, will stand man in good stead in the face of almost any hardship. Moreover, through learning and activity, it is in man's power to positively improve himself, his city, and its government. *De re aedificatoria* provides the blueprint for an architecture that is yet to come, one that may have positive social effects. Alberti himself was engaged in constructing the new architecture in bricks, mortar, and marble.

The question remains, however, of whether the positive positions that Alberti takes can ever be entirely freed from the immense force of his pessimism—whether it is possible for him to convincingly reaffirm the dignity of man once it has been so powerfully undermined. To say that Alberti was a divided thinker might seem unsatisfying, but it is surely true. On more than one occasion, he circles back on his own arguments and subjects them to satire, irony, or skepticism. Alberti's thinking regarding the city is ultimately not fully resolved—nor, in truth, should we necessarily expect it to be. Cities are, above all, problematic in Alberti's thought. They are as problematic as mankind, whose nature they both mirror and affect. As Hercules reflects, peering down from heaven at his former home, "The amazing thing about mortals was that, as individuals, they were almost all wise and aware of what was right; but when they formed themselves into a group, they fell into a frenzied rage and spontaneously behaved like madmen."[29]

Notes

Regarding translations from the Latin and Italian, I have quoted from published English translations when they were available, noting any instances in which I have modified them. Unless otherwise specified, all other English translations are my own.

Introduction

1. Alberti, *On the Art of Building* 4.2, 95 (references are to book, chapter, and page numbers in Rykwert, Leach, and Tavernor's translation).

2. On the rise of the notary, see Waley, *Italian City-Republics*, 29–30.

3. It was, of course, a central contention of Burckhardt's *Civilization of the Renaissance in Italy* that rulers and governing bodies of Italian city-states, lacking the kind of legitimacy enjoyed by the rulers of other European states, were compelled to think in a more conscious and reflective manner about the nature of the state and its governance. Burckhardt saw this as leading to a new approach to the state as a "work of art."

4. On this, see Choay, *The Rule and the Model*, 6.

5. Garin, *Umanesimo Italiano*, 86: "L'occhio dell'Alberti vagheggia una città terrena armoniosa come uno dei suoi palazzi, ove la natura si piega all'intenzione dell'arte come la obbediente pietra serena dei colli fiorentini." Garin's view of Alberti would later change considerably.

6. Eden, "Studies in Urban Theory"; G. Simoncini, *Città e società*, 1:28–29; and Westfall, *In This Most Perfect Paradise*.

7. Holmes, *Florentine Enlightenment*, 169.

8. Westfall, *In This Most Perfect Paradise*, 58.

9. Shirwood probably purchased his copy in Florence and seems to have regarded it as a highly prized possession. The book was passed on to his successor at Durham, Richard Fox, and went on to form part of Fox's Corpus Christi foundation library. This information is derived from Jonathan Foyle's "Italian Architectural Treatises in England Prior to 1520" (lecture, Renaissance Architecture and Theory Scholars' Day, Courtauld Institute, London, May 4, 2002). I am grateful to Jonathan Foyle for subsequently clarifying some points of the story further for me.

10. This elaborately illustrated edition followed the (short-lived) success of Leoni's earlier publication of Palladio. It included parallel Italian and English texts and also incorporated Alberti's shorter treatises on painting and sculpture. Leoni's edition was reprinted in 1739 and again in 1755 without the Italian text. It was reprinted a third time in 1955, in London, edited by Joseph Rykwert. For details of editions of Alberti's treatise, see Rykwert's introduction to Alberti, *On the Art of Building*, xviii–xxii.

11. Roscoe, *Life of Lorenzo de' Medici*, 1:86.

12. Ibid., 1:88. Roscoe follows Vasari in judging Alberti to have been primarily a theorist who was found somewhat wanting in artistic and architectural practice.

13. Burckhardt, *Civilization*, 103.

14. Eliot, *Romola*, 295.

15. Gadol, *Leon Battista Alberti*, xiii.

16. This may owe to the particular difficulties of finding an Italian term for master builder that would adequately describe Alberti. *Capomaestro* would be entirely wrong.

17. Quoted in Celenza, *Renaissance Humanism*, 156–57: "Et aequalem meum Baptistam Albertum, cuius ingenium ita laudo ut hac laude cum eo neminem comparem, ita admiror ut magnum mihi nescio quid portendere inposterum videatur. Est enim eiusmodi ut ad quancumque se animo conferat facultatem, in ea facile ac brevi ceteris antecellat."

18. For Alberti's biography, see Mancini, *Vita*; Grayson, "Leon Battista Alberti: Vita e opera"; and more recently Grafton, *Leon Battista Alberti*. For a discussion regarding the current state of biographical studies, see Boschetto, "Tra biografia e autobiografia."

19. This is not to say, of course, that the Alberti accepted exile. On the contrary, they made repeated attempts to be readmitted, sometimes having recourse to arms.

20. On Alberti's illegitimacy, see Kuehn, "Reading Between the Patrilines" and "Leon Battista Alberti come illegittimo." Kuehn emphasizes that at various stages of his life, Alberti suffered profoundly negative consequences as a result of his illegitimacy.

21. Watkins, "Leon Battista Alberti in the Mirror," 8.

22. This is the title given to them by their modern translator, David Marsh.

23. Marsh, "Aesop and the Humanist Apologue."

24. Boschetto, "Tra biografia e autobiografia," 101–3, explores how Alberti's account of his switch from law to mathematics relates to a literary tradition regarding the conduct of students and teachers.

25. The source is Johannes Regiomontanus, quoted in Grafton, *Leon Battista Alberti*, 245.

26. Alberti, *Treatise on Ciphers*, 4.

27. For a thorough analysis of Alberti's architectural career that examines how, when, and why Alberti became an architect, see Calzona, "Leon Battista Alberti e l'architettura."

28. For Michelet, great men were the proof of a great age, and in his *Histoire de France: Renaissance* of 1885, he pointed to artists such as Raphael as proof of the Renaissance's special worth. By contrast, he condemned the Middle Ages for failing to produce such giants. It was, he said, a "great desert of men." See Michelet, *Ouevres complètes*, 4:250–51.

29. Grafton, *Leon Battista Alberti*, 23–25, points out the parallels between the *Vita* and Diogenes Laertius's life of Thales.

30. Engels wrote in his introduction to the *Dialectics of Nature* that the Renaissance was "the greatest progressive revolution that mankind had so far experienced, a time which called for giants and produced giants—giants in power of thought, passion and character, in universality and learning. The men who founded the modern rule of the bourgeoisie had anything but bourgeois limitations. On the contrary, the adventurous character of the time imbued them to a greater or less degree. There was hardly any man of importance then living who had not traveled extensively, who did not command four or five languages, who did not shine in a number of fields. Leonardo da Vinci was not only a great painter but also a great mathematician, mechanician and engineer, to whom the most diverse branches of physics are indebted for important discoveries." Marx and Engels, *Selected Works*, 2:57–58.

31. Mancini, *Vita*, 548 (1st ed.): "Incominciò il funesto periodo delle servitù straniere. . . . Egli aveva insegnato il modo, col quale uomini, famiglie e nazioni primeggiano, prosperano, resistono alle calamità: non l'ascoltarono, ed i posteri pagarono a misura di lacrime e di sangue le colpe degli avi." The closeness to Alberti's own account of Italian history in the prologue to the *Della famiglia* is striking.

32. Ibid., 551: "Nella prima gioventù mi posi a cercare notizie di lui, ed invaghitomi di narrarne la vita m'accinsi a mettere in atto l'ardito divisamento. Poi per lungo tempo m'impedirono d'incarnare il giovanile disegno le cure della famiglia, gli affari privati, e la patria che nel ricostruirsi chiedeva l'opera di tutti i suoi figli, e fu da me servita ne' consigli del comune e della provincia, nel Parlamento, e colle armi ne' corpi volontari." Unless otherwise stated, all following references to Mancini's *Vita* are to the second edition.

33. See Alberti, *Momus; o, Del principe*, published in 1942. Despite the fascist publisher, the introduction to this edition is singularly apolitical and scholarly.

34. Baron, *Crisis*, 6, 35, 37, 42.

35. Ibid., 40.

36. Ibid., 10.

37. Baron, *In Search of Florentine Civic Humanism*, 1:258–88.

38. For an account of the development of the idea of the Renaissance and how thinkers such as Voltaire and Pater fit into it, see Bullen, *Myth of the Renaissance*.

39. See Holmes, *Florentine Enlightenment*, 1–67.

40. Barker, introduction to Bowra, *Golden Ages of the Great Cities*, 1.

41. Acton, "Medicean Florence," in Bowra, *Golden Ages of the Great Cities*, 106.

42. In the introduction to Bowra, *Golden Ages of the Great Cities*, 5, Barker writes that New York "is not yet one of the golden cities of culture—that will yet come, because political and economic greatness generally fosters, as the history of cities shows, the rise and growth of great art and architecture—but even so it could not be omitted from the plan of this book." Indeed, the book "serves to show to America what Europe has given in the past to the accumulated treasure of civilization, and what, if it is true to its past, it will still continue to give; but it must, as it ends, serve also to show Europe what America is already giving and will continue increasingly to give."

43. A remarkably similar undertaking was attempted, on a grand scale, by the new Tate Gallery in London. In 2001, a large exhibition entitled *Century City* proposed to offer a slice of twentieth-century cultural and urban history by looking at nine cities that had undergone particular moments of cultural vibrancy over the last one hundred years. In addition to featuring revolutionary Moscow and avant-garde Paris, the Tate signaled its desire to break with a Eurocentric history of art by including, among other cities, Rio di Janeiro in the 1950s and 1960s, Lagos from 1955 to 1970, and Mumbai from 1992 to 2001. Bravely, but not entirely convincingly, the exhibition ended not just with Mumbai but also with contemporary London, suggesting that the visitor was living in one of these cultural peaks. The high point was exemplified, of course, in the enormous new Tate Gallery itself and other redevelopments going on in London. This example must be considered in the context of the contemporaneous attempt by the government to "rebrand" postcolonial Britain as "cool Britannia," a country undergoing a "renaissance" of its own.

44. Urban Task Force, *Towards an Urban Renaissance*, 26.

45. For Ruskin, the Renaissance heralded the onset of modernity, and the journey from the reviled Palladio to the despised Gower Street—architecturally, ethically, and socially—was a direct one. Ruskin did not, however, view the Renaissance as a natural progression from the classical era. He argued that in ancient Greece, art and architecture excelled because they were born out of their own culture and were

endowed with authentic meaning. Gothic art and architecture held the same relation to the wider culture of the Middle Ages. The fundamental mistake of the Renaissance was to revive classical forms in an age in which they had no function other than as ornament. Art and architecture were therefore bereft of relevance, belief, or cultural significance, effectively becoming alienated from society.

46. Westfall, *In This Most Perfect Paradise*, 57.

47. For a particularly clear-sighted rebuttal of Alberti as a civic humanist, see Tenenti, "Leon Battista Alberti umanista," 38–45.

48. Trachtenberg, *Dominion of the Eye*, 1.

49. Edgerton, *Renaissance Rediscovery*, 32–33.

50. Trachtenberg, *Dominion of the Eye*, esp. 1–8.

51. Alberti, *On Painting and On Sculpture*, 33.

52. For a penetrating analysis of this preface, see Smith, *Architecture in the Culture of Early Humanism*, 80–97.

53. Alberti, *Opere volgari*, 2:204; quoted in Rykwert's introduction to Alberti, *On the Art of Building*, xv.

54. This has been stressed by Luca Boschetto, who argues that Alberti's attitude toward Florence varied considerably over time, according to political factors, family affairs, and his relationship to Florentine humanism. He even suggests that when Alberti stresses the excellence of the fine arts in the preface to *De pictura*, contrasting it to poor cultural development in general, it may not be so much to praise Florentine art as to put down Florentine literary culture. See Boschetto, *Leon Battista Alberti e Firenze*, 101.

55. Garin, "Il pensiero," 502: "L'artista, la cui immagine suole collocarsi sotto il segno dell'armonia e della misura, col referimento d'obbligo alla 'monumentalità' della *Famiglia* e dell'*Architettura*, in realtà è scrittore inquietante, imprevedibile e bizzarro, tutto giuochi di fantasia sfrenata e preziosismi stilistici."

56. Cardini, "Alberti scrittore e umanista," 26.

57. Aluffi Begliomini, "Note sull'opera dell'Alberti," in particular argued that in both *Momus* and *De re aedificatoria*, Alberti envisaged a perverse and difficult world where God was absent and human endeavor was mostly fruitless. In doing so, she succeeded in infuriating J. H. Whitfield, who dubbed her "slightly hysterical"; see Whitfield, "*Momus* and the Language of Irony," 39. Revisionist works that followed include Jarzombek, *On Leon Baptista Alberti*, and Marolda, *Crisi e conflitto.*

58. The case is well made by Cardini, "Alberti scrittore e umanista."

59. Ibid., esp. 29.

60. Cardini, *Mosaici*; Alberti, *Opere volgare*, 2:160–62.

61. In the architectural treatise, *On the Art of Building*, Alberti in fact twice directs the reader to his nonarchitectural writings: *Pontifex* at 5.6, 126, and *Theogenius* at 10.1, 321.

62. That this position has become orthodox is demonstrated by Cesare de Seta's almost verbatim reproduction of Choay's remark about the *Theogenius* and the *Della famiglia* in his "Come in un specchio," 35. De Seta argues that one may indeed seek ideals regarding the city in the *Theogenius*, *Villa*, or *Famiglia*, but not in *De re aedificatoria*, which is neutral and technical in character. Tavernor, *On Alberti*, 19, agrees that Alberti presents no ideal city.

63. Alberti, *Della famiglia*, 190, and *Opere volgari*, 1:188: "E a che conosceresti voi la terra quanto fosse atta a queste tutte cose? Non sarebbe egli difficile non solo conoscerla, ma trovarla?" I have mostly followed Guarino's translation of Alberti's *I libri della famiglia*. Unless otherwise specified, references to the *Della famiglia* refer to this translation.

64. Alberti, *Della famiglia*, 191, and *Opere volgari*, 1:189: "Nimici, né casi avversi né ira di Dio."

65. Alberti, *Della famiglia*, 191, and *Opere volgari*, 1:189:

LIONARDO: E dove si troverrebbe mai una sì fatta terra compiuta di tante lode? Se già a voi, il quale vi dilettate abitare in Vinegia, quella una terra non vi paresse in tutte queste meno che l'altre viziosa; certo credo sarebbe difficile trovarla.

GIANNOZZO: E io pur ne cercherei. Non vorrei avermi a pentire della negligenza mia. E quella ove io trovassi le più e le migliori di tutte quali dissi cose, ivi mi fermerei.

Chapter 1

The epigraph is drawn from Herodotus, *Histories* 1.5, 1:9 (references are to book, section, and page numbers in Godley's translation).

1. Martines, *Power and Imagination*, 72.

2. Later, Villani relates how in 1347, just before the disastrous plague that would end his life, Florence was struck by a series of terrible fires and devastating storms: "E nota, lettore, quante tempeste occorsono in questo anno all nostra città di Firenze, fame, mortalità, ruine, tempeste, folgori, fuochi e discordie tra'cittadini, per lo soperchio de'nostri difetti e peccati." Villani, *Cronica*, 2:89–91; see also 4:141.

3. On such disasters, see Goldthwaite, *Building of Renaissance Florence*, 19. As a provision against fire, it was suggested that rope and sacks should be kept around all houses so that the occupants could speedily remove themselves and their goods in case of an outbreak.

4. Heywood, *History of Perugia*, 186–87.

5. Fifty-one earthquakes were recorded in Italy during the fourteenth century and sixty-one during the fifteenth. The most important period of seismic activity in the fifteenth century is recorded between the years 1445 and 1449, exactly the period when Alberti was composing his architectural treatise. Earthquakes were widespread throughout the peninsula, with many recorded in Venice, where Alberti spent a large portion of his childhood. See Doutreleau, "Les tremblements," 225–31.

6. For all of these examples, see Figliuolo, *Il terremoto del 1456*, 1:3–29. On the earthquake in Naples, the author comments, "Lo spaventoso terremoto che la notte tra sabato 4 e domenica 5 dicembre—un giorno ed un mese, curiosamente, governati dal maligno Saturno—devastò gran parte del regno di Napoli, sembrò infine venire a porre il proprio sinistro suggello ad un anno di disgrazie" (1:20). The appearance of Halley's Comet in May 1456 convinced some observers, particularly among the common people, that the storms, flooding, famine, plague, and earthquake were all due to a single cause. Stefano Borsi, *Leon Battista Alberti e Napoli*, 208–10, notes that although the Naples earthquake is mentioned in the correspondence of a number of people whom Alberti knew, the event does not appear to have any specific echoes in *De re aedificatoria*. See also S. Borsi, *Leon Battista Alberti e Roma*, 125.

7. Hanska, *Strategies of Sanity*, 169–70. Hanska argues that while many local disasters have left little by way of source material and have not generally received much scholarly attention, such events "might have been the worst disaster ever from the point of view of the local population. For the victims, these local disasters were more serious than the *Black Death*, which they might never have heard of."

8. For example, Alberti, *On the Art of Building* 8.8, 279, observes of the Circus Maximus that "at present it is so dilapidated as not to offer the least impression of its original appearance."

9. Mancini, *Vita*, 486.

10. Alberti, *Della famiglia*, 31–32, and *Opere volgari*, 1:8: "E le barbare nazioni, le serve remotissime genti . . . subito queste tutte presero audacia di irrumpere in mezzo el tuo seno santissimo, Italia, sino ad incendere el nido e la propria antica sedia dello imperio de tutti li imperii." I have slightly modified the translation.

11. Rather as Joseph Michael Gandy did in his 1830 image of Soane's Bank of England in ruins.

12. Quoted in Baxandall, *Giotto and the Orators*, 67.

13. Garin, "Il pensiero," 520, notes Alberti's preoccupation with the tendency of things toward death, decay, and dissolution. The theme is also taken up by Aluffi Begliomini, "Note sull'opera dell'Alberti," 275–77.

14. Alberti, *On the Art of Building* 10.1, 320.

15. Ibid., prologue, 3.

16. Ibid., 1.2, 8.

17. Ibid., 4.1, 92.

18. Vitruvius, *On Architecture* 2.1, 1:77 (references are to book, chapter, and page numbers in Granger's translation): "Homines vetere more ut ferae in silvis et speluncis et nemoribus nascebantur ciboque agresti vescendo vitam exigebant."

19. Ibid., 2.1, 78–79: "Ligna adicientes et id conservantes alios adducebant et nutu monstrantes ostendebant, quas haberent ex eo utilitates. In eo hominum congressu cum profunderentur aliter e spiritu voces, cotidiana consuetudine vocabula, ut optigerant, constituerunt, deinde significando res saepius in usu ex eventu fari fortuito coeperunt et ita sermones inter se procreaverunt. Ergo cum propter ignis inventionem conventus initio apud homines et concilium et convictus esset natus, et in unum locum plures convenirent habentes ab natura praemium praeter reliqua animalia, ut non proni sed erecti ambularent mundique et astrorum magnificentiam aspicerent, item manibus et articulis quam vellent rem faciliter tractarent, coeperunt in eo coetu alii de fronde facere tecta, alii speluncas fodere sub montibus, nonnulli hirundinum nidos et aedificationes earum imitantes de luto et virgulis facere loca quae subirent."

20. Alberti, *Momus*, 306–9: "'O te philosophum quidem bonum, qui siderum cursus teneas et quae hominum sint ignoras! Ex Charonte adeo portitore disce ipsum te nosse. Referam quae non a philosopho—nam vestra omnis ratio nisi in argutiis et verborum captiunculis versatur—sed a pictore quodam memini audivisse. Is quidem lineamentis contemplandis plus vidit solus quam vos omnes philosophi caelo commensurando et disquirendo. Adsis animo: audies rem rarissimam. Sic enim aiebat pictor: tanti operis artificem selegisse et depurasse id quo esset hominem conditurus; id vero fuisse aliqui limum melle infusum, alii ceram tractando contepefactam. Quicquid ipsum fuerit, aiunt imposuisse sigillis aeneis binis quibus altero pectus, vultus et quae cum his una visuntur, altero occiput, tergum, nates et postrema istiusmodi impressarentur.'"

21. Ibid.: "'Multas formasse hominum species et ex his selegisse mancas et vitio insignes, praesertim leves et vacuas, ut essent feminae, feminasque a maribus distinxisse dempto ab iis paulo quantillo quod alteris adigeretur. Fecisse item alio ex luto variisque sigillis multiplices alias animantium species. Quibus operibus confectis, cum vidisset homines aliquos sua non usquequaque forma delectari, edixisse ut qui id praestare arbitrarentur quas placuerit in alias reliquorum animantium facies se verterent.'"

22. Ibid., 308–11: "'Dehinc suas quae obiecto in monte paterent aedes monstravit atque hortatus est ut acclivi directaque via quae pateret conscenderent: habituros illic omnem bonarum rerum copiam, sed iterum atque iterum caverent ne alias praeter hanc inirent vias—videri arduam initio hanc, sed continuo aequabilem successuram. His dictis abivisse. Homunculos coepisse conscendere, sed illico alios per stultitiam boves, asinos, quadrupedes videri maluisse, alios cupiditatis errore adductos in transversos viculos delirasse. Illic abruptis constreposisque praecipitiis sentibusque et vepribus irretitos pro loci difficultate se in varia vertisse monstra; et iterato ad primariam viam redisse, illic fuisse ab suis ob deformitatem explosos. Ea de re, comperto consimili quo compacti essent luto, fictas et aliorum vultibus compares sibi superinduisse personas, et crevisse hoc personandorum hominum artificium usu quoad paene a veris secernas fictos vultus ni forte accuratius ipsa per foramina obductae personae introspexeris: illinc enim contemplantibus varias solere occurrere monstri facies. Et appellatas personas hasce fictiones easque ad Acherontis usque undas durare, nihilo plus, nam fluvium ingressis humido vapore evenire ut dissolvantur. Quo fit ut alteram nemo ad ripam non nudatus amissa persona pervenerit.' Tum Gelastus: 'O Charon, fingisne haec ludi gratia an vera praedicas?' 'Quin' inquit Charon 'ex personarum barbis et superciliis rudentem hunc intorsi ipsoque ex luto cumbam obstipavi.'"

23. Brown and Knight, in Alberti, *Momus*, 397n20, cite as examples Dante, *Purgatorio*; Petrarch, *Epistole familiari* 4.1; and Seneca, *De providentia* 5. To this we might add Hesiod, *Works and Days*, lines 285–94; Xenophon, *Memorabilia* 2.1.21; an Aesopic fable concerning Prometheus and Zeus (fable 240 in Perry's index); and Silius Italicus, *Punica* 15.18–128, 2:326–35 (references are to book, line, and page numbers in Duff's translation), where Scipio Africanus dreams that the hero is first tempted by Voluptas and then exhorted by Virtus. Virtus tells him, "My household is pure; my dwelling is set on a lofty hill, and a steep track leads there by a rocky ascent. Hard at first—it is not my way to hold out false hopes—is the toil you must endure. If you seek to enter, you must exert yourself; and you must not reckon as good those things which fickle fortune can give and can also take away" (15.101–6, 2:332–33). The notion that the true nature of a person can be seen in the eyes might also relate to Matthew 6:22–23, which reads, "The light of the body is the eye: if therefore thine eye be single, thy whole body shall be full of light. But if thine eye be evil, thy whole body shall be full of darkness. If therefore the light that is in thee be darkness, how great is that darkness!" This is closely followed in Matthew 7:13–14 by the command "Enter ye in at the strait gate: for wide is the gate, and broad is the way, that leadeth to destruction, and many there be which go in thereat: Because strait is the gate, and narrow is the way, which leadeth unto life, and few there be that find it" (Authorized Version).

24. Marassi, *Metamorfosi della storia*, 51, argues, with reference to *Momus* and some of the *Intercenales*, that Alberti sees humanity as being essentially fallen.

25. In the *Della famiglia*, Lionardo ascribes to philosophers the opinion that in its original, uncorrupted nature, "da prima intera natura" is as perfect as it can possibly be. If this is so, Lionardo reasons, "then it seems to me that I can affirm that all mortals are given by nature what is necessary for loving and practicing the most commendable virtues." Given that not all humans do in fact love or practice virtue, this statement implies a turning away, on the part of some, from the "prima intera natura." See Alberti, *Della famiglia*, 80, and *Opere volgari*, 1:62.

26. Augustine, *City of God* 15.1, 635 (references are to book, chapter, and page numbers in Dyson's translation).

27. Dyson, introduction to Augustine, *City of God*, xvii.

28. Augustine, *City of God* 15.5, 639–40.

29. Ibid., 18.17, 843.

30. Alberti, *Opuscoli inediti*, 70: "Quid enim monstrum est perdito flagitiosoque homine maius? Certe nullum."

31. The preoccupation with *fortuna* and with the nature of man in the *Life of Saint Potitus* is characteristic of Alberti's work. Certainly, this notion of a man who turns out to be a monster and an animal, who represents the corruption of mankind and its foolish desire for the gifts of fortune, and who demonstrates that such men have in fact left the order of nature seems to find a strong echo in Charon's story in *Momus*.

32. Grafton, *Leon Battista Alberti*, 68.

33. Cassani, *La fatica del costruire*, 22–23, notes that Alberti considers matter to be, from the outset, corruptible; corruptibility is an ontological condition of matter, and matter carries within itself the principle of its own destruction. See also ibid., 111–21.

34. Alberti, *On the Art of Building* 1.4, 13.

35. Ibid., 1.5, 17.

36. Ibid., 1.5, 16.

37. Ibid., 1.8, 22.

38. Ibid., 1.6, 17.

39. Ibid., 1.5, 15. He continues, "I know of another town in Italy where there are so many born either with tumors, squints, and limps, or who are crippled, that there is scarcely a family that does not contain someone deformed or handicapped in some way."

40. Ibid., 1.5, 15–16.

41. Alberti, *Della famiglia*, 190–91, and *Opere volgari*, 1:188–89.

42. Alberti, *On the Art of Building* 1.8, 21.

43. Ibid. See also Orlandi's Latin edition, Alberti, *L'architettura*, 1:57.

44. Alberti, *On the Art of Building* 1.11, 26, and *L'architettura*, 1:75. Alberti goes on to observe, surely correctly, that "nor have as many buildings fallen into ruin by fire, sword, enemy hands, or by any other calamity, as have tumbled down for no other reason than human neglect, when left naked and deprived of the roof covering" (*On the Art of Building* 1.11, 26).

45. Alberti, *On the Art of Building* 2.8, 47, and *L'architettura*, 1:135.

46. Alberti, *On the Art of Building* 3.15, 87, and *L'architettura*, 1:251. On this topic, see also Cassani, *La fatica del costruire*, 115.

47. Alberti, *On the Art of Building* 1.11, 27.

48. On this topic, see also Cassani, *La fatica del costruire*, 115.

49. Ibid., 2.2, 35–36. Alberti's examples are taken from ancient sources. He mentions the ports of Claudius and Hadrian, while the bridge of ships might refer either to one constructed by Xerxes or to one that was built for Caligula. For the bridge of Xerxes, see Herodotus, *Histories* 7.33–37, 3:347–53; for Caligula's bridge, see Suetonius, *Caligula* 19. Both are examples of folly. The destruction of Xerxes's bridge led to an attempt to punish the sea, which involved precisely the kind of misunderstanding of the relationship between man and nature that Alberti warns against. In Caligula's case, the bridge episode was part of a series of incidents that led Suetonius to declare that Caligula was mentally ill.

50. See Genesis 11:3–8.

51. For a near-contemporary example of another use of this topos, see Valla, *On Pleasure* 1.13.5, 82–83 (references are to book, section, subsection, and page numbers in Hieatt and Lorch's translation). There, a character comments, "Idem est enim natura quod Deus aut fere idem," citing Ovid, *Metamorphoses* 1.21. See also Seneca, *De beneficiis* 4.7.

52. Alberti, *Momus*, 32–33: "Nullos inveniri deos, praesertim qui hominum res curasse velint; vel tandem unum esse omnium animantium communem deum, Naturam, cuius quidem sint opus et opera non homines modo regere, verum

et iumenta et alites et pisces et eiusmodi animantia. . . . Fungi idcirco quaecumque a Natura procreata sint certo praescriptoque officio, seu bona illa quidem, seu mala pensentur ab hominibus, quandoquidem invita repugnanteque Natura eadem ipsa per se nihil possint. Multa pensari peccata opinione, quae peccata non sint. Ludum esse Naturae hominum vitam."

53. Ibid., 34–37: "Ille, ut erat in omni suscepta controversia pervicax, suam durius tueri sententiam, negare deos, ac demum falli homines, qui quidem ob istum, quem caelo spectent, conversionum ambitum moti, praesides deos ullos praeter Naturam putent. Naturam quidem ultro ac sponte suesse erga genus hominum innato et suo uti officio, eamque haud usquam egere nostris rebus, sed ne eam quidem nostris moveri precibus."

54. On this distinction, see Gabbey, "Spinoza on the Natural," 225, and Lagrée, *Juste Lipse*, 52. Lagrée notes that Seneca touches on the theme of *Natura sive Deus* in *De beneficiis* 4.7 and *Naturales quaestiones* 2.45.

55. Alberti, *Opere volgari*, 1:133.

56. Alberti, *On the Art of Building* 4.3, 102.

57. Alberti devotes a lengthy passage of the *Pontifex* to a discussion of the negative effects of ambition.

58. Alberti, *Della famiglia*, 279, and *Opere volgari*, 1:288: "Occisioni e ruine delle terre." I have modified the translation. In the same passage, Adovardo observes that history only ever recounts the troubles suffered by states, the overthrow of republics, and the inconstancy and volubility of fortune.

59. Alberti, *On the Art of Building* 4.3, 102.

60. Vitruvius, *On Architecture* 1.3, 1:33.

61. Hale, *Renaissance Fortification*, 13–14, points out, "The tradition that artists and 'art' architects should turn naturally to fortification was an old one. Vasari's statement that Arnolfo designed the third circuit of Florence's walls has not been disproved. We have Giotto's contract of 1334 as their supervisor. Moreover, we know that the sculptor Andrea Pisano helped to complete them. . . . Florence diverted Leonardo da Vinci, recently Cesare Borgia's 'architect and engineer general,' from his work on the *Battle of Anghiari* in the Palazzo Vecchio to inspect fortifications near Pisa and to design new ones at Piombino in 1503–4, and appointed Michelangelo in 1529 'governor and procurator general of the fortifications' of the city." Indeed, Michelangelo, while well advanced in his meteoric career, professed to know little of painting and sculpture but to be an expert on fortification. See Ackerman and Newman, *Architecture of Michelangelo*, 123.

62. Hale, *Renaissance War Studies*, 12. Hall, *Weapons and Warfare*, 161, similarly notes of some of Alberti's schemes for fortifications that "strangely, Alberti formulated his ideas without referring to gunfire at all, but the applicability of his general ideas only increased as the firepower of attackers became evident."

63. Alberti's treatise on the ship may have described more offensive modes of marine battle. He writes in *On the Art of Building* 5.12, 137, of some of the defensive mechanisms he has invented for ships, adding, "Here I shall not mention my other inventions for sinking and burning enemy ships and throwing the crew into confusion, and putting them to a wretched death. Perhaps there will be another occasion." Alberti had thus worked on offensive strategies, whether or not he ultimately incorporated them into a treatise.

64. Ibid., 4.2, 95.

65. Ibid., 4.2, 96. Alberti muses, "What should my example be? Egypt is praised above all for being so utterly inaccessible and so wonderfully fortified on all sides, protected on one by the sea, on the other by a vast desert, to the right by craggy mountains, and to the left by extensive marshes; so great is the fertility of the land,

that Egypt was known in antiquity as the common granary of the world, and the gods would retreat there for peace and enjoyment. Yet, although its natural fortification and fertility were so great that it could boast of being capable of sustaining all other mortals, and hosting and protecting even the gods themselves, the region was unable, according to Josephus, to remain free for ever."

66. Ibid., 5.10, 131.

67. Ibid., 4.5, 107. Mancini lamented the practice of building winding streets, calling it a precept unfortunately put into practice all too often in Italian cities (*precetto disgraziamente troppo praticato nelle città italiane*). Mancini, *Vita*, 338.

68. Alberti, *On the Art of Building* 4.5, 107. Although this may sound far-fetched, Landucci describes how the French king Charles VIII, while occupying Florence in 1494, suffered a loss of nerve when negotiating the urban fabric: "23rd November (Sunday). The king rode out with a great troop of horsemen, and came to the *Croce di San Giovanni*; and when he was near the steps of *Santa Maria del Fiore*, he turned back and went towards the *Servi*; but having gone a few paces, he turned round again, and again went to the *Croce di San Giovanni*, going at the back of *San Giovanni*, through that narrow *Chiassolino* [alley], and coming under the *Volta di San Giovanni, d' Cialdonai*; and those who saw him laughed, and said slighting things of him, causing his reputation to suffer. Then he went through the *Mercato Vecchio*, and on as far as *San Felice in Piazza*, to see the *festa* of San Felice, which they were having on his account; but when he reached the door he would not enter; and they repeated everything several times, but he did not enter once. Many people said that he was afraid, and did not wish to be shut in, and this proved to us that he was more afraid than we were; and woe to him if a disturbance had begun, although there would also have been great danger for us." Landucci, *Florentine Diary*, 69.

69. Alberti, *On the Art of Building* 4.5, 107.

70. Ibid., 4.8, 115. Of the harbor itself, Alberti writes, "One further relevant consideration must not be overlooked here: there have been, and there remain to this day, well-known examples of cities that are all the better defended for the inconsistency of the current at their harbor mouths and entrances; the current there is understood only by those who study its almost invisible, hourly changes in direction."

71. Ibid., 4.8, 116.

72. Deuteronomy 20:16–17 (Authorized Version).

73. The influence of the Old Testament, particularly Ecclesiastes, on Alberti's thought has been noted by Marolda, *Crisi e conflitto*, 106. See also Panza, *Leon Battista Alberti*, 33–34.

74. Alberti, *Opere volgari*, 2:87: "Constituta legge della fortuna pervertere ogni dì nuove cose."

75. Ibid., 2:88.

76. Ibid., 2:89: "Ne' tempi di Tiberio dicono in una notte ruinorono in Asia dodici grandissime e famose città, dove ancora e ne' tempi di Nerone più nobile città ruinarono, Apamea, Laodicia, Ieropoli e Colossa. E scrive Tacito in que' tempi stata in Campagna sì veemente tempesta che pel furore de' venti le ville, gli albori e onni pianta in tutta la provincia si trovò svelta e lungi asportata."

77. Ibid.: "Non adunque dobbiamo maravigliarci, omicciuoli mortali e sopra tutti gli altri animali infermissimi, se mai quando che sia riceviamo qualche calamità, poiché noi vediamo le terre e provincie intere suggette ad ultimi estermini e ruine."

78. Ibid., 2:90–91. Teogenio says, "Potrei estendermi in quante erbe, in quanti frutti, in quanti animali, in quante cose la natura vi ponesse contro di noi veneno e morte, e quasi possiamo affermare nulla trovarsi fra e' mortali in quale non sia forza di darci a morte." The Epicurean Vegio mocks this Stoic position in Valla, *On Pleasure*, 85.

79. Alberti, *Opere volgari*, 2:92: "Scrive Iustino e Paulo Orosio istorici ch' e' populi chiamati Obderite, e que' che si nominano Avienate, fuggirono e abandonarono el suo paese cacciati dalla moltitudine de' topi e dalle ranelle. E scrisse M. Varrone in Ispagna essere stata svelta una terra da' conigli, e in Tessaglia simile dalle talpe data in ruina un'altra città. E racconta Plinio quanto siano infestissimi inimici a' populi cirenaici e' grilli. E così troverai in le istorie spesso state a' mortali gravissime calamitate addutte da tali vilissimi animanti. Nè trovasi animale alcuno tanto da tutti gli altri odiato quanto l'uomo."

80. Ibid., 2:94: "L'uomo efferattissimo si truova mortale agli altri uomini e a se stessi. E troverai più uomini essere periti per cagion degli altri uomini che per tutte l'altre calamità ricevute. Cesare Augusto si gloriava in sue battaglie, senza la strage civile, avere uccisi uomini numero cento e due e novanta migliara. Paolo Orosio istorico raccolse in parte le miserie sofferte da' mortali persino a' tempi suoi, e benché fusse scrittore succinto e brevissimo, pur crebbero suoi libri in amplissimo volume, tanta trovò stata sofferta miseria da' populi e gente degna di memoria."

81. On this, see David Marsh's introduction to Alberti, *Dinner Pieces*, 7.

82. Ibid., 16.

83. Watkins, "Leon Battista Alberti in the Mirror," 9; Fubini and Menci Gallorini, "L'autobiografia di Leon Battista Alberti," 71; and Mancini, *Vita*, 169.

84. Alberti, *Dinner Pieces*, 27.

85. Ibid.

86. Ibid.

87. Alberti, *Opere volgari*, 2:160–62.

88. Alberti, *Dinner Pieces*, 211.

89. As Garin, "Il pensiero," 518, has written, Alberti does not claim that the virtuous man is somehow able to overcome the world and its events. Rather, he is able to overcome himself.

90. Alberti, *Opere volgari*, 2:107: "E certo questo tempio ha in sè grazia e maiestà: e quello ch'io spesso considerai, mi diletta ch'io veggo in questo tempio iunta insieme una gracilità vezzosa con una sodezza robusta e piena, tale che da una parte ogni suo membro pare posto ad amenità, e dall'altra parte compreendo che ogni cosa qui è fatta offirmata a perpetuità. Aggiungi che qui abita continuo la temperie, si può dire, della primavera: fuori vento, gelo, brina; qui entro socchiuso da' venti, qui tiepido aere e quieto: fuori vampe estive e autunnali; qui entro temperatissimo refrigerio. E s'egl'è, come e' dicono, che le delizie sono quando a' nostri sensi s'aggiungono le cose quanto e quali le richiede la natura, chi dubiterà appellare questo tempio nido delle delizie?" I have used the English translation of this passage by Smith, *Architecture in the Culture of Early Humanism*, 5–6. Smith provides a highly effective and original analysis of the passage.

91. I am paraphrasing Rinaldi, *Melancholia christiana*, 10–11.

92. Ibid.: "Le tessere del mosaico allora, le fonti albertiane, finiscono per apparire come i relitti di un'apocalittica distruzione del sapere, compiuta dal tempo e dalla stoltezza umana."

93. Marsh, *Dinner Pieces*, 110.

94. Alberti, *Momus*, 84–85: "Quantas clades, quantas urbium eversiones, quanta gentium excidia futura intueor!"

95. Ibid.: "Refertum cadaveribus mare, cruentatas provincias, foedata astra flagrantium urbium fuligine visurus sum." I have slightly modified the translation.

96. Ibid., 122–23: "Quid et quod magis oderis? Vota audebant facere quibus urbium provinciarumque ultimum exitium atque excidium flagitarent."

97. Ovid, *Metamorphoses* 1.236–39, 8 (references are to book, line, and page numbers in Melville's translation).

98. Alberti, *Dinner Pieces*, 186.

99. Alberti, *Opere volgari*, 2:94: "Lupo dicea Plauto poeta essere l'uomo agli altri uomini." See Plautus, *Asinaria* 2.495.

100. Smith, "Apocalypse Sent Up," S167, points out that in the proems to each of the four books of *Momus*, Alberti emphasizes that Momus was intent on the destruction of the world, the gods, and humanity and almost plunged the whole of creation into catastrophe. Seneca, *Natural Questions* 3.27.13–14, warns that the destruction of the world is not a fitting subject for humor.

Chapter 2

1. Alberti, *On the Art of Building* 5.1, 117, and *L'architettura*, 1:333.

2. Alberti, *On the Art of Building* 5.1, 117.

3. For further elaboration on the issues surrounding the tyrant's city, see Pearson, "Poulterers, Butchers, and Cooks," 303–33.

4. Plato, Aristotle, the Roman Stoics, and Thomas Aquinas are among notable contributors to the discourse.

5. See Baron, *Crisis, From Petrarch to Leonardo Bruni*, and *In Search of Florentine Civic Humanism*, which includes a perceptive essay on Alberti's relationship to civic humanism.

6. One of the few surviving pieces of Alberti's correspondence is a letter from Bruni; see Gorni, "Storia del certame coronario," 148–50. The letter, written in the wake of the 1441 Certame Coronario, is not warm in tone and seems to refer to a confrontation between the two men at Santa Croce in Florence in connection with the contest. David Marsh suggests that Bruni, who had a miserly reputation, was offended by Alberti's dedication to him of a book of the *Intercenales* on the subject of avarice and prodigality. See Alberti, *Dinner Pieces*, 223n, 232n. On Bruni and Alberti, see also Tavoni, *Latino, grammatica, volgare*, xiii. Regarding Alberti and the general ambience of Florentine humanism, Boschetto, *Leon Battista Alberti e Firenze*, 100, has argued that the ferocious satire to which Alberti often subjects Florence in many of the *Intercenales* suggests that he was not, as a young scholar, much preoccupied with winning the favor of the city's cultural establishment—or that he soon found himself at odds with it. Later, he notes that Alberti never hesitated to articulate his critical view of Florentine humanistic culture and his profound skepticism toward the idea that the city had a cultural mission.

7. Alberti, *On the Art of Building* 5.1, 118, and *L'architettura*, 1:337: "Itaque his tyrannorum urbs a regum urbe differt."

8. Burroughs, *From Signs to Design*, 173, 182, also comments on this ambiguity. Alberti himself was employed by rulers such as Sigismondo Malatesta of Rimini and the Este in Ferrara, who could be classified as tyrants according to many definitions.

9. Alberti, *On the Art of Building* 5.1, 117.

10. Ibid., 5.1, 118. I have slightly modified the translation. The reference is to Terence, *Eunuchus* 2.2.

11. Walls were a fundamental element of the urban topography, and they loom large in descriptions of cities throughout the Middle Ages; see Hyde, "Medieval Descriptions." Successive wall-building campaigns might serve to differentiate the inner and outer zones of a city. Alberti would have been aware of such campaigns in Rome and Florence.

12. Salutati's most obvious sources are John of Salisbury's *Polycraticus* and Bartolo di Sassoferrato's *De tyranno*.

13. Emerton, *Humanism and Tyranny*, 78.

14. Ibid., 85.

15. Ibid., 93; these are Ephraim Emerton's words. The figure of Julius Caesar in the writings of Salutati and others is explored by Canfora, *Prima di Machiavelli*, 5–19.

16. Emerton, *Humanism and Tyranny*, 93–116.

17. Ibid., 93; these are Emerton's words.

18. Baron, *Crisis*, 100–120, seeks to explain Salutati's position with reference to concepts of medieval and Renaissance minds. Salutati, he says, fell between the two and expresses to some degree "the vitality of medieval thought still preserved on the threshold of the new century" (103). Proof of Salutati's medieval character, he says, is found in the quality of his Latin and his preference for the *vita contemplativa*, which was rejected by the Renaissance. He argues that Salutati became a monarchist in later life because he was ultimately unable to disagree with Dante. According to Baron, Salutati's *De tyranno*, with its pattern of starting in a rather republican vein and ending on a monarchical (even a tyrannical) note, is typical of trecento thinking. Salutati, he notes, is the last of such thinkers, because the Milanese war made this position untenable. It might be argued, however, that Baron's thesis relies too heavily on rather rigid concepts of the "psyches" of the Middle Ages and the Renaissance. On Salutati's approach to the *vita contemplativa*, see Kahn, "Coluccio Salutati."

19. Emerton, *Humanism and Tyranny*, 74. Salutati clearly reveals himself here, as elsewhere in his treatise, as a monarchist. For a fuller discussion of Salutati's views on monarchy, see Ullman, "Coluccio Salutati on Monarchy." Ullman argues that Salutati favored a resurrection of the Roman Empire.

20. Alberti, *On the Art of Building* 5.1, 117.

21. Ibid. For a detailed analysis of these examples and their sources, as well as a very particular argument, see Burroughs, *From Signs to Design*, 171–84.

22. Alberti, *On the Art of Building* 5.1, 117–18.

23. Ibid., 5.1, 118.

24. Ibid. Alberti's concentric city appears to draw inspiration from Herodotus's description of Babylon in the *Histories* 1.181.

25. Burroughs, *From Signs to Design*, 176. We should note, however, that Leonardo da Vinci did suggest to Ludovico Sforza that he should divide Milan into ten cities in order to avoid potential mass gatherings. See G. Simoncini, *Città e società*, 1:38.

26. White, *Italy*, 144. Many commentators have seen Alberti as in some ways anticipating Machiavelli. Hale, *Renaissance War Studies*, 192–93, argues that in Alberti's discussion of security "were hints which, if known, could have been more suggestive than anything to be found in pre-Machiavellian writers on politics: the occasions and justification of war; the use of armies and the character of the soldier; the need for and the nature of defenses, the qualities of the tyrant and discussion as to whether it is better to be loved or feared." Machiavelli devotes a section of *The Prince* (completed early 1514) to the pros and cons of building fortresses and dividing the population of a city. See Machiavelli, *The Prince*, 114–19.

27. Di Stefano, *L'altro sapere*, 90, suggests that Alberti's treatise was aimed above all at refined patrons in the Italian courts. Stefano Borsi, *Leon Battista Alberti e Roma*, 234, notes that Alberti specifies in *De re aedificatoria* 2.9 that his text is not intended merely for those involved in construction but rather for a wider public of men of culture. Marolda, *Crisi e conflitto*, 132–33, recognizes that Alberti's interests extend beyond buildings for rulers and the elite in *De re*, taking in infrastructure such as streets and waterways. However, despite Alberti's claim that he treats buildings for all kinds of individuals, buildings for the lower orders receive scant attention and Alberti sometimes simply advises that they should approximate, so far as possible, buildings for the elite.

28. From a letter written in 1484, quoted by Rykwert in his introduction to Alberti, *On the Art of Building*, xviii.

29. Alberti, *Opere volgari*, 2:78: "Dicea Assioco, presso a Platone, la plebe altro essere nulla che inconstanza, inferma, instabile, volubile, lieve, futile, bestiale, ignava, quale solo si guidi con errore, inimica sempre alla ragione, e piena d'ogni corrotto iudizio."

30. Ibid., 1:291: "La Luna conciti viaggi e movimenti feminili e plebei." See also Trexler, *Public Life*, 16. Alberti is renowned for his disdain for women.

31. Alberti, *Della famiglia*, 251–52, and *Opere volgari*, 1:259:

GIANNOZZO: Quanto io, della amistà, che so io? Forse potrebbesi dire che chi è ricco truova più amici che non vuole.

ADOVARDO: Io pur veggo e' ricchi essere molto invidiati dagli altri, e dicesi che tutti e' poveri sono inimici de' ricchi, e forse dicono il vero. Volete voi vedere perché?

GIANNOZZO: Voglio. Dì.

ADOVARDO: Perché ogni povero cerca d'aricchire.

GIANNOZZO: Vero.

ADOVARDO: E niuno povero, se già non gli nascessono sotto terra le ricchezze, niuno povero arricchisce se a qualche altro non scemano le sue ricchezze.

32. Adovardo's sentiments appear to be reflected in Libripeta's assertion in the intercenale "Religion" that "no goods can come to you but those snatched from others who own them." Alberti, *Dinner Pieces*, 19.

33. Alberti, *Della famiglia*, 251–52, and *Opere volgari*, 1:259:

ADOVARDO: E' poveri sono quasi infiniti.

GIANNOZZO: Vero. Molto più ch'e' ricchi.

ADOVARDO: Tutti s'argomentano d'avere più roba, ciascuno con sua arte, con inganni, fraude, rapine, non meno che con industria.

GIANNOZZO: Vero.

ADOVARDO: Le ricchezze adunque assediate da tanti piluccatori v'arrecano elle amistà pure o nimistà?

34. For statutes regarding influxes into Parma and Perugia, see Dean, *Towns of Italy*, 138–39. Controls were put in place in Parma "lest in every respect all peasants become citizens" (139).

35. For various opinions of the nature of the Ciompi revolt, see Antal, *Florentine Painting*, 23–24; Brucker, *Renaissance Florence*, 68, and "Ciompi Revolution," 356; and Cohn, *Laboring Classes*, 129–44.

36. Dean, *Towns of Italy*, 176–82.

37. Antal, *Florentine Painting*, 70–72. On the Fraticelli in Florence, see Stephens, "Heresy in Medieval and Renaissance Florence," 36, and Weinstein, "Myth of Florence," 26–28, 30–32.

38. The major guilds did not govern the city as they did at Florence, and by the time Alberti arrived in Rome, the guilds appear to have had little importance, although there is scant evidence as to their membership. See Burroughs, *From Signs to Design*, 28, and Maire-Vigueur, "Classe dominante."

39. Pastor, *History of the Popes*, 1:294–95.

40. Farenga, "I Romani," 292: ". . . in visinanza de Cortesanj, che altramente mi bisognava andare fora di logi dove sono riducti per esser più siccuri."

41. Ibid., 302: "nel corpo della terra"; "un menare queste gente alla beccaria."

42. Cicero, *De officiis* 1.150, 152–55 (references are to book, chapter, and page numbers in Miller's translation): "Minimeque artes eae probandae, quae ministrae sunt voluptatum: / Cetarii, lanii, coqui, fartores, piscatores, / Ut ait Terentius; adde huc, si placet, unguentarios, saltatores, totumque ludum talarium." I have slightly modified the translation. Cicero's translator, Walter Miller, describes the *ludus talarius* as "a kind of low variety show, with loose songs and dances and bad music" (155n1).

43. Palmieri, *Vita civile*, 187: "In nell'arti sono inhoneste quelle che nuocono et sono inutili a costumi degl'huomini et minestre di non necessario dilecto, come taverne, cuochi, venditori di liscio, scuole di balli o d'altre lascivie et qualunche giuoco di dadi."

44. Celenza, *Renaissance Humanism*, 182–83. Celenza provides a complete parallel English translation of the Latin text. Lapo's own words are "coquos, fartores, pulmentarios." Alberti must have known Lapo's work, not least because, as we saw earlier, Lapo included a passage in his treatise that praised Alberti generously.

45. Brucker, *Renaissance Florence*, 153, states that during the fourteenth century, "the most unruly element of the *arti minori* were the butchers, who by tradition and temperament were prone to violence." Becker and Brucker, "*Arti Minori*," 99, describe how the butchers were "traditionally the most unruly and ubiquitous of the *arti minori*, eager to take the lead in popular movements and insurrections against authority."

46. Becker and Brucker, "*Arti Minori*," 99–100.

47. *Statuti*, 1:238: "Statutum et ordinatum est quod non patiatur dominus Capitaneus nec dominus Potestas Florentie quod aliqua persona, masculus vel femina, Communis, nec etiam aliquis vendens panem vel vinum seu carnes vel pisces coctos vel aliqua commestibilia moretur vel stet prope palatium dominorum Potestatis et Capitanei per ducenta brachia."

48. See Trexler, *Public Life*, 51–52, esp. n. 26.

49. Modigliani, *Mercati*, 109–16.

50. Antonio Pucci's poem "Proprieta di Mercato Vecchio" describes the rabble of Florence's central marketplace. Pucci says that one might see "miserable youths," butchers, poulterers, women who argue and swear at one another, gamblers, pimps, and prostitutes. One can observe all kinds of ne'er-do-wells, from both city and country, and fights often occur, sometimes resulting in fatalities. The crowds include professional swindlers, raucous people who sing all day, and the destitute, who, being completely without clothes, crouch naked in the cold. See Sapegno, *Poeti minori del Trecento*, 403–10, and Dean, *Towns of Italy*, 121–24, for an English translation of Pucci's text. Fanelli, *Firenze*, 58, describes how at the trecento Mercato Vecchio of Florence "one could find every kind of merchandise and every type of person: peasants, gentlemen, the simply curious, gamblers, prostitutes and pimps, usurers, money lenders, and secondhand dealers." (Si possono trovare ogni genere di merce, e ogni genere di persone: contadini, gentiluomini, semplici curiosi, giocatori, meretrici e ruffiani, usurai, cambiatori, rigattieri.) See Modigliani, *Mercati*, 187–91, for an account of the mixture of persons and the problems of public order in the Campo de' Fiori in Rome.

51. Cohn, *Laboring Classes*, 89; see also Cherubini, "La taverna," 552–55.

52. Cohn, *Laboring Classes*, 89.

53. Celenza, *Renaissance Humanism*, 180–81: "... formosos etiam ministros ad ministrandas epulas, catamitos quoque et calamistratos studiose quaerunt eosque splendidis vestibus indutos, leves maximeque inberbes esse volunt, Alexandri, credo, Macedonis auctoritatem secuti."

54. Ibid., 178–79: "Ex hac plurimae voluptatum libidines maximaeque venereae excitantur, quae ea sublata refrigescunt, ut est apud Terentium: 'Sine Cerere et Libero.'"

Alberti visits the same commonplace in *Della famiglia*, 80, and *Opere volgari*, 1:63. The source is Terence, *Eunuchus* 4.5.733.

55. *Statuti*, 1:243: "Cum propter multitudinem tabernarum in quibus venduntur et fiunt cibaria commestibilia et gulosa multi pueri et homines devient et assuescant et actus suos convertant ad vitia et ad peccata turpia pertractanda que sunt abhominabilia apud deum et homines."

56. Ibid., 1:244.

57. Cohn, *Laboring Classes*, 89n36, quotes Paolo da Certaldo's admonition to take great care not to visit taverns but to visit churches instead, both on feast days and at any other time that one might legitimately leave the workshop or the warehouse. In the *Della famiglia*, Lionardo describes how a child may stray from the path to fame and glory, "just as although one might be on the good, straight road to go to the temple, yet one can stop at the theater and watch and waste time" (come benché uno sia per la buona e dritta via a 'ndare al tempio, al teatro pure può fermarsi e badare e perdere tempo). Alberti, *Opere volgari*, 1:64.

58. Bernardino laments, "O tavern keepers, because of you, men go to your tavern instead of to mass!" (O taverneiri, che se' principio che l'uomo non va a la messa per la tua taverna!) Cherubini, "La taverna," 536. Cherubini summarizes Bernardino's position neatly, observing that for the Franciscan preacher, "the tavern is a kind of anti-church, of anti-parish, in which the parish priests are the tavern keepers, vicars are the swindlers, incense is the odor of cooking pig's liver, the parishioners are the drunks who frequent these counter-churches that are contrary to God, priests are gamblers, canonesses are prostitutes, and canons are pimps." (La taverna è una sorta di controchiesa, di contropieve, e pievani vengano da lui definiti i tavernieri, vicari i bari, incenso l'odore dei fegatelli, parrochiani gli ubriachi che frequentano queste chiese contrarie a Dio, preti sono i giocatori, canonichesse le meretrici, canonici i ruffiani.)

59. Cherubini, "La taverna," 562.

60. Alberti, *Della familia*, 63, and *Opere volgari*, 1:43: "Onde non senza grandissimo biasimo di negligenza saranno e' padri quali aranno e' figliuoli non corretti, ma disviati e scelerati."

61. Alberti, *Opere volgari*, 2:201: "Impazzano se non possono quel che vorrebbono, diventano rattori, ottrettatori, calunniatori, insidiatori, perfidi, e fanno in sé abito d'ogni corruttela."

62. Ibid., 2:202: "... furto, sacrilegio, latrocinio, lenocini, venefici, conducere con fraudolenza e tradimento persone a farli perdere la roba, l'onore, la vita, vendere l'onestà sua e de' suoi."

63. Sullivan, "Aertsen's Kitchen and Market Scenes," provides an extensive bibliography regarding food traders and popular perception of them from the ancient to the early modern period; see especially 249–51 for a very rich account of kitchens, markets, and food in ancient satire.

64. Celenza, *Renaissance Humanism*, 182–83: "... quos unctos sordidos in media culina, in fumo et nidore volutari videris."

65. *Statuti*, 1:244: "... tabernarius sive coquus sive quocumque nomine censeatur."

66. Ibid.

67. Palmieri, *Vita civile*, 187.

68. Jeanneret, *Feast of Words*, 201, observes that "since the comedies of Plautus, the cook has traditionally been at the bottom of the servant hierarchy; he is in constant contact with raw material and flesh, is uneducated and speaks like a peasant."

69. Plato, *Complete Works*, 808 (465a). Plato goes on to condemn cosmetics, the art of adorning the body, which he also classifies as a part of "flattery." It is, he says, "a mischievous, deceptive, disgraceful and ill-bred thing, one that perpetrates

deception by means of shaping and coloring, smoothing out and dressing up, so as to make people assume an alien beauty and neglect their own, which comes through gymnastics." Cicero, it should be remembered, lists *unguentarii* (dealers in perfumes and unguents) among the trades to be disparaged, and cosmetics might be considered part of the same category. Cosmetics are clearly condemned by Christian thinkers such as Tertullian and Aquinas and singled out for disapproval by Palmieri. Alberti condemns the application of cosmetics in a well-known passage of Book III of *Della famiglia* and returns to the theme in *Momus*, 57–61.

70. Alberti, *Opere volgari*, 2:201: "Obbrobio della città, meritano essere portati in qualche insula deserta a ciò che tanta peste non vizi gli altri."

71. In Florence, certainly, while many families possessed property in the *contado*, very few members of the ruling group were prepared to construct their urban palaces outside of the old city center in the large stretches of land enclosed within the third ring of walls constructed between 1284 and 1333, despite generous tax incentives. Goldthwaite, *Building of Renaissance Florence*, 16–17, notes that "these vast blocks of private property were inserted in the congested center of the city, not in the open areas of the periphery.... Subsequently, legislation was designed to promote building in the vast outlying area between the populated center of the city and the third circle of walls, which had never been built up and was turned over instead to gardens and farms." This took the form of tax breaks. Twenty years later, however, not a single person had taken advantage of them. See also Cohn, *Laboring Classes*, 127.

72. Passerini, *Gli Alberti*; Mancini, *Vita*, 1–16; and Cancro, *Filosofia ed architettura*, 49–96. See also Grafton, *Leon Battista Alberti*, 6, 33, and Goldthwaite, *Building of Renaissance Florence*, 35, 39. Boschetto, *Leon Battista Alberti e Firenze*, 101, supplies much detail about the Albertis' commercial activities and, interestingly, demonstrates how, in Florence, Battista himself was very much socialized into the mercantile world and integrated into a tight web of social and economic relations.

73. Alberti, *Della famiglia*, 62, and *Opere volgari*, 1:41: "Né anche fa la terra nostra troppo pregio de' litterati, anzi più tosto pare tutta studiosa al guadagno e cupida di ricchezze. O questo il paese che lo dia, o pure la natura e consuetudine de' passati, tutti pare crescano alla industria del guadagno, ogni ragionamento pare che senta della masserizia, ogni pensiero s'argomenta ad acquistare, ogni arte si stracca in congregare motle ricchezze.... Come scrive Platone, quel principe de' filosofi, che ogni costume de' Lacedemoniesi era infiammato di cupidità di vincere, così stimo alla terra nostra il cielo produce gl'ingegni astuti a discernere el guadagno, el luogo e l'uso gl'incende non a gloria in prima, ma ad avanzarsi e conservarsi roba, e a desiderare ricchezze."

74. Alberti, *Della famiglia*, 147, and *Opere volgari*, 1:141: "Adunque ora cominceremo ad accumulare ricchezze. Forse questo tempo, che già siamo presso al brunire della sera, s'aconfarà a questi ragionamenti. Niuno essercizio, a chi hane l'animo magno e liberale, pare manco splendido che paiono quegli instituti essercizi per coadunare ricchezze. Se voi qui considererete alquanto e discorrerete, riducendo a memoria quali siano essercizii accomodati a fare roba, voi gli troverete tutti posti non in altro che in comperare e vendere, prestare e riscuotere. E io stimo che a voi, e' quali, quanto giudico, pur non avete l'animo né piccolo né vile, que' tutti essercizii suggetti solo al guadagno potranno parervi bassi e con poco lume di lode e autorità. Già poiché in verità el vendere non è se non cosa mercennaria, tu servi alla utilità del comperatore, paghiti della fatica tua, ricevi premio sopraponendo ad altri quello che manco era costato a te.... El prestare sarebbe lodata liberalità, se tu non ne richiedessi premio, ma non sarebbe essercizio d'aricchirne. Né pare ad alcuni questi essercizii, come gli chiameremo, pecuniarii mai stieno netti, sanza molte bugie, e stimano non poche volte in quegli intervenire patti spurchi e scritture non oneste."

75. Alberti, *Della famiglia*, 147, and *Opere volgari*, 1:141: "Però dicono al tutto questi come brutti e mercenarii sono a' liberali ingegni molto da fuggire."

76. Poggio put this argument into the mouth of Antonio Loschi in his *De avaritia*. See Kohl and Witt, *Earthly Republic*, 262–63.

77. Alberti, *Della famiglia*, 147, and *Opere volgari*, 1:141: "Ma costoro, quali così giudicano di tutti gli essercizii pecuniarii, a mio parere errano. Se l'acquistare ricchezza non è glorioso come gli altri essercizii maggiori, non però sarà da spregiar colui el quale non sia di natura atto a ben travagliarsi in quelle molto magnifiche essercitazioni, se si trametterà in questo al quale essercizio conosce sé essere non inetto, e quale per tutti si confessa alle republice essere molto e alle famiglie utilissimo."

78. Watkins, "Leon Battista Alberti in the Mirror," 9; Fubini and Menci Gallorini, "L'autobiografia di Leon Battista Alberti," 71; and Mancini, *Vita*, 168–69.

79. Kuehn, "Reading Between the Patrilines," 167, argues that Alberti's treatise on the family was actually "a subtle and learned form of vendetta against those Alberti who had harmed him."

80. Alberti, *Della famiglia*, 151, and *Opere volgari*, 1:146: "Ora mancano e' padri; ora seguano e' parenti invidiosi, duri, inumani: ora t'asalisce povertà, ora cadi in qualche infortunio."

81. Alberti, *Dinner Pieces*, 17.

82. The rupture between Battista and other members of the *consorteria* should not be viewed too simplistically. Boschetto, *Leon Battista Alberti e Firenze*, 75–76, 128, has stressed that Alberti's grievances related only to the cousins Benedetto and Antonio and that he maintained good relationships with other members of the clan. Even the rupture that did occur cannot, he continues, be dated to before the middle years of the 1430s. Where Kuehn has interpreted the *Della famiglia* as a subtle vendetta against part of the family, Boschetto sees the author as keen, above all else, to defend the family at every turn. Nonetheless, he suggests that the optimism shown in Book II, where the Alberti appear as great merchants and are praised as such, does not continue, because by the time Alberti began the third book, the troubles that were to engulf the family business were already beginning to manifest themselves. As argued above, however, there does appear to be an implied critique of the relatives whom Alberti felt had wronged him.

83. Alberti, *Della famiglia*, 148, and *Opere volgari*, 1:142: ". . . e in questo modo siamo in Italia e fuor d'Italia, in Ispagna, in Ponente, in Soria, in Grecia, e a tutti e' porti conosciuti grandissimi mercatanti." I have slightly modified the translation.

84. Irmscher, "*Ministrae voluptatum*," 219–32, considers Cicero's distinction in relation to sixteenth-century Netherlandish painting and, to some degree, the broader culture of early modern Europe. On the same topic, see Sullivan, "Aertsen's Kitchen and Market Scenes."

85. Cicero, *De officiis* 1.42, 152–55.

86. Alberti, *On the Art of Building* 4.3, 102.

87. Indeed, the term seems always to have had this double meaning and was sometimes used in the Middle Ages specifically to denote a greedy person. For an example of such usage that is contemporary with Alberti's *De re aedificatoria*, see Porcellius Napolitanus's *Commentarii comitis Jacobi Picinini* of 1452, column 81: "Illuc [Florentiam] ergo cupedenarii per multi concurrebant, quorum nulla exstare gloria potest, quando quidem laudi bonæque famæ pecuniam anteponunt." Varro, *De lingua Latina* 5.146, writes, "Ubi variae res ad Corneta Forum Cuppedinis a cupedio, id est a fastidio, quod multi Forum Cupidinis a cupiditate." Ambrosius Calepinus, in his fifteenth-century Latin dictionary, repeats this etymology, adding that some believe the word *cupedinarij* to originate from the Roman consul Cupedius, who, having been convicted of robbery,

had his property torn down. A forum for sellers of confectionary was then constructed where his buildings had stood. A version of this story is repeated in Tomaso Garzoni's *La piazza universale*, where the word *cupedinarii* is characterized as coextensive with *lardaruoli*, sellers of fatty delicacies such as "salamis, hams, ox tongues, fine fat, pork lard, cheese from Piacenza, cheeses from Monferrato, sardines, anchovies, fish eggs, poultry, and also birds of various types" (salami, persciutti, lingue di bue, onto sottile, lardo di porco, formaggio piacentino, formelle di Monferrato, puine fresche, sardelle, anchioe, caviaro, pollami, et anco uccelli di varie sorti). Garzoni, who knew Alberti's treatise, goes on to connect such traders with *fartores* and *pollaruoli*, and comments that although the *lardaruolo* serves a useful purpose, "on the other hand, he has so much of the guzzler and the greedy in him that you will not find a more comfortable dive for gluttons than a *lardaruolo*'s workshop. It is also a dirty and vile occupation because they are always greasy like cooks, and you will find little or no difference between them and a dogsbody." (Dall'altro canto ha tanto del ghiotto et del leccardo, che non si trova bettola per i golosi più commoda quanto la bottega d'un lardaruolo. È anco mestiero sporco, et vile, perché sempre son onti come cuochi, e da sguattari a loro si trova poco, o nulla di differenza.) See Garzoni, *La piazza universale*, 2:1005.

88. Alberti, *On the Art of Building*, prologue, 3.

89. See, for example, Buonaccorso Pitti's fruitless efforts to recover a loan from the count of Savoy, recounted by Brucker, *Two Memoirs*, 44–45, 64. We may also note the case of Rinieri Davanzati, who complained in 1427 that he could not recover debts that had been owed to his grandfather from business dealings in Dalmatia because some of the debtors "are lords and counts in these regions and have no superiors, and whoever ventures there does so at great risk, and instead of repayment, he may receive blows and be robbed and killed, as has happened to others." Quoted in Brucker, *Renaissance Florence*, 78; for the difficulties faced by the international merchant, see 68–78.

90. Alberti, *Della famiglia*, 149, and *Opere volgari*, 1:143: "Pare in la terra nostra niuna, se non sola la nostra famiglia Alberta, gran ricchezza, niuna giugnesse mai a' suoi nipoti eredi. In pochi dì sono inanite e ite, come dicono e' vulgari, in fummo, e di qualche una di loro rimasone povertà, miseria e infamia. Non mi piace qui stendere a recitare essempli, né investigare che cagione o che infortunio così tra' nostri concittadini dilegui le grandissime ricchezze. . . . Cerchi, Peruzzi, Scali, Spini e Ricci, e infinite altre famiglie nella terra nostra amplissime e oggidì ornatissime di virtù e nobilissime, le quali già abondavano di grandissime e ismisurate ricchezze, si vede quanto subito, ingiuria della fortuna, sieno cadute in infelicità e parte in grandissime necessitati."

91. Del Fante, *La città di Leon Battista Alberti*, 34, and Eckstein, *District of the Green Dragon*, 9.

92. Alberti, *On the Art of Building* 5.3, 121–22.

93. Ibid., 5.3, 122.

94. Ibid., 5.4, 123. Stefano Borsi, *Momus, o Del principe*, 9–10, relates the form of the tyrant's arx to the humorous episode in *Momus* in which Apollo, conversing with Democritus, dissects an onion to reveal the letters C and O. Apollo interprets this as referring to the words *corruiturum orbem*—"the world will collapse." We might read this as an acknowledgment of the inevitable destruction of even the strongest of buildings (although Apollo's prediction is brushed aside by the pragmatic philosopher, who asks where the gods would be able to put the raw material of the world if they destroyed it). See Alberti, *Momus*, 252–53.

95. Alberti, *On the Art of Building* 5.4, 123.

96. Ibid., 5.5, 125.

97. Ibid., 5.3, 122.

98. Frommel, "Papal Policy," 39.

99. Westfall, *In This Most Perfect Paradise*, 100–101; Burroughs, *From Signs to Design*, 72–74, 77–78, and "Below the Angel," 94–124. It has been argued that the passage of *Momus* that describes the collapse of the Arch of Juno may be read as a satire on the Torrione, or New Tower, that Nicholas V constructed at the Vatican palace. The tower collapsed on August 31, 1454. See Grafton, *Leon Battista Alberti*, 309, and Fubini, "Leon Battista Alberti, Niccolò V," 463.

100. Westfall, *In This Most Perfect Paradise*, 107–9, 143–48.

101. Ibid., 100.

102. The parallels with Alberti's tyrant's city have, of course, been remarked upon. See Cassanelli, Delfini, and Fonti, *Le mura di Roma*, 96–102; Burroughs, "Alberti e Roma"; and S. Borsi, *Leon Battista Alberti e Roma*, 84, and *Momus, o Del principe*, 12.

103. Alberti, *On the Art of Building* 5.5, 125.

104. Watkins, *Humanism and Liberty*, 112.

105. Ibid., 114–15.

106. Fubini, "Leon Battista Alberti, Niccolò V," argues that, following Poggio's lead, Alberti undermines the notion of the pope's maestas in *Momus*. Maestas was traditionally held to exempt the ruler from being subject to fortune and unhappiness. Fubini contends that *Momus* ultimately argues for the dignity of power rather than for its majesty, in much the same way that Alberti argued for a functional architecture as opposed to the triumphalist building projects favored by Nicholas. See especially p. 460.

107. Alberti, *On the Art of Building* 5.3, 122.

108. Rubinstein, "Fortified Enclosures," 2. Rubinstein also points out that "when, at Naples, in 1535, Florentine exiles presented to Charles V a list of complaints about the rule of Duke Alessandro de' Medici, among the evidence to prove the tyrannical nature of that rule, they cited his building of a large fortress near the Porta a Faenza.... The exiles argued that: 'avere edificato una fortezza, [era] cosa tutta aliena a qualunche città libera,' as was shown by the example of Venice, Siena, Lucca and Genoa" (1).

109. Manetti, "The Testament of Nicholas V," section T4, in Smith and O'Connor, *Building the Kingdom*, 474–75. Nicholas emphasized that such action was necessary to preserve the government of the church against enemies who conspired continually: "Adversos externos hostes ac domesticos novarum rerum cupidos quotidie diripiendi gratia conspirantes et in grave ecclesiasticarum gubernationum damnum insurgentes munitiores redduntur."

110. Watkins, *Humanism and Liberty*, 114.

111. Tafuri's essay is available in English in his *Interpreting the Renaissance*.

112. This argument is explored in detail by Stefano Borsi, *Momus, o Del principe*, and *Leon Battista Alberti e Roma*. See also S. Simoncini, "Roma come Gerusalemme," esp. 327; Smith and O'Connor, *Building the Kingdom*, 230–40; and Fubini, "Leon Battista Alberti, Niccolò V," 455–69.

113. The notion of *aedificandi libido* in Alberti's works has been widely commented on. See particularly Cassani, "*Libertas, frugalitas, aedificandi libido*." Fubini, "Leon Battista Alberti, Niccolò V," 458–59, explores the relationship of this term to others used by Alberti, such as *aedificandi insania*.

114. The collapse of the Arch of Juno may also relate to the destruction by Nicholas of a triumphal arch that stood in the area of Rome in which Alberti lived. The materials were used for paving. See Burroughs, "Alberti e Roma," 148; S. Borsi, *Momus, o Del principe*, 62; and Smith and O'Connor, *Building the Kingdom*, 213.

115. Stefano Borsi explores the issue in detail in *Momus, o Del principe*, and *Leon Battista Alberti e Roma*. See also Smith and O'Connor, *Building the Kingdom*, 237–39.

116. Stefano Borsi, *Alberti e Roma*, 36–37, notes that Alberti moved to Rome immediately upon Nicholas V's election. In contrast, when Eugenius IV returned to the city, Alberti waited several months before following the pope. Borsi suggests that this reflects Alberti's lack of faith in Eugenius's ability to govern. On Alberti as a spurned advisor, see ibid., 69–81. Boschetto, *Leon Battista Alberti e Firenze*, 158, notes that shortly after Nicholas was elected, Alberti had a contract drawn up for the tenancy of his benefice at San Martino a Gangalandi, in which he stipulated that the conditions would no longer apply if he were to receive promotion. This suggests that Alberti might have had high hopes from the new pope, with whom he was well acquainted. If Alberti expected advancement, the benefice that he received two years later must have been a disappointment, as it did not represent an improvement economically or in terms of status.

117. S. Borsi, *Momus, o Del principe*, 84–85, and *Leon Battista Alberti e Roma*, 81.

118. Smith and O'Connor, *Building the Kingdom*, 198–200, provide a summary of the debate regarding the date of *Momus*. The authors' own view is that *Momus* was written soon after the death of Nicholas V in 1455 and is contemporary with Manetti's biography. Fubini, "Leon Battista Alberti, Niccolò V," 455–69, sees *Momus* as a response to Manetti's biography.

119. See S. Simoncini, "Roma come Gerusalemme"; Smith, "Apocalypse Sent Up"; and Smith and O'Connor, *Building the Kingdom*, 225–54.

120. Smith and O'Connor, *Building the Kingdom*, 231.

121. Ibid., 240–54.

122. Ibid., 254.

123. Burroughs, "Alberti e Roma," 153.

124. S. Borsi, *Leon Battista Alberti e Roma*, 98: "Viveva, in fondo, nel punto di giunzione tra la città dei Romani e quella dei chierici, quella Città Leonina che con Nicolò V vedeva emblematicamente completarsi il suo munito sistema di fortificazioni. E l'autore del *De re* sa bene che significato attribuire a simili iniziative."

125. Borsi, ibid., 106, 260–61, points out that sideswipes at the jubilee form a relatively minor part of *De re* and that Alberti's attitude toward the *renovatio* should not be oversimplified.

Chapter 3

1. Tavernor, *On Alberti*, 19, emphasizes the pragmatic and non-idealizing nature of Alberti's treatise, while Franco Borsi, *Leon Battista Alberti*, 14, argues that Alberti does not present an ideal city. This is also a major contention of Choay's *The Rule and the Model*.

2. Garin, "La cité idéale," 13–37.

3. Ibid., 30–31: "Alberti, à vrai dire, distingue les principautés nouvelles et les royaumes des républiques libres. Les nouvelles principautés doivent s'accrocher aux montagnes et rester sur la défensive, dans le soupçon et la peur, alors que les peuples libres peuvent habiter des cités commodes dans la plaine. Mais à part cette mention, la ville d'Alberti est construite de manière à marquer fortement les différences de classes, à réaliser par les murailles et les édifices une structure politique précise. Ainsi architecte devient synonyme de régulateur, et de coordinateur de toutes les activités urbaines; reprenant librement l'expression d'Aristote, Alberti présente l'architecture comme l'art des arts, unificateur et roi de tous les autres. L'urbanisme est plus que lié à la politique, il fait corps avec elle et pour ainsi dire l'exprime de manière exemplaire." I have used the English translation of this passage by F. Borsi, *Leon Battista Alberti*, 14.

4. Alberti, *On the Art of Building*, prologue, 3.

5. In the ninth book, Alberti says that it is not necessary for the architect to have a detailed knowledge of many disciplines: "Of the arts the ones that are useful, even vital, to the architect are painting and mathematics. I am not concerned whether he is versed in any others" (ibid., 9.10, 317). Notably, these two disciplines contribute to the arts of drawing, design, and the determination and representation of *lineamenta*. There are hints in both *De re aedificatoria* and *Momus* that Alberti accorded lineamenta a particular epistemological importance. Particularly in *Momus*, the man who understands painting is able to understand the fundamental truths of the world.

6. Foucault, *Discipline and Punish*, 27, writes, "We should admit . . . that power produces knowledge (and not simply by encouraging it because it serves power or by applying it because it is useful); that power and knowledge directly imply one another; that there is no power relation without the correlative constitution of a field of knowledge, nor any knowledge that does not presuppose and constitute at the same time power relations."

7. Cassani, "Et flores quidem negligitis," esp. 68–77, examines the opposition between philosophers and architects in *Momus* and points out that both are found wanting in one way or another.

8. The extent to which Alberti actually formulated these rules himself, rather than merely transcribing them, is unclear. The tradition that Brunelleschi was the inventor of pictorial perspective has been challenged. Thomas Puttfarken, *Discovery of Pictorial Composition*, 84, points out that "Brunelleschi's experiments would not necessarily have suggested that precise perspective would work if it was not seen under the conditions of a peephole show." Lubbock, *Storytelling in Christian Art*, 177–90, conducts a forensic examination of the evidence regarding the "discovery" of perspective and concludes that the version set down by Alberti was his own invention.

9. See Carpo, "*Descriptio urbis romae*," 123.

10. Alberti, *On the Art of Building* 5.14, 140.

11. Ibid., 1.9, 23.

12. Ibid., 5.2, 119–20.

13. Ibid., 5.17, 145–51.

14. Ibid., 5.7, 127–28. In fact, he says, "A military camp with its rampart and ditches need not be defended as strongly as this, fortified, as it should be, with a high, unbroken wall, not even pierced by a single aperture through which temptations of the eye or incitement of the tongue might enter to weaken resolve, let alone actual people with designs on their chastity" (128).

15. Ibid., 5.2, 120–21.

16. Ibid., 5.17, 149.

17. Garin, "La cité idéale," 16–17: "hygiène publique, sécurité intérieure, défense contre les attaques venues de l'extérieur"; "les épidémies toujours renouvelées, les désordres populaires, les luttes pour la suprématie, les sièges, les sacs de ville, la famine. C'est ainsi que les traités d'urbanisme deviennent des traités de politique."

18. Throughout the communal and signoral periods, much legislation dealt with hygiene, the maintenance of streets, and prevention of private interests taking over or obstructing public spaces. See, for example, Waley, *Italian City-Republics*, 99; Dean, *Towns of Italy*, 50–54; Carmichael, *Plague and the Poor*, 96–98; and Bocchi, "Normativa urbanistica." De Seta has stressed that Alberti's treatise is strongly related to the discourse of planning legislation and civic ordinances; see his "Come in un specchio," 25–27.

19. Again, Foucault's work, although concerned with the eighteenth century, is interesting in this context. He remarks that "doctors at that time [the eighteenth

century] were among other things the specialists of space. They posed four fundamental problems. That of local conditions (regional climates . . .); that of the coexistences (either between men, questions of density and proximity, or between men and things, the question of water, sewage, ventilation, or between men and animals . . .); that of residences (the environment, urban problems); that of displacements (the migration of men, the propagation of diseases)." Foucault, *Power/ Knowledge*, 150–51.

20. Alberti, *On the Art of Building* 4.7, 113, denounces the filthy state of Siena and discusses the construction of drainage and sewers.

21. Carmichael, *Plague and the Poor*, 97, 99.

22. Ibid., 99, 108.

23. This information is derived from John Henderson, "Filth Is the Mother of Corruption" (paper presentation, Air in the Renaissance conference, Warburg Institute, June 28, 2002). See also his "Black Death," 143.

24. Chaucer, *Canterbury Tales*, general prologue, 379–87:

> A cook they hadde with hem for the nones
> To boille the chiknes with the marybones,
> And poudre-marchant tart and galyngale.
> Wel koude he knowe a draughte of Londoun ale.
> He koude rooste, and sethe, and broille, and frye,
> Maken mortreux, and wel bake a pye.
> But greet harm was it, as it thoughte me,
> That on his shyne a mormal hadde he.
> For blankmanger, that made he with the beste.

25. The Latin text is reproduced by D'Onofrio, *Visitiamo Roma*, 17–18: "Et (sicut accepimus) nonnulli ex civibus, habitatoribus et incolis Urbis et districtus praedicti, macellarii videlicet, piscarii, sutores, pelamantellarii, diversisque artifices, loca ac etiam ergasteria Urbis inhabitantes, suasque inibi artes exercentes, viscera, intestina, capita, pedes, ossa, cruores, necnon pelles, carnes et pisces corruptos, resque alias foetidas atque corruptas in viis, stratis, plateis et locis publicis atque privatis huiusmodi proiicere atque occultare . . . non verentur." The bull goes on to describe how residents of the city also expropriate and destroy public property without regard, and how all such behavior damages the health of humans, corrupts the air, and is even harmful to the salvation of the soul.

26. Dean, *Towns of Italy*, 50.

27. Henderson, "Black Death," 143, and Carmichael, *Plague and the Poor*, 121–26.

28. It is this connection that caused Foucault to begin his discussion of the Panopticon with a description of the orders that were enacted when the plague struck a town at the end of the seventeenth century. He writes that "the plague as a form, at once real and imaginary, of disorder had as its medical and political correlative discipline. Behind the disciplinary mechanisms can be read the haunting memory of 'contagions,' of the plague, of rebellions, crimes, vagabondage, desertions, people who appear and disappear, live and die in disorder. . . . The plague-stricken town, traversed throughout with hierarchy, surveillance, observation, writing; the town immobilized by the functioning of an extensive power that bears in a distinct way over all individual bodies—this is the utopia of the perfectly governed city." Foucault, *Discipline and Punish*, 198.

29. This preoccupation with plague and measures for its control coincides with contemporary developments. At the time that Alberti was writing, the issue of how to

control the plague was receiving fresh attention and new measures were being adopted, including the employment of guards to enforce order during outbreaks and the building of special hospitals to isolate plague victims (as well as greater enforcement of isolation in the home). Ann Carmichael has commented that "as much as a century [after 1348] little had changed in this sequence of responses [to the plague] despite the frequent recurrence of plague. Then in the mid-fifteenth century, as if by consensus, Italian legislators decided to isolate plague sufferers by building or designating a lazaretto (pest house)." See Carmichael, *Plague and the Poor*, 108.

30. Alberti, *On the Art of Building* 1.6, 17–18.

31. Ibid., 7.1, 191.

32. Ibid., 7.1, 191–92.

33. Ibid., 4.1, 93–94.

34. Ibid., 4.1, 94.

35. Paoli, "Battista e i suoi nipoti," 533–35. See also S. Borsi, *Momus, o Del principe*, 23–24.

36. Paoli, "Battista e i suoi nipoti," 533–34.

37. Ibid., 535–38. Stefano Borsi, *Momus, o Del principe*, 55, explores the same themes in relation to the intercenale "The Lake."

38. See Boschetto, *Leon Battista Alberti e Firenze*, 117. Boschetto argues that Alberti's vernacular dialogues written later than the *Della famiglia* all seem to take a critical line with regard to the Medici, and some of Alberti's positions in the *Theogenius* and *Profugiorum* are close to those of Filelfo and his anti-Medicean faction; see ibid., 140. See also S. Borsi, *Leon Battista Alberti e Napoli*, 121–27.

39. See Cassani, "*Libertas, frugalitas, aedificandi libido*," 299–300.

40. See Boschetto, *Leon Battista Alberti e Firenze*, 142.

41. Ibid. See also Cassani, "*Libertas, frugalitas, aedificandi libido*," 299.

42. On this, see Borsi, *Leon Battista Alberti e Napoli*, 120–21.

43. Alberti, *On the Art of Building* 5.6, 125.

44. Ibid., 5.8, 129. Nonetheless, they should be isolated from workmen, foul smells, and the distractions of the idle—all of the things that are also to be escaped from in the tyrant's city.

45. Ibid., 5.9, 130–31.

46. Ibid., 5.11, 134.

47. Ibid., 5.13, 138.

48. Del Fante, *La città di Leon Battista Alberti*, 47–48. This is perhaps the best illustration of the fact that if one were to combine all of Alberti's statements about the city in an attempt to create an "ideal city," the result would be riddled with incoherence and contradiction.

49. Alberti, *On the Art of Building* 7.1, 190–91. Alberti refers to the founding of Tigranocerta by Tigranes, the son-in-law of Mithridates, related in Plutarch, *Lucullus* 26.

50. See Jarzombek, *On Leon Baptista Alberti*, 112–17.

51. Alberti, *On the Art of Building* 8.6, 261.

52. Ibid., 8.6, 263.

53. The project that Nicholas V planned for the Borgo, as outlined by Giannozzo Manetti, was also to include the zoning of activities, with the currency market considered among the highest. Manetti writes, "Each of the three streets was intended to be distinguished from the others by the various types of dwellings, shops, and workshops on it, in the following way. The street on the right was to have been furnished on both sides with almost identical types of premises for different kinds of smaller craftsmen. The central street was to have differed from that on the left in that it was planned to

provide facilities for money-changers, drapers, and various other more important crafts, also situated on both sides. But on the one on the left, and as far as the wall which was to be constructed along the Tiber, there were to be laid out on both sides of the street shops for various types of minor craftsmen." It has often been alleged that Alberti was a key figure in the formulation of this plan. Magnuson, "Project of Nicholas V," 92–94.

54. Alberti, *On the Art of Building* 8.8, 281. On open spaces within the city, see Bertinelli Ferrari, "Gli spazi aperti."

55. Jarzombek, On Leon Baptista Alberti, 112–117.

56. Alberti, *On the Art of Building* 8.7, 268.

57. This has also been highlighted by Cesare de Seta, "Come in un specchio," 33–34, who points out that in the earlier books, Alberti deals with ancient and contemporary cities on an equal footing. However, de Seta contends that in the eighth book Alberti's city no longer accords with contemporary realities, concluding that this book must have been written some time after the earlier ones.

58. Alberti juxtaposes the difficulties of the two cities in his intercenale "Discord." He also comments on the ruined and devastated nature of Rome.

59. Alberti, *On the Art of Building* 5.6, 125–26.

60. Ibid., 7.1, 192. I have modified the translation slightly.

61. Michel, *Un idéal humain*, 256. Vasoli, "Potere e follia," 44, sees this passage as the climax of the second book of *Momus*, and perhaps even of the entire work. Responding to Garin's treatment of the passage, Whitfield, "*Momus* and the Language of Irony," 43, argues contrarily that "it is inadmissible to take the bravura passage of Momus (the person, not the book) lauding the vagabond, and mistake it for the doctrine of Alberti in some agony of nihilism. The doctrine of Alberti is written everywhere and it is positive."

62. Alberti, *Momus*, 132–33: "Erronum theatra, erronum porticus, erronum quicquid ubique publici est. Alii in foro ne considere neve altercari quidem voce paulo elatiori audebunt, et censoria veriti patrum supercilia publico ita versantur ut nihil sine lege et more, nihil pro voluntate et arbitrio audeant. Tu, erro, transverso foro prostratus iacebis, libere conclamitabis, faciesque ex animi libidine quaecumque collibuerint." I have slightly modified the translation.

63. Grafton, *Leon Battista Alberti*, 310. The opposite was argued by Whitfield, "*Momus* and the Language of Irony," 41. He saw Garin's attention to and interpretation of the figure of the vagabond as inexplicable, "because, of course, in the meantime, Alberti wrote the *De re aedificatoria*."

64. Alberti, *Momus*, 132–33: "Malo regnante principe alii diffugient errabuntque exilio, tu arcem tyranni concelebrabis."

65. Ibid., 134–35: "At hac in sola una erraria (ut ita loquar) disciplina et arte nihil umquam offendi quod quidem ulla ex parte minus placuerit. Nudos vides errones sub divo atque duro in solo accubare: eos contemnis, despicis una cum vulgo atque fastidis. Vide ne teque vulgusque errones ipsi contemnant atque despiciant!"

66. Terence, *Eunuchus* 2.2.255–57, 1:258–59 (references are to act, scene, line, and page numbers in Sargeaunt's translation): "Dum haec loquimur, interea loci ad macellum ubi adventamus, / concurrunt laeti mi obviam cuppedinarii omnes, / cetarii, lanii, coqui, fartores, piscatores . . ."

67. Ibid., 2.2.264, 1:258–59.

68. For a penetrating analysis of Alberti as a political thinker and his influence on subsequent writers, see Canfora, "Leon Battista Alberti modello di letteratura." Canfora highlights the influence of Poggio Barcciolini on Alberti's political thought, a theme that has been pursued by a number of other scholars. See, for example, Fubini, "Leon Battista Alberti, Niccolò V."

Chapter 4

1. For the most important antique sources for the town/country topos, see Lillie, *Florentine Villas*, 291n1; Lillie also lists many examples of the satirical treatment of the theme. See also Ackerman, *Villa*, 35–43.

2. Rinaldi, *Melancholia christiana*, 13.

3. The rental of a *casa da signore* was also rare among the Strozzi. Lillie, *Florentine Villas*, 17–21.

4. Ibid., 23.

5. Alberti, *On the Art of Building* 5.18, 152.

6. See Grayson, "Studi su Leon Battista Alberti: *Villa*," 45–53, for the dating of the work. Grayson suggests 1438 as a likely date (p. 48). Alberti's knowledge of Hesiod may not have been firsthand. See Pavan, "Il mito della villa," 317–25. The importance of Pliny the Elder's *Natural History* as a model for the text is emphasized by Damonte Medini, "Osservazioni sulla *Villa* di Leon Battista Alberti," 81–95.

7. Alberti, *Opere volgari*, 1:359: "Compera la villa per pascere la famiglia tua, non per darne diletto ad altri."

8. Ibid. See also Lillie, *Florentine Villas*, 24.

9. This was undoubtedly the most popular of the four books of *Della famiglia*, sometimes being circulated on its own as a separate work. Generally, the circulation of Alberti's *Della famiglia* seems to have been relatively small, and certainly not as wide as that of Leonardo Bruni's commentary on the *Economics* of the pseudo-Aristotle.

10. Alberti, *Della famiglia*, 194–95, and *Opere volgari*, 1:193:

GIANNOZZO: Non comperrei, no, imperoché non sarebbe masserizia. Chi vende le cose sue stimi tu venda testé quello che potrebbe più oltre serbare? Che credi tu che si cavi di casa, il migliore o pur il piggiore?

LIONARDO: Il piggiore, e quello quale pensa non potere bene serbare. Ma ancora alcuna volta per necessità del danaio si vendono le cose buone e utili.

GIANNOZZO: Così confesso. Ma se costui sarà savio, e' prima venderà il piggiore; e vendendo il migliore, non fa egli di venderlo più che non viene a sé? Non cerca egli con ogni astuzia fartelo parere migliore che non è?

LIONARDO: Spesso.

11. Alberti, *Della famiglia*, 195, and *Opere volgari*, 1:193–94: "Vorrei, sì, avere quello che in casa si può senza pericolo, senza grande fatica bene serbare. . . . Móstrotelo. Così. Darei io modo d'avere la possessione la quale per sé con molto minore spesa che comperandole in piazza fusse atta a tenermi la casa fornita di biave, vino, legne, strame e simili cose, ove farei alevarvi suso pecugli, colombi e polli, ancora e pesce."

12. Alberti, *Della famiglia*, 195, and *Opere volgari*, 1:193: "Però, vedi tu, chi compera spende quello superchio, e stassi a rischio di non avere tolto cosa falsificata, male durabile e poco buona. Vero? E quando mai vi fusse altra cagione, a me avermi presso tutto quello mi bisogna, a me avere provato più anni le cose mie e conoscerle quanto e in che stagione siano buone, più mi giova che cercarne altrove."

13. It seems that the necessity to import basic foodstuffs as a matter of routine may have expired after the city's population was halved by the plague in 1348. See Goldthwaite, *Building of Renaissance Florence*, 54. There is thus some accuracy to Leonardo Bruni's statement that the local country provided adequate food for the city, though his claims are highly exaggerated. See Kohl and Witt, *Earthly Republic*, 145.

14. De Grazia, "Ideology of Superfluous Things," 255–56. De Grazia goes on to argue that King Lear displays a resistance and anxiety toward this separation. My argument regarding Giannozzo's position is indebted to her work.

15. Alberti, *Della famiglia*, 40–41, and *Opere volgari*, 1:15: "Pure questa dolcezza del vivere, questo piacere d'avermi e ragionarmi con voi e con gli amici, questo diletto di vedermi le cose mie, pur mi duole lasciarlo. Non vorrei inanzi tempo esserne privato."

16. Alberti, *Della famiglia*, 196, and *Opere volgari*, 1:194: "Per questo proprio e per altre cagioni assai io mi comperrei la possessione de' miei danari, che fusse mia, poi e de' figliuoli miei, e così oltre de' nipoti miei, acciò che io con più amore la facessi governare bene e molto cultivare, e acciò che e' miei rimanenti in quella età prendessono frutto delle piante e delle opere quali io vi ponessi."

17. Giannozzo would also buy his town house rather then rent it, although the reasons he gives for this are rather more straightforwardly financial. He says, "I should certainly not rent it, for with the years you would have spent the money and yet not own the house." Alberti, *Della famiglia*, 192, and *Opere volgari*, 1:190: "A pigione certo no, però che in tempo l'uomo si truova più volte avere comperata la casa e non averla." The whole notion of the family *consorteria*, we should bear in mind, depended on the link between property and identity. This point is emphasized in Alberti's *De commodis literarum atque incommodis*, where, having just finished his studies at Bologna, he argues that one of the worst aspects of the student's plight is his separation from family property. This will result in a financial loss for the father "whose sons are living in distant cities, where none of the fruit of the family's land can be used to sustain them, where not the least thing can be had without cash, where physical needs and care of the body must all be paid for by draining the father's coffers." Alberti, *Use and Abuse of Books*, 30. The passage highlights not only the student's financial plight but also his *alienation*, living in a city away from family lands, having to use the cash economy for everything, and therefore becoming utterly alienated from the commodities he handles.

18. Alberti, *Della famiglia*, 196, and *Opere volgari*, 1:195: "A volere il buono vino, bisogna la costa e il solitìo; a fare buono grano si richiede l'aperto piano morbido e leggiere; le buone legne crescono nell'aspero e alla grippa; il fieno nel fresco e molliccio. Tanta adunque diversità di cose come troverresti voi in uno solo sito? Che dite, Giannozzo? Stimate voi si truovino simili molti siti atti a vigna, sementi, boschi e pascoli? E trovandoli, crederresti voi averli a pregio non carissimo?"

19. Alberti, *Della famiglia*, 196, and *Opere volgari*, 1:195: "Quanto sì! Ma pure, Lionardo mio, io mi ricordo a Firenze quanto siano degli altri assai, e ancora quelli nostri luoghi, quelli di messer Benedetto, quelli altri di messere Niccolaio, e quelli di messer Cipriano, e quelli di messere Antonio, e gli altri de' nostri Alberti, a' quali tu non desiderresti cosa più niuna, posti in aere cristallina, in paese lieto, per tutto bello occhio, rarissime nebbie, non cattivi venti, buone acque, sano e puro ogni cosa."

20. Alberti, *Della famiglia*, 196, and *Opere volgari*, 1:195: "Ma tacciamo di quelli, e' quali più sono palagi da signori, e più tengono forma di castella che di ville. Non ci ricordiamo al presente delle magnificenze Alberte, dimentichianci quelli edificii superbi e troppo ornatissimi, ne' quali molti vedendovi testé nuovi abitatori trapassano sospirando, e desiderandovi l'antiche fronti e cortesie nostre Alberte."

21. Kohl and Witt, *Earthly Republic*, 145.

22. Alberti, *Della famiglia*, 240, and *Opere volgari*, 1:246–47: "Si vede il danaio essere di tutte le cose o radice, o esca, o nutrimento. Il danaio niuno dubita quanto e' sia nervo di tutti e' mestieri. . . . Se adunque il danaio supplisce a tutti i bisogni, che fa mestiere occupare l'animo in altra masserizia che in sola questa del danaio?"

23. Alberti, *Della famiglia*, 241, and *Opere volgari*, 1:247: "Ma io non ti confesserò però, benché io avessi danari, che ancora a me non manchino molte e molte cose, le quali non si truovano tutte ora apparecchiate a' bisogni, o sono non sì buone, o costano superchio. E quando le bene costassino vili, a me sarà più grato pigliarmi fatica piacevole in governare le mie possessioni, la mia cosa io stessi, e ricormi quello mi bisogna, che d'avere prima al continuo fatica in contenere e' danari, poi avere travaglio in trovare le cose di dì in dì, e in quelle spendere molto più che se io me l'avessi stagionate in casa."

24. Alberti, *Della famiglia*, 241–42, and *Opere volgari*, 1:248: "Ove tu truovi te manco avere perduto danari che possessioni, ti pare egli però ch'e' danari si possino meglio serbare che le cose stabili? Parti però più stabile ricchezza quella del danaio che quella della villa? Parti più utile frutto quello del danaio che quello de' terreni? Quale sarà cosa alcuna più atta a perdersi, più difficile a serbare, più pericolosa a trassinalla, più brigosa a riavella, più facile a dileguarsi, spegnersi, irne in fummo? Quale a tutti quelli perdimenti tanto sarà atta quanto essere si vede il danaio?"

25. Alberti, *Della famiglia*, 242, and *Opere volgari*, 1:248: "Fatica incredibile serbar e' danari, fatica sopra tutte l'altre piena di sospetti, piena di pericoli, pienissima di infortunii. Né in modo alcuno si possono tenere rinchiusi e' danari; e se tu gli tieni serrati e ascosi, sono utili né a te né a' tuoi. . . . E potrei ancora racontarti a quanti pericoli sia sottoposto il danaio: male mani, mala fede, malo consiglio, mala fortuna, e infinite simili altre cose pessime in uno sorso divorano tutte le somme de' danari, tutto consumano, mai più se ne vede né reliquie né cenere."

26. Alberti, *Della famiglia*, 242–43, and *Opere volgari*, 1:249: "Considera, Adovardo, che né mani di furoni, né rapine, né fuoco, né ferro, né perfidia de' mortali, né, che ardirò io dire, non le saette, il tuono, non l'ira d'Iddio ti priva della possessione. Se questo anno vi cascò tempesta, se molte piove, se troppo gelo, se venti, o calure, o secco corruppero o riarsero le semente, a te poi seguita uno altro anno migliore fortuna, se non a te, a' figliouli tuoi, a' nipoti tuoi. A quanti pupilli, a quanti cittadini sono più state utili le possessioni ch'e' denari! Per tutto se ne vede infiniti essempli. E quanti falliti, e quanti corsali, e quanti rapinatori hanno saziati e' danari de' nostri Alberti! Somme inestimabili, somme infinite, ricchezze da nolle credere tutte fatte con nostra perdita. E volesse Dio si fussero spesi in praterie, in boschi o grippe più tosto, che almanco pur sarebbono dette nostre, almanco si potrebbe sperare a migliore nostra fortuna di riavelle."

27. The permanence of land is stressed in the Old Testament. Of particular interest is God's instruction to Jeremiah to buy a field, despite the destruction to be visited on the land. For no matter how great the destruction, a remnant will return. Jeremiah's purchase of the field and his signing and burying of the deed are described in detail. Afterward, the word of God comes to him, showing him that the field will stand as a symbol of permanence: "For thus saith the LORD; Like as I have brought all this great evil upon this people, so will I bring upon them all the good that I have promised them. And fields shall be bought in this land, whereof ye say, It is desolate without man or beast; it is given into the hand of the Chaldeans. Men shall buy fields for money, and subscribe evidences, and seal them, and take witnesses in the land of Benjamin, and in the places about Jerusalem, and in the cities of Judah, and in the cities of the mountains, and in the cities of the valley, and in the cities of the south: for I will cause their captivity to return, saith the LORD" (Jeremiah 32:42–44, Authorized Version). The notion of the permanence of land also exists in Cicero. In the *Philippics*, commenting on funerary monuments, Cicero says, "Our ancestors indeed decreed statues to many, public funerals to few. But statues perish by weather, violence, and age; of sepulchers the sanctity is in the very soil, which cannot be moved or obliterated

by violence; and so, while other things come to an end, sepulchers become more sanctified by age." Cicero, *Philippics* 9.14, 412–15 (references are to book, section, and page numbers in Ker's translation). Alberti knew this passage, making specific reference to it in *De re aedificatoria*, where he says that "according to Cicero, the sanctity of a sepulcher lies in the very ground, which cannot be destroyed or removed: while everything else becomes extinguished, the sanctity of the sepulcher increases with age." Alberti, *On the Art of Building* 8.2, 246.

28. This sentiment has shown great persistence through time. Heidegger uses the terms "care" or "concern" in a somewhat similar manner to describe the being of *Dasein* within the world. He asserts, "Dasein's facility is such that its Being-in-the-world has always dispersed itself or even split itself up into definite ways of Being-in. The multiplicity of these is indicated by the following examples: having to do with something, producing something, attending to something and looking after it, making use of something. . . . All these ways of Being-in have *concern* as their kind of Being." He adds, "This term has been chosen not because Dasein happens to be proximally and to a large extent 'practical' and economic, but because the Being of Dasein itself is to be made visible as *care*. . . . Because Being-in-the-world belongs essentially to Dasein, its Being towards the world is essentially concern." Heidegger, *Being and Time*, §§56–57, pp. 83–84. The point of contact between the two is Hesiod, a major source of inspiration for Alberti's *Villa* (probably indirectly) as well as Heidegger's *Building, Dwelling, Thinking*.

29. I am grateful to Dr. Simon Richards for useful discussions on architecture and the self.

30. See Cato, *On Agriculture*, opening remarks, sections 1–4; Varro, *On Agriculture*, bk. 2, opening remarks, section 1, and bk. 3, sections 1.1–10; Columella, *On Agriculture*, bk. 1, preface; and Pliny the Elder, *Natural History* 18.1.5. For an examination of Alberti's use of the agricultural treatise writers, and Varro, Columella, and Palladius in particular, see Sberlati, "*Rerum rusticarum scriptores*."

31. Cato, *On Agriculture*, opening remarks, sections 1–4. The quote is located on p. 3 of Hooper and Ash's translation.

32. Hesiod, *Works and Days*, 70, line 365.

33. Alberti, *Della famiglia*, 199, and *Opere volgari*, 1:198–99: "Quale uomo fusse, il quale non si traesse piacere della villa? Porge la villa utile grandissimo, onestissimo e certissimo. E pruovasi qualunque altro essercizio intoparsi in mille pericoli, hanno seco mille sospetti, seguongli molti danni e molti pentimenti: in comperare cura, in condurre paura, in serbare pericolo, in vendere sollicitudine, in credere sospetto, in ritrarre fatica, nel commutare inganno. E così sempre degli altri essercizii ti premono infiniti affanni e agonie di mente." I have slightly modified the translation. Guarino routinely translates Alberti's term *villa* as "country," while Watkins alternates between "farm," "country estate," and "country." The term *villa* can signify all of these things (and more). I have mostly left it in the original Tuscan.

34. Alberti, *Della famiglia*, 199–200, and *Opere volgari*, 1:199: "La villa sola sopra tutti si truova conoscente, graziosa, fidata, veridica. Se tu la governi con diligenza e con amore, mai a lei parerà averti satisfatto; sempre agiunge premio a' premii. Alla primavera la villa ti dona infiniti sollazzi, verzure, fiori, odori, canti; sforzasi in più modi farti lieto, tutta ti ride e ti promette grandissima ricolta, émpieti di buona speranza e di piaceri assai. Poi e quanto la truovi tu teco alla state cortese! Ella ti manda a casa ora uno, ora un altro frutto, mai ti lascia la casa vòta di qualche sua liberalità. Eccoti poi presso l'autunno. Qui rende la villa alle tue fatiche e a' tuoi meriti smisurato premio e copiosissime mercé, e quanto volentieri e quanto abundante, e con quanta fede! Per uno dodici. . . . Poi neanche il verno si dimentica teco essere la

villa liberale. . . . La villa ti fa parte del suo splendissimo sole, e porgeti la leprettina, il capro, il cervo, che tu gli corra drieto, avendone piacere e vincendone il freddo e la forza del verno. Non dico de' polli, del cavretto, delle giuncate e delle altre delizie, quali tutto l'anno la villa t'alieva e serba. Al tutto così è: la villa si sforza a te in casa manchi nulla, cerca che nell'animo tuo stia niuna malinconia, émpieti di piacere e d'utile. E se la villa da te richiede opera alcuna, non vuole come gli altri essercizii tu ivi te atristi, né vi ti carchi di pensieri, né punto vi ti vuole affannato e lasso, ma piace alla villa la tua opera ed essercizio pieno di diletto, il quale sia non meno alla sanità tua che alla cultura utilissimo." I have modified the translation.

35. Xenophon, *Oeconomicus* 5.2–12, 6.8–10; Cicero, *Senectute* 15.51, 16.56; Hesiod, *Works and Days*, 66; and Virgil, *Georgics* 2.458.

36. Alberti, *Della famiglia*, 200, and *Opere volgari*, 1:200: "Che bisogna dire, Lionardo? Tù non potresti lodare a mezzo quanto sia la villa utile alla sanità, commoda al vivere, conveniente alla famiglia."

37. Alberti, *Della famiglia*, 200, and *Opere volgari*, 1:200: "Non ti conviene, come negli altri mestieri, temere perfidia o fallacie di debitori o procuratori. Nulla vi si fa in oscuro, nulla non veduto e conosciuto da molti, né puoi esservi ingannato, né bisogna chiamare notari e testimoni, non seguire litigii e l'altre simili cose acerbissime e piene di malinconie, che alle più fiate sarebbe meglio perdere che con quelle suste d'animo guadagnare."

38. Nonetheless, Alberti by no means held back from initiating litigation himself. He was repeatedly involved in legal wrangles over his benefice of San Martino a Gangalandi, and in 1436, he was recorded as proceeding against fifteen *fittavoli*, requesting that magistrates take action against their persons and their property (*nelle loro persone e nei loro beni*). None of these fifteen was worth much, and the poorest could almost be counted among the *miserabili*. Interestingly, these lawsuits related not to the city and trade or politics, but to country property and peasants. See Boschetto, *Leon Battista Alberti e Firenze*, 109.

39. Virgil, *Georgics* 2.500–503, 93 (references are to book, line, and page numbers in Wilkinson's translation).

40. Alberti, *Della famiglia*, 200–201, and *Opere volgari*, 1:200: "Agiugni qui che tu puoi ridurti in villa e viverti in riposo pascendo la famigliuola tua, procurando tu stessi a' fatti tuoi, la festa sotto l'ombra ragionarti piacevole del bue, della lana, delle vigne o delle sementi, senza sentire romori, o relazioni, o alcuna altra di quelle furie quali dentro alla terra fra' cittadini mai restano—sospetti, paure, maledicenti, ingiustizie, risse, e l'altre molte bruttissime a ragionarne cose, e orribili a ricordarsene." I have slightly modified the translation.

41. Virgil, *Georgics* 2.462, 92, says in a somewhat similar vein that the city "belches a mighty tide of morning callers."

42. Alberti, *Use and Abuse of Books*, 36.

43. Ibid.

44. Ibid., 38.

45. Ibid., 47.

46. Alberti, *Della famiglia*, 201, and *Opere volgari*, 1:200: "Di tutte si ragiona con diletto, da tutti se' con piacere e volentieri ascoltato. Ciascuno porge in mezzo quello che conosce utile alla cultura; ciascuno t'insegna ed emenda, ove tu errassi in piantare qualche cosa o sementare. Niuna invidia, niuno odio, niuna malivolenza ti nasce dal cultivare e governare il campo." Giannozzo's words somewhat echo those of Horace in his second epode. Similar sentiments appear in the *De commodis*, where Alberti likewise emphasizes the practical and straightforward nature of country life: "Or if you practice agriculture? What way of life is more blessed? What more fruitful, profitable,

and respected occupation could you find? Only agriculture can give comfort, peace, and freedom to the ignorant but can also make learned men happy. For no expectation of returns is surer than that given by a well-cultivated field, while at the same time the country provides leisure to live well and blessedly away from all noise and bother. In addition, there is nothing more valuable and perennially useful than what is gained by agriculture." Alberti, *Use and Abuse of Books*, 32. Giannozzo's claim that, in the country, people are always ready to correct you in helpful and constructive ways is of particular interest. Grafton, in his *Leon Battista Alberti*, argues that collegial emendation was central to Alberti's conception of how humanistic scholarly debate ought to be conducted.

47. Alberti, *Della famiglia*, 201, and *Opere volgari*, 1:200: "E anche vi godete in villa quelli giorni aerosi e puri, aperti e lietissimi; avete leggiadrissimo spettacolo rimirando que' colletti frondíti, e que' piani verzosi, e quelli fonti e rivoli chiari, che seguono saltellando e perdendosi fra quelle chiome dell'erba." I have slightly modified the translation.

48. Alberti, *Della famiglia*, 201, and *Opere volgari*, 1:200–201: "Sì, Dio, uno proprio paradiso. E anche, quello che più giova, puoi alla villa fuggire questi strepiti, questi tumulti, questa tempesta della terra, della piazza, del palagio. Puoi in villa nasconderti per non vedere le rubalderie, le sceleraggine e la tanta quantità de' pessimi mali uomini, quali pella terra continuo ti farfallano inanti agli occhi, quali mai restano di cicalarti torno all'orecchie, quali d'ora in ora seguono stridendo e mugghiando per tutta la terra, bestie furiosissime e orribilissime. Quanto sarà beatissimo lo starsi in villa: felicità non conosciuta!" I have slightly modified the translation. Again, these lines are reminiscent of Hesiod, *Works and Days*, 60, lines 27–29.

49. Alberti, *Opuscoli inediti*, 69: "Etenim pulchrius intra feras belluas versari arbitrabatur quam intra crudeles, nefarios immanesque homines, quorum nulla pene urbs non refertissima est."

50. Alberti, *Della famiglia*, 182, and *Opere volgari*, 1:179: "Niuna cosa manco, Lionardo mio; niuna cosa manco figliuoli miei. Niuna cosa a me pare in uno uomo meno degna di riputarsela ad onore che ritrovarsi in questi stati."

51. Alberti, *Della famiglia*, 164, and *Opere volgari*, 1:158. Giannozzo's role as a reluctant political operator may relate to the Platonic notion that those who wish to have no part of politics, but engage with it out of a sense of duty, are actually the best and most honest politicians.

52. Alberti, *Della famiglia*, 182–83, and *Opere volgari*, 1:179–80: "Vita molestissima, piena di sospetti, di fatiche, pienissima di servitù. Che vedi tu da questi i quali si travagliono agli stati essere differenza a publici servi? Pratica qui, ripriega quivi, scapùcciati a questo, gareggia con quello, ingiuria quell'altro; molti sospetti, mille invidie, infinite inimistà, niuna ferma amicizia, abundanti promesse, copiose proferte, ogni cosa piena di fizione, vanità e bugie. E quanto a te più bisogna, tanto manco truovi chi a te serbi o promessa o fede. E così ogni tua fatica e ogni speranza a uno tratto con tuo danno, con dolore e non senza tua ruina, rimane perduta."

53. Alberti, *Della famiglia*, 183, and *Opere volgari*, 1:180: "Che n'hai tu d'utile se none uno solo: potere rubare e sforzare con qualche licenza?"

54. Alberti, *Della famiglia*, 183, and *Opere volgari*, 1:180: "Odivi continui richiami, innumerabili accuse, grandissimi tumulti, e intorno a te sempre s'aviluppano litigiosi, avari, ingiustissimi uomini, empionti l'orecchie di sospetti, l'animo di cupidità, la mente di paure e perturbazioni."

55. Alberti, *Della famiglia*, 183, and *Opere volgari*, 1:180: "Ciascuno giudica la volontà sua essere onesta . . . e l'opinione sua migliore che gli altri. Tu seguendo l'errore comune o l'arroganza d'altrui acquisti propria infamia, e se pur t'adoperi in servire,

compiaci a uno, dispiaci a cento. Au! furia non conosciuta, miseria non fuggita, male non odiato da ciascuno quanto e' merita."

56. Alberti, *Della famiglia*, 183–84, and *Opere volgari*, 1:180–81: "O pazzi, fummosi, superbi, proprii tiranneschi, che date scusa al vizio vostro! Non potete sofferire gli altri meno ricchi, ma forse più antichi cittadini di voi, essere pari a voi quanto si richiede: non potete vivere senza sforzare e' minori, però desiderate lo stato. E per avere stato, stolti, che fate voi? Pazzi, che vi sponete a ogni pericolo, porgetevi alla morte; bestiali, che chiamate onore così essere assediato da tutti i cattivi. . . . E chiamate onore essere nel numero de' rapinatori, chiamate onore convenire e pascere e servire agli uomini servili! O bestialità! Uomini degni di odio, se così pigliate a piacere tanta perversità e travaglio quanto trabocca adosso a chi sia in questi uffici e amministrazioni pubbliche!"

57. Alberti, *Della famiglia*, 131–33, and *Opere volgari*, 1:121–24. Lionardo advises fleeing to the country to avoid the plague.

58. Watkins, "Leon Battista Alberti in the Mirror," 12.

59. Alberti, *Della famiglia*, 184, and *Opere volgari*, 1:181: "E che piacere d'animo mai può avere costui, se già e' non sia di natura feroce e bestiale, il quale al continuo abbia a prestare orecchie a doglienze, lamenti, pianti di pupilli, di vedove, e di uomini calamitosi e miseri? Che contentamento arà colui il quale tutto il dì arà a porgere fronte e guardarsi insieme da mille turme di ribaldi, barattieri, spioni, detrattori, rapinatori e commettitori d'ogni falsità e scandolo? E che recreamento arà colui al quale ogni sera sia necessario torcere le braccia e le membra agli uomini, sentirli con quella dolorosa voce gridare misericordia, e pur convenirli usare molte altre orribili crudeltà, essere beccaio e squarciatore delle membra umane? Au! cosa abominevole a chi pur vi pensa." I have slightly modified the translation.

60. Freud, commenting on a repetition in the notebooks of Leonardo da Vinci, notes that "such cases of . . . repetition are significant. . . . [It] is a case in which [the author] was unsuccessful in suppressing his affect and in which something that had long been concealed forcibly obtained a distorted expression. . . . We call a repetition of this kind a perseveration. It is an excellent means [in literature] of indicating affective color." He offers as an example Saint Peter's words in Dante's *Paradiso*: "He who usurps on earth my place, / My place, my place, which is vacant / In the presence of the son of God, / Has made a sewer of the ground where I am buried." Freud, *Leonardo da Vinci*, 164–65. For the quotation from Dante, see *Paradiso* 27.22–25: "Quelli ch'usurpa in terra il luogo mio, / il luogo mio, il luogo mio, che vaca / ne la presenza del Figliuol di Dio, / fatt'ha del cimitero mio cloacca."

61. Alberti, *Opuscoli inediti*, 83.

62. See, for example, Catte, Delmolino, and Held, *Catalogo della mostra di strumenti di tortura*. The authors emphasize the frequency and extreme cruelty of torture throughout the cities of Europe during this period.

63. Alberti, *Della famiglia*, 200, and *Opere volgari*, 1:200: "Nulla vi si fa in oscuro, nulla non veduto e conosciuto da molti."

64. A remark by Foucault concerning eighteenth-century political theorists also seems appropriate in Alberti's case: "What in fact was the Rousseauist dream that motivated many of the revolutionaries? It was the dream of a transparent society, visible and legible in each of its parts, the dream of there no longer existing any zones of darkness." Foucault, *Power/Knowledge*, 152. Alberti is clearly troubled by the darkness and secrecy of the city. Nonetheless, he sometimes displays an attraction to it (as, for instance, with his recommendation of making a secret part of the wall of the inner citadel from clay). Alberti appears to doubt the city's capacity to become truly visible and transparent, accounting in part for his anti-urban sentiment. As we have seen, he is also sometimes willing to forego transparency in favor of deliberate confusion, in the cause of defense.

65. Alberti, *Della famiglia*, 196, and *Opere volgari*, 1:195. I have slightly modified the translation. The language used in this section was first brought to my attention when Amanda Lillie read the passage aloud in the original Tuscan, from her paper "Designing for the Weather: Microclimates and Environmental Strategies in Fifteenth-Century Florentine Country" (Air in the Renaissance conference, Warburg Institute, June 28, 2002).

66. Alberti, *Della famiglia*, 201, and *Opere volgari*, 1:200. I have slightly modified the translation.

67. Alberti, *Della famiglia*, 201, and *Opere volgari*, 1:201:

LIONARDO: Lodate voi abitare in villa più che in mezzo alla città?

GIANNOZZO: Quanto io, a vivere con manco vizio, con meno maninconie, con minore spesa, con più sanità, maggiore suavità del vivere mio, sì bene, figliuoli miei, che io lodo la villa.

68. Alberti, *Della famiglia*, 201, and *Opere volgari*, 1:201: "Chi non conosce il suono della cornamusa non può bene giudicare se lo strumento sia buono o non buono." As I shall discuss in chapter 6, Alberti is fond of using musical analogies when talking about both society and the individual. In the *Theogenius*, Genipatro says, "E fu in questa sapientissimo chi disse el populo essere una tromba rotta quale si possa mai ben sonare." Alberti, *Opere volgari*, 2:78. The *popolo* are a broken trumpet that can never be well played. The sound of the bagpipe (at least in these texts) is a bad one.

69. Alberti, *Della famiglia*, 202, and *Opere volgari*, 1:201: "E anche, Giannozzo, nella terra la gioventù impara la civilità, prende buone arti, vede molti essempli da schifare e' vizii, scorge più da presso quanto l'onore sia cosa bellissima, quanto sia la fama leggiadra, e quanto sia divina cosa la gloria, gusta quanto siano dolci le lode, essere nomato, guardato e avuto virtuoso. Destasi la gioventù per queste prestantissime cose, commove e sé stessi incita a virtù, e proferiscesi ad opere faticose e degne di immortalità; quali ottime cose forse non si truovano in villa fra' tronchi e fra le zolle." I have slightly modified the translation.

70. Alberti, *Della famiglia*, 202, and *Opere volgari*, 1:202: "Con tutto questo, Lionardo mio, dubito io quale fusse più utile, allevare la gioventù in villa o nella terra. Ma sia così, abbiasi ciascuna cosa le sue proprie utilità, siano nelle terre le fabriche di quelli grandissimi sogni, stati, reggimenti, e fama, e nella villa si truovi quiete, contentamento d'animo, libertà di vivere e fermezza di sanità." I have slightly modified the translation.

71. Alberti, *Della famiglia*, 202, and *Opere volgari*, 1:202: "Io per me così ti dico: se io avessi villa simile quale io narrava, io mi vi starei buoni dì dell'anno, dare'mi piacere e modo di pascere la famiglia mia copioso e bene."

72. Alberti, *Della famiglia*, 185, and *Opere volgari*, 1:183: ". . . perché cresciuti in antichissima libertà della patria e con animo troppo pieno d'odio acerbissimo contro a ogni tiranno, non contenti della commune libertà vorrebbono più che gli altri libertà e licenza."

73. Alberti, *Della famiglia*, 186, and *Opere volgari*, 1:183: "Ma neanche quelle republiche medesime si potranno bene conservare, ove tutti e' buoni siano solo del suo ozio privato contenti. Dicono e' savi ch'e' buoni cittadini debbono traprendere la republica e soffrire le fatiche della patria e non curare le inezie degli uomini."

74. Alberti, *Della famiglia*, 186, and *Opere volgari*, 1:183–84: "E poi vedete, Giannozzo, che questo vostro lodatissimo proposito e regola del vivere con privata onestà qui solo, benché in sé sia prestante e generoso, non però a' cupidi animi di gloria in tutto sia da seguire. Non in mezzo agli ozii privati, ma intra le publiche esperienze nasce la fama;

nelle publiche piazze surge la gloria; in mezzo de' popoli si nutrisce le lode con voce e iudicio di molti onorati. Fugge la fama ogni solitudine e luogo privato, e volentieri siede e dimora sopra e' teatri, presente alle conzioni e celebrità; ivi si collustra e alluma il nome di chi con molto sudore e assiduo studio di buone cose sé stessi tradusse fuori di taciturnità e tenebre, d'ignoranza e vizii."

75. Alberti, *Della famiglia*, 187, and *Opere volgari*, 1:185: "Mai lasciate di reggere voi stessi; per guidare le cose publiche non lasciate però le vostre private."

76. Alberti, *Della famiglia*, 21, 337n31.

77. Garin, "Il pensiero," 505, writes, "Né si repeterà mai abbastanza che nei dialoghi—e non a caso gran parte di questa produzione è dialogata—non è lecito identificare l'autore con uno solo dei personaggi, quando invece il suo pensiero vive soltanto nel giuoco delle parti." For a similar approach, see Baron, *In Search of Florentine Civic Humanism*, 1:258–88, and Marolda, *Crisi e conflitto*, 15–26.

78. Alberti, *Della famiglia*, 167–68, and *Opere volgari*, 1:162: "L'altra gioventù, com'è corrotto ingegno de' giovani trarre più tosto a' sollazzosi luoghi che alla bottega, ridursi più tosto tra giovani spendenti che tra vecchi massai." One should also bear in mind that young men were, by a wide margin, the cause of most violence and unrest in the city-states and that in Florence, at least, their behavior may have been affected by the relatively small number of older males and women able to offer a restraining influence. There is also much evidence of the sons of wealthy merchants living scandalous lives, spending profligately, and falling out with their fathers. For age and gender ratios in Florence and their relationship to violence, see Herlihy, "Some Psychological and Social Roots of Violence."

79. Alberti, *Della famiglia*, 192, and *Opere volgari*, 1:190:

LIONARDO:	Sono contento. Ma in prima che parrebbe a voi bene atto alla sanità?
GIANNOZZO:	Quella quale, voglia tu o no, tale ti conviene usarla quale tu la truovi: l'aria.
LIONARDO:	Poi apresso?
GIANNOZZO:	L'altre buone cose al cibo e al vivere nostro, e fra esse il buono vino. Lionardo mio, tu ridi.
LIONARDO:	E quivi vi fermeresti?

I have slightly modified the translation.

80. Alberti, *Opere volgari*, 2:108: ". . . d'età maggiori in senato, d'autorità primi, d'integrità soli." Indeed, there is some suggestion that Alberti saw Giannozzo as a father figure, for Niccola says that by comparing Pandolfini to Giannozzo, he wants to demonstrate that Battista looks upon Pandolfini as a father: "Voglio inferire che a Battista, qual sempre v'appella padre, e védevi e odevi con avidità e volentieri, e' vostri ragionamenti saranno, come e' sono a me, accettissimi e gratissimi" (ibid., 2:108–9).

81. Giannozzo's thinking is entirely in key with the words of Virgil's second *Georgic* (2.493–99, 93):

But happy too is he who knows the gods
Of the countryside, knows Pan and old Silvanus
And the sister Nymphs. Neither the people's gift,
The fasces, nor the purple robes of kings,
Nor treacherous feuds of brother against brother
Disturb him, not the Danube plotting raids
Of Dacian tribesmen, nor the affairs of Rome

> And crumbling kingdoms, nor the grievous sight
> Of poor to pity and of rich to envy.

The reference to feuds between brothers should remind us of the classical and biblical tradition of cities being founded through fratricides—including Rome.

82. This point is even emphasized in the *Profugiorum*, where only a few sentences are devoted to Giannozzo. Continuing the comparison between Giannozzo and Pandolfini, Niccola says, "Se a Giannozzo fusse molta cognizione di lettere, direi: qual due uomini altrove si troverebbono o sì compiuti d'ogni pregio, o sì insieme simili in ogni laude?" See Alberti, *Opere volgari*, 2:108.

83. Alberti, *Della famiglia*, 241, and *Opere volgari*, 1:247: "Bene a me sogliono questi vostri litterati parere troppo litigiosi. Niuna cosa si truova tanto certa, niuna sì manifesta, niuna sì chiara, la quale voi con vostri argomenti non facciate essere dubia, incerta, e oscurissima. Ma testé meco o piacciavi come tra voi solete disputare, o piacciavi vedere in questo che opinione sia la mia, conosco a me essere debito risponderti più per contentarne te, Adovardo, che per difendere alcuna opinione." I have slightly modified the translation.

84. Alberti, *Della famiglia*, 242, and *Opere volgari*, 1:248: "Quanto io, non però vorrei non sapere quali mi dilettano lettere."

85. Alberti, *Della famiglia*, 242, and *Opere volgari*, 1:249: "Ancora mi piace, com'e' pratichi buoni combattenti adoperano per vincere non meno astuzia che forza, e tale ora monstrano fuggire per condurre il nimico in qualche disavantaggio, così tu meco qui mostri accedermi, e pur ti fortifichi più tosto d'astuzia che di fermezza. . . . Non temo da voi alcune insidie come forse dovrei."

86. Alberti, *Della famiglia*, 243, and *Opere volgari*, 1:250: "Che pure miri tu, Adovardo, quasi come stupefatto a questi detti di Giannozzo? Se tu avessi udito e' suoi ragionamenti sopra, tu confesseresti e' suoi detti alle famiglie quasi oraculi divini essere."

87. Alberti, *Della famiglia*, 244, and *Opere volgari*, 1:250:

LIONARDO:	Crederesti tu potere errare, Adovardo, nella masserizia consentendo al giudicio di Giannozzo?
ADOVARDO:	Anzi sarebbe in grande errore chi credesse il giudicio e sentenze di Giannozzo non essere verissimo, ma in alcuna cosa, Lionardo, benché le siano vere, tale ora non mi pare biasimo dubitarne.

88. It should also be remembered that Alberti was unusual among humanist scholars for his interest in practical wisdom. He stressed that he learned a great deal from experience, watching craftsmen, measuring buildings, and so on. In one of the strangest and most fantastical of the *Intercenales*, "The Dream," he viciously satirized scholars of the type of Niccolò Niccoli, who did not write but only criticized others.

89. Alberti, *Della famiglia*, 99–100, and *Opere volgari*, 1:83: "Quanta sia incerta e varia cosa el ragionare." This gives Lionardo the opportunity to discourse on the subject of eloquence, making direct reference to Cicero. The highly self-consciously rhetorical nature of Lionardo's speech is more apparent here than ever.

90. On the satirizing of philosophers, see Michel, *Un idéal humain*, 235–38.

91. Gelastus must be seen, on some level, as a figure for Alberti since his long lament about the state of man and the world is familiar as Alberti's own and includes a number of autobiographical features.

92. Alberti, *Momus*, 300–301: "'Num' inquit Gelastus 'quaeris 'quid' sapimus? Etenim omnia novimus, siderum, imbrium, fulminum, causas et motum; novimus

terras, caelum, maria. Nos artium optimarum inventores; nos quae ad pietatem, ad vitae modum, ad hominum gratiam conciliandam faciant nostris monitis quasi lege data praescribimus.'"

93. Ibid.: "'Tu igitur officio legique hoc dato' inquit Charon 'hanc praegravem cumbam adiutato ut feram.'"

94. An example of this selfishness and the "all against all" nature of Florentine society is Giannozzo's statement that when developing his property, he would "never stop planting trees on the border, where they would shade my neighbors' fields rather than my own" (mai resterei di piantarvi così in sulle margini, onde s'auggiasse il vicino campo non il mio). Furthermore, when discussing political participation, he says, "One must live for himself, not for everyone else." (E' si vuole vivere a sé, non al comune.) Alberti, *Della famiglia*, 198, 184, and *Opere volgari*, 1:198, 182.

95. Alberti, *Della famiglia*, 213–14, and *Opere volgari*, 1:215–16: "Voi litterati . . . e' quali trattando della prudenza e vivere umano solete adurre essemplo dalle formiche, e dite che da loro si debba prendere amonimento provedendo oggi a' bisogni di domane; e così constituendo il principe solete prendere argomento dall'api, le quali tutte a uno solo obediscono, e pella publica salute tutte con fortissimo animo e ardentissima opera s'essercitano. . . . E sia testé ancora lecito a me con qualche mia similitudine non tanto apropriatissima quanto le vostre, ma certo non in tutto inetta, per meglio e più aperto narrarvi, e quasi dipignere, e qui in mezzo porvi inanzi agli occhi quello che a me pare in uno padre di famiglia sia necessario, sia, dico, testé a me licito seguire ne' miei ragionamenti la vostra lodata e nobile consuetudine. Voi vedete el ragno quanto egli nella sua rete abbia le cordicine tutte per modo sparse in razzi che ciascuna di quelle, benché sia in lungo spazio stesa, pure suo principio e quasi radice e nascimento si vede cominciato e uscito dal mezzo, in quale luogo lo industrissimo animale osserva sua sedia e abitacolo; e ivi, poiché così dimora, tessuto e ordinato il suo lavoro, sta desto e diligente, tale che, per minima ed estremissima cordicina quale si fosse tocca, subito la sente, subito s'apresenta e a tutto subito provede. Così faccia il padre della famiglia. Distingua le cose sue, pongale in modo che a lui solo tutte facciano capo, e da lui s'adirizzino e ferminsi ai più sicuri luoghi; e stia il padre della famiglia in mezzo intento e presto a sentire e vedere il tutto, e dove bisogni provedere subito provegga."

96. Aristotle praises bees in his *History of Animals*, as does Pliny the Elder in his *Natural History*. Cato, Varro, and Columella devote much attention to bees in their agricultural treatises, and Xenophon refers to them in his *Oeconomicus* (7.32–34), as do many other classical authors. Bees feature, in the same way, in medieval literature. See Guldentops, "Sagacity of the Bees," 275–96.

97. The spider is also portrayed positively by Alberti in the *Intercenales*. In "The Spider," the creature is shown to be just and eloquent, defending a helpless man against an enraged elephant. This cannot necessarily be used to determine Alberti's attitude toward spiders, however. The fable does not resemble Alberti's treatment of the spider in the *Della famiglia* or in his *Musca* (discussed below). It appears to be a reworking of a traditional Aesopian theme of a small creature overcoming a large one. See Alberti, *Dinner Pieces*, 186–89, 258n1.

98. Pliny the Elder, *Natural History* 11.4.11, 3:438–39 (references are to book, section, subsection, and page numbers in Rackham's translation). Importantly, however, he describes them separately. He never directly links bees, spiders, and ants together as Aristotle does (see below).

99. Ibid., 11.28.79, 480–81.

100. The claim appears to be untrue.

101. Pliny the Elder, *Natural History* 11.28.79, 480–81.

102. Beavis, *Insects and Other Invertebrates*, 39. He provides a detailed list of references to spiders in classical antiquity.

103. Dundas, *The Spider and the Bee*, 1–5.

104. Pliny the Elder, for example, employs the Greek term, distinguishing between *phalangia* and *areneae*.

105. Aristotle, *History of Animals* 8.622b, 3:327 (references are to book, section, and page numbers in Peck and Balme's translation). Aristotle is also the source of Pliny's claim about spiders hunting lizards; see 8.623b, 3:333.

106. Ibid., 8.623a, 3:329–31.

107. Alberti refers to poisonous spiders in *On the Art of Building* 1.4, 14–15, where he warns of the bite of the tarantula: "But good heavens, what about our own times in Apulia, here in Italy, where small land-spiders are common, with an incredibly poisonous bite which can send men into various forms of delirium, as though driven mad? Most surprisingly, there is no swelling, no telltale mark appears anywhere on the body to show the bite or sting of a poisonous insect; but to begin with men lose consciousness, fainting from the shock, and then, if there is no one to help them they soon die. They may be treated with a remedy of Theophrastus, who maintained that snake bites could be healed by the sound of the flute." He adds that "we read a similar event that befell the Albanians who fought against Pompey with a large cavalry force. For it is said that spiders were found there which would cause the death of anyone who touched them, either by laughing or by crying." Rykwert, Leach, and Tavernor (ibid., 369n43) comment that although the bite of the European tarantula is not severe, it was believed to be so. It was also commonly held that victims could be cured by the music of the tarantella.

108. Alberti, *Apologhi ed elogi*, 192–94.

109. Ibid., 194.

110. Burroughs, *From Signs to Design*, 77, 260, has also commented on the spider in Alberti's work as an image of central authority that can be applied to the city as well as to the house. He links the image to the Foucauldian theory of panopticism, with the central authority maintaining total surveillance. However, we should bear in mind that panopticism relies on transparency to achieve a condition in which individuals will internalize the panoptic gaze, providing their own surveillance and thus achieving a greater economy of power. It is not clear in any of Alberti's writings that people surveyed by the central authority should actually be aware of the gaze. That is to say, the listening tubes in Bentham's Panopticon would be overtly positioned so that the prisoner might know he was being heard and learn to condition his behavior accordingly. In the castle of Alberti's tyrant, the listening tubes are secret; they are not meant to condition behavior but simply to gather information. This emphasis on secrecy makes Alberti's proposals far removed from the Panopticon, despite certain outward resemblances. The case is more persuasive, however, as Burroughs presents it in relation to Nicholas V's positioning of the giant statue of the Archangel Michael on the Castel Sant'Angelo.

111. Emerton, *Humanism and Tyranny*, 77.

112. Vitruvius says in *De architectura* 2.1 that humans first made their dwellings in imitation of swallows' nests; Alberti states that architects can learn from swallows in *On the Art of Building* 3.10, 76.

113. Kemp, "From 'Mimesis' to 'Fantasia,'" 354. Kemp lists many examples from classical literature and some from the Middle Ages. He points out that Francesco di Giorgio used the constructions of swallows, bees, and spiders to differentiate the human capacity of invention from that of animals. Humans may invent an infinite variety of forms, whereas these animals build in the same way every time. See di

Giorgio, *Trattati di architettura*, 2:505, as well as Dickerman, "Some Stock Illustrations," 123–30.

114. Pliny the Elder, *Natural History* 11.28.82, 3:482–83.

115. Aristotle, *History of Animals* 8.623a, 3:329.

116. Aelian, *On the Characteristics of Animals* 6.57, 2:77–79 (references are to book, section, and page numbers in Scholfield's translation).

117. Alberti, *On the Art of Building* 5.2, 120.

118. Alberti, *Use and Abuse of Books*, 25.

119. This point has been noted by Garin, "Il pensiero," 510. Jarzombek has also paid particular attention to this aspect of Alberti; see his "*Enigma* of Leon Battista Alberti's *Dissimulatio*," 741–48, and *On Leon Baptista Alberti*, 157.

120. Alberti, "*Philodoxus*," 99.

121. Watkins, "Leon Battista Alberti in the Mirror," 9.

122. See Bremmer, "Walking, Standing, and Sitting."

123. Watkins, "Leon Battista Alberti in the Mirror," 11. Interesting in this context is Agnolo Pandolfini's praise of Ulysses in the *Profugiorum ab aerumna.* The character of Ulysses, although admired, was also often perceived as morally dubious because of his habit of lying and hiding his true self behind a mask. For his fraudulent deeds, Dante placed him in one of the lowest circles of hell, inside an eternal flame (although he portrayed the character with some admiration, as neither suffering nor repentant, and recounted a heroic story). See Dante, *Inferno* 26.56–142. In the *Profugiorum*, by contrast, Ulysses is held up as an example of self-control on account of his patient scheming to avenge himself on the suitors in his house. Agnolo comments on Ulysses's incredible patience and unprecedented steadfastness. Despite all of the insults and ill treatment that he had received in his own house, he never gave himself away in word or deed. Rather, he dissimulated with everyone, chose to bear his suffering, and waited for time or the stupidity of his enemies to offer him the occasion for revenge. See Alberti, *Opere volgari*, 2:151–52. Thus, it is Ulysses's dissimulation that is praised—precisely the thing for which he had traditionally been condemned. The idea that one should behave in this manner, disguising his true feelings and waiting for the opportune moment to strike against his enemies, is also, as we shall see, voiced by Momus. It is interesting that Agnolo and Momus, usually seen as occupying opposing ends of the moral spectrum, should share this view.

124. Alberti, *Momus*, 60–61: "Atqui hoc mihi ex acerbo exilio obtigisse voluptati est, quod vafre et gnaviter versipellem atque tergiversatorem praebere me simulando ac dissimulando perdoctus peritissimusque evaserim."

125. Ibid., 100–101: "Et quaenam ea erit persona, Mome? Nempe ut comem, lenem affabilemque me exhibeam. Item oportet discam praesto esse omnibus, benigne obsequi, per hilaritatem excipere, grate detinere, laetos mittere. Ne tu haec, Mome, ab tua natura penitus aliena poteris? Potero quidem, dum velim."

126. Ibid., 100–103: "Quid tum? Igiturne vero nos insitum et penitus innatum lacessendi morem obliviscemur? Minime; verum id quidem moderabimur taciturnitate, pristinumque erga inimicos studium nova quadam captandi laedendique via et ratione servabimus. Demum sic statuo oportere his quibus intra multitudinem atque in negotio vivendum sit, ut ex intimis praecordiis numquam susceptae iniuriae memoriam obliterent, offensae vero livorem nusquam propalent, sed inserviant temporibus, simulando atque dissimulando."

127. Ibid., 102–3: "Alia ex parte sua ipsi studia et cupiditates callida semper confingendi arte integant; vigilantes, sollertes, accincti paratique occasiones praestolentur vindicandi sui, praestitam ne deserant; sempiterne sui sint memores. . . . Omnium sermones aeque esse insidiosos deputent; credent

nemini, sed credere omnibus ostentabunt. Nullos vereantur, sed coram quibusque applaudere atque assentari omnibus condocefiant."

128. Ibid., 104–5: "Omnino illud unum iterum atque iterum iuvabit meminisse, bene et gnaviter fuscare omnia adumbratis quibusdam signis probitatis et innocentiae. Quam quidem rem pulchre assequemur si verba vultusque nostros et omnem corporis faciem assuefaciemus ita fingere atque conformare, ut illis esse persimiles videamur qui boni ac mites putentur, tametsi ab illis penitus discrepemus. O rem optimam nosse erudito artificio fucatae fallacisque simulationis suos operire atque obnubere sensus!"

129. Ibid., 148–49: "Momus, etsi acrem animo ex ea re indignationem concepisset, tamen, quod simulare dissimulareque omni in causa decrevisset, tenui oratione et levibus dictis Minervam ab se missam fecit."

130. Indeed, it is Momus who presents Jupiter with a text depicting how the world could be remade and properly governed. Jupiter tosses it aside and forgets it, coming across it again at the end of the story, where the reader is left with little hope that any of its proposals will ever be implemented. This rejection by a ruler of a text on planning has been seen as highly significant by commentators such as Jarzombek, Tafuri, and Stefano Borsi (who, following Tafuri, argues that Alberti was hostile to Nicholas V's renovation of Rome and estranged from the center of power). Certainly, *Momus* seems to articulate a deep cynicism toward the activity of planning, with which Alberti is so concerned in *De re aedificatoria*.

131. Jarzombek, *On Leon Baptista Alberti*, 145, argues that the "Baptista" of Alberti's literary works may never be confused as identical with Alberti himself.

Chapter 5

1. Varro, *On Agriculture* 1.4.1, 184–85 (references are to book, section, subsection, and page numbers in Hooper and Ash's translation).

2. Alberti, *Della famiglia*, 197, and *Opere volgari*, 1:195: "Dico, cercherei comperare la possessione ch'ella fusse tale quale l'avolo mio Caroccio . . . solea dire voleano essere le possessioni, che portandovi uno quartuccio di sale ivi si potesse tutto l'anno pascere la famiglia."

3. Alberti, *Della famiglia*, 202, and *Opere volgari*, 1:202: "Se io avessi villa simile quale io narrava, io mi vi starei buoni dì dell'anno." This also appears to be the position of the Roman agricultural authors, who all display distinctly anti-urban feelings (especially Columella) yet argue for the necessity of having a farm in close proximity to the city.

4. Lillie, *Florentine Villas*, 27–28.

5. Alberti, *Della famiglia*, 197, and *Opere volgari*, 1:196.

6. Crescenzi, *Trattato della agricoltura* 11.8, cited in Lillie, *Florentine Villas*, 25. Crescenzi speaks of the "'mportuna voracità de'lavoratori."

7. Herlihy, "Distribution of Wealth," 150–51.

8. See Boschetto, *Leon Battista Alberti e Firenze*, 109.

9. Herlihy, "Distribution of Wealth," 134.

10. Alberti, *On the Art of Building* 5.15, 141.

11. Ibid.

12. Ibid., 5.17, 145.

13. Ibid. Alberti later expressed disapproval of this kind of villa in his last work, *De iciarchia*.

14. Coffin, *The Villa*, 14.

15. Alberti, *Opere volgari*, 2:64: "Erano le mani a Genipatro callose per lo essercitarsi alla coltura dell'orto suo quando ogni dì esso dava opera qualche ora alla sanità."

16. Ibid., 2:74: "Se m'agrada conoscere le cagioni e principi di quanto io vedo vari effetti prodotti della natura, s'io desidero modo a discernere el vero dal falso, el bene dal male, s'io cerco conoscere me stesso e insieme intendere le cose prodotte in vita per indi riconoscere e reverire il padre, ottimo e primo maestro e procuratore di tante maraviglie, non a me mancano i santissimi filosofi, apresso de' quali io d'ora in ora a me stessi satisfacendo me senta divenire più dotto anche e migliore."

17. Ibid.: "La amplitudine tua e pompa civile, la frequenza di molti salutatori mai a me più piacerà che la mia quieta solitudine."

18. Ibid., 2:138–39: "E certo s'io avessi edificio sì atto e sì magnifico in luogo sì grato e sì salubre come voi, Agnolo, non so dove traducessi molta parte de' miei dì altrove che solo ivi."

19. Ibid., 2:157: "Dicono che nulla si truova fidissimo quanto la terra. Ella ciò che tu gli accomandasti rende, secondo el precetto di Esiodo, non a pari ma a maggior misura. Ancora più troverai fedele la industria e vigilanza tua, *presertim* quella qual tu porrai a cose oneste e degne, quando in queste e' cieli e ogni fato si adopera in satisfare a' tuoi meriti. Mai fu la virtù senza premio di lode e grazia."

20. The same sentiment can be found in Columella's *On Agriculture*.

21. Alberti, *On the Art of Building* 9.2, 294–95. It should be noted that the word "suburban," which appears before the first use of the term *hortus* in this passage, is an addition by Rykwert, Leach, and Tavernor.

22. Ibid., and Alberti, *L'architettura*, 2:793.

23. Mumford, *City in History*, 485. The suburb is also discussed in Eden, "Studies in Urban Theory," 27, where the author notes that "having to make a choice between two good things, town and country, he [Alberti] takes the logical course and chooses both—what Ebenezer Howard calls 'town-country.'" He adds, "Alberti would no doubt have been greatly surprised if he could have known how widely his idea, which he himself drew from the classics, was destined to spread in the next five centuries." Morris, *History of Urban Form*, 134, also stresses the modern nature of Alberti's proposals, writing, "It is also possible to see the germ of twentieth-century suburbia in [Alberti's] observation that there is a great deal of satisfaction in a convenient retreat near the town, where a man is at liberty to do just what he pleases."

24. Mumford, *City in History*, 485.

25. Alberti, *Opere volgari*, 2:68: "Somma certo felicità viversi sanza cura alcuna di queste cose caduche e fragili della fortuna coll'animo libero da tanta contagione del corpo, e fuggito lo strepito e fastidio della plebe in solitudine parlarsi colla natura."

26. Alberti, *On the Art of Building* 9.2, 295.

27. Bruni, *Panegirico*, 24: "Quare et ville longinquos aspectus, et suburbia villas, et urbs ipsa suburbia pulcritudine vincit." See also Kohl and Witt, *Earthly Republic*, 142.

28. Kohl and Witt, *Earthly Republic*, 144–45.

29. See Mazzini and Martini, *Villa Medici*, 167–72.

30. Coffin, *Villa*, 16.

31. Eckstein, *District of the Green Dragon*, 20.

32. Ibid., 21.

33. Tafuri, *Interpreting the Renaissance*, 32.

34. Eckstein, *District of the Green Dragon*, 11: ". . . di tagliare i ponti e fare città per noi." See also Kent and Kent, *Neighbours and Neighbourhood*, 4.

35. Cohn, *Laboring Classes in Renaissance Florence*, 127.

36. Ackerman, *Villa*, 10.

37. Alberti, *On the Art of Building* 5.18, 151.

38. Coffin, *Villa*, 21, asserts that Alberti elaborates a hierarchy of building types in which the villa stands near the bottom, below the urban palace.

39. Alberti, *On the Art of Building* 5.18, 151.

40. Ibid., 5.18, 152.

Chapter 6

1. Vitruvius, *On Architecture* 1.3.2, 1:36.

2. Alberti, *On the Art of Building* 6.1, 155, and *L'architettura*, 2:445.

3. Alberti, *On the Art of Building* 6.2, 155.

4. Westfall, "Society, Beauty, and the Humanist Architect," 67. Many scholars have stressed Alberti's independence from Vitruvius. Choay, "Alberti and Vitruvius," 26, asserts that Alberti "has not simply improved Vitruvius' text: insofar as he uses it at all, he transforms it completely." See also her *The Rule and the Model*, 19–20, 112–31.

5. Manetti, "The Testament of Nicholas V," sections T2, T3, in Smith and O'Connor, *Building the Kingdom*, 472–75.

6. Alberti, *On the Art of Building* 6.2, 155.

7. Ibid., 6.2, 158.

8. Bialostocki, "Power of Beauty," 13–14.

9. Alberti, *On the Art of Building* 8.3, 249.

10. Ibid., 10.1, 320.

11. Bialostocki, "Power of Beauty," 14.

12. We might remember here Alberti's remarks on the Circus Maximus. See Alberti, *On the Art of Building* 8.8, 279.

13. Alberti acknowledges that sculptures made from precious metals are likely to be melted down, regardless of artistic worth. Ibid., 7.16, 243.

14. For the influence of this event on *Momus* and *De re*, see S. Borsi, *Leon Battista Alberti e Roma*, 256–59, and *Momus, o Del principe*, 28–29. Borsi argues that Alberti's references to Constantinople in *De re* have a detached nature, suggesting that they date from before the fall of the city. The case of *Momus* is quite different.

15. Quoted in Fortini Brown, *Venice and Antiquity*, 16.

16. Bialostocki, "Power of Beauty," 14.

17. I am grateful to Chris Siwicky for this suggestion. On the issue of Alberti's relationship to Roman antiquity, in the broadest sense, see Stefano Borsi's major study, *Leon Battista Alberti e l'antichità romana*.

18. Alberti, *On the Art of Building* 6.2, 156. I have slightly modified the translation. See also Alberti, *L'architettura*, 2:447.

19. Alberti, *On the Art of Building* 6.2, 156.

20. Di Stefano, *L'altro sapere*, 46–50, examines, in a complex and sophisticated analysis, the negative connotations attached to ornament as something additional and nonessential in relation to rhetorical models. She notes that Alberti describes ornament not only as *affictum* (additional) but also as *compactum* (united with).

21. Alberti, *On the Art of Building* 6.2, 156–57.

22. This attack on the ignorant and those who lack understanding may be in the same vein as certain Vasari's anecdotes regarding Giotto, Donatello's *St. Mark*, or the nose of Michelangelo's *David*, where it is demonstrated that those who are ignorant about art lack the required judgment to comment on it.

23. Alberti, *On the Art of Building* 6.3, 157.

24. Ibid., 6.3, 157–58.

25. Ibid., 6.3, 158.

26. Ibid., 6.1, 154.

27. Ibid.

28. Ibid., 6.1, 155. A good example of Alberti's willingness to value his own measurements equally or above those of Vitruvius is to be found at 6.5.

29. Ibid., 6.3, 159.

30. Ibid.

31. Choay, *The Rule and the Model*, 93.

32. Mitrović, *Serene Greed*, 112, argues that although he labels it as Socratic, Alberti in fact derives his maxim from Aristotle's *Nicomachean Ethics* (1106b9–35), via Leonardo Bruni's translation.

33. Regarding architecture, see Thomson, *Renaissance Architecture*, 4–5. Thomson quotes Saint Bernard of Clairvaux as asking, "What has gold to do with holiness?" and why should people try to "arouse the devotion of fleshy people with adornments, seeing they [the bishops and monks] cannot do so with things of the spirit?" (4). Alexander Neckham cries, "Behold the superfluous and vain contrivances connected with buildings, clothing, food, trappings, furniture, and finally various adornments, and rightly you will be able to say: O vanity! O superfluity!" (5). Pierre Le Chantre comments that "men sin even in building churches" (5). On frugality in Alberti's writings, see Cassani, "*Libertas, frugalitas, aedificandi libido.*" Stefano Borsi, *Leon Battista Alberti e Roma*, 44–45, offers some suggestions as to the sources of Alberti's *frugalitas* (see also p. 68).

34. Alberti, *On the Art of Building* 9.1, 291.

35. Ibid., 9.1, 292.

36. Ibid., 7.10, 220.

37. Ibid., 7.12, 223. In the following chapter, Alberti voices criticisms of certain contemporary practices within churches and especially the profusion of altars, which were sufficient to earn his treatise a place on the Index in the following century.

38. Ibid., 9.1, 293.

39. Ibid., 7.1, 190.

40. Ibid., 7.1, 191, and Alberti, *L'architettura*, 2:535: "Nanque amoto quidem ordine nihil prorsus erit, quod sese aut commodum aut gratum aut dignum praestet."

41. Alberti, *On the Art of Building* 8.6, 262.

42. Ibid., 8.6, 263–68.

43. Ibid., 9.5, 301, and Alberti, *L'architettura*, 2:811.

44. Alberti, *On the Art of Building* 9.5, 301.

45. Ibid., 9.5, 302. Rykwert, Leach, and Tavernor, in their notes to this passage, elaborate on these translations: "*Numerus*/number means quantity, and also quality— in the Pythagorean-Platonic sense and as interpreted through various Christian commentaries, such as Augustine's *City of God. . . . Finitio* we have translated as 'outline,' though 'measured outline' is possibly more precise. . . . *Collocatio*, or position, relates to decisions that determine the arrangement of a building" (ibid., 422). For a more detailed examination of the terms, see Tavernor, *On Alberti*, 44–45. He examines *numerus* in the context of the Renaissance notion of number, argues that *finitio* relates to Alberti's alleged practice of starting from ground plans, and interprets *collocatio* as relating to composition in a broad sense. On Alberti's use of ground plans, see Lang, "*De lineamentis*," 331–35.

46. Alberti, *On the Art of Building* 9.5, 302.

47. Vagnetti, "Concinnitas: Riflessioni," 139–61, examines the various translations and interpretations of *concinnitas* by all of Alberti's translators and the major commentators on his text up to the time at which the article was written.

48. Cicero, *Orator* 44.149, 49.164, 65.220; and *Brutus* 83.287, 95.325. See also Tavernor, *On Alberti*, 43–44, and "Concinnitas, o la formulazione della bellezza," 300–315; Lücke, "Alberti, Vitruvio e Cicerone," 70–95; and Santinello, *Leon Battista Alberti*, 224–38.

49. Tavernor, *On Alberti*, 43–44. He argues that Wittkower, in particular, interpreted Alberti's notion in too Vitruvian a way. For Wittkower's views on Alberti's theory of beauty, see his *Architectural Principles*, 7.

50. Santinello, *Leon Battista Alberti*, 224–38, charts the appearances of *concinnitas* in Alberti's writings, starting with the *Commentarium Philodoxus fabulae* and moving to "Defunctus" (one of the *Intercenales*), *Pontifex*, and *Della famiglia*. The term first appears in the architectural treatise, Alberti, *On the Art of Building*, at 2.1, 35.

51. Alberti, *On the Art of Building* 9.5, 302–3.

52. Ibid.

53. Ibid., 9.5, 303. Alberti says, "All that has been said our ancestors learned through observation of Nature herself; so they had no doubt that if they neglected these things, they would be unable to attain all that contributes to the praise and honor of the work; not without reason they declared that Nature, as the perfect generator of forms, should be their model. And so, with the utmost industry, they searched out the rules that she employed in producing things, and translated them into methods of building. By studying in Nature the patterns both for whole bodies and for their individual parts, they understood that at their very origins bodies do not consist of equal proportions, with the result that some are slender, some fat, and others in between; and observing the great difference in purpose and intention between one building and another, as we have already observed in earlier books, they concluded that, by the same token, each should be treated differently."

54. Ibid.

55. Di Stefano, *L'altro sapere*, 93, emphasizes that this entails imitating not only natural forms but also the way in which nature works. See also S. Borsi, *Leon Battista Alberti e Roma*, 229.

56. Nonetheless, Alberti does concede that nature creates ugliness as well as beauty.

57. These passages are discussed by Cassani, "Et flores quidem negligitis." See also Pearson, "Visions of the City," 220–22.

58. Alberti, *Momus*, 302–3: "Est Charon sensibus acutissimus, visu, auditu et huiusmodi supra quam possis credere. Cum igitur ad eius nares florum, qui passim in prato aderant, applicuisset odor, illico se ad flores ipsos colligendos et contemplandos dedit tanta voluptate et admiratione ut ab iis aegre ferret abstrahi. Admonebat enim Gelastus plus itinerum superesse quam ut puerilibus florum deliciis legendis insisteret: maiora enim esse quae aggrediantur, flores quidem suppeditari mortalibus adeo ut etiam ab invitis conculcentur. Ille etsi nihil invitus magis posset audire, ductori tamen parendum ducebat. Dehinc inter proficiscendum Charon tantam in natura rerum amoenitatem et varietatem spectans, colles, convalles, fontes, fluenta, lacus et huiusmodi, de Gelasto coepit quaerere unde tanta vis pretiosissimarum rerum manarit mundo."

59. Ibid., 310–13: "Medio in theatro illi cum advenissent, 'Enim et quid tibi haec, o Charon?' inquit Gelastus. Negavit Charon videri sibi aut theatrum aut ornamenta istiusmodi talia ut ulla ex parte cum floribus quos apud pratum excerpserat essent comparanda. Et mirari quidem professus est quod pluris faciant homines quae possint vilissimorum manu assequi quam ea quae ne cogitatione quidem satis queant attingere. 'Et flores' inquit 'neglegitis: saxa admirabimur? In flore ad venustatem, ad gratiam omnia conveniunt. In his hominum operibus nihil invenies dignum admiratione praeter id, ut vituperes tantorum laborum tam stultam profusionem.'" I have slightly modified the translation.

60. Ibid., 262–63. Describing the theater in an earlier passage, Alberti says that the top of it was swathed in gold-embroidered veils and that it included statues of the great gods, which shone with gold and jewels. However, he notes, "what surpassed the

gold and gems in beauty, as much as they themselves were surpassed in value, were the flowers: the flowers strewn over the statues, adding to their charm; the flowers woven into garlands, girdling the statues and perfuming them with delicious incense." (Et quod aurum gemmasque vinceret specie quantum ab iis dignitate vincebantur, omnia floribus conspersa ad venustatem conveniebant, omnia sertis fumorumque deliciis odorata et redimita.)

61. Alberti, *On the Art of Building* 6.2, 155.

62. Ibid., 6.2, 155–56.

63. On this, see S. Borsi, *Momus, o Del principe*, 43.

64. Alberti, *On the Art of Building* 9.7, 310.

65. Smith's translation, *Architecture in the Culture of Early Humanism*, 5–6.

66. Alberti, *Opere volgari*, 2:57–58: "Ma sediamo, se così ti piace, qui fra questi mirti, luogo non meno delizioso che i vostri teatri e templi amplissimi e suntuosissimi. Qui colonne fabricate dalla natura tante quante tu vedi albori ertissimi. Qui sopra dal sole noi copre ombra lietissima di questi faggi e abeti, e atorno, dovunque te volgi, vedi mille perfettissimi colori di vari fiori intessuti fra el verde splendere in fra l'ombra, e vincere tanto lustro e chiarore del cielo; e da qualunque parte verso te si muove l'aura, indi senti venire a gratificarti suavissimi odori. E poi la festività di questi quali tu in presenza vedi uccelletti con sue piume dipintissimi e ornatissimi, a chi non delettasse? Bellissimi, che d'ora in ora vengono con nuovi canti lodando i cieli a salutarmi! E questo qui presso argenteo e purissimo fonte, testimone e arbitro in parte delli studi mei, sempre m'arride in fronte, e quanto in lui sia, attorno mi si avolge vezzeggiando, ora nascondendosi fra le chiome di queste freschissime e vezzosissime erbette, ora con sue onde sollevandosi e dolce immurmurando bello m'inchina e risaluta, ora lieto molto e quietissimo mi s'apre, e soffre ch'io in lui me stesso contempli e specchi. Agiungi che qui niuno invido, niuno maledico, niuno ottrettatore fallace, qui iniquo niuno perturba la nostra quiete e tranquillità. Ma sediamo."

67. Numerous authors have discussed the relationship of Alberti's architectural theory to rhetoric. See, for example, Onians, "Alberti and ΦΙΛΑΡΕΤΗ"; Smith, *Architecture in the Culture of Early Humanism*; Van Eck, "Architecture, Language, and Rhetoric"; Dunlop, "Rhetoric and the City"; and Di Stefano, *L'altro sapere*, esp. 27–51. Wolf, "Body and Antiquity," 175, highlights the importance of rhetorical models for Renaissance writings on art theory and suggests that this derives from their being the only elaborate account of any art at all to survive from antiquity.

68. Alberti, *On the Art of Building* 7.3, 194.

69. Augustine, *City of God* 1.1, 4.

70. As Wittkower, *Architectural Principles*, 27, puts it, specifically citing Alberti, "Renaissance artists firmly adhered to the Pythagorean concept 'All is Number' and, guided by Plato and the Neo-Platonists and supported by a long chain of theologians from Augustine onwards, they were convinced of the mathematical and harmonic structure of the universe and all creation." This is not to say that Alberti adopted Platonic or Neo-Platonic metaphysics, however. Gadol's remark in *Leon Battista Alberti*, 106, that "in *De re aedificatoria*, the idea of beauty has all the characteristics of a Platonic Form" rather overstates the case, since Alberti never elaborates his thought in this direction and continually argues that beauty is to be found above all in nature. On Alberti's use of the term *idea delle bellezze* in Book III of *De pictura*, see Panofsky, *Idea*, 58–59.

71. Alberti, *On the Art of Building* 9.5, 305.

72. Ibid.

73. Iamblichus, *On the Pythagorean Life*, §§64–65, p. 27. See also Cavarnos, *Pythagoras on the Fine Arts*, 36.

74. Basil, *Letters*, "To Young Men," 9.9–10, 4:419 (references are to section, subsection, and page numbers in Defarrari's translation). Basil also notes that David was able to cure Saul of his madness with song. See also Cavarnos, *Pythagoras on the Fine Arts*, 39.

75. Iamblichus, *On the Pythagorean Life*, §112, p. 49–50.

76. Alberti, *On the Art of Building* 1.4, 15. Rykwert, Leach, and Tavernor (ibid., 369n44) comment that Alberti's source is Gellius (*The Attic Nights* 4.13), who in turn points to Democritus.

77. Virgil, *Georgics* 4.467–72, 140, and 4.481–84, 140–41.

78. This is also emphasized by Ovid, *Metamorphoses* 10.40–47, 226:

> So to the music of his strings he sang,
> And all the bloodless spirits wept to hear;
> And Tantalus forgot the fleeing water,
> Ixion's wheel was tranced; the Danaids
> Laid down their urns; the vultures left their feast,
> And Sisyphus sat rapt upon his stone.
> Then first by that sad singing overwhelmed,
> The Furies' cheeks, it's said, were wet with tears;
> And Hades' queen and he whose scepter rules
> The underworld could not deny the prayer. . . .

The lasting appeal of this powerful image is demonstrated by Schopenhauer. Seeking to describe how art may move the human soul and deliver it from the tyranny of the will, he writes, "It is the painless state, prized by Epicurus as the highest good and as the state of the gods; for that moment we are delivered from the miserable pressure of the will. We celebrate the Sabbath of the penal servitude of willing; the wheel of Ixion stands still." Schopenhauer, who believed music to be the highest form of art, was clearly inspired by the story of Orpheus. See Schopenhauer, *The World as Will and Representation*, bk. 3, §38, p. 196.

79. Scavizzi, "Myth of Orpheus," 111–62.

80. Macrobius, *On the Dream of Scipio*, 2.3.7–9, quoted in Brumble, *Classical Myths*, 250–51.

81. Alberti, *On the Art of Building* 6.2, 155.

82. *Chess of Love Commentary*, 281, quoted in Brumble, *Classical Myths*, 24.

83. Alberti, *Della famiglia*, 201, and *Opere volgari*, 1:200–201: ". . . la tanta quantità de' pessimi mali uomini, quali pella terra continuo ti farfallano inanti agli occhi, quali mai restano di cicalarti torno all'orecchie, quali d'ora in ora seguono stridendo e mugghiando per tutta la terra, bestie furiosissime e orribilissime." Orpheus was, of course, famous precisely for attracting and pacifying wild beasts by the sound of his music. Between 1437 and 1439, Luca della Robbia sculpted a relief for the campanile of Florence Cathedral symbolizing music, in which Orpheus is shown surrounded by lions and swans. Pythagoras was also adept at "relaxing tension and giving instruction in what he said which reached even non-rational animals," according to Iamblichus. Although he did this through speech rather than music, Iamblichus says that he had "the command of Orpheus over wild creatures, charming them and holding them fast with the power of his voice." Iamblichus, *On the Pythagorean Life*, §60, pp. 24–25.

84. Stahel, "Cristoforo Landino's Allegorization," 54.

85. I am here paraphrasing Szilágyi, "Amphion Playing the Lyre," 478–79.

86. Horace, *Ars Poetica*, 391–401, 482–83 (references are to line and page numbers in Fairclough's translation).

87. Marvin Trachtenberg has demonstrated how architectural proportions might be reflected in music with regard to Dufay's *Nuper rosarum flores*, commissioned for the dedication of Florence Cathedral on March 25, 1436. Alberti would likely have been present at the ceremony. See Trachtenberg, "Architecture and Music Reunited," 740–75.

88. I am grateful to Professor Peter Vergo for bringing this point to my attention. Vitruvius, for example, notes that "a man must know music that he may have acquired the acoustic and mathematical relations and be able to carry out rightly the adjustments of *ballistae, catapultae* and *scorpiones*." Vitruvius's *De architectura* also includes a section on harmonics, which precedes that on acoustics. However, he does not discuss in any further detail the application of harmonic proportions to architecture and never claims that musical harmonies might be visually perceptible. See Vitruvius, *On Architecture* 1.1.8–9, 1:12–15; 5.4–5, 1:268–83; and 5.8, 1:292–95.

89. Grayson, *Studi su Leon Battista Alberti*, 166: "Le misure et proportioni de' pilastri tu vedi onde elle naschono: ciò che tu muti si discorda tutta quella musica." On the proportions of Alberti's buildings, see Tavernor, *On Alberti*, 74, 173.

90. This point is emphasized by Mitrović, *Serene Greed*, 118.

91. Plato, *Complete Works*, 1037–38 (400d–401a).

92. Watkins, "Leon Battista Alberti in the Mirror," 15, 16.

93. As Smith and O'Connor have shown in *Building the Kingdom*, there was a long tradition in which large and impressive buildings—fortifications above all—were seen as overawing a populace and deterring attack. In some ways, Alberti's position must be viewed as related to these ideas. However, he does not aim at intimidation, but rather persuasion, through the beauty of nature. Politically and ethically speaking, the gulf between the two conceptions is enormous.

94. Alberti's criticisms of certain medieval urban practices, such as the building of excessive numbers of towers and churches, perhaps express the notion that such things, apart from concerns about use, are fundamentally disproportionate and, in that sense, are opposed to nature. In *On the Art of Building* 8.5, 257, Alberti seems to include a cautionary note regarding the idea of an architecture and a city that are yet to come, as he comments, "What is this we now see, the whole of Italy competing for renewal? How many cities, which as children we saw all built of wood, have now been turned into marble?" There is perhaps an allusion here to modern rulers who see themselves as new emperors, eager to write their own *res gestae*. This relates to Alberti's distrust of immoderate building schemes and grand political projects.

Conclusion

1. Alberti, *Momus*, 101–3. The issue has recently been discussed by Catanorchi, "Tra politica e passione," 137–77.

2. In "The Dream," which contains some of the most vivid imagery to be found in the *Intercenales*, Libripeta enters a wide meadow of human and animal hair, where people are digging up roots that will make them appear learned even though they are not. He is then nearly devoured by a swarm of lice. Here, too, the physicality of the body, and hair specifically, is employed in the mockery of human pretensions.

3. Alberti, *Opere volgari*, 2:234: "Chi potrà mirare un maledico ottrettatore, calunniatore, e non avere orrore della rabbia sua? Omini ancora e ancora pessimi, degni d'essere persequitati da tutto el populo, non dirò con l'arco e colle saette, ma co' funali e face infiammate, e brustulati tanto che l'ossa rimangono denudate, acciò che niuna fizione possa più in quel mostro essere latente!" The language here is similar to

that used in Charon's story, where men adopt *fictos vultus* but finally end up *nudatus*. The passage is also commented on by Catanorchi, "Tra politica e passione," 163.

4. Smith, "Apocalypse Sent Up," S167.

5. Alberti, *Momus*, 92–93: ". . . paene ultimum in discrimen deos et homines et universam orbis machinam adduxerit."

6. Ibid., 198–99: "Videbis enim quo pacto salus hominum deorumque maiestas et orbis imperium fuerint ultimum paene in discrimen adducta."

7. Smith, "Apocalypse Sent Up," argues with some force that *Momus* in fact constitutes a parody of the Apocalypse. See also Smith and O'Connor, *Building the Kingdom*, 225–54, and S. Simoncini, "Roma come Gerusalemme."

8. Michel, *Un idéal humain*, 148–49, and Mitrović, *Serene Greed*, 143.

9. Alberti, *Opere volgari*, 2:266. "Ma furono poi le città constituite forse a caso, e non per altro ragione che solo per vivere con sufficienza e commodità insieme."

10. Alberti, *On the Art of Building* 8.8, 281.

11. Alberti, *Momus*, 309.

12. Watkins, "Leon Battista Alberti in the Mirror," 15. See also Fubini and Menci Gallorini, "L'autobiografia di Leon Battista Alberti," 36, 76: "Ex solo intuitu plurima cuiusque praesentis vitia ediscebat" (76).

13. Alberi, *Opere volgari*, 2:245. Mitrović, *Serene Greed*, 49, notes that in *De re aedificatoria*, Alberti, with the exception of one sentence, appears to use the term *lineamenta* to refer only to things made by human beings. The use of the vernacular *lineamenti* in the *De iciarchia* suggests, however, that he saw its scope as being much broader. Indeed, while the masks that the painter observes in Charon's story are man-made, it seems that his knowledge is gained from observing lineamenta more generally—that is to say, the lineamenta of both human being and mask, though this is not specified.

14. Here, "body" is not to be understood in the sense of a living body, according to Mitrović's argument.

15. Mitrović, *Serene Greed*, 31. Wolf, "Body and Antiquity," 183, already makes much the same observation, noting that *lineamenta* "can refer to the building in the mind of the artist, to the building as projected or represented in designs or models, to the existing building itself, or to the 'reconstruction' of ruined edifices such as those of Roman antiquity."

16. Mitrović, *Serene Greed*, 35.

17. Alberti, *On the Art of Building* 6.13, 188. I have substituted the Latin *lineamenta* for the translators' "lineaments."

18. Ibid., 7.1, 189.

19. On this topic, see Di Stefano, *L'altro sapere*, 79, and Wolf, "Body and Antiquity," 184. Alina Payne, "Alberti and the Origins of the Paragone," 360, offers a more skeptical view. For the relationships between the visual arts in Alberti's writings, see Cassani, "Il pittore, lo scultore e l'architetto."

20. Mitrović, *Serene Greed*, 75, persuasively argues that Alberti considered the shape of a building, as defined by its lineamenta, to be the totality of that building's *forma*, or essence.

21. In *De pictura*, Alberti relates that the Greek painter Zeuxis gave his works away since "he did not believe any price could be found to recompense the man who, in modeling or painting living things, behaved like a god among mortals. The virtues of painting, therefore, are that its masters see their works admired and feel themselves almost to be like the creator." Alberti, *On Painting and On Sculpture*, 2.25–26, 61 (references are to book, section, and page numbers in Grayson's translation). For the story of Zeuxis, see Pliny the Elder, *Natural History* 35.36.62.

22. Tafuri, *Interpreting the Renaissance*, 46.

23. Garin, *Rinascite e rivoluzioni*, 145. Nonetheless, Garin's observations do not appear to be entirely accurate. He describes the creator in Charon's story as impervious and as amused by the spectacle of the humans below, who are trying to disguise themselves with mud. Yet there is nothing in the text to suggest the creator's amusement. Garin also describes the painter as off to one side, taking note of the goings-on, but it is not clear from Alberti's text that the painter was present at these events. Rather, it is surely the painter's specialty in the realm of images and knowledge of lineamenta that allow him knowledge of what went on before. On the painter as a specialist in imagery in the wider context of *Momus*, see Rinaldi, *Melancholia christiana*, 133.

24. Flemming, "Natura ridens," 7.

25. Vitruvius, *On Architecture* 2.1, 1:78–79: ". . . habentes ab natura praemium praeter reliqua animalia, ut non proni sed erecti ambularent mundique et astrorum magnificentiam aspicerent."

26. Alberti, *Opere volgari*, 1:131 and 2:122.

27. Conrad, *Lord Jim*, 195. This contrast between the act of stargazing and careless attention to the ground has a long pedigree. Diogenes Laertius recounts how Thales was led out of his house by an old woman to look at the stars. When Thales fell into a ditch and began to complain, the woman rebuked him, asking how he could hope to understand what is in heaven when he could not see what was under his own feet. See Diogenes Laertius, *Life of Thales* 1.1.34. The same author relates that Diogenes of Sinope used to berate mathematicians for gazing at the sun and moon but having little idea of what was going on around them. See Diogenes Laertius, *Lives of Eminent Philosophers* 2.2.27.

28. Alberti, *Opere volgari*, 2:92–93: "Gli altri animali contenti di quello che li si condice: l'omo solo sempre investigando cose nuove sé stessi infesta. . . . Che stoltizia de' mortali, che vogliamo sapere e quando e come e per qual consiglio e a che fine sia ogni instituto e opera di Dio, e vogliamo sapere che materia, che figura, che natura, che forza sia quella del cielo, de' pianeti, delle intelligenze, e mille secreti vogliamo essere noti a noi più che alla natura." See also Tafuri, *Interpreting the Renaissance*, 43.

29. Alberti, *Momus*, 278–79: "Et quod magis miretur, in hominum numero sapere quidem per se ferme singulos atque nosse quid rectum sit; cum tamen coiverint, omnes simul facile insanire sponteque delirare."

Bibliography

Ackerman, James, and John Newman. *The Architecture of Michelangelo, with a Catalogue of Michelangelo's Works.* Harmondsworth: Penguin, 1970.

———. "The Planning of Renaissance Rome, 1450–1580." In *Rome in the Renaissance: The City and the Myth; Papers of the Thirteenth Annual Conference of the Center for Medieval and Early Renaissance Studies, State University of New York at Binghamton,* edited by P. A. Ramsey, 2–17. Binghamton, N.Y.: Medieval and Renaissance Texts and Studies, Center for Medieval and Early Renaissance Studies, 1982.

———. *The Villa: Form and Ideology of Country Houses.* Princeton: Princeton University Press, 1990.

Aelian. *On the Characteristics of Animals.* Translated by A. F. Scholfield. 3 vols. Cambridge, Mass.: Harvard University Press; London: W. Heinemann, 1958–59.

Aiken, Jane Andrews. "Leon Battista Alberti's System of Human Proportions." *Journal of the Warburg and Courtauld Institutes* 43 (1980): 68–96.

Alberti, Leon Battista. *The Albertis of Florence: Leon Battista Alberti's "Della Famiglia."* Translated with an introduction and notes by Guido A. Guarino. Lewisburg: Bucknell University Press, 1971.

———. *Apologhi ed elogi.* Edited by Rosario Contarino. Genoa: Edizioni Costa & Nolan, 1984.

———. *L'architettura.* Edited and translated by G. Orlandi, with an introduction and notes by Paolo Portoghese. 2 vols. Milan: Edizioni Il Polifilo, 1966.

———. *De iure.* Edited by Cecil Grayson. Translated into French with a postface by Pierre Caye. *Albertiana* 3 (2000): 157–248.

———. *Descriptio urbis Romae: Edition critique.* Translated with commentary by Martine Furno and Mario Carpo. Geneva: Droz, 2000.

———. *Dinner Pieces.* Translated by David Marsh. Binghamton, N.Y.: Medieval and Renaissance Texts and Studies, in conjunction with the Renaissance Society of America, 1987.

———. *The Family in Renaissance Florence.* Translated with an introduction by Renée Neu Watkins. Columbia: University of South Carolina Press, 1969.

———. "Leon Battista Alberti's *Philodoxus* (c. 1424): An English Translation." Translated by Joseph R. Jones and Lucia Guzzi. *Celestinesca* 17, no. 1 (Spring 1993): 87–134.

———. *Leonis Battistae Alberti Opera inedita et pauca separatim impressa.* Edited by Girolamo Mancini. Florence: J. C. Sansoni, 1890.

———. *Momus.* Latin text edited by Virginia Brown and Sarah Knight. Translated into English by Sarah Knight. Cambridge, Mass.: Harvard University Press, 2003.

———. *Momus; o, Del principe.* Edited and translated with an introduction and notes by Giuseppe Martini. Bologna: N. Zanichelli, 1942.

———. *On Painting.* Translated by Cecil Grayson, with an introduction and notes by Martin Kemp. Harmondsworth: Penguin, 1991.

————. *On Painting and On Sculpture: The Latin Texts of "De pictura" and "De statua."* Edited and translated with an introduction and notes by Cecil Grayson. London: Phaidon, 1972.

————. *On the Art of Building in Ten Books.* Translated by Joseph Rykwert, Neil Leach, and Robert Tavernor. Cambridge, Mass.: MIT Press, 1988.

————. *Opere volgari.* Edited by Cecil Grayson. 3 vols. Bari: G. Laterza, 1960–73.

————. *Opuscoli inediti: "Musca," "Vita S. Potiti."* Edited by Cecil Grayson. Florence: L. S. Olschki, 1954.

————. *Ten Books on Architecture.* Edited by Joseph Rykwert. Translated into Italian by Cosimo Bartoli and into English by James Leoni. London: A. Tiranti, 1965.

————. *A Treatise on Ciphers.* Edited by David Kahn, based on a partial translation by Charles J. Mendelsohn in 1939. Turin: Galimberti Tipografi Editori, 1997.

————. *The Use and Abuse of Books.* Translated with an introduction by Renée Neu Watkins. Prospect Heights, Ill.: Waveland Press, 1999.

Alighieri, Dante. *La divina commedia.* Edited by Natalino Sapegno. Milan: Riccardo Ricciardi Editore, 1979.

Aluffi Begliomini, Lorenza. "Note sull'opera dell'Alberti: Il *Momus* e il *De re aedificatoria.*" *Rinascimento,* n.s., 12 (1972): 267–83.

Antal, Frederick. *Florentine Painting and Its Social Background: The Bourgeois Republic Before Cosimo de' Medici's Advent to Power; XIV and Early XV Centuries.* London: Kegan Paul, 1948.

Aristotle. *History of Animals.* Translated by A. L. Peck and D. M. Balme. 3 vols. Cambridge, Mass.: Harvard University Press, 1965–91.

————. *Politics.* Translated by T. A. Sinclair. London: Penguin, 1982.

Augustine. *The City of God Against the Pagans.* Edited and translated by R. W. Dyson. Cambridge: Cambridge University Press, 1998.

Babrius and Phaedrus. *Babrius and Phaedrus.* Edited and translated by Ben Edwin Perry. Cambridge, Mass: Harvard University Press, 1975.

Baron, Hans. *The Crisis of the Early Italian Renaissance: Civic Humanism and Republican Liberty in an Age of Classicism and Tyranny.* Princeton: Princeton University Press, 1966.

————. *From Petrarch to Leonardo Bruni: Studies in Humanistic and Political Literature.* Chicago: University of Chicago Press, 1968.

————. *In Search of Florentine Civic Humanism: Essays on the Transition from Medieval to Modern Thought.* 2 vols. Princeton: Princeton University Press, 1988.

Basil. *St. Basil: The Letters.* Translated by Roy J. Defarrari. 4 vols. London: W. Heinemann; New York: G. P. Putnam's Sons, 1926–34.

Baxandall, Michael. "Alberti's Self." *Fenway Court,* 1990–91, 31–37.

————. *Giotto and the Orators: Humanist Observers of Painting in Italy and the Discovery of Pictorial Composition, 1350–1450.* Oxford: Clarendon Press, 1971.

————. *Painting and Experience in Fifteenth-Century Italy: A Primer in the Social History of Pictorial Style.* Oxford: Oxford University Press, 1974.

Beavis, Ian C. *Insects and Other Invertebrates in Classical Antiquity.* Exeter, Devon: University of Exeter, 1988.

Becker, Marvin, and Gene Brucker. "The *Arti Minori* in Florentine Politics, 1342–1378." *Medieval Studies* 18 (1956): 93–104.

Bek, Lise. "Ideal to Reality: An Aspect of Florentine Renaissance Modernism Expressed Through Alberti's Ciceronianism and Brunelleschi's Approach to Perspective." *Analecta Romana Instituti Danici* 8 (1977): 159–66.

Bertinelli Ferrari, Francesca. "Gli spazi aperti e il paesaggio nel *De re aedificatoria.*" In *Leon Battista Alberti (1404–72) tra scienze e lettere: Atti del convegno organizzato in collaborazione con la Société internationale Leon Battista Alberti (Parigi) e l'Istituto italiano per gli studi filosofici (Napoli), Genova, 19–20 novembre 2004,* edited by Alberto Beniscelli and Francesco Furlan, 177–94. Genoa: Academia ligure di scienze e lettere, 2005.

Bialostocki, Jan. "The Power of Beauty: A Utopian Idea of Leon Battista Alberti." In *Studien zur toskanischen Kunst: Festschrift für Ludwig Heydenreich,* edited by W. Lotz and L. L. Möller, 13–19. Munich: Prestel-Verlag, 1964.

Blunt, Anthony. *Artistic Theory in Italy, 1450–1600.* Oxford: Clarendon Press, 1962.

Bocchi, Francesca. "Normativa urbanistica, spazzi pubblici, disposizioni antinquinamento nella legislazione comunale delle città emiliane." In *Cultura e società nell'Italia medievale: Studi per Paolo Brezzi,* 1:91–115. Rome: Istituto storico italiano per il Medio Evo, 1988.

Borsi, Franco. *Leon Battista Alberti.* Translated by Rudolf G. Carpanini. Oxford: Phaidon, 1977.

Borsi, Stefano. *Leon Battista Alberti e l'antichità romana.* Florence: Edizioni Polistampa, Fondazione Spadolini Nuova Antologia, 2004.

———. *Leon Battista Alberti e Napoli.* Florence: Edizioni Polistampa, Fondazione Spadolini Nuova Antologia, 2006.

———. *Leon Battista Alberti e Roma.* Florence: Edizioni Polistampa, Fondazione Spadolini Nuova Antologia, 2003.

———. *Momus, o Del principe: Leon Battista Alberti, i papi, il giubileo.* Florence: Edizioni Polistampa, Fondazione Spadolini Nuova Antologia, 1999.

Boschetto, Luca. "Democrito e la filosofia della follia: La parodia della filosofia e della medicina nel *Momus* di Leon Battista Alberti." *Rinascimento,* n.s., 35 (1995): 3–29.

———. "Un iciarco albertiano: Paolo di Lapo Niccolini." In *Alberti e la cultura del Quattrocento: Atti del Convegno internazionale del Comitato nazionale VI centenario della nascita di Leon Battista Alberti, Firenze, 16–18 dicembre 2004,* edited by Roberto Cardini and Mariangela Regoliosi, 1:441–65. Florence: Edizioni Polistampa, 2007.

———. *Leon Battista Alberti e Firenze: Biografia, storia, letteratura.* Florence: Olschki, 2000.

———. "Tra biografia e autobiografia: Le prospettive e i problemi della ricerca introno alla vita di L. B. Alberti." In *La vita e il mondo di Leon Battista Alberti: Atti dei convegni internazionali del Comitato Nazionale VI Centenario della Nascita di Leon Battista Alberti, Genova, 19–21 febbraio 2004,* 1:85–116. Florence: Olschki, 2008.

Bouwsma, William J. "The Renaissance and the Drama of Western History." *American Historical Review* 84, no. 1 (1969): 1–15.

Bowra, Cecil Maurice, ed. *Golden Ages of the Great Cities.* London: Thames and Hudson, 1952.

Bremmer, Jan. "Walking, Standing, and Sitting in Ancient Greek Culture." In *A Cultural History of Gesture,* edited by Jan Bremmer and Herman Roodenburg, 15–35. New York: Cornell University Press, 1991.

Brucker, Gene. "The Ciompi Revolution." In *Florentine Studies: Politics and Society in Renaissance Florence,* edited by N. Rubinstein, 314–56. London: Faber, 1968.

———. *Renaissance Florence.* Berkeley: University of California Press, 1983.

———, ed. *Two Memoirs of Renaissance Florence: The Diaries of Buonaccorso Pitti and Gregorio Dati.* New York: Harper and Row, 1976.

Brumble, H. David. *Classical Myths and Legends in the Middle Ages and Renaissance: A Dictionary of Allegorical Meanings.* London: Fitzroy Dearborn, 1998.

Bruni, Leonardo. *Panegirico della città di Firenze.* Translated by Frate Lazaro di Padova. Florence: La Nuova Italia, 1974.

Bullen, J. B. *The Myth of the Renaissance in Nineteenth-Century Writing.* Oxford: Clarendon Press, 1994.

Burckhardt, Jacob. *The Architecture of the Italian Renaissance*. Edited by Peter Murray. Translated by James Palmes. Chicago: University of Chicago Press, 1985.

———. *The Civilization of the Renaissance in Italy*. Translated by S. G. C. Middlemore. London: Penguin, 1990.

Burroughs, Charles. "Alberti e Roma." In *Leon Battista Alberti*, edited by Joseph Rykwert and Anne Engel, 134–57. Milan: Electa, 1994.

———. "Below the Angel: An Urbanistic Project in the Rome of Pope Nicholas V." *Journal of the Warburg and Courtauld Institutes* 45 (1982): 94–124.

———. *From Signs to Design: Environmental Process and Reform in Early Renaissance Rome*. Cambridge, Mass.: MIT Press, 1990.

———. "A Planned Myth and a Myth of Planning: Nicholas V and Rome." In *Rome in the Renaissance: The City and the Myth; Papers of the Thirteenth Annual Conference of the Center for Medieval and Early Renaissance Studies, State University of New York at Binghamton*, edited by P. A. Ramsey, 197–207. Binghamton, N.Y.: Medieval and Renaissance Texts and Studies, Center for Medieval and Early Renaissance Studies, 1982.

Calzona, Arturo. "Leon Battista Alberti e l'architettura: Un rapporto complesso." In *La vita e il mondo di Leon Battista Alberti: Atti dei convegni internazionali del Comitato Nazionale VI Centenario della Nascita di Leon Battista Alberti, Genova, 19–21 febbraio 2004*, 2:471–515. Florence: Olschki, 2008.

Cancro, Cesare. *Filosofia ed architettura in Leon Battista Alberti*. Naples: Morano, 1978.

Canfora, Davide. "Leon Battista Alberti modello di letteratura politica in età umanistica." In *Alberti e la cultura del Quattrocento: Atti del Convegno internazionale del Comitato nazionale VI centenario della nascita di Leon Battista Alberti, Firenze, 16–18 dicembre 2004*, edited by Roberto Cardini and Mariangela Regoliosi, 2:699–717. Florence: Edizioni Polistampa, 2007.

———. *Prima di Machiavelli: Politica e cultura in età umanistica*. Bari: Editore Laterza, 2005.

Cardini, Roberto. "Alberti scrittore e umanista." In *La vita e il mondo di Leon Battista Alberti: Atti dei convegni internazionali del Comitato Nazionale VI Centenario della Nascita di Leon Battista Alberti, Genova, 19–21 febbrai 2004*, 1:23–40. Florence: Olschki, 2008.

———. *Mosaici: Il "nemico" dell'Alberti*. Roma: Bulzoni Editore, 1990.

Carmichael, Ann G. *Plague and the Poor in Renaissance Florence*. Cambridge: Cambridge University Press, 1986.

Carpo, Mario. "*Descriptio urbis romae*: Ekfrasis geografica e cultura visuale all'alba della rivoluzione tipografica." *Albertiana* 1 (1998): 121–42.

———. *Metodo ed ordini nella teoria architectonica dei primi moderni: Alberti, Raffaello, Serlio e Camillo*. Geneva: Droz, 1993.

Cassanelli, Luciana, Gabriella Delfini, and Daniela Fonti. *Le mura di Roma: L'architettura militare nella storia urbana*. Rome: Bulzoni, 1974.

Cassani, Alberto G. "Et flores quidem negligitis: Saxa admirabimur? Sul conflitto natura-architettura in L. B. Alberti." *Albertiana* 8 (2005): 57–83.

———. *La fatica del costruire: Tempo e materia nel pensiero di Leon Battista Alberti*. Milan: Edizioni Unicopli, 2000.

———. "*Libertas, frugalitas, aedificandi libido*: Paradigmi indiziari per Leon Battista Alberti a Roma." In *Le due Rome del Quattrocento: Melozzo, Antoniazzo e la cultura artistica del '400 romano*, edited by Sergio Rossi and Stefano Valeri, 296–321. Rome: Lithos, 1997.

———. "Il pittore, lo scultore e l'architetto: Un paragone fra le arti." In *Leon Battista Alberti (1404–72) tra scienze e lettere: Atti del convegno organizzato in collaborazione con la Société internationale Leon Battista Alberti (Parigi) e l'Istituto italiano per gli studi filosofici (Napoli), Genova, 19–20 novembre 2004*, edited by Alberto Beniscelli and Francesco Furlan, 83–144. Genoa: Academia ligure di scienze e lettere, 2005.

Catanorchi, Olivia. "Tra politica e passione: Simulazione e dissimulazione in Leon Battista Alberti." *Rinascimento*, n.s., 45 (2005): 137–77.

Cato, Marcus Porcius. *On Agriculture*. Translated by William Davis Hooper and Harrison Boyd Ash in *Marcus Porcius Cato: "On Agriculture"; Marcus Terentius Varro: "On Agriculture."* Cambridge, Mass.: Harvard University Press; London: W. Heinemann, 1967.

Catte, Tabatha, Tobia Delmolino, and Robert Held. *Catalogo della mostra di strumenti di tortura, 1400–1800: Nella Casermetta di Forte Belvedere, Firenze, dal 14 maggio a metà settembre, 1983*. Florence: Qua d'Arno, 1983.

Cavarnos, Constantine. *Pythagoras on the Fine Arts as Therapy: A Lecture Delivered in 1993 at Wellesley College*. Belmont, Mass.: Institute for Byzantine and Modern Greek Studies, 1994.

Celenza, Christopher S. *Renaissance Humanism and the Papal Curia: Lapo da Castiglionchio the Younger's "De curiae commodis."* Ann Arbor: University of Michigan Press, 1999.

Chaucer, Geoffrey. *The Works of Geoffrey Chaucer*. Edited by F. N. Robinson. London: Oxford University Press, 1957.

Cherubini, Giovanni. "La taverna nel basso medioevo." In *Il tempo libero, economia e società (loisirs, leisure, tiempo libre, Freizeit): Secc. 13–18; Atti della ventiseiesima settimana di studi, 18–23 aprile 1994*, edited by Simonetta Cavaciocchi, 525–63. Grassina, Bagno a Ripoli: Le Monnier, 1995.

Chittolini, Giorgio. "Civic Religion and the Country in Late Medieval Italy." In *City and Countryside in Late Medieval and Renaissance Italy: Essays Presented to Philip Jones*, edited by Trevor Dean and Chris Wickham, 69–80. London: Hambledon, 1990.

Choay, Françoise. "Alberti and Vitruvius." *Architectural Design* 49, nos. 5–6 (1979): 26–35.

———. *The Rule and the Model: On the Theory of Architecture and Urbanism*. Edited by Denise Bratton. Cambridge, Mass.: MIT Press, 1997.

Cicero, Marcus Tullius. *"Brutus" and "Orator."* Translated by G. L. Hendrickson and H. M. Hubbell, respectively. Cambridge, Mass.: Harvard University Press; London: W. Heinemann, 1939.

———. *De natura deorum: Academica*. Translated by H. Rackham. London: W. Heinemann; New York: G. P. Putnam's Sons, 1933.

———. *De officiis*. Translated by Walter Miller. London: W. Heinemann; New York: Macmillan, 1913.

———. *De oratore*. Translated by E. W. Sutton, with an introduction by H. Rackham. 2 vols. London: W. Heinemann; Cambridge, Mass.: Harvard University Press, 1942.

———. *Philippics*. Translated by Walter C. A. Ker. London: W. Heinemann; New York: G. P. Putnam's Sons, 1926.

Coffin, David. *The Villa in the Life of Renaissance Rome*. Princeton: Princeton University Press, 1979.

Cohn, Samuel Kline, Jr. *The Laboring Classes in Renaissance Florence*. New York: Academic Press, 1980.

Cole, Alison. "The Perception of Beauty in Landscape in the Quattrocento." In *Concepts of Beauty in Renaissance Art*, edited by Francis Ames-Lewis and Mary Rogers, 28–43. Aldershot, Hampshire: Ashgate, 1998.

Columella, Lucius Junius Moderatus. *On Agriculture*. Translated by Harrison Boyd Ash. 3 vols. Cambridge, Mass.: Harvard University Press; London: W. Heinemann, 1941–55.

Conrad, Joseph. *Lord Jim*. London: Penguin, 2000.

Crescenzi, Pietro de'. *Trattato della agricoltura di Piero de'Crescenzi*. 3 vols. Milan: Società Tipografica de'Classici Italiani, 1805.

Damonte Medini, Silvana. "Osservazioni sulla *Villa* di Leon Battista Alberti." In *Miscellanea di studi Albertiani: A cura del Comitato genovese per le onoranze a Leon Battista Alberti nel quinto centenario della morte*, 81–95. Genoa: Tilgher, 1975.

Davidsohn, Robert. *Storia di Firenze*. 8 vols. Florence: Sansoni, 1956–68.

da Vinci, Leonardo. *Leonardo on Painting: An Anthology of Writings by Leonardo da Vinci with a Selection of Documents Relating to His Career as an Artist*. Edited by Martin Kemp. Translated by Martin Kemp and Margaret Walker. New Haven: Yale University Press, 1989.

Dean, Trevor, ed. and trans. *The Towns of Italy in the Later Middle Ages*. Manchester: Manchester University Press, 2000.

Debby, Nirit Ben-Aryeh. *Renaissance Florence in the Rhetoric of Two Popular Preachers: Giovanni Dominici (1356–1419) and Bernardino da Siena (1380–1444)*. Turnhout: Brepols; Cheltenham: European Schoolbooks, 2001.

de Grazia, Margreta. "The Ideology of Superfluous Things: *King Lear* as a Period Piece." In *Shakespeare's Tragedies*, edited by S. Zimmerman, 255–84. Basingstoke: Macmillan, 1998.

del Fante, Luigi. *La città di Leon Battista Alberti*. Florence: Alinea, 1982.

Denley, Peter. "Giovanni Dominici's Opposition to Humanism." In *Religion and Humanism: Papers Read at the Eighteenth Summer Meeting and the Nineteenth Winter Meeting of the Ecclesiastical History Society*, edited by Keith Robbins, 103–14. Studies in Church History 17. Oxford: Basil Blackwell, 1981.

de Seta, Cesare. "Come in un specchio: La città rinascimentale nel *De re aedificatoria* e nelle tarsie." In *Imago urbis: Dalla città reale alla città ideale*, by Cesare de Seta, Massimo Ferretti, and Alberto Tenenti, 25–55. Milan: Franco Maria Ricci, 1986.

de Seta, Cesare, and Jacques Le Goff, eds. *La città e le mura*. Rome: Editori Laterza, 1989.

Dickerman, Sherwood Owen. "Some Stock Illustrations of Animal Intelligence in Greek Psychology." *Transactions and Proceedings of the American Philological Association* 42 (1911): 123–30.

di Giorgio, Francesco. *Trattati di architettura ingegneria e arte militare*. Edited by Corrado Maltese. Transcribed by Livia Maltese Degrassi. 2 vols. Milan: Il Polifilo, 1967.

Diogenes Laertius. *Lives of Eminent Philosophers*. Translated by R. D. Hicks. 2 vols. Cambridge, Mass.: Harvard University Press; London: W. Heinemann, 1856–79.

Di Stefano, Elisabetta. *L'altro sapere: Bello, arte, immagine in Leon Battista Alberti*. Palermo: Centro internazionale studio di estetica, 2000.

D'Onofrio, Cesare. *Visitiamo Roma nel quattrocento: La città degli umanisti*. Rome: Romano Società editrice, 1989.

Doutreleau, Véronique. "Les tremblements de terre Italiens du XIIe au XVe siècle." In *Les catastrophes naturelles dans l'Europe médiévale et moderne: Actes des XVe Journées Internationales d'Histoire de l'Abbaye de Flaran, 10, 11 et 12 septembre 1993*, 223–32. Toulouse: Presses universitaires du Mirail, 1996.

Dundas, Judith. *The Spider and the Bee: The Artistry of Spenser's "Faerie Queene."* Urbana: University of Illinois Press, 1985.

Dunlop, Kirsten. "Rhetoric and the City: Reading Alberti, Reading Urban Design." Ph.D. diss., University of East Anglia, 1999.

Eckstein, Nicholas. *The District of the Green Dragon: Neighbourhood Life and Social Change in Renaissance Florence*. Florence: Olschki, 1995.

Eden, W. A. "Studies in Urban Theory: The *De re aedificatoria* of Leon Battista Alberti." *Town Planning Review* 19, no. 1 (1943): 10–28.

Edgerton, Samuel Y. *The Renaissance Rediscovery of Linear Perspective.* New York: Basic Books, 1975.

Eliot, George. *Romola.* Edinburgh: William Blackwood and Sons, ca. 1891.

Emerton, Ephraim. *Humanism and Tyranny: Studies in the Italian Trecento.* Cambridge, Mass.: Harvard University Press, 1925.

Fanelli, Giovanni. *Firenze.* Rome: Laterza, 1981.

Farenga, Paola. "I Romani sono periculoso populo ..." In *Roma capitale, 1447–1527: Atti del IV convegno di studio del Centro Studi sulla Civiltà del Tardo Medioevo, 27–31 ottobre 1992, San Miniato, Pisa,* edited by Sergio Gensini. Pisa: Pacini, 1994.

Ferguson, Wallace K. *The Renaissance in Historical Thought: Five Centuries of Interpretation.* Cambridge, Mass.: Houghton Mifflin, 1948.

Figliuolo, Bruno. *Il terremoto del 1456.* 2 vols. Altavilla Silentina: Studi storici meridionali, 1988–89.

Flemming, John V. "Natura lachrymosa." In *Man and Nature in the Middle Ages,* edited by Susan J. Ridyard and Robert G. Benson, 19–35. Sewanee, Tenn.: University of the South Press, 1995.

———. "Natura ridens." In *Man and Nature in the Middle Ages,* edited by Susan J. Ridyard and Robert G. Benson, 1–18. Sewanee, Tenn.: University of the South Press, 1995.

Fortini Brown, Patricia. *Venice and Antiquity: The Venetian Sense of the Past.* New Haven: Yale University Press, 1997.

Foucault, Michel. *Discipline and Punish: The Birth of the Prison.* Translated by Alan Sheridan. London: Penguin, 1977.

———. *Power/Knowledge: Selected Interviews and Other Writings, 1972–1977.* Edited by Colin Gordon. Translated by Colin Gordon, Leo Marshall, John Mepham, and Kate Soper. Harlow: Prentice Hall, 1980.

Fox-Genovese, Elizabeth. *The Origins of Physiocracy: Economic Revolution and Social Order in Eighteenth-Century France.* Ithaca: Cornell University Press, 1976.

Freud, Sigmund. *Leonardo da Vinci and a Memory of His Childhood.* Translated by Alan Tyson, with an introduction by Brian Farrell. Harmondsworth: Penguin, 1963.

Friedman, David. *Florentine New Towns: Urban Design in the Late Middle Ages.* Cambridge, Mass.: MIT Press, 1988.

Frommel, Christoph L. "Papal Policy: The Planning of Rome during the Renaissance." *Journal of Interdisciplinary History* 17, no. 1 (1986): 39–65.

Frugoni, Chiara. *A Distant City: Images of Urban Experience in the Medieval World.* Translated by William McCuaig. Princeton: Princeton University Press, 1991.

Fubini, Riccardo. "Leon Battista Alberti, Niccolò V e il tema della 'infelicità del principe.'" In *La vita e il mondo di Leon Battista Alberti: Atti dei convegni internazionali del Comitato Nazionale VI Centenario della Nascita di Leon Battista Alberti, Genova, 19–21 febbraio 2004,* 2:441–69. Florence: Olschki, 2008.

Fubini, Riccardo, and Anna Menci Gallorini. "L'autobiografia di Leon Battista Alberti: Studio e edizione." *Rinascimento,* n.s., 12 (1972): 21–78.

Gabbey, Alan. "Spinoza on the Natural and the Artificial." In *The Artificial and the Natural: An Evolving Polarity,* edited by Bernadette Bensaude-Vincent and William R. Newman, 225–37. Cambridge, Mass.: MIT Press, 2007.

Gadol, Joan. *Leon Battista Alberti: Universal Man of the Early Renaissance.* Chicago: University of Chicago Press, 1969.

Garin, Eugenio. "La cité idéale de la Renaissance italienne." In *Les utopies à la Renaissance: Colloque international (avril 1961) sous les auspices de la Fédération internationale des instituts et sociétés pour l'étude de la Renaissance et du Ministère de l'éducation nationale et de la culture de Belgique,* 13–37. Brussels: Presses Universitaires de Bruxelles; Paris: Presses Universitaires de France, 1963.

————. *Filosofi italiani del quattrocento*. Florence: Le Monnier, 1942.

————. "Il pensiero di Leon Battista Alberti e la cultura del quattrocento." *Belfagor* 27 (1972): 502–21.

————. *Rinascite e rivoluzioni: Movimenti culturali dal XIV al XVIII secolo*. Roma: Laterza, 1975.

————. *L'umanesimo Italiano: Filosofia e vita civile nel Rinascimento*. Bari: Laterza, 1952.

Garzoni, Tomaso. *La piazza universale di tutte le professioni del mondo*. Edited by Giovanni Battista Bronzini, with the collaboration of Pina de Meo and Luciano Carcereri. 2 vols. Florence: Olschki, 1996.

Goldthwaite, Richard. *The Building of Renaissance Florence: An Economic and Social History*. Baltimore: Johns Hopkins University Press, 1982.

Gorni, Guglielmo. "Storia del certame coronario." *Rinascimento*, n.s., 12 (1972): 135–81.

Grafton, Anthony. *Leon Battista Alberti: Master Builder of the Italian Renaissance*. London: Penguin, 2001.

————. "Un passe-partout ai segreti di una vita." In *La vita e il mondo di Leon Battista Alberti: Atti dei convegni internazionali del Comitato Nazionale VI Centenario della Nascita di Leon Battista Alberti, Genova, 19–21 febbraio 2004*, 1:3–21. Florence: Olschki, 2008.

Grayson, Cecil. "Leon Battista Alberti: Vita e opera." In *Leon Battista Alberti*, edited by Joseph Rykwert and Anne Engel, 28–37. Milan: Electa, 1994.

————. *Studi su Leon Battista Alberti*. Florence: Olschki, 1998.

————. "Studi su Leon Battista Alberti: Villa; Un opuscolo sconosciuto." *Rinascimento* 4 (1953): 45–53.

Guldentops, Guy. "The Sagacity of the Bees: An Aristotelian Topos in Thirteenth-Century Philosophy." In *Aristotle's Animals in the Middle Ages and Renaissance*, edited by Carlos Steel, Guy Guldentops, and Pieter Beullens, 275–96. Leuven: Leuven University Press, 1999.

Hale, John R. *The Civilization of Europe in the Renaissance*. London: HarperCollins, 1993.

————. *Renaissance Fortification: Art or Engineering?* London: Thames and Hudson, 1977.

————. *Renaissance War Studies*. London: Hambledon Press, 1983.

————. *War and Society in Renaissance Europe, 1450–1620*. London: Fontana Paperbacks, 1985.

Hall, Bert S. *Weapons and Warfare in Renaissance Europe: Gunpowder, Technology, and Tactics*. Baltimore: Johns Hopkins University Press, 1997.

Hall, Marcia. "Savonarola's Preaching and the Patronage of Art." In *Christianity and the Renaissance: Image and Religious Imagination in the Quattrocento*, edited by Timothy Verdon and John Henderson, 493–522. Syracuse: Syracuse University Press, 1990.

Hanska, Jussi. *Strategies of Sanity and Survival: Religious Responses to Natural Disasters in the Middle Ages*. Helsinki: Finnish Literature Society, 2002.

Heidegger, Martin. *Being and Time*. Translated by John Macquarrie and Edward Robinson. Oxford: Basil Blackwell, 1995.

Hemsoll, David, and Paul Davies. "Leon Battista Alberti." In *The Dictionary of Art*, edited by Jane Turner, 1:555–69. New York: Grove, 1996.

Henderson, John. "The Black Death in Florence: Medical and Communal Responses." In *Death in Towns: Urban Responses to the Dying and the Dead, 100–1600*, edited by Steven Bassett, 136–50. Leicester: Leicester University Press, 1992.

Herlihy, David. "The Distribution of Wealth in a Renaissance Community." In *Towns in Societies: Essays in Economic History and Historical Sociology*, edited by Philip Abrams and E. A. Wrigley, 131–57. Cambridge: Cambridge University Press, 1978.

———. "Some Psychological and Social Roots of Violence in the Tuscan Cities." In *Violence and Civil Disorder in Italian Cities, 1200–1500*, edited by Lauro Martines, 129–54. Berkeley: University of California Press, 1972.

Herodotus. *Histories*. Translated by A. D. Godley as *Herodotus*. 4 vols. London: W. Heinemann; New York: G. P. Putnam's Sons, 1921–24.

Hesiod. *Works and Days*. Translated with an introduction by Dorothea Wender in *Hesiod: "Theogony" and "Works and Days"; Theognis: "Elegies."* London: Penguin, 1973.

Heywood, William. *A History of Perugia*. Edited by R. Langton Douglas. London: Methuen, 1910.

Holmes, George. *The First Age of the Western City, 1300–1500: An Inaugural Lecture Delivered Before the University of Oxford on 8 November 1989*. Oxford: Clarendon Press, 1990.

———. *The Florentine Enlightenment, 1400–1450*. Oxford: Clarendon Press, 1992.

Horace. *Horace: The "Odes" and "Epodes."* Translated by C. E. Bennett. London; W. Heinemann; New York: Macmillan, 1914.

———. *Satires, Epistles, and Ars Poetica*. Translated by H. Rushton Fairclough. London: W. Heinemann; New York: G. P. Putnam's Sons, 1926.

Howard, Donald Roy. *The Idea of the Canterbury Tales*. Berkeley: University of California Press, 1976.

Hyde, John Kenneth. "Medieval Descriptions of Cities." *Bulletin of the John Rylands University Library of Manchester* 48 (1965–66): 308–40.

Iamblichus. *On the Pythagorean Life*. Translated with an introduction and notes by Gillian Clark. Liverpool: Liverpool University Press, 1989.

Irmscher, Günter. "*Ministrae voluptatum*: Stoicizing Ethics in the Market and Kitchen Scenes of Pieter Aertsen and Joachim Beuckelaer." *Simiolus: Netherlands Quarterly for the History of Art* 16, no. 4 (1986): 219–32.

Jarzombek, Mark. "The *Enigma* of Leon Battista Alberti's *Dissimulatio*." In *Leon Battista Alberti: Actes du congrès international de Paris, Sorbonne, Institut de France, Institut culturel italien, Collège de France, 10–15 avril 1995*, edited by Francesco Furlan, with the collaboration of A. P. Filotico, I. Giordano, P. Hicks, S. Matton, and L. Vallance, 2:741–48. Turin: Nino Aragno Editore; Paris: J. Vrin, 2000.

———. *On Leon Baptista Alberti: His Literary and Aesthetic Theories*. Cambridge, Mass.: MIT Press, 1989.

Jeanneret, Michel. *A Feast of Words: Banquets and Table Talk in the Renaissance*. Translated by Emma Hughes and Jeremy Whiteley. Cambridge: Polity Press, 1991.

Kahn, Victoria. "Coluccio Salutati on the Active and Contemplative Lives." In *Arbeit, Musse, Meditation: Betrachtungen zur "Vita activa" und "Vita contemplativa,"* edited by Brian Vickers, 153–79. Zürich: Verlag der Fachvereine, 1985.

Kanerva, Liisa. *Defining the Architect in Fifteenth-Century Italy: Exemplary Architects in Leon Battista Alberti's "De re aedificatoria."* Helsinki: Suomamalainen Tiedeakatemia, 1998.

Katz, M. Barry. *Leon Battista Alberti and the Humanist Theory of the Arts*. Washington, D.C.: University Press of America, 1978.

Kemp, Martin. "From 'Mimesis' to 'Fantasia'": The Quattrocento Vocabulary of Creation, Inspiration, and Genius in the Visual Arts." *Viator: Medieval and Renaissance Studies* 8 (1977): 347–98.

———. *The Science of Art: Optical Themes in Western Art from Brunelleschi to Seurat*. New Haven: Yale University Press, 1990.

Kent, Dale V., and F. W. Kent. *Neighbours and Neighbourhood in Renaissance Florence: The District of the Red Lion in the Fifteenth Century*. Locust Valley, N.Y.: J. J. Augustin, 1982.

Klein, Francesca. "Considerazioni sull'ideologia della città di Firenze tra trecento e quattrocento (Giovanni Villani–Leonardo Bruni)." *Ricerche Storiche* 10 (1980): 311–36.

Kohl, Benjamin G., and Ronald G. Witt, eds. and trans. *The Earthly Republic: Italian Humanists on Government and Society.* With contributions by Elizabeth B. Welles. Philadelphia: University of Pennsylvania Press, 1978.

Krautheimer, Richard. "Alberti and Vitruvius." In *Studies in Western Art: Acts of the Twentieth International Congress of the History of Arts,* edited by Millard Meiss, Richard Krautheimer, George Kubler, Rensselaer W. Lee, Rudolf Wittkower, and Ida E. Rubin, vol. 2, *The Renaissance and Mannerism,* 42–52. Princeton: Princeton University Press, 1963.

Kristeller, Paul Oskar. "The Active and Contemplative Life in Renaissance Humanism." In *Arbeit, Musse, Meditation: Betrachtungen zur "Vita activa" und "Vita contempla- tiva,"* edited by Brian Vickers, 138–52. Zürich: Verlag der Fachvereine, 1985.

———. *Renaissance Thought and the Arts.* Princeton: Princeton University Press, 1980.

Kuehn, Thomas. "Leon Battista Alberti come illegittimo Fiorentino." In *La vita e il mondo di Leon Battista Alberti: Atti dei Convegni internazionali del Comitato nazio- nale VI centenario della nascita di Leon Battista Alberti, Genova, 19–21 febbraio 2004,* 1:147-171. Florence: Olschki, 2008.

———. "Reading Between the Patrilines: Leon Battista Alberti's *Della Famiglia* in Light of His Illegitimacy." *I Tatti Studies* 1 (1985): 161–87.

Lagrée, Jacqueline. *Juste Lipse: La restauration du stoïcisme.* Paris: Librairie Philosophique J. Vrin, 1994.

Landauer, Carl. "Erwin Panofsky and the Renascence of the Renaissance." *Renaissance Quarterly* 47 (1994): 255–81.

Landucci, Luca. *A Florentine Diary from 1415–1516, by Luca Landucci, Continued by an Anonymous Writer till 1542.* Translated by Alice De Rosen Jervis, with notes by Iodoco del Badia. London: J. M. Dent and Sons; New York: Dutton, 1927.

Lang, Susan. *"De lineamentis:* L. B. Alberti's Use of a Technical Term." *Journal of the Warburg and Courtauld Institutes* 28 (1965): 331–35.

———. "The Ideal City from Plato to Howard." *Architectural Review* 112 (1952): 90–101.

Lee, Edgmont. "Workers and Work in Quattrocento Rome." In *Rome in the Renaissance: The City and the Myth; Papers of the Thirteenth Annual Conference of the Center for Medieval and Early Renaissance Studies, State University of New York at Binghamton,* edited by P. A. Ramsey, 141–52. Binghamton, N.Y.: Medieval and Renaissance Texts and Studies, Center for Medieval and Early Renaissance Studies, 1982.

Lillie, Amanda. *Florentine Villas in the Fifteenth Century: An Architectural and Social History.* Cambridge: Cambridge University Press, 2005.

Lubbock, Julius. *Storytelling in Christian Art from Giotto to Donatello.* New Haven: Yale University Press, 2006.

———. "Walter Pater's *Marius the Epicurean:* The Imaginary Portrait as Cultural History." *Journal of the Warburg and Courtauld Institutes* 46 (1983): 166–90.

Lücke, Hans-Karl. *Alberti Index: Leon Battista Alberti, "De re aedificatoria," Florenz 1485; Index verborum.* Munich: Prestel, 1975.

———. "Alberti, Vitruvio e Cicerone." In *Leon Battista Alberti,* edited by Joseph Rykwert and Anne Engel, 70–95. Milan: Electa, 1994.

Machiavelli, Niccolò. *The Prince.* Translated by George Bull. Harmondsworth: Penguin, 1982.

Mack, Charles R. *Pienza: The Creation of a Renaissance City.* With a section of texts trans- lated by Catherine Castner. Ithaca: Cornell University Press, 1987.

Magnuson, Torgil. "The Project of Nicholas V for Rebuilding the Borgo Leonino in Rome." *Art Bulletin* 36, no. 2 (1954): 89–115.

Maire-Vigueur, Jean-Claude. "Classe dominante et classes dirigeants à Rome à la fin du Moyen Age." *Storia Della Città* 1 (1976): 4–26.

———. "Les rapports ville-campagne dans l'Italie communale: Pour une révision des problèmes." In *La ville, la bourgeoisie et la genèse de l'état moderne, XIIe–XVIIIe siècles: Actes du colloque de Bielefeld, 29 novembre–1er décembre 1985*, edited by Neithard Bulst and J.-Ph. Genet, 21–33. Paris: Editions du Centre national de la recherche scientifique, 1988.

Mancini, Girolamo. *Vita di Leon Battista Alberti*. Florence: G. C. Sasoni, 1882. 2nd ed., Rome: Bardi Editore, 1971.

Manetti, Giannozzo. *De vita ac gestis Nicolai Quinti summi pontificis*. Edited and translated by Anna Modigliani. Rome: Istituto storico italiano per il Medio Evo, 2005.

Marassi, Massimo. *Metamorfosi della storia: "Momus" e Alberti*. Milan: Mimesis, 2004.

Marolda, Paolo. *Crisi e conflitto in Leon Battista Alberti*. Rome: Bonacci, 1988.

Marsh, David. "Aesop and the Humanist Apologue." *Renaissance Studies* 17, no. 1 (2003): 9–26.

———. *Lucian and the Latins: Humor and Humanism in the Early Renaissance*. Ann Arbor: University of Michigan Press, 1998.

———. *The Quattrocento Dialogue: Classical Tradition and Humanist Innovation*. Cambridge, Mass.: Harvard University Press, 1980.

———. *Renaissance Fables: Aesopic Prose by Leon Battista Alberti, Bartolomeo Scala, Leonardo da Vinci, Bernardino Baldi*. Translated with an introduction and notes by David Marsh. Tempe, Ariz.: Arizona Center for Medieval and Renaissance Studies, 2003.

Martines, Lauro. *Power and Imagination: City-States in Renaissance Italy*. London: Allen Lane, 1980.

———. *The Social World of the Florentine Humanists, 1390–1460*. London: Routledge and Kegan Paul, 1963.

———. *Violence and Civil Disorder in Italian Cities, 1200–1500*. Berkeley: University of California Press, 1972.

Marx, Karl, and Frederick Engels. *Selected Works*. 2 vols. Moscow: Foreign Languages Publishing House; London: Lawrence and Wishart, 1951.

Mastrorosa, Ida. "L. B. Alberti 'epidemiologo': Esiti umanistici di dottrine classiche." *Albertiana* 4 (2001): 21–44.

Mazzini, Donata, and Simone Martini. *Villa Medici a Fiesole: Leon Battista Alberti e il proto-tipo di villa Rinascimentale*. Edited by Donata Mazzini. Florence: Centro Di, 2004.

McLaughlin, Martin L. *Literary Imitation in the Italian Renaissance: The Theory and Practice of Literary Imitation in Italy from Dante to Bembo*. Oxford: Clarendon Press, 1995.

Michel, Paul-Henri. *Un idéal humain au XVe siècle: La pensée de L. B. Alberti (1404–1472)*. Paris: Societé d'éditions "Les belles lettres," 1930.

Michelet, Jules. *Oeuvres complètes*. 16 vols. Edited by Paul Viallaneix. Paris: Flammarion, 1971–80.

Miotto, Luciana. "Natura, campagna e paesaggio nella teoria albertiana dell'architettura." In *La campagna in città: Letteratura e ideologia nel Rinascimento; Scritti in onore di Michel Plaisance*, edited by Giuditta Isotti Rosowsky, 11–29. Florence: F. Cesati, 2002.

Mitrović, Branko. *Serene Greed of the Eye: Leon Battista Alberti and the Philosophical Foundations of Renaissance Architectural Theory*. With a preface by Mario Carpo. Munich: Deutscher Kunstverlag, 2005.

Modigliani, Anna. *Mercati, botteghe e spazi di commercio a Roma tra medioevo ed età moderna*. Rome: Roma nel Rinascimento, 1998.

Morris, Anthony Edwin James. *History of Urban Form: Before the Industrial Revolution.* London: Godwin, 1979.

Mumford, Lewis. *The City in History: Its Origins, Its Transformations, and Its Prospects.* New York: Harbinger, 1961.

Nicholas, David. *The Growth of the Medieval City: From Late Antiquity to the Early Fourteenth Century.* London: Longman, 1997.

———. *The Later Medieval City, 1300–1500.* London: Longman, 1997.

Onians, John. "Alberti and ΦΙΛΑΡΕΤΗ: A Study in Their Sources." *Journal of the Warburg and Courtauld Institutes* 34 (1971): 96–114.

———. *Bearers of Meaning: The Classical Orders in Antiquity, the Middle Ages, and the Renaissance.* Princeton: Princeton University Press, 1988.

Ovid. *Metamorphoses.* Translated by A. D. Melville. New York: Oxford University Press, 1986.

Palmieri, Matteo. *Vita civile.* Edited by Gino Belloni. Florence: Sansoni, 1982.

Panizza, Letizia A. "Active and Contemplative in Lorenzo Valla: The Fusion of Opposites." In *Arbeit, Musse, Meditation: Betrachtungen zur "Vita activa" und "Vita contemplativa,"* edited by Brian Vickers, 181–223. Zürich: Verlag der Fachvereine, 1985.

Panofsky, Erwin. *Idea: A Concept in Art Theory.* Columbia: University of South Carolina Press, 1968.

Panza, Pierluigi. *Leon Battista Alberti: Filosofia e teoria dell'arte.* With an introduction by Dino Formaggio. Milan: Guerini Studio, 1994.

Paoli, Michel. "Battista e i suoi nipoti: Il 'conservatorismo' Albertiano nel *De iciarchia* e le ultime opera." In *Leon Battista Alberti umanista e scrittore: Filologia, esegesi, tradizione; Atti del Convegno internazionale VI centenario della nascita di Leon Battista Alberti, Arezzo, 24–25 giugno 2004,* edited by Roberto Cardini and Mariangela Regoliosi, 2:523–40. Florence: Polistampa, 2007.

———. *L'idée de nature chez Leon Battista Alberti 1404–1472.* Paris: Champion, 1999.

Passerini, Luigi. *Gli Alberti di Firenze: Genealogia, storia e documenti.* 2 vols. Florence: Tipi di M. Cellini e c., 1869.

Pastor, Ludwig. *The History of the Popes from the Close of the Middle Ages: Drawn from the Secret Archives of the Vatican and Other Original Sources.* Edited by Frederick Ignatius Antrobus. 40 vols. Nendeln: Kraus Reprint, 1969.

Pater, Walter. *Renaissance.* Oxford: Oxford University Press, 1998.

Pavan, Lydia. "Il mito della villa." In *Leon Battista Alberti: Actes du congrès international de Paris, Sorbonne, Institut de France, Institut culturel italien, Collège de France, 10–15 avril 1995,* edited by Francesco Furlan, with the collaboration of A. P. Filotico, I. Giordano, P. Hicks, S. Matton, and L. Vallance, 1:317–25. Turin: Nino Aragno Editore; Paris: J. Vrin, 2000.

Payne, Alina. "Alberti and the Origins of the Paragone Between Architecture and the Figural Arts." In *Leon Battista Alberti teorico delle arti e gli impegni civili del "De re aedificatoria": Atti dei Convegni internazionali del Comitato Nazionale VI centenario della nascita di Leon Battista Alberti, Mantova, 17–19 ottobre 2002/Mantova, 23–25 ottobre 2003,* edited by Arturo Calzona, Francesco Paolo Fiore, and Cesare Vasoli, 1:347–68. Florence: Olschki, 2007.

Pearson, Caspar. "Poulterers, Butchers, and Cooks: Concepts of the Rabble in Leon Battista Alberti's *De re Aedificatoria.*" In *Armut und Armenfürsorge in der italienischen Stadtkultur zwischen 13. und 16. Jahrhundert: Bilder, Texte und soziale Praktiken,* edited by Philine Helas and Gerhard Wolf, 303–33. Frankfurt: Peter Lang, 2006.

———. "Visions of the City in Leon Battista Alberti's *De re aedificatoria.*" Ph.D. diss., University of Essex, 2002.

Pinto, Giuliano. "'Honor' and 'Profit': Landed Property in Medieval Siena." In *City and Countryside in Late Medieval and Renaissance Italy: Essays Presented to Philip Jones*, edited by Trevor Dean and Chris Wickham, 81–91. London: Hambledon, 1990.

Plato. *Complete Works*. Edited with an introduction and notes by John M. Cooper. Indianapolis, Ind.: Hackett, 1997.

Pliny the Elder. *Natural History*. Translated by H. Rackham. 10 vols. Cambridge, Mass.: Harvard University Press; London: W. Heinemann, 1938–63.

Plutarch. *Plutarch's Lives*. Translated by Bernadotte Perrin. 11 vols. Cambridge, Mass.: Harvard University Press; London: W. Heinemann, 1914–26.

Ponte, Giovanni. *Leon Battista Alberti: Umanista e scrittore*. Genoa: Tilgher, 1981.

Puttfarken, Thomas. *The Discovery of Pictorial Composition: Theories of Visual Order in Painting, 1400–1800*. New Haven: Yale University Press, 2000.

Quintilian. *The Institutio Oratoria of Quintilian*. Translated by H. E. Butler. 4 vols. London: W. Heinemann; New York: G. P. Putnam's Sons, 1921–22.

Rerum italicarum scriptores. Edited by Antonio Muratori. 28 vols. Milan: Societas Palatina, 1723–51.

Rinaldi, Rinaldo. *"Melancholia christiana": Studi sulle fonti di Leon Battista Alberti*. Florence: Olschki, 2002.

Robin, Diana Maury. *Filelfo in Milan: Writings, 1451–1477*. Princeton: Princeton University Press, 1991.

Roscoe, William. *The Life of Lorenzo de' Medici Called the Magnificent*. London: Printed for A. Strahan, T. Cadell Jun., and W. Davies in the Strand, and J. Edwards in Pall Mall, 1796.

Rosenau, Helen. *The Ideal City in Its Architectural Evolution*. London: Routledge and Paul, 1959.

Rubinstein, Nicolai. "Florentine Constitutionalism and Medici Ascendancy in the Fifteenth Century." In *Florentine Studies: Politics and Society in Renaissance Florence*, edited by Nicolai Rubinstein, 442–62. London: Faber, 1968.

———. "Fortified Enclosures in Italian Cities Under *Signori*." In *War, Culture, and Society in Renaissance Venice: Essays in Honor of John Hale*, edited by David S. Chambers, Cecil H. Clough, and Michael E. Mallett, 1–8. London: Hambledon Press, 1993.

Rykwert, Joseph. "Theory as Rhetoric: Leon Battista Alberti in Theory and in Practice." In *Paper Palaces: The Rise of the Renaissance Architectural Treatise*. Edited by Vaughan Hart and Peter Hicks, 33–50. New Haven: Yale University Press, 1998.

Santinello, Giovanni. *Leon Battista Alberti: Una visione estetica del mondo e della vita*. Florence: Sansoni, 1962.

Sapegno, Natalino, ed. *Poeti minori del Trecento*. Milan: Riccardo Ricciardi Editore, 1952.

Sberlati, Francesco. *"Rerum rusticarum scriptores* in Alberti." In *Alberti e la tradizione: Per lo "smontaggio" dei "mosaici" albertiani; Atti del Convegno internazionale del Comitato nazionale VI centenario della nascita di Leon Battista Alberti, Arezzo, 23–24–25 settembre 2004*, 1:157–79. Florence: Polistampa, 2007.

Scavizzi, Giuseppe. "The Myth of Orpheus in Italian Renaissance Art, 1400–1600." In *Orpheus: The Metamorphoses of a Myth*, edited by John Warden, 111–62. Toronto: University of Toronto Press, 1982.

Schopenhauer, Arthur. *The World as Will and Representation*. Translated by E. F. J. Payne. New York: Dover, 1969.

Seneca, Lucius Annaeus. *Moral Essays*. Translated by John W. Basore. 3 vols. Cambridge, Mass.: Harvard University Press, 1958.

Silius Italicus. *Punica*. Translated by J. D. Duff. 2 vols. London: W. Heinemann; New York: G. P. Putnam's Sons, 1934.

Simoncini, Giorgio. *Città e società nel Rinascimento*. 2 vols. Turin: Giulio Einaudi, 1974.

Simoncini, Stefano. "L'avventura di Momo nel Rinascimento: Il nume della critica tra Leon Battista Alberti e Giordano Bruno." *Rinascimento*, n.s., 38 (1998): 405–54.

———. "Roma come Gerusalemme nel giubileo del 1450: La *renovatio* di Nicolò V e il *Momus* di Leon Battista Alberti." In *Le due Rome del Quattrocento: Melozzo, Antoniazzo e la cultura artistica del '400 romano*, edited by Sergio Rossi and Stefano Valeri, 322–45. Rome: Lithos, 1997.

Sismondi, Jean-Charles-Léonard Simonde de. *A History of the Italian Republics, Being a View of the Origin, Progress, and Fall of Italian Freedom.* London: Printed for Longman, Brown, Green, and Longmans, 1832.

Smith, Christine. "The Apocalypse Sent Up: A Parody of the Papacy by Leon Battista Alberti." *MLN* 119, no. 1 (2004): S162–S177.

———. *Architecture in the Culture of Early Humanism: Ethics, Aesthetics, and Eloquence, 1400–1470.* Oxford: Oxford University Press, 1992.

Smith, Christine, and Joseph F. O'Connor. *Building the Kingdom: Giannozzo Manetti on the Material and Spiritual Edifice.* Tempe: Arizona Center for Medieval and Renaissance Studies; Turnhout: Brepols, 2006.

Sombart, Werner. *The Quintessence of Capitalism: A Study of the History and Psychology of the Modern Business Man.* Edited and translated by M. Epstein. New York: H. Fertig, 1967.

Stahel, Peter. "Cristoforo Landino's Allegorization of the *Aeneid*: Books III and IV of the *Camaldolese Disputations.*" Ph.D. diss., Johns Hopkins University, 1968.

Statuti della repubblica fiorentina. Edited by Romolo Caggese. 2 vols. Florence: Galileiana, 1910–21.

Stephens, J. N. "Heresy in Medieval and Renaissance Florence." *Past and Present* 54 (1972): 25–62.

Sullivan, Margaret A. "Aertsen's Kitchen and Market Scenes: Audience and Innovation in Northern Art." *Art Bulletin* 81, no. 2 (1999): 236–66.

Szilágyi, András. "Amphion Playing the Lyre." In *Renaissance Studies in Honor of Craig Hugh Smyth*, edited by Andrew Morrough, Fiorella Superbi Gioffredi, Piero Morselli, and Eve Borsook, 2:478–79. Florence: Giunti Barbèra, 1985.

Tafuri, Manfredo. *Interpreting the Renaissance: Princes, Cities, Architects.* Translated by Daniel Sherer, with a foreword by K. Michael Hays. New Haven: Yale University Press, 2006.

Tavernor, Robert. "Concinnitas, o la formulazione della bellezza." In *Leon Battista Alberti*, edited by Joseph Rykwert and Anne Engel, 300–315. Milan: Electa, 1994.

———. *On Alberti and the Art of Building.* New Haven: Yale University Press, 1998.

Tavoni, Mirko. *Latino, grammatica, volgare: Storia di una questione umanistica.* Padua: Antenore, 1984.

Tenenti, Alberto. "Leon Battista Alberti umanista." In *Leon Battista Alberti*, edited by Joseph Rykwert and Anne Engel, 38–45. Milan: Electa, 1994.

———. "The Merchant and the Banker." In *Renaissance Characters*, edited by Eugenio Garin and translated by Lydia G. Cochrane, 154–79. Chicago: University of Chicago Press, 1991.

Terence. *Eunuchus.* In *Terence*, translated by John Sargeaunt. 2 vols. London: W. Heinemann; New York: Macmillan, 1912.

Thomson, David. *Renaissance Architecture: Critics, Patrons, Luxury.* Manchester: Manchester University Press, 1993.

Toker, Franklin D. "Alberti's Ideal Architect: Renaissance—or Gothic?" In *Renaissance Studies in Honor of Craig Hugh Smyth*, edited by Andrew Morrough, Fiorella Superbi Gioffredi, Piero Morselli, and Eve Borsook, 2:667–74. Florence: Giunti Barbèra, 1985.

Trachtenberg, Marvin. "Architecture and Music Reunited: A New Reading of Dufay's *Numper Rosarum Flores* and the Cathedral of Florence." *Renaissance Quarterly* 54, no. 3 (2001): 740–75.

———. *Dominion of the Eye: Urbanism, Art, and Power in Early Modern Florence.* Cambridge: Cambridge University Press, 1997.

Trexler, Richard. *Public Life in Renaissance Florence.* New York: Academic Press, 1980.

Ullman, Berthold Louis. "Coluccio Salutati on Monarchy." *Mélanges Eugène Tisserant* 5 (1944): 401–11.

Urban Task Force. *Towards an Urban Renaissance.* London: Spon, 1999.

Vagnetti, Luigi. "Concinnitas: Riflessioni sul significato di un termine Albertiano." *Studi e documenti di architettura* 2 (1973): 137–61.

Valla, Lorenzo. *On Pleasure: De voluptate.* Translated by A. Kent Hieatt and Maristella Lorch. New York: Abaris Books, 1977.

Van Eck, Caroline. "Architecture, Language, and Rhetoric in Alberti's *De re aedificatoria*." In *Architecture and Language: Constructing Identity in European Architecture, 1000–c. 1650*, edited by Georgia Clarke and Paul Crossley, 72–81. Cambridge: Cambridge University Press, 2000.

Varro, Marcus Terentius. *On Agriculture.* Translated by William Davis Hooper and Harrison Boyd Ash in *Marcus Porcius Cato: "On Agriculture"; Marcus Terentius Varro: "On Agriculture."* Cambridge, Mass.: Harvard University Press; London: W. Heinemann, 1967.

Vasari, Giorgio. *Lives of the Painters, Sculptors, and Architects.* Translated by Gaston du C. de Vere. 2 vols. London: Everyman's Library, 1996.

Vasoli, Cesare. "Alberti e la cultura filosofica." In *Alberti e la cultura del Quattrocento: Atti del Convegno internazionale del Comitato nazionale VI centenario della nascita di Leon Battista Alberti, Firenze, 16–18 dicembre 2004*, edited by Roberto Cardini and Mariangela Regoliosi, 1:19–57. Florence: Polistampa, 2007.

———. "Potere e follia nel Momus." In *Leon Battista Alberti, actes du congrès international de Paris, Sorbonne, Institut de France, Institut culturel italien, Collège de France, 10–15 avril 1995*, edited by Francesco Furlan, with the collaboration of A. P. Filotico, I. Giordano, P. Hicks, S. Matton, and L. Vallance, 1:443–63. Turin: Nino Aragno Editore; Paris: J. Vrin, 2000.

Villani, Giovanni. *Cronica di Giovanni Villani: A miglior lezione ridotta.* With notes by I. Moutier and a historico-geographical appendix by Francesco Gherardi Dragomanni. 4 vols. Florence: Sansone Coen Tipografo-Editore, 1845.

Virgil. *The Georgics.* Translated by L. P. Wilkinson. London: Penguin, 1982.

Vitruvius. *On Architecture.* Edited and translated by Frank Granger. 2 vols. London: W. Heinemann; New York: Putman, 1931–34.

Von Naredi-Rainer, Paul. "La bellezza numerabile: L'estetica architettonica di Leon Battista Alberti." In *Leon Battista Alberti*, edited by Joseph Rykwert and Anne Engel, 292–99. Milan: Electa, 1994.

Waley, Daniel. *The Italian City-Republics.* London: Longman, 1988.

Watkins, Renée Neu, ed. *Humanism and Liberty: Writings on Freedom from Fifteenth-Century Florence.* Columbia: University of South Carolina Press, 1978.

———. "Leon Battista Alberti in the Mirror: An Interpretation of the *Vita* with a New Translation." *Italian Quarterly* 30, no. 117 (1989): 7–22.

Weinstein, Donald. "The Myth of Florence." In *Florentine Studies: Politics and Society in Renaissance Florence*, edited by N. Rubinstein, 15–44. London: Faber, 1968.

Westfall, Caroll William. *In This Most Perfect Paradise: Alberti, Nicholas V, and the Invention of Conscious Urban Planning in Rome, 1447–55.* University Park: Pennsylvania State University Press, 1974.

————. "Society, Beauty, and the Humanist Architect in Alberti's *De re aedificatoria.*" *Studies in the Renaissance* 16 (1969): 61–78.

————. *The Two Ideal Cities of the Early Renaissance: Republican and Ducal Thought in Quattrocento Architectural Treatises.* Ph.D. diss., Columbia University, 1967.

White, Jonathan. *Italy: The Enduring Culture.* London: Leicester University Press, 2000.

Whitfield, J. H. "*Momus* and the Language of Irony." In *The Languages of Literature in Renaissance Italy,* edited by Peter Hainsworth, Valerio Lucchesi, Christina Roa, David Robey, and J. R. Woodhouse, 31–43. Oxford: Clarendon Press, 1988.

Wittkower, Rudolf. *Architectural Principles in the Age of Humanism.* London: Alec Tiranti, 1962.

Wolf, Gerhard. "The Body and Antiquity in Alberti's Art Theoretical Writings." In *Antiquity and Its Interpreters,* edited by Alina Payne, Anne Kuttner, and Rebekah Smick, 174–90. Cambridge: Cambridge University Press, 2000.

Xenophon. *"Memorabilia" and "Oeconomicus."* Translated by E. C. Marchant. London: W. Heinemann; New York: G. P. Putnam's Sons, 1923.

Zoubov, V. P. "Leon Battista Alberti et les auteurs du Moyen-Age." *Medieval and Renaissance Studies* 4 (1958): 245–66.

Index

Acton, Harold, 13
Aelian, 136
agriculture, 116, 144
air quality, 125
Alberti, Leon Battista. *See also related topics*
    background, 6–10
    lawsuits, 144, 226n38
    perception preoccupation, 137–39
    personality descriptions, 139
    pseudonyms used by, 8, 137–38
    recent scholarship on, 17–23
    reputation in history, 4–6, 12–13
    themes, overview, 188–91
    writings of, overview, 8–9
Albertiana (journal), 18
Amphion, 181, 183–85
amphitheaters, 99
animal analogies, 131–41
ants, 132, 133, 134
Apologi centum (Alberti), 8
arches, 170
architects, 87–88
architecture
    animal analogies and, 136
    beauty and rules of, 162–66, 170
    history of, 163–64
    nature's relationship with, 174–77
    origin of, 28–35
aristocrats, 71, 77, 88, 91, 95, 152.
    See also rulers
Aristotle, 134, 135, 136
arsenals, 98
Athens (Greece), 13, 14
Augustine, 35–38, 100, 180
Augustus (emperor), 62

Barker, Sir Ernest, 13
Baron, Hans, 10–12, 57
Barzizza, Gasparino, 6
baths, 99

Baxandall, Michael, 179
beauty
    architectural rules and, 161–66
    definitions, 161
    elements of, 170–73
    functions of, 157–60, 179–80, 194
    importance of, 98, 156
    music and, 180–87
    nature and, 173–78
    ornamentation compared to, 160–62
    overview, 191
    rhetoric and, 178–80
Beavis, Ian C., 133
bees, 132, 133, 134, 136
Begliomini, Aluffi, 200n57
Bernardino of Sienna, Fra, 69
Bernardo, Benedetto di, 7, 214n82
Bialostocki, Jan, 158, 159, 160
Bible, 47–48, 182, 224n27
Bisticci, Vespasiano da, 147
Bonatto, Bartolomeo, 66
Borgo, 80, 220–21n53
Borsi, Stefano, 19, 84
Boschetto, Luca, 19, 144
Bracciolini, Poggio, 28, 113
bridges, 99
Brunelleschi, Filippo, 167, 218n8
Bruni, Leonardo, 10, 57, 150–51
Burckhardt, Jacob, 5, 12, 111, 138
Burroughs, Charles, 62, 84, 86
butchers, 66, 67, 91

Caesar, Julius, 59
Caligula (emperor), 204n49
The Canterbury Tales (Chaucer), 91
Cardini, Roberto, 19
care, concept of, 115
Carrae (Egypt), 60–61, 93
Cassani, Alberto, 19, 54
Castel Sant'Angelo, 80